# Handbook of Bioentrepreneurship

# International Handbook Series on Entrepreneurship

## VOLUME 4

*Series Editors*

Zoltan J. Acs, *George Mason University*, U.S.A.

David B. Audretsch, *Max Planck Institute of Economics, Jena, Germany, and Indiana University*, U.S.A.

## SERIES FORWARD

Interest in entrepreneurship has surged in the last decade. Scholars across a broad spectrum of fields and disciplines have responded by generating new research approaches uncovering a wealth of new findings and insights about entrepreneurship. This new research spans not just a diverse set of fields, such as management, finance, psychology, economics, sociology, and geography but also a wide range of countries reflecting the fact that entrepreneurship is a global phenomenon. The exceptionally cross-disciplinary nature of entrepreneurship has made it difficult for scholars in any one particular field to become aware of and understand the leading contributions and insights emerging in other disciplines. The purpose of this series is to compile a series of handbooks, each devoted to a particular issue in the entrepreneurship. Each handbook will draw upon the leading international scholars from the entire range of disciplines contributing to entrepreneurship to articulate the state of knowledge about a particular topic. The contribution should identify the fundamental questions, which are being posed, the methodological approaches, types of data bases used for empirical analyses, the most important empirical regularities to emerge in the literature, major policy conclusions, and the most promising research direction. Thus, each handbook will reflect the interdisciplinary nature of entrepreneurship that has proven to be elusive to discipline-based scholars. A goal of the *International Handbook Series on Entrepreneurship* is not only to provide a state-of-the-art coverage of what has been learned about entrepreneurship, but that when viewed in its entirety, entrepreneurship is emerging as a bona fide academic discipline.

The particular topics in the Series will be drawn from discussions with the leading scholars. Each handbook will be directed and compiled by a Handbook Editor. (S)he will work closely with the Series Editors to ensure that the contents and contributions are appropriate, and that there is consistency with the other volumes in the Series.

*The titles published in this series are listed at the end of this volume.*

Holger Patzelt   Thomas Brenner
Editors

# Handbook of
# Bioentrepreneurship

 Springer

*Editors*
Holger Patzelt
Max Planck Institute of Economics
07745 Jena
Germany
Patzelt@econ.mpg.de

Dr. Thomas Brenner
Philipps University Marburg
Marburg
Germany
brenner@mpiew-jena.mpg.de


*Series Editors*
Zoltan J. Acs
George Mason University
Fairfax, VA
USA

David B. Audretsch
Max Planck Institute of Economics
Jena
Germany

and

Indiana University
Indiana
USA

ISBN: 978-0-387-48343-6      e-ISBN: 978-0-387-48345-0
DOI: 10.1007/978-0-387-48345-0

Library of Congress Control Number: 2008926123

Printed on acid-free paper

9 8 7 6 5 4 3 2 1

springer.com

# Contents

# List of Contributors

T.T. Aldridge
Max Planck Institute of Economics
Kahlaische Str. 10
07745 Jena
Germany

D.B. Audretsch
Max Planck Institute of Economics
Kahlaische Str. 10
07745 Jena
Germany

S. Bhaduri
Centre for Studies in Science Policy
Jawaharlal Nehru University
New Delhi
India

M. Brannback
Eugenio Pino and Family Global Entrepreneurship Center
Florida International University
11110 Southwest 11th Street, University Park – VH 130
Miami, FL, USA

T. Brenner
Philipps University Marburg
Deutschhausstr. 10
35032 Marburg
Germany

P. Bubenzer
WHU – Otto Beisheim School of Management
Burgplatz 2
56179 Vallendar
Germany

A.L. Carsrud
Eugenio Pino and Family Global Entrepreneurship Center
Florida International University
11110 Southwest 11th Street, University Park – VH 130
Miami, FL
USA

D. Catherine
Grenoble Ecole de Management
12 rue Pierre Sémard – BP 127
38003 GRENOBLE Cedex 01
France

P. Cooke
Centre for Advanced Studies and Centre for Economic
and Social Analysis of Genomics (CESAGen)
Cardiff University
44-45 Park Place, Cathays Park, Cardiff CF10 3BB
UK

D. Engel
Rheinisch-Westfälisches Institut fuer Wirtschaftsforschung (RWI)
Hohenzollernstr. 1-3
45128 Essen
Germany

D. Fornahl
Institut für Wirtschaftspolitik und Wirtschaftsforschung
Universität Karlsruhe (TH)
Kaiserstraße 12, 76128 Karlsruhe
Germany

O. Heneric
Center for European Economic Research (ZEW)
L 7, 1
68161 Mannheim
Germany

M.J. Lynskey
Institute of Innovation Research
Hitotsubashi University
2-1 Naka, Kunitachi
Tokyo 186-8603
Japan

A.L. Oliver
Department of Sociology and Anthropology
The Hebrew University of Jerusalem, Mt. Scopus
Jerusalem 91905
Israel

H. Patzelt
Max Plank Institute of Economics
Kahlaische Str. 10
07745 Jena
Germany

M. Perry
　　School of Public and Environmental Affairs
　　Indiana University
　　Bloomington
　　USA

M. Renko
　　Eugenio Pino and Family Global Entrepreneurship Center
　　Florida International University
　　11110 Southwest 11th Street, University Park – VH 130
　　Miami, FL
　　USA

P.P. Saviotti
　　UMR GAEL, Universitè Pierre Mendès-France
　　BP 47 38040 Grenoble Cedex 9, and
　　GREDEG CNRS, I2C, 250 rue Albert Einstein
　　06560 Valbonne
　　France

L. Schweizer
　　Johann Wolfgang Goethe-University Frankfurt am Main
　　Mertonstr. 17
　　60325 Frankfurt am Main
　　Germany

O. Sorenson
　　Rotman School of Management
　　University of Toronto
　　105 St. George Street, Toronto M5S 3E6
　　Canada

M. Sytch
　　Kellogg School of Management
　　Northwestern University
　　2001 Sheridan Rd., Leverone 395
　　Evanston, IL 60201
　　USA

D. Zu Knyphausen-Aufsess
　　Otto-Friedrich University of Bamberg
　　Feldkirchenstr. 21
　　96045 Bamberg
　　Germany

# 1 Introduction to the Handbook of Bioentrepreneurship

Holger Patzelt[1] and Thomas Brenner[1,2]

[1]Max Planck Institute of Economics, Jena, Germany
[2]Philipps University Marburg, Marburg, Germany

Biotechnology is one of *the* most booming industries at the beginning of the twenty first century. According to the 2006 Annual Biotechnology Report of Ernst & Young (one of the leading industry observers), the world's publicly traded biotech companies had revenues greater than US $70 billion in 2006, representing growth rates of 22% in Canada, 14% in the USA, and 14% in Europe, as compared with those in 2005. Moreover, biotech companies raised more than US $27 billion at the global capital markets, an annual growth of 42%. The average premium pharmaceutical incumbents paid for acquiring biotech firms with values more than US $500 million was 60%. Biotech firms had 36 new drugs approved in the USA alone. Glen Giovannetti, Ernst & Young's Global Biotechnology Leader, concludes: "The industry in the US has never been stronger and we're seeing its success story spreading to other parts of the world – particularly Europe" (Ernst & Young 2007).

These numbers are even more impressive when we consider that the biotech industry is only 30 years old. Genentech, which is often referred to as the first modern biotech firm, was founded in 1976 in California. Genentech used recombinant DNA technology, a radically new biotechnological technique to genetically modify living organisms, to produce human insulin, which, after market introduction by its pharmaceutical partner Eli Lilly in 1982, formed the basis of Genentech's overwhelming economic success. Motivated by this success, people founded thousands of bioentrepreneurial ventures in the USA in the 1980s. The European biotech industry is even younger than the US sector because governmental regulations, missing societal acceptance, and an insufficiently developed capital market made it difficult for bioentrepreneurs in most countries to start a new firm before the 1990s. Thus, most biotech firms are still entrepreneurial ventures. For example, although the US sector is the most developed biotech industry worldwide, less than one quarter of all the 1,400 US biotech firms are traded at the stock markets. In Europe, only about 100 of more

H. Patzelt and T. Brenner (eds.), *Handbook of Bioentrepreneurship*,
doi: 10.1007/978-0-387-48345-0_1, © Springer Science + Business Media, LLC 2008

than 1,800 biotech firms are publicly traded, and the average firm employees are less than 60 people (Ernst & Young 2003a, 2003b).

Although the development of the US industry and the individual firms such as Genentech demonstrate that biotechnology can be an extremely successful business, starting a biotech venture is among the most complex entrepreneurial tasks. Biotechnology firms are characterized by high knowledge intensity, long product development cycles, high technological and market uncertainties, and an extraordinary need for capital. For example, the development of biopharmaceutical drugs takes, on an average, more than 12 years and several hundreds of millions of US dollars (DiMasi et al. 2003; Kellog and Charnes 2000), and only one of 5,000 initial drug candidates reaches market launch (Evans and Varaiya 2003). Thus, particularly in the case of drug development, biotechnology is an extremely risky and money-consuming business, and many bioentrepreneurial firms fail before they bring any product to the market. Indeed, most existing biotech ventures do not earn any profits yet, and the sector as a whole is still not profitable (Ernst & Young 2007).

The extraordinary success potential on one hand and the high failure rates of bioentrepreneurial firms on the other hand make biotechnology a fascinating field of study for academic research, and the sector has attracted considerable scholarly attention. For example, management researchers have analyzed the success factors and strategies of bioentrepreneurial ventures; sociologists have studied the extensive web of collaborations between biotech firms, universities, and incumbent companies; and scholars from the disciplines of economics and political sciences have identified regional and political factors that promote or hinder the development of a local biotech industry. Indeed, biotechnology appears to be one of the most researched industries over the last decade. For instance, a Business Source Premier search for publications that match the word *biotechnology* and appeared in scholarly, peer-reviewed journals yielded more than 3,200 articles. While these articles have advanced our understanding of bioentrepreneurship at the firm, industry, and regional level considerably, the pure amount of research that has been conducted to date demonstrates that, particularly for scholars new to the field of bioentrepreneurship, it is difficult to gain an overview and understanding of what has been researched and within which discipline, where the field stands, and what the challenges are for the going forward researchers focusing on this fascinating industry.

Based on these observations, the purpose of the *Handbook of Bioentrepreneurship* is twofold. First, it provides an overview of the current state of the academic field. It was our goal to bring leading bioentrepreneurship researchers from various disciplines together and have them review and summarize past research in their fields. Second, based on these reviews, the scholars identify important gaps in our knowledge and suggest avenues how these gaps may be filled in by future bioentrepreneurship research. Thus, this book is not so much a guide for practitioners, but is mainly addressed to academic researchers. Since the efficient generation of new knowledge requires building on existing knowledge (Kuhn 1974), we expect that the book will not only help to inform those who have a general interest in academic bioentrepreneurship research, but will also serve as a starting point for further studies, based on the research gaps identified by leading scholars in the field.

The 11 chapters of this book are organized into four parts. These parts address (i) the geography of biotechnology and regional networks, (ii) strategic and managerial perspectives, (iii) university bioentrepreneurship, and (iv) legal frameworks and bioentrepreneurship policy. Each chapter contains a separate introduction to its topic, a summary and assessment of past research, and closes with suggestions for future directions.

Part I focuses on geographic issues and networks in biotechnology and contains three chapters. Chapter 2, by Phil Cooke, gives an overview on the spatial distribution of the biotech industry in the world. It starts by providing information and a number of tables about economic relevance and size of the biotech industries in the major countries in which biotech firms are active. The chapter then moves to a more detailed geographic perspective and describes a number of regions, namely Cambridge, Boston, San Diego, San Jose, and San Francisco (USA), Cambridge (UK), and Munich (Germany), that are strongholds in biotechnology. Information about the size, the focus, and the local interaction patterns among organizations is given for these regions, and the regions are compared. Furthermore, the state and dynamics of the biotech industry in Canada, Sweden, Switzerland, Singapore, and Israel are described. All this shows that biotechnological activities are spatially concentrated and occur mainly in a few hot spots.

The reasons for this geographic concentration of biotechnological activities are examined in Chap. 3. Two different explanations for the geographic concentration of industries are usually given in the literature: agglomeration externalities and the geographic characteristics of start-up processes. Dirk Fornahl and Olav Sorenson focus in their chapter on the latter explanations. They argue that social networks and relationships play an important role in this process. This argument is substantiated by providing the reader with an overview on the scientific knowledge about a number of mechanisms that are involved. This is done in several steps. First, the influence of spatial aspects on social networks is discussed. Then, the role of social networks for entrepreneurship is examined. On the basis of these two discussions, it is investigated why this might lead to the concentration of biotechnological activities in space. In addition, some empirical evidence on this issue is discussed. Finally, policy implications are deduced.

While networks are one topic among others in Chap. 3, Chap. 4 focuses exclusively on networks, especially innovation networks. Pier Paolo Saviotti and David Catherine give a comprehensive overview of the literature. This overview includes a discussion of the historic developments in which networks became a significant phenomenon in industrial organization as well as a reflection on the theoretical explanations – including a list of all the reasons that are claimed in the literature – and the methods that are used to analyze networks. The chapter also contains a description of the specific developments of networks in biotechnology and the role of universities therein. Furthermore, the chapter lists the empirical findings about how firms benefit from being part of an innovation network. The second part of Chap. 4 presents the results of an empirical study of networks in biotechnology. It focuses on how networking has changed within the last 20–30 years in the biotechnology sector.

Part II of this volume takes a managerial perspective and consists of four chapters. In Chap. 5, Alan Carsrud, Malin Brännback, and Maija Renko investigate research on strategic thinking and strategy making in young biotech ventures. After providing an overview of the diversity of biotechnology business, intersections with other industries, and the meaning of innovation for bioventures, the authors identify components of strategy making in these firms. They identify proactive deeds and market foresight, a fit between (financial) resource availability and the market environment, reactiveness in case of diminishing financing opportunities, and the historic business model of the firm as important determinants of strategic choice. They conclude with how bioventures can gain and maintain competitive advantage.

Chapter 6 concentrates on strategic alliances in the biotech industry. Maxim Sytch and Philipp Bubenzer provide a comprehensive overview of alliance motives, governance, and outcomes. Their review of the literature shows that access to knowledge and other complementary resources as well as the desire to enhance legitimacy are main drivers of alliance formation. Moreover, they identify factors that influence alliance partner choice such as, for example, the partners' resource endowments and the social capital of the biotech firms' top managers. Sytch and Bubenzer also demonstrate how levels of behavioral, task, and technological uncertainties of alliance projects influence the modes of alliance governance. Finally, they illustrate both positive and negative potential consequences of alliance formation for young bioventures.

In Chap. 7, Lars Schweizer and Dodo zu Knyphausen-Aufsess summarize research on mergers and acquisitions (M&As) in the context of biotechnology. They take a different perspective to demonstrate the need for M&A activities in the biotech sector. First, from a scientific perspective, they analyze how the scientific advance and development in the industry motivate M&A activities. Second, the organizational perspective focuses on the bioventures' needs for organizational resources and strategic flexibility and their effects on M&A motivations. Finally, a financial perspective investigates how the biotech firms' high financing needs triggers M&As. The authors then, in more detail, elaborate on M&A activities among biotech companies, and on M&As between biotech firms and pharmaceutical incumbents, and they identify motives and potential outcomes of these deals. Finally, they offer a host of interesting research questions for continuing with this underdeveloped field of research.

Chapter 8 closes Part II and is written by Michael Lynskey. This chapter stands out from the rest of the book, in which it addresses a topic where basically no research is available so far – the entrance of nonbiotechnology incumbent firms into the biotechnology sector via unrelated diversification. Consequently, Lynskey draws on a comprehensive case study of the Japanese Kirin Brewery, which decided to enter the market for biopharmaceuticals in the 1980s. The chapter describes the factors that motivated this decision and the early efforts of the company. Moreover, Lynskey highlights the central role of tacit knowledge, entrepreneurial individuals, and key collaborations – particularly Kirin's joint venture with Amgen – for making the entry into the biotech sector successful. Subsequently, the chapter describes Kirin's strategy in selecting research projects related to different therapeutic fields and scientific techniques. Finally, the author highlights implications for bioentrepreneurship research.

Part III of the book addresses the issue of university entrepreneurship in biotechnology and consists of two chapters. In Chap. 9, David Audretsch, Taylor Aldridge, and Marcus Perry focus on the process in which scientific research leads to entrepreneurial commercialization. They start with an extensive review of the theoretical literature on entrepreneurial decision making to answer the question of why researchers become entrepreneurs. They discuss the two common views – the discovery and creationist view – and the influence of personal characteristics. They come to the conclusion that the context – whether the potential entrepreneur working in a firm is a user or a scientist – matters for the entrepreneurial decision. Then they focus on scientists and give a comprehensive overview on all the factors and circumstances that are found in the literature to influence the decision of the scientists to become entrepreneurs.

The second chapter of Part III (Chap. 10) is written by Amalya Oliver and summarizes research related to university-based biotechnology spin-off companies. Oliver explores the role and properties of an entrepreneurial university in creating knowledge that can be transformed into private ventures, and she illustrates how changes in academic science over the last decades and the development of a triple helix approach connecting universities, industry, and governments impact the creation of spin-off companies. After distinguishing university spin-offs from university-based spin-offs, the chapter goes more into detail and discusses how characteristics of individual academic entrepreneurs, the network surrounding them, and the institutional framework impact the motivation of these entrepreneurs to start a spin-off venture. Finally, Oliver highlights complexities that arise in the context of academic spin-off formation and discusses how future bioentrepreneurship research may advance our understanding of these complexities.

The fourth and final part of this book contains two chapters that elaborate on legal frameworks and policy in the bioentrepreneurship context. Saradindu Bhaduri presents in Chap. 11 an overview on patent law and the meaning of patents for the biotech industry. The starting point of this chapter is a comprehensive discussion of the characteristics of biotechnological research and innovations and the historical development of patent laws in the field of biotechnology. Then, a number of issues are discussed, among them are the patentability of life forms, patent length, and patent scope. Besides a general economic discussion of the patent scope, the chapter also provides an examination of the implications of different patent scopes for the catch-up processes of countries and the hold-up problem. Finally, the controversy between biodiversity mainly found in southern countries and indigenous science mainly conducted in northern countries is discussed.

The last chapter of the book is written by Dirk Engel and Oliver Heneric, who draw on the case of Germany to demonstrate the profound impact the legal framework and public support can have on the commercialization of biotechnological inventions. The authors review rationales for state intervention in the context of the biotech industry and summarize empirical studies that have analyzed the effects of such interventions and state funding on industry development. Subsequently, they provide a detailed description of framework changes that have occurred in the German context, which is followed by an empirical assessment of how these changes affected foundations of bioentre-preneurial ventures. The chapter concludes by identifying blind spots of our understanding of the impact of policy tools on the development of the biotech industry. These blind spots constitute important areas for future bioentre-preneurship research.

## References

DiMasi JA, Hansen RW, Grabowski HG (2003) The price of innovation: New estimates of drug development costs. Journal of Health Economics 22: 151–185

Ernst & Young (2003a) Endurance – The European Biotechnology Report 2003, Cambridge, UK

Ernst & Young (2003b) Resilience – Americas Biotechnology Report 2003, New York

Ernst & Young (2007) Beyond borders 2006. Ernst & Young, Boston

Evans AG, Varaiya NP (2003) Anne Evans: Assessment of a biotech market opportunity. Entrepreneurship: Theory & Practice 28: 87–105

Kellog D, Charnes JM (2000) Real-options valuation for a biotechnology company. Financial Analyst Journal 56: 76–84

Kuhn TS (1974) The structure of scientific revolutions. University of Chicago, Chicago

# 2 Biotechnology Dynamics at the Global Scale

Philip Cooke

Centre for Advanced Studies and Centre for Economic and Social Analysis
of Genomics (CESAGen), Cardiff University, UK

## 2.1 Introduction

In this chapter, a new knowledge-based theory of economic geography is worked
out utilising a variety of economic indicators regarding the medical biotechnology
sector and bioscientific knowledge metrics. It will be shown that biotechnology
has proved something of a pioneer sector that other industries emulate for its
innovative industry organisation. The medical biotechnology sector is only one of
the bioscientific 'family' that together account for a significant share of GDP in
the advanced countries, and a growing share in countries such as India and China
Within such sectors, which include agro-food, energy and environmental biotechnology, sub-sectors such as bioprocessing,[1] bioengineering, bioinformatics,
bioimaging and so on are also growing in significance in certain regional
economies. It is a science-driven, knowledge-intensive and widely applicable
group of interacting platforms that are already evolving certain pervasive characteristics for different functions, including health and safety testing and
standardisation (bioanalysis), civil and military security (DNA fingerprinting,
biometrics) and applications in mechanical, electronic and civil engineering
(nanobiotechnology) rather as ICT became pervasive during the 1990s.

To that extent they have the character of platform technologies and even
general purpose technologies as discussed by inter alia Helpman (1998). Traditional
natural resource-based theories in economic geography explained the microeconomics of agglomerative economic activity relatively well. However, knowledge-based economic growth is less easy to explain and predict, although there
are some aspects of knowledge economy agglomerations that are less uncertain
than others. Thus the chapter is able to point with reasonable confidence at the
leading global bioregions and offer a rationale for their current prominence.
However, such regions may be said to arise through a process not of direct

---

[1] A broad term that describes the use of microbial, plant or animal cells for the production
of chemical compounds.

H. Patzelt and T. Brenner (eds.), *Handbook of Bioentrepreneurship*,
doi: 10.1007/978-0-387-48345-0_2, © Springer Science + Business Media, LLC 2008

comparative or even competitive advantage, not least because markets do not explain much of the rationale for their existence. Rather, bioregions are exemplars of a modern tendency for regional accomplishment to be a product of 'constructed advantage' (Smith 1776; Foray and Freeman 1993). Constructed regional advantage occurs in substantial measure because of the influence of public goods upon a region.[2] Thus, in bioscience, a university and medical school is a key factor, not only for its role in the production of talent, but the innovative research and entrepreneurial businesses it sustains. Similarly, large research hospitals, for patient trials of new treatments, add to regional constructed advantage. Notably, most of these facilities are the product of initial *public* provision and are sustained by public teaching and research subventions. Thereafter, nearby pharmaceuticals and agro-chemicals facilities may provide intermediate markets as they adjust to meet the new exigencies of 'open innovation' (Chesbrough 2003).

In this chapter, the first section discusses recent industry dynamics in medical biotechnology at a global scale. A global bioscientific market analysis is performed, followed by an in-depth analysis of the UK sector, Europe's leading and the world's second biotechnology economy. Of importance here are such issues as the lengthy lead times to actual products reaching the market, efforts to moderate the regulatory regime to hasten drug-trialing, and the relative and continuing laggardliness of European biotechnology in generating therapeutic products on the market. Even global shortage of capacity in bioprocessing further holds up the appearance of new products.[3] Finally, the rise of R&D outsourcing from large to small firms, which is particularly pronounced in the USA and Europe, leads to an investigation of the impact this has in the emergence of key 'spatial knowledge domains' and the extent this sustains biotechnology clusters and knowledge networks among them.

---

[2] A number of key terms have been introduced. In definitional terms, their usage here is as follows. 'Region' is a governance unit between national and local levels. A 'regional economy' is '…the production, distribution and consumption of goods and services in a particular geographic region.' The 'knowledge economy' is measured, currently inadequately, as high technology manufacturing added to knowledge-intensive services. A 'bioregion' has no standard definition, although regarding biotechnology 'clusters', a location quotient of 1.25 is considered sufficient. 'Knowledge' differs from 'information' in that it is creative and informed by meaning and understanding, whereas information is passive and, without the application of knowledge, meaningless. To 'develop', as in 'regional development,' means to evolve and augment, or enrich. Hence 'regional development' involves the cultural, economic and social enrichment of a region and its people. Here it mainly, but not exclusively, entails *economic* growth arising from increased efficiency and effectiveness in use and exchange of the productive factors of an openly trading regional economy. 'Constructed advantage' may or may not purposively cause clusters, but in health-care biotechnology no examples exist of clusters that do not have these public goods underlying them; hence, it is a necessary but not sufficient condition for growth to occur.

[3] A drug from Immunex, a US biotechnology firm, was delayed in reaching the health-care market because of a global shortage of bioprocessing capacity. Immunex's inability to produce sufficient quantities of its 'star' rheumatoid arthritis and psoriasis treatment *Enbrel* cost more than $200 million in lost revenue in 2001 alone; see Malik et al. (2002).

## 2.2 The Global Health Care Market in Relation to Biotechnology

Biotechnology has become a global sector of the health care, agro-food and respective industries referred to. However, health care takes the lion's share of investment, turnover and sales. Because of the relative novelty of the consolidated category 'health-care industry' compared to the long-established industry association status in most advanced countries of the pharmaceutical industry, new efforts are being made to define it and estimate its scale. In the discussion in this and the following paragraph, along with Table 2.1 we follow the Healthcare Industries Task Force (HITF 2004), who define health-care industries to mean manufacturers of everything used in health care *except medicines*. Subsequently, we shall combine key statistics for both, giving a baseline number expressing the scale of the key world markets for health-care products *and pharmaceuticals* to justify the effort devoted to an initial investigation of its global and local dynamics.

Thus health-care industries means manufacture of all products except medicines used in diagnosis, prevention, monitoring or treatment of illnesses in humans. This covers consumables, hospital supplies and equipment ranging from syringes to diagnostic test kits (a mainstay of the biotechnology industry), pacemakers and CAT scanners. In Europe, all are regulated by European Medical Devices Directives and in the USA the regulator is the Food and Drug Administration (FDA) Centre for Devices and Radiological Health. Interestingly, it is a sector that, unlike pharmaceuticals (but not biotechnology), is overwhelmingly SME in character. Hence there are estimated to be some 7,000 medical technology firms in Europe. In the UK, for example, where some 4,800 firms operate, 85% have an annual turnover of less than €7 million. A comparable picture exists in the USA, where there are some 5,100 firms, of which 83% employ less than 100 persons. Annual sales for 2001 was €73 billion ahead of Europe at €47 billion, as shown for major world markets in Table 2.1.

**Table 2.1.** Key world markets for medical technologies, 2001

| Key market | € bn |
|------------|------|
| World market | 170 |
| USA | 73 |
| Europe | 47 |
| Germany | 18 |
| France | 8 |
| Italy | 6 |
| UK | 4 |
| Japan | 24 |

*Source:* Healthcare Industries Task Force (2004)

Now, to give a rounded picture of the key world markets, these data are augmented by those for medicines in general, involving pharmaceuticals and other firms that produce or market both chemically derived traditional drugs and those focused solely on the production of biotechnologically derived products. If we summarise the picture for bioscience firms only (Table 2.2), we see that a long-established picture of USA–UK hegemony with regard to the key industry indicator of number of pipeline products prevails, with only Switzerland challenging the latter. Notable in the Swiss case is that only five public companies employ on average 1,600 persons each. This is a very different profile from that of the UK, whose firm employment profile averages some 500 persons, closer to the USA with some 620. Germany's public companies have a more Swiss profile. France is also similar to Switzerland in employment per firm, but like Germany, it displays a much lower productivity measured in terms of revenue and pipeline products.

**Table 2.2.** Main international biotech competitors, 2003

| Country | Companies | Public companies | Market capitalisation[a] (€ bn) | Revenues[a] (€ bn) | Employees[a] | Pipeline[a] |
|---|---|---|---|---|---|---|
| USA | 1,457 | 307 | 205 | 27 | 191,000 | 872 |
| UK | 331 | 46 | 9.4 | 3 | 22,000 | 194 |
| Switzerland | 129 | 5 | 7.3 | 2 | 8,000 | 90 |
| France | 239 | 6 | 0.5 | 0.3 | 9,655 | 31 |
| Germany | 369 | 13 | 0.5 | 0.5 | 13,386 | 15 |

*Source:* Bioscience Innovation and Growth Team (2004)
[a]Public company data only

Regarding pipeline product abundance, Table 2.3 supplies far greater detail on this key indicator and shows how the USA easily outperforms the rest of the world, with the UK leading a badly trailing pack.[4] It is partly a matter of early entry, the first US biotechnology firm being Genentech in 1976 and partly a matter of very large R&D budgets in the USA, compared to elsewhere on a per capita or per firm basis. But more important for public companies it reveals the importance of private investment by biotechnology venture capitalists. These have the greatest impact on the capabilities of firms actually to realise the fruits of significant injections of R&D expenditure. However, this is high-risk investment and approved new drug treatments follow lengthy and expensive trialing of up to 10 years and in many cases more. Many of these products fail in trials. Table 2.3 is interesting since it shows that while individual European countries are behind on most key indicators of pipeline performance, when added together (plus Israel) they constitute approximately half the innovation impact of the USA. Moreover,

---

[4] According to Ernst & Young (2007), Germany has 22% of all European biotechnology businesses but only 11% of Europe's *public* biotechs. Europe's leader in share of public biotechs is the UK at 40% of the European total. The report indicates that many of Germany's *privately* owned firms have pipeline products, but that these are in their early stage and relatively unattractive to investors at this time.

proportionally speaking, Europe has more drugs in late stage trialing than does the USA. Some explanation for this imbalance is given in Table 2.4, which reveals a significant surge of new chemical entities (NCEs) towards the end of the 1990s but a rather stagnant position previous to the late 1990s technology boom.

**Table 2.3.** Product pipeline of public bioscience companies worldwide

| Country | Pre-clinical | Phase 1 | Phase 2 | Phase 3 | Pipeline |
|---|---|---|---|---|---|
| USA | 584 | 96 | 148 | 44 | 872 |
| UK | 65 | 50 | 56 | 23 | 194 |
| Switzerland | 45 | 23 | 11 | 11 | 90 |
| Sweden | 14 | 8 | 10 | 0 | 32 |
| France | 16 | 8 | 6 | 1 | 31 |
| Denmark | 14 | 5 | 5 | 4 | 28 |
| Italy | 9 | 0 | 4 | 3 | 16 |
| Israel | 2 | 3 | 6 | 4 | 15 |
| Germany | 7 | 4 | 3 | 1 | 15 |
| Norway | 8 | 2 | 2 | 3 | 15 |
| Netherlands | 9 | 1 | 1 | 0 | 11 |
| Finland | 9 | 1 | 0 | 0 | 10 |
| Ireland | 2 | 0 | 2 | 3 | 7 |
| Belgium | 2 | 0 | 1 | 0 | 3 |
| Total Europe | 202 | 94 | 107 | 53 | 456 |

*Source:* Bioscience Innovation and Growth Team (2004)

Put simply, it was easier to find risk capital to take firms out beyond Phase 3 trials at that point than hitherto or since. Hence the USA has many more approved drugs available for sale than does Europe. However, Europe may take a larger share of world markets if the requisite funding is made available in the near future. This will be a great relief to many in the industry and government who have seen many false dawns in the European biotechnology sector's market performance. A key requisite, in a period when venture capitalists are risk-averse and in other respects not seen as the preferred partner by biotechnology firms, is for small firms to seek scale to finance the late stages of pipeline development. Here, the Swiss model of a few large, successful firms, notably the world's number three in market capitalisation, Serono, is something of an exemplar. That France and Germany also follow this route, presently less successfully, is revealed in Table 2.3. As noted, the UK seems to have a firm size profile more comparable to that of the USA, showing that the 'varieties of capitalism' thesis retains some purchase (Hall and Soskice 2001). Nevertheless, UK and US firms were, in the first half of the present decade, also seen to be pursuing scale through numerous acquisitions and mergers. Thus in 2003–2004, the UK's Celltech was acquired by Belgian chemicals giant UCB, Powderject by Chiron, and British Biotech by Cold Spring Harbor spinout OSI. Meanwhile, US leaders Biogen and IDEC merged. Simultaneously, risk-averse venture capitalists were also challenged by direct funding of promising pipeline spinouts by large pharmaceuticals firms, small firms thus avoiding the venture capital route entirely.

The point was made earlier that the venture-capital-driven boom of the 1990s squeezed a significantly larger number of NCEs on to the market in the late 1990s than hitherto. This observation is supported by the data in Table 2.4. However, it was bought at the cost of a considerable decline in productivity in relation to hugely increasing R&D expenditure by private industry. This was matched also by US public R&D funding from, particularly, the National Institutes of Health (NIH), for whom expenditure rose to $37 billion in 2003 from $14 billion in 1999. The US lead has been fuelled by such expenditures of public and private R&D funding, reaching some $70 billion in the USA by 2005. Thus, step changes occurred in public and private investments in US bioscientific R&D, especially during the 1990s, with the output effects in terms of NCE peaking around 1997 but at a far lower productivity, given the continued exponential rise of US bioscience R&D expenditure even thereafter.

**Table 2.4.** Declining pharmaceutical productivity over time

| Year | US NCE approvals | R&D expenditure, $ bn (2001) |
|---|---|---|
| 1963 | 19 | 2 |
| 1967 | 20 | 2 |
| 1971 | 18 | 3 |
| 1975 | 17 | 3 |
| 1979 | 16 | 3 |
| 1983 | 16 | 4 |
| 1987 | 19 | 5 |
| 1991 | 25 | 8 |
| 1995 | 25 | 15 |
| 1996 | 45 | 17 |
| 1997 | 37 | 18 |
| 1998 | 23 | 22 |
| 1999 | 32 | 25 |
| 2001 | 23 | 30 |

*Source:* Bioscience Innovation and Growth Team (2004)
*NCE* new chemical entity

To conclude this section, the following three summary points will carry through the argument of this chapter, which is that these relatively recent events have revealed a new global economic arrangement in which 'knowledge capabilities' rooted in specific 'knowledge domains' are producing a new global economic geography. The data show biotechnology to be an important driver and absorber of massive public and private sector R&D expenditures, signifying an innovative lead role of *research* in economic development. Second, research magnitude produces results in terms of innovations but the correlations are far from perfect, since other variables, notably risk capital, intervene in producing realised NCEs. Finally, we see Europe, though traditionally behind the US numbers, closing an important gap in commercialisation by having relative, and regarding Phase 3 pipeline products absolute, leads over the USA on a firm capacity basis.

It now remains to incorporate the pharmaceuticals sector of the industry to evolve a number representing the scale of the health care plus bioscientific and pharmaceuticals sectors in global terms. Industry estimates for 2003, shown in Table 2.5, put this figure at some $400 billion, excluding biotechnology (Jack 2005). Hence the resulting value of the three sectors on the global economy measured in 2001–2003 average market revenue is $400 billion + $170 billion + $33 billion = $603 billion. As succeeding sections of this chapter show, although the world constitutes 'the market', that market is well-captured in Table 2.1 as North America, Europe and Japan. However, the originating production locations of that market are overwhelmingly American and European, and within both, highly localised in a few 'megacentres' that account for huge portions of the global value-chain.

**Table 2.5.** World trade (£ m) in pharmaceuticals, 2003

| Country | Exports | Imports | Balance |
|---|---|---|---|
| Ireland | 8,756 | 1,258 | 7,498 |
| Switzerland | 9,754 | 5,044 | 4,711 |
| France | 4,001 | 10,552 | 6,551 |
| UK | 11,926 | 8,293 | 3,634 |
| Sweden | 3,928 | 1,315 | 2,613 |
| Italy | 13,213 | 11,453 | 1,760 |
| Netherlands | 5,291 | 4,536 | 755 |
| Australia | 5,464 | 5,569 | −105 |
| Germany | 873 | 1,999 | −1,126 |
| Spain | 1,482 | 3,245 | −1,763 |
| Japan | 2,346 | 4,176 | −1,830 |
| Canada | 1,417 | 3,508 | −2,091 |
| USA | 9,753 | 16,998 | −7,245 |

*Source:* http://www.abpl.org.uk

## 2.3 Global Bioregions

These data refer to countries, but the main locations of knowledge exploration and examination, that is, basic and applied research with trialing and testing of therapeutic and services products, are, as we shall see, in specific clusters within regional innovation systems such as those of Massachusetts, northern and southern California, East Anglia (UK) and Bavaria (Germany). These host more localised biotechnology clusters such as those of Cambridge and Boston, San Diego, San Jose and San Francisco, Cambridge (UK) and Munich, respectively. Why this high proximity with accompanying inter-nodal 'distant networking'? It is because of knowledge capabilities. Theoretically speaking, the 'knowledge economy' has given rise to the following:

- Specific knowledge domains whereby places evolve, asymmetrically, expertise in specific and inter-connected knowledge – examples include genomics and post-genomic research, support services in genomic bioinformatics, biosoftware, gene sequencing, patent attorney, business angel and venture capital services in close proximity, as at the two Cambridges.

- The evolutionary stimulus is supplied by the attraction of a variety of imitative and innovative *talent* to the region, a Schumpeterian 'swarming' realising increasing returns to *related variety* where innovation may move swiftly through various parts of the innovation 'platform'. Related variety nourishes absorptive capacity because cognitive distance between platform sub-fields is low as with 'general purpose innovations' (Helpman 1998).

- Such clusters have spatial quasi-monopolistic or 'club' characteristics, exerting exclusion and inclusion mechanisms to aspirant 'members' consequent upon their knowledge value to the club. In such industries, firms are willing to pay super-rents of 100% to locate in clusters – even when they are professed non-collaborators, to access anticipated localised knowledge spillovers (Cooke 2006).

- Large firms able to pay for localised knowledge spillovers then induce what Chesbrough (2003) calls 'open innovation' as they outsource their R&D to purchase 'pipeline' knowledge and access via informal 'club channels' the required regional knowledge capabilities (Owen-Smith and Powell 2004).

**Table 2.6.** Core biotechnology firms and key clusters, 2000: Comparative US and European performance indicators

| Location | DBFs | Life scientists | VC ($ m) | Big pharma funding ($ m) |
|---|---|---|---|---|
| Boston | 141 | 4,980 | 601.5 | 800 per annum (1996–2001) |
| San Francisco | 152 | 3,090 | 1,063.5 | 400 per annum (1996–2001) |
| San Diego | 94 | 1,430 | 432.8 | 320 per annum (1996–2001) |
| Toronto | 73 | 1,149 | 120.0 | 89 (2002) |
| Montreal | 72 | 822 | 60.0 | 120 (2002) |
| Munich | 120 | 5,500 | 266.0 | 54 (2001) |
| Berlin | 100 | 3,700 | 122.0 | 30 (2001) |
| Rhein–Neckar | 37 | 3,200 | 40.0 | 20 (2000) |
| Rhineland | 54 | 1,250 | 30.0 | 40 (2000) |
| Stockholm–Uppsala | 87 | 2,998 | 90.0 | 250 (2002) |
| Lund–Medicon | 104 | 5,950 | 80.0 | 300 (2002) |
| Cambridge | 54 | 2,650 | 250.0 | 105 (2000) |
| Oxford | 46 | 3,250 | 100.0 | 90 (2002) |
| Scotland | 24 | 3,600 | 35.0 | 125 (2002) |
| Zurich | 70 | 1,236 | 57.0 | 85 (2002) |
| Singapore | 38 | 1,063 | 200.0 | 88 (2001) |
| Jerusalem | 172 | 1,015 | 300.0 | 54 (2002) |

*Source:* Cortright and Mayer 2002; National Institutes of Health; NRC; BioGenTec 1998; BioM, Munich; BTH, Heidelberg; BioTop, Berlin; VINNOVA, Sweden; Dorey 2003; Eastern Region Biotechnology Initiative (ERBI), UK; Kaufmann et al. 2003; Oxford Bioscience Network 2003; Scottish Enterprise 2003
*DBFs* dedicated biotechnology firms, *VC* venture capital

The resulting global pattern of the leading biotechnology clusters is as represented in Table 2.6. Key benchmarking indicators such as the numbers of core biopharmaceuticals firms and life scientists as well as funding streams such as those that come from service platforms such as venture capital in its numerous forms (e.g. pre-seed, seed, and business angel or other equity finance) and licensing income from pharmaceuticals customers produce a rough benchmarking profile of the main clusters. Except for the US entries (Cortright and Mayer 2002), the data in Table 2.6 were collected from diverse sources. Nevertheless, every effort to define terms and interrogate sources in similar ways has been made in collecting them.

But knowledge does not remain locked-in to the clusters, rather they are clubs that give overseas membership to each other based on reputation of the bioscientific capabilities and specific knowledge domains demonstrated by the 'star' scientists and high-impact research institutes and firms in the clusters. The high-impact scientists and the institutions they inhabit as conveyors of knowledge between the world's key clusters are remarkably hierarchically networked in that the key US ones dwarf most of the rest. Finally, some locations that are clearly not what might be termed 'global cities', such as Jerusalem or Zurich, are key parts of the inter-nodal knowledge exchange system, while some so-called global cities such as Paris or Tokyo are of no greater status.

## 2.4 The World Leaders in Brief: Top Bioclusters in the USA

We have already seen that Boston is perhaps the leading biosciences megacentre, not because it has the heaviest medical or even bioscientific research budgets, but because it is presently the leading centre for exploration research.[5] For example, Swiss drug company Novartis first announced in 2000 a path-breaking agreement to spend $25 million on first access to the results of plant and microbial biology research conducted at the University of California, Berkeley, in the heart of the northern California biotechnology cluster. However, in 2002 the company announced the establishment of a $250 million Novartis Institutes for Biomedical Research in Cambridge, Massachusetts, with a $4 billion research budget for the next 10 years. This was on the grounds that Cambridge is the leading exploration and exploitation centre for genomics and post-genomics knowledge. Boston's current primacy has not been the product of the operations of the market mechanism alone. In 1999, $770 million of NIH funding was earned for medical and bioscientific research. That figure was more than $1.1 billion by 2000, $1.5 billion by 2002 and $2.1 billion in 2003. As Table 2.7 shows, Boston exceeded all of California by 2002 and by 2003 the gap widened to $476 billion

---

[5] A distinction is being made here between 'exploration' and 'exploitation' knowledge. Clearly the first refers to basic research and the second to commercialisation. This may involve commercialisation of technology as well as therapeutics. The distinction was made by March (1991). It has been augmented with a third concept 'examination' knowledge to cover the important expertise involved in trialing, testing and prototyping.

($2021 cf. 1545 billion). Interestingly, this is a recent turnaround since the 1999 Massachusetts total was marginally less than the amount of NIH funding alone passing through the northern California cluster in 1999, a statistic that increased to $893 million in 2000.[6] Most of the exploration research conducted in both Cambridge/Boston and northern California is conducted in institutions that are dependent on public funding, though private research foundations are also functional in both.[7] In Boston, the Massachusetts Biotechnology Council is an active and successful biotechnology association that lobbies industry and political forums at State and Federal levels, pressing for an FDA presence in Boston to offset the advantage enjoyed by emergent firms and research institutes located in Maryland, near the head offices of both NIH and FDA.

Let us look more closely at the manner in which the assets of biosciences megacentres[8] such as those in northern and southern California are now packaged in documentation that promotes the image intended to appeal to investors of all kinds into the regional innovation system. The following two examples, from northern and southern California, are produced by a non-profit association (The California Healthcare Institute) and a consultancy (Michael Porter's *Monitor*), respectively. The California Healthcare Institute is a public policy institute for California's 200 leading biotechnology firms and research institutes. It is thus comparable to the Massachusetts Biotechnology Council. Its political brief is expressed clearly by CEO Gollaher, who despite noting '…funding for basic science is strong…' bemoans the fact that '…many federal and state lawmakers advocate policies that would impede medical innovation. Our greatest threats include a total ban on human cloning and severe restrictions on stem cell research; a Medicare administration that… effectively excludes new products… and a leaderless FDA facing the greatest wave of new inventions in history' (Gollaher in CHI/PWC 2002). The demand is for collaboration among members of the biosciences innovation system to change laws that are perceived as threatening the evolution of the industry in the post-genomic era.

Northern California is perceived as the birthplace of biotechnology, which, along with biomedical innovations such as cardiac stents, has a strong base of some 819 biomedical/biotechnology firms of which only some 20% are pure biotechnology firms, employing 86,000 people (28,000 in biotechnology), total R&D of $1.1 billion, NIH grants of $893 million and $4.1 billion in worldwide revenues, including $2.7 billion exports. New infrastructure projects include

---

[6] This is a further reason for rejecting the Milken Institute's ranking of San Diego first. We have seen that questionable research funds are not excluded. The Institute also deploys a spurious methodology based on research dollars per metropolitan inhabitant to promote San Diego's ranking. The research was commissioned by local San Diego interests (Deloitte's San Diego) and excludes 'big pharma' funding, on which San Diego performs less than half as well as Boston.

[7] For example, we shall see how Swiss firms Novartis and Roche are symbiotically linked to the Californian clusters, both directly and, especially in San Diego, through GNF in the case of Novartis.

[8] A 'megacentre' is more than simply a cluster in the sense of a market-driven complex of firms. Rather it is a location in which all the key drivers, public and private, required to make it function are in place from exploration to exploitation of innovation.

University of California (San Francisco) Medical School's new $1.4 billion Mission Bay bioscience research campus, the new California Institutes for Science and Innovation, and the California State University CSUPERB joint ventures programme where universities and the private sector collaborate in bioscience research, technology transfer, business and even residential development. Much emphasis is placed on survey results, showing that significant interaction occurs among firms and the institutional research base in northern California.

In southern California, the San Diego biotechnology cluster has larger claims to be considered a leading biosciences centre than even that in the North. In Porter's (2002) competitiveness study San Diego's biopharmaceuticals cluster is presented as long established and among the most significant outside Boston, especially for R&D. Cluster employment growth was more than 8,000 from 1988–1997, and San Diego had the most rapid growth in patent output, compared with that in the 20 largest US biotechnology clusters. There are some 400 SMEs, focusing mainly on one or two preferred drug targets, the University of California, San Diego (UCSD), with numerous specialist research centres, and finally, some globally known research institutes, the Salk Institute, the Scripps Research Institute, the Burnham Institute and the La Jolla Institute for Allergies and Immunology, each focusing upon aspects of life science, medical or clinical research. The Scripps Institute, since establishment in the 1950s, required its researchers to raise their own funds, encouraging collaborative innovation with larger firms (like Novartis). By contrast, the Salk Institute does not conduct corporate research but licenses its discoveries and takes equity stakes in companies. UCSD emphasised medical research and academic entrepreneurship. One early fruit of that approach was Hybritech, a 1978 biotechnology start-up, from which more than 50 other local biotechnology DBFs were spun out. In 1986 it was sold to Eli Lilly for $400 million. A further feature of this cluster is its strong and long-established networking propensity, signified by the establishment since 1985 of the UCSD CONNECT network, a model for cluster integration in many other new economy clusters such as Scotland's and Cambridge's (UK) (ICT) networking associations.

Thus, California's academic research institutions are credited with playing a central role in the growth of nearly one third of biomedical/biotechnology firms; 42% of firms had at least one research contract with a California research institution, 56% of firms planned to broaden or maintain such agreements, and up to 70% of firms having patent license agreements planned to maintain or broaden them in future. The key northern California life sciences and clinical research institutes cited include Stanford University (Biomedical Technology Information Programme), Lawrence Berkeley and Lawrence Livermore National Laboratories, and the University of California (San Francisco) Medical School, Berkeley (BioSTAR industry–academic collaboration), Santa Cruz (with Berkeley, the California Institute for Bioengineering, Biotechnology and Quantitative Biomedical Research, QB3) and Davis (Life Sciences Information programme). More than 19,000 are employed in research in the region, and nowadays two of the top ten NIH R&D grant recipients in the USA are University of California (San Francisco) and Stanford. A picture of this cluster that is developing the characteristics of a biosciences megacentre rather than just a cluster thus emerges. But the judgement as to whether it yet is, is occluded by the lobbying points that although some larger firms such as Abbot Laboratories and Genentech are present, most are SMEs, 49% without products on the market, 45% with no revenue in 2000. Finally, of the pharmaceutical pipeline products reported, 53% are in pre-clinical trials. This is by no means unusual, but nevertheless testifies to the apparent fragility of the *exploitation* aspect of the northern California cluster, once its strength, but never adequately backed up with strong bioscience *exploration* capabilities and now, belatedly perhaps, seeking to embed them.

**Table 2.7.** Comparison of bioregion National Institutes of Health (NIH) funding, 2002

| Rank (top 300) | Institution | NIH Research ($ m) | Rank (top 300) | Institution | NIH research ($ m) |
|---|---|---|---|---|---|
| *Massachusetts* | | | *N. California* | | |
| 12 | Harvard Univ. | 248.6 | 4 | UCSF Med. S. | 319.7 |
| 18 | Mass Gen. | 232.1 | 16 | Stanford Univ. | 226.3 |
| 22 | Brig. & W. | 192.4 | 47 | UC Davis | 103.1 |
| 34 | Boston Univ. | 132.3 | 53 | UC Berkeley | 81.6 |
| 51 | Dana-Farber | 96.3 | 117 | UC Law. Labs | 33.3 |
| 52 | Beth Israel | 94.8 | 144 | N. Cal. Inst. | 22.5 |
| 57 | Whitehead Inst. | 91.1 | 169 | Children's Hos. Oakl. | 14.7 |
| 60 | Univ. Mass. Med. | 87.6 | 206 | UC Santa Cruz | 11.5 |
| 63 | MIT | 77.8 | 247 | UC Livermore | 8.8 |
| 76 | Children's Hos. | 62.8 | 253 | N. Cal. Cancer C. | 5.2 |
| 88 | Tufts Univ. | 49.9 | 270 | Chiron | 2.2 |
| 120 | N. Eng. M.C. | 27.7 | *N. California total* | | *829.0* |
| 133 | Boston M.C. | 27.2 | | | |
| 148 | Joslin Diabetes | 20.9 | *S. California* | | |
| 166 | N. Eng. Rsch. Inst. | 14.7 | 17 | UCSD | 244.7 |
| 200 | Mass Eye–Ear | 11.9 | 25 | Scripps Inst. | 185.6 |
| 210 | UM Amherst | 11.3 | 96 | Salk Inst. | 44.9 |
| 228 | Boston Biomed. | 8.5 | 108 | Burnham Inst. | 37.2 |
| 290 | Boston College | 6.3 | 167 | SD State Univ. | 16.2 |
| | | | 199 | Loma Linda Univ. | 13.3 |
| *Massachusetts total* | | *1,494.2* | 227 | La Jolla Inst. | 10.6 |
| *California total* | | *1,381.5* | *S. California total* | | *552.5* |

*Source:* National Institutes of Health
*UCSF* University of California, San Francisco; *UC* University of California;
*UCSD* University of California, San Diego

Funding for basic research is higher in the Cambridge–Boston Bioregion – the heartland of the Massachusetts cluster – than in San Francisco and San Diego – the equivalent biotechnology cores in California. Data on NIH allocations for 2002 (Table 2.7) confirm the strengthening of the former since 2000. Clearly, the statistics reveal that it retains its lead over California with regard to research funding won from the NIH. This is because its institutional base is far broader and deeper. This is revealed in the large number of substantial mid-range institutions that are independent universities, research institutes, research hospitals and specialist centres such as Dana-Farber, Joslin, Beth Israel, and Whitehead in Boston and Cambridge. Both California bioregions are heavily dependent upon the University of California system, although independent Stanford University makes a significant showing and the Torrey Pines Mesa research institutes in La Jolla, San Diego, make a significant research income impact in otherwise institutionally thin San Diego. Nevertheless, San Diego's institutional base is tightly knit, not least through the activities of UCSD-CONNECT, and although UC San Diego is the catalyst of the Bioregion and its cluster, only 26 biotechnology firms were actually university spinouts. Faculty members privately founded 35, and 29 firms were indirectly connected.

## 2.5 Comparison of UK and German Clusters

The Cambridge biocluster specialises in health-care biotechnology. The two categories of 'biopharmarceuticals, including vaccines' and 'pharmaceuticals largely from chemical synthesis' registered 14 and 9 Cambridge firms, respectively, in 1998, reaching 47 and 20 in 2006, evidence of the rapid rise of biotechnology over fine chemistry in the pharmaceutical industry more generally. Examples of the former are Acambis, Alizyme, Amgen, Cambridge Antibody Technology, Domantis and Xenova, and of the latter, Argenta, UBC and Mundipharma. In addition to these two key categories are direct biotechnology services such as clinical trails, diagnostics and reagent supply.

**Table 2.8.** Core pharmaceutical biotechnology companies in the leading UK clusters

| Location | 2000 | 2004 | 2006 |
|---|---|---|---|
| Cambridge Core Therap. | 54 | 70 | 109 |
| Cambridge Genomic | – | 30 | 47 |
| Oxford Core Therap. | 46 | 50 | 63 |
| Scotland Core Therap. | 24 | 30 | 38 |

*Sources:* Eastern Region Biotechnology Initiative (ERBI) 1999; Oxford Biosciences Network; Scottish Enterprise

Detailed research on Cambridge's genomics sector (Table 2.8) has revealed the collaborative aspect of biotechnology innovation to be substantial. Regarding co-publication in journals, Casper and Karamanos (2003) showed that only 36% of firms were 'sole authors' while the majority (64%) partnered with firm founders, current incumbents and/or their laboratory. Academic collaborators are equally shared between Cambridge and the rest of the UK, with international partners a sizeable minority. Hence, the sector is associative in its interactive knowledge realisation, at least in respect of the all-important publication of results that firms will likely seek to patent. Moreover, they will, in many cases, either have or anticipate milestone payments from 'pharma' companies with whom they expect to have licensing agreements. Yet of all known genomics DBF (dedicated biotechnology firm) foundings (1990–2002), totaling 30, only nine were spinouts from Cambridge University laboratories, a further five were spinouts from the Medical Research Council's Cambridge Molecular Biology Laboratory, while others came from outside universities such as Imperial College, London University (3), the University of Wales, Cardiff (2), others and industry (6). Casper and Karamanos (2003) hold that Cambridge functions as an 'ideas market' with a good scientific image and much scholarly collaboration as well as academic membership of DBF boards and advisory committees. Yet a third of interactions are with academic and entrepreneurial partners elsewhere in the UK, and a further third are abroad, mainly in the USA.

The science base, mentioned earlier, is a key attraction and Lawton Smith (2004) sees this operating in three ways. First, Oxfordshire's clinical research strengths in medicine and medical research are echoed in the biopharmaceuticals and diagnostics DBF specialisations. Diverse service firms occupy niche roles within pharmaceutical research, development and production, and some drug development DBFs conduct this alongside service functions. Those in the diagnostics sub-sector report little competition between co-located firms. Second, a quarter of the companies originated in Oxford University. Other firms such as Prolifix were spinouts from elsewhere, in this case the National Institute for Medical Research in London. Through Isis Innovation, the university's technology transfer office, Oxford University has spun out 17 firms in biopharmaceuticals out of a total of 32 spinouts by 'star scientists', including Professors Ed Southern and Raymond Dwek (biochemistry), Brian Bellhouse and Mike Brady (Engineering) and John Bell, Nuffield Department of Clinical Medicine. Of these, 3 are medical diagnostics and 14 are biotechnology firms.

Oxford's advantage is that the cluster enabled firms to be close to a top university and other research institutes possessing 'talent'. The availability of clinical trial facilities was not a major sector challenge for Oxford DBFs, which hints that access to hospital units is satisfactory. However, research shows that local information sources not being the most important source of information, conferences score highest and other important sources were the Internet, published sources and trade fairs. Oxford DBFs clearly place a high valuation upon codified knowledge which fits its reputation as a strong clinical biotechnology bioregion, whereas Cambridge is thought of as stronger in medical biopharmaceutical, especially post-genomic research and exploitation. Clinical research is more patient-focused, including patient trials, diagnostics, software, bioinformatics and biochips, and technology-oriented as Oxford's DBF profile tends to show. Universities are thus not the prime source of information. They were ranked ninth, along with local sector networks, national trade associations, technology transfer departments and independent research organisations. Least important were education and training councils, general business services, consultancy services, regional sector networks and government research associations. Yet in spite of the evidence of interaction, firms themselves saw proximity to Oxford University and the local research base as an unimportant factor in the development of interactions, other than those of an informal nature. The local labour market was the next most important attraction factor, especially the availability of highly qualified human capital. DBFs in such surveys appear schizophrenic, locating near research excellence but denying it by stressing higher-status global connections.

Munich's biotechnology companies continue to focus mainly on therapeutics. Their turnover was expected to rise to €250 million in 2005, compared to €170 million in 2004. The consolidation phase in the region will continue over this year but know-how and expertise, especially in cancer research, and a well-supplied pipeline are factors that justify cautious hopes of cluster recovery. The science base in Munich is broad, but with special expertise in health-related and, less, agro-food biotechnology. There are three Max Planck Institutes of relevance, in Biochemistry, Psychiatry and the MPI Patent Agency. GSF is the Helmholtz Research Centre for Environment and Health, and the German Research Institute for Food Chemistry is a Leibniz Institute.**** There are three Fraunhofer Institutes, one of Germany's four Gene Centres, two universities and two polytechnics. The main research-oriented big pharma company following Sanofi's absorption of Hoechst AG as a subsidiary is Roche Diagnostics (formerly Boehringer Mannheim). The work areas of the broader bioscience community include three-dimensional structural analysis, biosensors, genomics, proteomics, combinatorial chemistry, gene transfer technologies, vaccines, bioinformatics, genetic engineering, DNA methods, primary and cell cultures, microorganisms, proteins, enzymes and gene mapping. In 1995, the State of Bavaria, the administrative district of Munich and local authorities of Planegg, together with the IZB Innovation and Start-Up Centre for Biotechnology Martinsried GmbH, established one of the first private business enterprise companies in Bavaria. This is a mostly public initiative, as with the IZB as a combination of incubator and technology park in proximity to the Gene Centre and two of the Max Planck Institutes conducting biotechnology research. Vertical networks from science through (public) funding to start-up are, in principle, strong, though, as elsewhere, given what looked a low-risk funding regime, due to public co-funding, the numbers of start-ups are not overwhelming, perhaps because of the quest for 'quality' start-ups in which substantial sums may be individually invested.

As to whether Munich's biotechnology constitutes a cluster, the answer is probably positive, although there are conflicting reports as to whether three key firms commercialising biotechnology from Max Planck Institutes are interacting, collaborating companies or not. Two of the firms MorphoSys and Micromet were collaborating on the development of an antibody-based treatment for micrometastatic cancer. MorphoSys was the first firm to receive a BioRegio grant and had previously collaborated successfully with Boeringer Mannheim on the development of a diagnostic reagent. MorphoSys's business strategy was to focus on the development of horizontal networking. They had no plans then to develop therapeutics themselves, aiming to remain a science discovery firm, but to let partners carry the risk of drug development. Thus MorphoSys worked with a variety of companies, minimising its risk-profile, but potentially benefiting from substantial injections of capital from research funding, milestone payments and royalties. Already in 1999 MediGene planned to become a fully integrated biopharmaceutical company, an ambition that is unlikely to be fulfilled, although as we have seen, MediGene marketed the first new biotechnologically derived drug since *Reteplase* from Boehringer Mannheim many years ago. MediGene was a spinout from Gene Centre in 1994 and initially raised €8 million venture capital, state and federal funds. Its expertise is in gene therapy for cancer and cardiovascular diseases, with a research partnership at the time with Hoechst. Academic–clinical partnerships included the Munich Gene Centre, the Munich University Hospital, German Cancer Centre at Heidelberg and, in the USA, the NIH and Princeton University. Its co-founder, Horst Domdey, gave up a chair at Munich University to become head of BioM. Another firm, Mondogen, spun out of the Virus Research department at the Martinsried Max Planck Institute for Biochemistry.

A sketch comparison of the cases examined is provided in Table 2.6, but by way of introduction it is important to stress the following three key points of comparison that are both qualitative and quantitative. First, the German cluster firms are not as interactive at the firm level as those in the UK clusters and this may be problematic but it also may be a function of firm maturity. In leading bioclusters worldwide, there is a high degree of formal and informal interaction, sometimes collaboration, sometimes competition among the same firms. This seems not to have developed in Germany – somewhat strangely given the concertation culture in business affairs more generally – and it may not evolve very much either in three of the four German clusters. In Heidelberg information was supplied in interview to suggest that the 'creative destruction' in recent years had destroyed many established linkages and that new businesses were extremely small, immature and often in similar and competing fields (e.g. diagnostics and platform technologies). In the cases of Rhineland and Berlin, firms are also small but in very diverse segments of biotechnology markets such as health care, agro-food and environmental biotechnologies where 'related diversity' is low.

Second, and building on the previous point, too many German clusters specialise in low-value, highly competitive and rapidly changing diagnostics segments and insufficiently specialise in therapeutic biotechnology. This contrasts with the UK clusters, where numerous firms specialise not only in therapeutics but also in the most advanced post-genomic bioscientific innovation, especially but not exclusively in Cambridge, the UK's leading biotechnology cluster. This means there is always likely to be rapid emergence and decline of market opportunities for these small German firms, although in some cases the fact that they are active in more than one line and the extra line involves at least therapeutics research is a promising indicator. To put it starkly, only Munich is remotely competitive in this regard in a European, let alone a global, context. Other research on co-publications (Cooke 2004) clearly shows that German bioscientists are not active in biotechnology co-publication with scientists elsewhere in Europe, Asia or North America. Only Munich displays such connectivity in the leading European and US bioscience journals, and such links as Munich bioscientists demonstrate are few and far between.

Finally, it is evident that Germany's biotechnology clusters demonstrate a marked dependence upon public support, with purely private enterprise support being at a premium. This contrasts markedly with Cambridge and Oxford, but less so with Scotland. However, even in Scotland, which is located relatively peripherally to the main markets, there is active private venture capital and business angel activity. Also, contrasting in particular Scotland with its large element of public support with the German bioclusters, that support seems to have been more innovative. Thus Scotland was the first region in Europe to hire Michael Porter to advise on their cluster policy for biotechnology back in the early 1990s. Moreover, Scotland pioneered the 'Proof of Concept' fund that has assisted spinout companies from universities by allowing professors to 'buy out' their teaching and administration time with the grant-funding they have won. Finally, not satisfied with an above-average start-up rate and a booming services and supply sector (see Table 2.6), the Scottish Executive and its economic development agency *Scottish Enterprise* established and funded a special intermediary organisation, the ITI for Life Sciences, to increase the general rate of exploitation and commercialisation of bioscientific discoveries over a 10-year period. This is a positive sign of real commitment that was politically controversial at the time because apologists for market solutions found it unacceptable that there should be even more intervention in Scotland's biotechnology from the public sector. However, as it turned out, an entrepreneur from Wales, John Chiplin, who had been an academic entrepreneur in the early days of San Diego's biotechnology cluster and made his fortune by establishing and selling both of his spinout companies 20 years later, was found to head the Life Sciences ITI and he applies complete market norms to the activities of his institution. Moreover, he and others involved are themselves somewhat critical of the content of some public policies, showing scepticism, as we have seen, about the cluster concept itself.

## 2.6 Bioregions and Their Key Characteristics Elsewhere

In this section we shall briefly examine developments in five developing network nodes, most of which were mentioned in the previous section of this chapter as having research or market relationships with UK firms (and conceivably US firms) which, it can be hypothesized, were less pronounced hitherto. The countries in question are Canada, Sweden, Switzerland, Singapore and Israel. For the present, space does not allow investigation of scientific and market developments in two key biologics supplier countries of the future, India and China. How have these five nodal countries positioned themselves globally? What specialisation, if any, characterises their activity? To what extent are institutional and economic geographic patterns established in the USA and UK being repeated? For example, in EU countries considered elsewhere, clustering near major knowledge centres such as Munich (Germany) and Paris (France) characterises the institutionalised economic geography of the sector (Cooke 2002; Kaiser 2003; Lemarié et al. 2001).

Literature on which the following brief accounts are drawn ostensibly shows the same, with Canada's biotechnology dominated by clusters of Montreal and Toronto; Sweden having concentrations in Stockholm–Uppsala and Lund–Malmö, now bridged formally to Denmark's nearby Medicon Valley cluster in Copenhagen; Switzerland's concentrations are at Zurich, Geneva and Basel; Singapore is tightly drawn to the National University of Singapore campus; and Israel's main concentration is in Jerusalem, near to the Hebrew University and *Hadasit* incubator (Niosi and Bas 2003; McKelvey et al. 2003; VINNOVA 2003; Nelund and Norus 2003; Finegold et al. 2004; Kaufmann et al. 2003). However, as will be shown, the trajectories by which these concentrations reached fruition are distinctive. One group has, in individually distinctive ways, an origin in close relationships with 'big pharma'. In Sweden and Denmark corporate spinout and supply, the former even before Pharmacia's acquisition by Pfizer, combine with university research and associated start-up DBFs. In Switzerland, close links to Roche and Novartis, the latter with its own incubator and VC fund, influence the focus in Basel. But Zurich and Geneva also have biotechnology and university research as a key progenitor. While Singapore's growth is based on a determined foreign direct investment (FDI) strategy to attract global leaders, but also interact through university research with DBFs, in Canada and Israel the origins of their metropolitan clusters lie primarily in public research funding and academic entrepreneurship. Let us now explore in a little more depth the experiences, linkage specificities and global knowledge network patterns and processes in the two broad categories.

### 2.6.1 Economic Geography of Clusters Spawned by Pharmaceuticals Firms

In the three instances under the spotlight here – Sweden/Denmark, Switzerland and Singapore – the influence of big pharma is, as noted, pronounced. Thus the first commercial exploitation of modern biotechnology in Sweden was based on technology from Genentech, licensed by the Swedish company Kabi in 1978. Kabi merged with Pharmacia in 1990. Pharmacia later merged with two US companies Upjohn and Monsanto, to form Pharmacia Corporation. In the spring of 2003 Pfizer, the US pharmaceutical company, acquired Pharmacia Corporation. The other major pharmaceutical company in Sweden, Astra (now a Swedish–UK firm AstraZeneca), has headquarters in Södertälje near Stockholm, with Swedish research based in Södertälje, Gothenburg and Lund started using recombinant DNA technology in the 1980s. From then, and increasingly in the 1990s, new DBFs were founded in Sweden. Most of these new companies were either spin-offs from university research or from existing large pharmaceutical companies. Swedish biotechnology ranks fourth in Europe in terms of number of companies and ninth in the world according to the Swedish Trade Council in 2002.

The number of Swedish DBFs increased by 35% from 135 in 1997 to 183 in 2001, and the number of employees increased by 48% to about 4,000 (VINNOVA 2003). The two pharmaceutical companies AstraZeneca and Pharmacia Corporation were the dominant large companies engaged in biotechnology activities. Many Swedish DBFs serviced them in the biopharmaceuticals application sector, but also in such industries as food processing and agriculture.[9] These DBFs are highly research-led and knowledge-intensive. Between 10 and 20% of employees in these companies have doctoral degrees. Of company presidents responding to VINNOVA's questionnaire, 93% stated that their companies collaborated with academic research groups. From our earlier results, this appears to differentiate Swedish DBFs somewhat from those in the USA and UK, where research interactions are more among firms or distinctively among PROs. This is possibly an indicator of the relative immaturity of many Swedish DBFs, formed as we have seen in the 1990s for, according to the VINNOVA study, a majority of companies were small in 2001, that is, they had fewer than 200 employees. Almost 90% of the companies had less than 50 employees, and a good half had less than 10 employees. However, the category of small and medium-sized biotechnology companies is growing such that in 2001 Swedish DBFs totaled about 4,000 employees, a 35% increase since 1997.

These are mostly found clustered in Sweden's metropolitan regions and in cities with large universities conducting substantial medical research. Fifty-six DBFs are located in the Stockholm region, followed by the Lund/Malmö and Uppsala regions, with 36 and 31, respectively; 24 are located in the Gothenburg region. The smallest cluster is in the Umeå region, with fewer than ten biotechnology DBFs. The Swedish pharmaceutical industry annually spends around 25% of its revenues on R&D, higher than the global standard of 17.5%. This high percentage by international standards mainly reflects AstraZeneca's large expenditures in its Swedish research centres, with around one third of the group's total R&D investments, $3.1 billion, occurring in Sweden. Of this some 20% or $540 million is spent extramurally in Sweden (Benner and Sandström, 2000). Stockholm–Uppsala, in particular, contributes to Sweden's relative strength in biotechnology research, mainly through the Karolinska Institute, Uppsala University, Stockholm University, SLU[10] and the Royal Institute of Technology.

---

[9] 'Swedish DBFs are noted suppliers and R&D partners to leading foreign pharmaceuticals firms (e.g. Carlsson Research and Merck; BioVitrum and Amgen; Kario Bio and Wyeth). However, the official http://www.sweden.se website notes that the following: 'Both AstraZeneca and Pharmacia collaborate with numerous biotech companies, some of them Swedish.... The pharmaceutical companies Astra (now AstraZeneca) and Pharmacia (today part of Pfizer) have stimulated the growth of the Swedish biotech industry, not only in the pharmaceutical and medical sub-sectors but also, for example, in biotech tools and supplies. Examples are Prevas Bioinformatics contract solutions for AstraZeneca, Biovitrum and GE Healthcare while blockbuster drugs like *Losec* (AstraZeneca) and *Celebrex* (Pharmacia) were clinically trialled by Swedish clinical research organisations as were many others originating abroad (e.g. Lipitor, Norvasc and Zoloft for Pfizer; Lipovas for Merck; and Paxil for Glaxo SmithKline).

[10] SLU is the Swedish University of Agricultural Sciences.

These produce annually some 8,000 publications, co-host some 4,000 PhD students and employ some 2,200 scientists.

However, on publication interactions, Sweden's collaborations revealed that 70% of co-authorships (1986–1997) were with other Swedish PROs, while 12% were with US institutions and an equivalent share with UK and German co-authors together. Regarding R&D projects, McKelvey et al. (2003) found the opposite, that is, of 215 collaborations made by 67 actors (firms, universities and research institutes), 52 were between Swedish institutions and the rest involved overseas partners, these again being mainly with the USA and UK. This undoubtedly reflects the relative thinness of the pharmaceuticals and DBF market, particularly the former, in Sweden, which perforce stimulates links for industrial research with larger economy incumbents. This is underlined to a limited degree for patenting where Swedish biotechnology patents registered in the USA involved 62 jointly with US inventors. However, 202 were products of Swedish-only collaborations: a similar pattern prevailed for pharmaceuticals joint-patenting (VINNOVA 2003).

Hence, Sweden may be said to display a relatively typical European introversion in much of its exploration or basic research activity, including to some extent patenting, but is more outgoing where applied research with industry is concerned. Stockholm–Uppsala is the stronger with 56 firms and 1,126 employees, at least five strong research universities and around 1,640 employees in smaller biotechnology businesses in four Science Parks. However, Lund–Malmö is a larger concentration at 104 than Stockholm–Uppsala. Medicon Valley is well placed in this respect, being home to 11 universities, 70 biopharmaceuticals companies (60% of the turnover of the Nordic pharmaceutical market) and 26 hospitals. Its academic institutions include, among others, Copenhagen and Lund universities, The Danish University of Pharmaceutical Sciences, and The Royal Veterinary and Agricultural University, as well as centres for diabetes and stem cell research, and a multidisciplinary centre for stem cell biology and cell therapy. There are also 135,000 students in the area, more than 300 research groups, 4,000 Life Science employees and 27 local venture capital firms (Dorey 2003). Pharmaceuticals firms have been key to the growth on the Danish side through the likes of Hansen Laboratories, Carlsberg Laboratory and Novo Nordisk, a global insulin supplier and partner of Biogen in early bioengineering of human insulin. Medicon Valley Academy was formed in 1997 to 'create, transfer and exploit knowledge' with the aim of making it the most attractive bioregion in Europe by 2005. This academy is largely responsible for creating a sense of identity in the region, arranging networking events and also building relationships with other clusters in Scandinavia such as the Stockholm–Uppsala region.

Singapore's government biotechnology initiatives started in 1987 with the establishment of the Institute of Molecular and Cellular Biology at the National University of Singapore, but became industrially serious within the 2000–2004 period. The aim was to build a biotechnology cluster around FDI, a policy that worked well in previous developmental stages, such as the policies in support of petrochemicals, electronics and ICT. Four new institutes in bioinformatics, genomics, bioprocessing and nanobiotechnology now exist at a cost of $150 million to 2006. Public venture capital of $200 million has been committed to three bioscience investment funds to fund start-ups and attract FDI. A further $100 million is earmarked for attracting up to five globally leading corporate research centres. The *Biopolis* is Singapore's intended world-class R&D hub for the georegion. The *Biopolis* is dedicated to biomedical R&D activities and designed to foster a collaborative culture among the institutions present and with the nearby National University of Singapore, the National University Hospital and Singapore's Science Parks. Internationally celebrated scientists, such as Nobel laureate Sidney Brenner, Alan Colman, leading transgenic animal cloning scientist from Scotland's Roslin Institute, Edison Liu, former head of the US National Cancer Institute, and leading Japanese cancer researcher Yoshaki Ito, have also been attracted.

These are 'magnet' appointments meant to attract talent and create cluster conventions and practices among research centres and DBFs. The sector now numbers 38 firms of which 15 are indigenous start-ups and 23 FDI R&D, manufacturing, clinical research organisations and other services. Johns Hopkins, MIT, Duke University, Columbia University and the Indian Institute of Technology have established facilities in Singapore. Singapore's Bioethics Advisory Committee advised acceptance of embryonic stem cell but not human cloning research, which is also a globally attractive locational factor, shared as we shall see with Israel, among others. Pharmaceuticals firms from overseas manufacturing in Singapore include Glaxo since 1989, Schering-Plough (1997), Genset (now Serono) (1997), Aventis (2000), Merck (2001), Wyeth (2002) and Pfizer (2004). R&D centres of the following firms are also present: Genelabs (1985), Becton Dickenson (1986), Oculex (1995), Perkin Elmer (1998), Sangui (1988), Cell Transplants (2000), Schering-Plough (2000), Eli Lilly (2001), Surromed (2001), Affymetrix (2001), Novartis (2002), ViaCell (2002), PharmaLogicals (2002). Finally, clinical research organisation services are available from Quintiles (1995), Novo Nordisk (1999), Covance (2000) and Pharmacia-Upjohn (now Pfizer) (2000). Joining ViaCell in stem cells are indigenous DBFs ES Cell and CordLife, a few genomics firms such as APGenomics and Qugen, and a variety of drug discovery, bioinformatics and diagnostics firms mostly established since 2000. In brief, Singapore is host to a large number of mainly US and, to a lesser extent, European R&D laboratories of big pharma businesses. It has strength in public research activity and small signs of growth in stem cells exploration and exploitation activity. The benign regulatory environment allowing embryonic stem cells research is undoubtedly an attraction, which contextuated by Singapore's celebrated 'developmentalist state' capabilities, will stimulate cluster growth as an 'offshore' research and production platform targeting the burgeoning Asian market.

Switzerland is another small country in which multinationals generally, and in big pharma specifically, are a notable feature of the economic landscape. Roche (Hoffmann La Roche) and Novartis (formerly Sandoz and Ciba-Geigy) are indigenous Swiss multinationals, the latter in the global top ten by market capitalisation, the former having slipped down the rankings in later years rather like Bayer and, to some extent, Aventis among former European majors. The Swiss government too in 2002 announced in favour of embryonic stem cells research while banning embryo-creation purely for research purposes. Apart from Novartis and Roche, Switzerland also hosts one of the world's largest biotechnology companies Serono, which in 2001 had a market capitalisation of $18 billion, ranking it third behind Amgen and Genentech. Serono and Amgen signed a licensing and commercialisation deal for Serono to sell a Multiple Sclerosis drug in the USA it had developed with Immunex, a Cambridge (MA) firm subsequently acquired by Amgen. Other prominent firms are Actelion, Cytos, The Genetics Company, bio-T, CELLnTEC, Debiopharm, GeneBio and Solvias. In addition to Serono, Actelion, Berna Biotech, Debiopharm and Basilea have several pharmaceuticals in clinical testing. Lonza Biologics is also Swiss and one of the largest biosynthesis firms in the world. Debiopharm funds cancer research projects at Tulane University, New Orleans.

Of the 200 Swiss biotechnology companies listed in 2003, around 40 are pure biotechnology firms (DBFs), the others being instrumentation and services firms that nevertheless link to many of the forty. Some 22% of the 200 are located in the Geneva–Lausanne 'BioAlps' region, ~26% are in the Basel 'BioValley' region and about 35% are in the Greater Zurich region. Zurich has a Functional Genomics Research Centre. Since 2000, 45 new biotechnology businesses have been established, 15 of which were spinouts from the Swiss Federal Institute of Technology in Lausanne and Zurich and 10 were spinouts from other Swiss universities. The remainder came from domestic and foreign subsidiary industries. Of the 30 or so public companies, many such as Genedata (Basel), Cytos (Zurich) and GeneProt (Geneva), a proteomics DBF, have long-term collaborative research, opinion and licensing agreements with the likes of Novartis and Roche. International collaborations extend to the partnership between the University of Minnesota and the Swiss Federal Institute of Technology focused upon medical technology. This arises in part from Minneapolis devices firm Medtronic's subsidiary located in Switzerland and its collaboration with the likes of Disetronic, a leading Swiss insulin-pump manufacturer. In conclusion, Switzerland is a small, capable knowledge-intensive biosciences economy. It has leaders in big pharma, global DBF capability and numerous smaller DBFs and spinouts concentrating on leading-edge proteomics and other post-genomics treatments. It is highly connected globally, but especially to the US megacentres through big pharma and its leading clusters in Zurich, Basel and Geneva–Lausanne.

## 2.6.2 The Research and DBF-Led Clusters in Israel and Canada

By 2001 the Israeli biotechnology industry consisted of 172 firms, 7 of which were publicly traded. The whole sector had a total valuation of $3.5 billion and 4,000 employees, and 85% of firms employed less than 20 persons. These firms are clustered as follows: Rehovot (satellite of Tel Aviv) has 46 firms and some 1,290 life scientists, Jerusalem has 38 firms and 1,358 life scientists, and Tel Aviv has 32 firms and some 1,725 life scientists. Jerusalem's patent score is the highest at 209, followed by Rehovot at 176 and Tel Aviv at 64. Jerusalem has perhaps the more mature of the three clusters, something the patent data underline. Apart from generics drug manufacturer Teva, Israel lacks major pharmaceuticals firms and even clinical research organisation services. It is very much a research-led, university and incubator-based system in much need of finding co-incubation partners and consolidating links with big pharma. It is noteworthy that if Hebrew University, Jerusalem, were to appear in rankings on university royalty earnings it would be rather high because of its 2002 licensing income of over $20 million resulting from the invention in its biosciences faculty of the globally consumed 'cherry tomato' (Kaufmann et al. 2003).

An example of the Israeli bioincubator strategy is at the heart of the dynamic biotechnology cluster connected to the Hebrew University and related teaching hospitals. *Hadasit* is fundamentally a for-profit, incorporated company founded by the Hadasah Medical Organisation, a women's health foundation that owns 100% of Hadasit's shares. It offers a comprehensive, one-stop-shop service to its spinout firms. Hadasit's procedure involves screening firm candidates, agreement for pre-proof of concept funds, followed by an IPR assessment. If it passes muster a patent filing occurs conducted by Hadasit, leading to a final prototype, preparation of a business plan and auditioning for venture capital. Hadasit has US partners and also links to incubation facilities in Singapore and Australia. It offers firms the widest range of services and benefits from growth in its equity stake in incubated start-ups. The incubator has firms specialising in thrombosis, cancer care, rheumatoid arthritis and hormone research. Hadasit has taken on one-stop-shop functions perforce, because of the relative absence in Jerusalem, and Israel more generally, of a developed biotechnology services market.

The Canadian industry is split evenly between Toronto and Montreal, though Vancouver also has a presence. Toronto and Montreal together account for some 228 DBFs; Vancouver has 71. Space permits only limited discussion of both, starting with Toronto. According to Niosi and Bas (2001, 2003), Toronto has a stronger scientific base than Montreal even though each city has some 73 and 72 DBFs, respectively. Thus Toronto had 178 DBF patents (1989–1999), 61% of the total, while Montreal had 51 or 17%. Similarly, Toronto had 191 patents overall, including firms, universities and government (37%) and Montreal 96 (18%). Toronto has recently been named as the destination of Aventis's new $350 million Genomics Research Institute, adding to big pharmas' exodus of leading-edge research from continental Europe (Novartis has established its equivalent $250 million facility in the Boston region). Venture capital also reflects the variation in status of the two centres. Both cities have multinational pharmaceuticals firms such as Pfizer, Merck, Shire (formerly BioChem Pharma), Aventis, Novartis and Schering in Montreal and Aventis Pasteur, AstraZeneca, Bayer and Eli Lilly in Toronto. Each has main university research centres such as University of Toronto, York and McMaster in Toronto, and McGill, University of Montreal, University of Quebec at Montreal and Concordia universities in Montreal. Many government research laboratories also co-exist in both places.

Yet there is more of a struggle for the DBF sector in Montreal since the region experienced significant industrial restructuring, loss of traditional manufacturing industry and particularly financial services to Toronto during the 1970–2000 period. However, bioscientific research is deeply embedded in the region and commercialisation has produced world-class firms, notably and also at the Laval campus, BioChem Pharma discoverer of *Epivir*, the first AIDS treatment marketed through Glaxo. Since acquired by the UK firm Shire Pharmaceuticals, BioChem was, in late 2003, experiencing significant corporate re-positioning towards less costly therapeutic targets while advanced research was being focused more towards home base, the greater Montreal region. The region has a large biomedical cluster with leading companies and a strong research base with four universities in Montreal, an established biopharmaceuticals and diagnostics industry with 145 companies and 14,500 jobs and 50 biological research institutes, including the Canadian National Research Council Biotechnology Research Institute, an important federal biotechnology research centre. QBIC is located in the Laval Science and High Technology Park, Montreal. The Park was created in 1989 as the result of a strategic alliance between the INRS-Institut Armand-Frappier (a research centre of Quebec University), the City of Laval and Laval Technopole. The Laval Science and High Technology Park is the focus of 'Biotech City', a $100 million initiative launched in June 2001 to develop a business and science centre supported by the Quebec government, Investissement Québec, the Institut National de la Recherché Scientifique (INRS), the Laval Technopole and the City of Laval. Some 30 businesses, biotechnology and biopharmaceutical companies, research centres and IT firms exist in the Biotech City. QBIC had, in late 2003, six firms in its bioincubator.

We can say, in conclusion, that Canada's large pharmaceuticals firms have grown as established production, sales and marketing branches serving the Canadian market whether from the US or Europe. However, cluster-development has occurred mainly separately from this through academic entrepreneurship supported by well-found research infrastructure and local venture capital capabilities. Unlike Israel, where there are scarcely any pharmaceuticals firms with which DBFs might interact, in Toronto and Montreal, they have been perhaps equivalents of 'ships that pass in the night'. In relation to our earlier proposal of a Spatial Knowledge Capabilities theory of economic geography, the sketches provided earlier point to the emergence in some cases in concertation of DBFs and big pharma, and in others the largely or substantially independent emergence of DBF clusters in proximity to knowledge centres, notably universities where leading-edge research is commonly practised. To these centres are attracted investment and talent, including in recent years incumbent research talent in big pharma that also establishes its 'ahead of the curve' post-genomics research in look-out posts or embedded research facilities in the clusters. No longer does talent migrate to corporate headquarters in New Jersey or London, rather the magnets for large-scale knowledge investments are the privileged global network nodes represented in a brief benchmarking exercise in Table 2.6.

## 2.7 Conclusions

Thus the chapter, in focusing on the SME–research nexus that typifies bioregions and the strength of weak and strong ties among actors in such locales, pays due attention to the global reach of many of the connections characterising such companies, but also emphasises the importance of the public sector as customer through health systems and provider, along with big pharma and private foundations in fuelling modern bioscientific research and commercialisation. It further pays due attention to the varying strength of large corporations in bioregions, depending upon the type of biotechnology in which they specialise. It seems that, as a major global biotechnology player in terms of research, number of firms, clusters and even recent pipeline product performance, Europe could nevertheless learn some useful lessons from the USA in promoting its bioregions by the following five practices found there. These conclusions draw some critical lessons for European biotechnology from comparison of similar cluster-focused evolutionary processes there and in the USA, which admittedly has enjoyed a 20-year technological lead over most of Europe and at least a 10-year lead compared to Europe's leading practitioners.

- It is important to maintain a global presence in the pharmaceutical industry in geographical proximity to key bioscience clusters. This does not mean global companies that are only anchored in domestic locations. Clearly, accomplished firms must remain functionally close to key bioregions domestically and abroad. Helping create stronger links beyond presently reasonably healthy publishing collaborations from bioregions to the leading ones in the USA will also hasten non-firm-led knowledge transfer. Without these, it simply proves harder for European SMEs to build and maintain close links with, for example, pharmaceuticals R&D procurement offices when these relocate to the USA.
- Such knowledge transfer must be improved between research and firms by even better linkage around patenting and better funding opportunities for commercialisation by firms (but see later). Europe's innovative clusters, of which there are a relatively good number compared to the USA, seem to make fewer biotechnology 'breakthrough' innovations, presumably because the science is not found in sufficiently promising, possibly high-risk research areas.
- Although the USA has no significant lead in numbers of firms or clusters in biotechnology, it has a significant lead in the levels of investment by both risk capital investors and big pharma licensing of intellectual property for which they can see good prospects of a return on their investment – in both cases. This is a result of much European research being 'far from the market' but it may also be a function of the larger public investment in the USA in basic research, which now runs at more than double the European investment in public R&D in biotechnology.
- Incentives for commercialisation of innovative knowledge are weak in Europe, generally-speaking. Historically, only Cambridge and Sweden as a whole have operated such that intellectual property remained largely with the inventor,

usually a university scientist. The UK government policy more recently has been to dilute that, leaving only Sweden with such an incentive structure. It is perhaps no coincidence that Ernst & Young (2007) reveal Sweden to have Europe's largest number of biotechnology companies relative to GDP.

• It is possible that a stronger *licensing* orientation from both research institutes and firms may bring a more rapid return and progress to commercialisation than going mainly down the spinout route towards commercialisation.

These and related aspects of the knowledge gleaned from this survey of global bioregions will assist those with an already relatively strong showing in the global bioregion stakes to become even stronger in the foreseeable future. It will also assist those aspiring to evolve biotechnology clusters to understand better the challenges and opportunities that lie before them.[11]

# References

Benner M, Sandström U (2000) Internationalising the triple helix: Research funding and norms in the academic system. Research Policy 29: 291–301

BioGenTec (1998) BioGenTec Atlas. BioGenTec, Cologne

Bioscience Innovation and Growth Team (BIGT) (2004) Bioscience 2015: Improving national health, increasing national wealth. BIGT BIA/DTI/DoH, London

Casper S, Karamanos A (2003) Commercialising science in Europe: The Cambridge biotechnology cluster. European Planning Studies 11: 805–822

Chesbrough H (2003) Open innovation. Harvard Business School Press, Boston

California Healthcare Institute and PriceWaterhouseCoopers (CHI/PWC) (2002) Biomedicine: The new pillar in northern California's economy. CHI/PWC, La Jolla and San José

Cooke P (2002) Biotechnology clusters as regional, sectoral innovation systems. International Regional Science Review 25: 8–37

Cooke P (2004) The molecular biology revolution and the rise of bioscience megacentres in North America and Europe. Environment and Planning C: Government and Policy 22: 161–177

Cooke P (2006) Entrepreneurs, innovation systems and policy platforms. Report to the Constructing Regional Advantage Commission. EU Directorate General Research, Brussels

Cortright J, Mayer H (2002) Signs of life: The growth of biotechnology centres in the US. The Brookings Institute, Washington, DC

Dorey E (2003, March) Emerging market Medicon Valley: A hotspot for biotech affairs. BioResource. http://www.investintech.com

Eastern Region Biotechnology Initiative (ERBI) (1999) Background information for Cambridge and Eastern Region biotechnology cluster. ERBI, Cambridge

Ernst & Young (2007) Beyond borders 2006. Ernst & Young, Boston

---

[11] Thanks to Ann Yaolu for assistance with the scientometrics and to David Knight for data on the UK genomics firms. Thanks also to Lennart Stenberg, VINNOVA, for discussing various concepts and hypotheses. Finally, thanks to colleagues in the CIND, CIRCLE and ISRN networks in Sweden and Canada who heard these observations in preliminary form and encouraged their development into a hopefully coherent analysis.

Finegold D, Wong P, Cheah T (2004) Adapting a foreign direct investment strategy to the knowledge economy: The case of Singapore's emerging biotechnology cluster. European Planning Studies (in press)

Foray D, Freeman C (1993) Technology and the wealth of nations: The dynamics of constructed advantage. Pinter, London

Hall P, Soskice D (2001) Varieties of capitalism: The historical foundations of comparative advantage. Oxford University Press, Oxford

Healthcare Industries Task Force (HITF) (2004) Better healthcare through partnership: A programme for action. HITF, London

Helpman E (1998) General purpose technologies and economic growth. MIT Press, Cambridge

Jack A (2005, 14 January) Focus turns to question of drugs advertising. Financial Times, p 3

Kaiser R (2003) Multi-level science policy and regional innovation: The case of the Munich cluster for pharmaceutical biotechnology. European Planning Studies 11: 841–858

Kaufmann D, Schwartz D, Frenkel A, Shefer D (2003) The role of location and regional networks for biotechnology firms in Israel. European Planning Studies 11: 823–840

Lawton Smith H (2004) The biotechnology industry in Oxfordshire: Enterprise and innovation. European Planning Studies 12: 985–1002

Lemarié S, Mangematin V, Torre A (2001) Is the creation and development of biotech SMEs localised? Conclusions drawn from the French case. Small Business Economics 17: 61–76

Malik A, Pinkus G, Sheffer S (2002) Biopharma's capacity crunch. McKinsey Quarterly, http://www.mckinsey.co.uk

March J (1991) Exploration and exploitation in organisational learning. Organization Science 2: 71–87

McKelvey M, Alm H, Riccaboni M (2003) Does co-location matter for formal knowledge collaboration in the Swedish biotechnology–pharmaceuticals sector? Research Policy 32: 485–501

Nelund R, Norus J (2003) Competitiveness and opportunities: Building an island of innovation apart from Europe's innovative centre. In: Hilpert U (ed) Regionalisation of globalised innovation. Routledge, London

Niosi J, Bas T (2001) The competencies of regions – Canada's clusters in biotechnology. Small Business Economics 17: 31–42

Niosi J, Bas T (2003) Biotechnology megacentres: Montreal and Toronto regional systems of innovation. European Planning Studies 11: 789–804

Owen-Smith J, Powell W (2004) Knowledge networks as channels and conduits: The effects of spillovers in the Boston biotechnology community. Organization Science 15: 5–21

Porter M (2002) Clusters of innovation: Regional foundations of US competitiveness. Council on Competitiveness, Washington

Smith A (1776) Wealth of nations. The Modern Library, New York

VINNOVA (2003) Swedish biotechnology-scientific publications, patenting and industrial development. VINNOVA (Swedish Agency for Innovation Systems), Stockholm

# 3 Geographic Clustering in Biotechnology: Social Networks and Firm Foundings

Dirk Fornahl[1] and Olav Sorenson[2]

[1] Universität Karlsruhe (TH) – Institute of Economic Policy Research (IWW), Germany
[2] Jeffrey S. Skoll Chair in Technical Innovation and Entrepreneurship, Professor of Strategic Management, Rotman School of Management, University of Toronto

## 3.1 Introduction

Even casual observation reveals that firms in a wide range of industries have a tendency to cluster together – from computer software and hardware in the region between San Francisco and San Jose ("Silicon Valley"), to motion picture production in Los Angeles, to investment banking in London and New York. Biotechnology is no exception. In the United States, one finds concentrations of biotechnology firms in San Diego, South San Francisco, the Research Triangle Park in North Carolina, and the region off Route 128, just north of Boston (Fig. 3.1; for a more detailed mapping, see Stuart and Sorenson 2003b). In Germany, biotechnology clusters are found in Bavaria and Baden Wuerttemberg (Fig. 3.2; for more details, see Zeller 2001). In the United Kingdom, concentrations appear in the regions around Cambridge and Oxford (Lawton Smith et al. 2000). In fact, one finds a significant degree of geographic concentration in every country with a major presence in biotechnology (for further information on Canada, see Niosi and Bas 2001; for more on France, see Lemarié et al. 2001; and for a worldwide map, see Rinaldi 2006).

H. Patzelt and T. Brenner (eds.), *Handbook of Bioentrepreneurship*,
doi: 10.1007/978-0-387-48345-0_3, © Springer Science + Business Media, LLC 2008

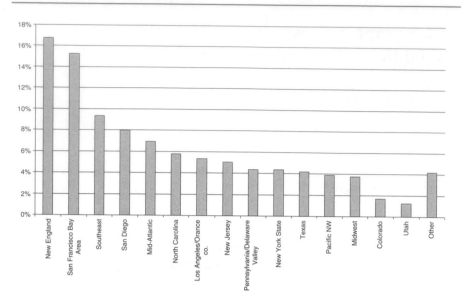

**Fig. 3.1.** Distribution of core biotechnology firms in the USA in 2003 (*Source:* Ernst & Young 2004)

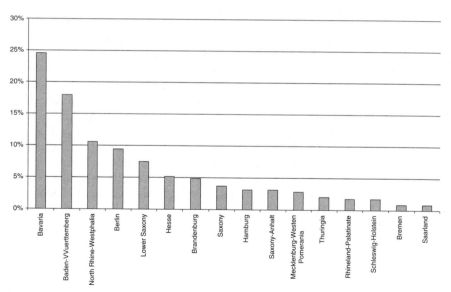

**Fig. 3.2.** Distribution of core biotechnology firms in Germany in 2001 (*Source:* Ernst & Young 2002)

Why does such agglomeration occur? Traditional explanations for geographic concentration based on transportation costs and the location of critical inputs hold little sway in this setting since biotechnology draws most crucially on knowledge, an input with no physical weight and no natural location.[1] Explanations for the geographic clustering of biotechnology firms, as well as other high-technology industries, have therefore focused primarily on accounts that recall Marshall's (1890) ideas on agglomeration externalities, claiming that colocation allows firms to operate more efficiently by sharing resources, such as information or the output of some supplier (e.g., reagents in biotechnology).[2] Others, however, have suggested that geographic concentration reflects more where entrepreneurs can and do found firms than the economic efficiency of agglomeration (Sorenson and Audia 2000; Stuart and Sorenson 2003b; Klepper and Sleeper 2005). In this chapter, we explain the logic behind and review the evidence for this second explanation.

Social networks – sets of relationships between individuals – are central to this explanation. One can conceive of the entrepreneurial process as composed of two stages. First, the potential entrepreneur must perceive a business opportunity worth pursuing. In biotechnology, such an opportunity might represent either a technology, such as a new technique for DNA sequencing, or an application, for example, a disease without existing treatments available. Once an opportunity has been identified, the would-be founder faces the challenge of assembling the resources necessary to pursue it – know-how, financial capital, and skilled labor in the form of both scientists and laboratory technicians. Social relationships influence both stages of this process, facilitating opportunity recognition and the acquisition of intellectual, financial, and human capital.

Because they play critical roles in the entrepreneurial process, these relationships shape the geographic distribution of industries. The social ties that individuals acquire and maintain do not appear at random. Rather, people must meet in space and time to bond. Although the nascent entrepreneur might form connections with others met at an academic or professional conference or on a vacation, relationships more commonly arise from situations that involve more sustained interaction – attending the same school, being employed at the same firm, or perhaps belonging to the same club. Even among initiated relationships, those most proximate tend to last longest since the cost of maintaining them declines with distance (Stouffer 1940; Zipf 1949). As a result, social networks primarily connect individuals to others in the regions in which they live and work. This social parochialism restricts the ability of entrepreneurs to found firms far from their existing locations, thereby ensuring that the geographic patterns of entry reinforce the existing distribution of economic activity in any industry (Sorenson and Audia 2000). Just as this dynamic promotes agglomeration in other industries, so too does it in biotechnology (Stuart and Sorenson 2003b).

The remainder of this chapter presents this idea and the evidence supporting it in greater detail. Section 3.2 discusses the local character of social relationships. Section 3.3 details the mechanisms through which these relationships influence firm founding. Section 3.4 reviews the empirical implications of and evidence for

---

[1] Zucker et al. (1998), however, recall this classical view by claiming that biotechnology firms must locate near elite universities to gain access to 'star' scientists.

[2] See Brenner (2004) for a review of the literature on agglomeration externalities.

this theory. Section 3.5 discusses its policy implications, and Section 3.6 concludes.

## 3.2 Social Networks and Geographic Proximity

Despite the press surrounding "globalization" and proclamations of the "death of distance," individuals by and large lead highly local lives. They work in close proximity to their places of residences. They socialize with people living in the same communities (Festinger et al. 1950), and even typically marry partners from these same regions (Bossard 1932). The ability to obtain information and secure resources from other parties, which depends on these relationships, therefore tends to decrease with distance (as we discuss in Sect. 3.3).

People live local lives not only in the geographic sense, but also in a social one (Lazarsfeld and Merton 1954; Blau 1977). Even among those residing in the same region, people most commonly interact with others similar to them on a variety of dimensions – for example, those employed in the same firms, industries, and fields, and those of the same social standing, educational level, ethnicity, and religion. Though social relationships can and do span geographic and social spaces, these "distant" ties remain the exception rather than the rule.

A number of factors contribute to the local character of social networks. First and foremost, the formation of a relationship requires that two individuals meet. Although in some cases people pursue specific contacts, more commonly they meet by chance.[3] Since these chance encounters require individuals to be in the same location at the same time, they tend to occur between people that frequent the same places. Two scientists employed in neighboring firms, for example, might meet at a favorite pub or lunch spot.

Formal organizations play an important role in this process, as they serve as "foci" for people with similar interests to meet and interact (Feld 1981). People work in firms, worship in congregations, and pursue hobbies in clubs. In biotechnology, universities, laboratories, and conferences all provide potential points of first contact. Fledgling fields and industries, however, typically lack formal organizations to serve as foci. Most such organizations in the US biotechnology industry, for example, did not emerge until the late 1980s and early 1990s, more than a decade after the critical scientific breakthroughs that enabled the industry (Stuart and Sorenson 2003b). As a result, industry-specific organizations play less of a role than more general ones during the emergence of an industry.

Enduring relations also require time to mature. People do not become fast friends, or even trusted colleagues, the first time they meet. Relationships emerge through repeated interactions (Blau 1964). Maintaining them also requires contact. Though friendships persist to some extent and rarely simply disappear in the

---

[3] This intentional path to relationship formation, however, may not represent an important source of interpersonal relationships. Recipients of such attention often reject these attempts to form connections, skeptical of the intentions of suitors. Repeated attempts even constitute a crime – stalking – in many jurisdictions.

absence of interaction, over time they nonetheless "grow distant" (i.e. weaker) without exchanges to reinforce them. Again, both geographic and social proximity affect the costs of interaction, and consequently the odds that relationships emerge from chance meetings and persist over time. Distance imposes two types of costs. First, distance raises the direct costs of interaction (Zipf 1949). Travel requires both time and money. Second, it also increases the opportunity costs. As the distance between two actors lengthens, the likelihood of an intervening opportunity – an equally preferred but closer contact – increases as well (Stouffer 1940).

Even among the individuals a person sees on a regular basis, he or she may favor some over others. In particular, research finds that people prefer to interact with others similar to them; that is, they exhibit "homophily" (for a review of this literature, see McPherson et al. 2001). A variety of factors may account for this tendency – common interests could provide topics for conversion, or cultural and social similarity might facilitate communication, thereby reducing the potential for misunderstanding and conflict. Regardless of its source, homophily further reinforces the clustering of social relationships.

Although research on this preference for similar others has focused on demographic characteristics, "place" has a number of important influences on interests and cultural similarity. Those from the same region, for example, might bond over common cultural references or a shared passion for a local sports club. It therefore seems reasonable to expect that this preference could similarly intensify the localization of social ties in geographic space.

Because these factors strongly shape relationship formation in general, they further imply that those tie-generating processes that operate endogenous to the network also result in local connections. Introductions through friends and colleagues, for example, simply lead to more connections to similar others. Time constraints and a desire for social cohesion likewise increase the density of these clusters of relationships. Groups of friends can socialize as group. Belonging to multiple social circles by contrast requires negotiation, and potentially choosing among them when the interests of the groups diverge.

Together these forces produce social networks with some important characteristics: Most people interact with a limited set of others, who themselves know each other or are friends of friends; in other words, they form clusters in the social network. These clusters of relations moreover tend to reside within regions, and to connect individuals with a high degree of similarity across many dimensions. Although true of all relations, individuals become even more tightly clustered and the clusters become increasingly homogenous as we consider groups connected by stronger relationships: close friends versus friends, friends vs. acquaintances, etc.

These features become important to the geography of industries because social relationships structure the flows of both information and resources. The next section reviews these effects.

## 3.3 Social Networks and Entrepreneurship

One can conceptually divide the entrepreneurial process into two stages. In the first stage, entrepreneurs identify opportunities for profit. In biotechnology, for example, an entrepreneur might see a need for an instrument to sequence DNA rapidly, or might notice the possibility of using a scientific breakthrough to treat some illness. In the second stage, entrepreneurs build firms to develop and provide products and services. Although one tends to expect that the first stage should always precede the second, it is not a necessity. Accounts of the origins of many successful firms, for example, suggest that sometimes an entrepreneur's efforts to create a firm precede any specific idea of what that firm should do (e.g., Hewlett-Packard; Packard 1995). Hence, we will discuss these stages as distinct, but not necessarily sequential.

Each of these stages captures a portion of the activities conceptualized as entrepreneurship in the literature. Opportunity recognition, for instance, seems consistent with the idea that entrepreneurs combine disparate ideas (Say 1821) and with the definition of the entrepreneur as innovator (Schumpeter 1934). The possibility of profit in both of these cases comes from unusual insight into an opportunity available for exploitation.

The second stage meanwhile captures better the common understanding of entrepreneurship, the notion that the entrepreneur builds and manages a firm. This stage resonates with a different set of definitions of entrepreneurship. For instance, it appears consistent with the conceptualizations of entrepreneurs as combiners of disparate resources (Say 1821; Burt 1992) and as bearers of uncertainty in the economy (Knight 1921). Let us consider the role of social relationships in each stage in turn.

### 3.3.1 Opportunity Perception

Identifying potentially profitable opportunities requires access to information. But not just any information; profitable opportunities generally arise from access to *private* information. Two factors contribute to this fact. On the one hand, if those who first discover some bit of data understand their value, they will try to reveal it to as few as possible. On the other hand, if they do not understand their value and disclose it to the public, many entrepreneurs may pursue the opportunity and consequently compete away much (if not all) of the available value. Regardless of which of these factors matters more, it is this need for private information that links opportunity recognition to relationships.

Social networks provide channels for the flow of private information. On the one hand, individuals may simply exchange data through the course of interaction. But even if information holders understand its value and wish to restrict access to it, they may still share it with some of their affiliates because they require these individuals' cooperation. The head of a laboratory, for instance, might keep those working for her up-to-date on the results of the entire team's efforts because of independencies in their activities. Though that channel would appear limited in its scope, once passed on to members of a laboratory or employees in an organization, information might continue to seep outside these organizational boundaries for other reasons.

Those with the information, for example, might provide it to others in their immediate social circles as a form of favor exchange. Gossiping typically involves a quid pro quo. I will tell you some "secrets" that you did not know if you tell me some that I did not. Despite the apparent innocuousness of such exchanges, they can result in the diffusion of valuable information far beyond its original source.

Although information can and does flow multiple "steps" away from its origin, closer connections – hearing from the source for example rather than from someone who heard it from the source or someone that heard it from someone that heard it from the source, etc. – provide better information. Those nearer to the source tend to receive information earlier than those further away (Burt 1992). Also, as a message passes through multiple individuals, it tends to accumulate errors (Sorenson et al. 2006). Each person in the chain may fail to recall or have understood the original message, or they may even have incentives to relay inaccurate information.

Because individuals vary in the information that they hold and because information flows more rapidly and with higher fidelity to those nearer in the network, connections to some prove more valuable than to others. In biotechnology, as in other settings, the most valuable connections are to those employed in the industry. Existing institutions generate most of the important information with respect to business opportunities in any industry. Among those employed in biotechnology, those at commercial biotechnology firms probably have access to more valuable information with respect to these opportunities than those in nonprofit organizations for at least two reasons. First, researchers in nonprofit settings tend to focus on technology that requires much more development before one could deploy it commercially. Second, the norms of publication in the academe mean that much less of the information produced in those organizations remains private (Bernal 1939; Merton 1942; Sorenson and Fleming 2004). Not only do these norms reduce the ability of potential entrepreneurs to profit from this information, but also to the extent that the information still has value, the publications serve as substitutes for social connections to these scientists (Sorenson and Singh 2007).

When one combines the fact that the most valuable information comes from within the industry with the local character of social relationships (in both geographic and social space), one can see that those best situated to identify opportunities for profit are those with prior experience in the industry (often referred to as "spin-offs" in the literature). These individuals have both industry-specific human capital (Agrawal et al. 2004; Klepper and Sleeper 2005) and dense social connections to others in the industry. It is not surprising therefore that a large share of the entrants into the biotechnology industry have prior experience at another biotechnology firm (Mitton 1990; Haug 1995). Moving beyond spin-offs, those that reside in a region with many biotechnology and pharmaceutical firms seem the next most likely to recognize an opportunity. These individuals tend to have more connections to those in these industries and therefore better access to relevant information flows.

### 3.3.2 Intellectual Capital

Biotechnology is a knowledge-based industry. As such, the single most important resource required for the success of a biotechnology firm is intellectual capital. Simply seeing the opportunity for a particular product or service is insufficient. The founder must have access to the scientific and technical knowledge necessary to develop it.

Acquiring such knowledge is not a trivial task. The knowledge used in biotechnology is not only complex, but also often tacit. Both of these factors increase the difficulty and costs of knowledge transfer. Complex knowledge – recipes in which the results depend sensitively on the steps involved in getting there – eludes easy transfer because the recipient of the knowledge cannot easily correct errors or omissions that may have occurred in the transmission process (Sorenson et al. 2006). The transferal of such knowledge therefore typically requires that the sender help the recipient to identify and correct mistakes in transmission. Similarly, the acquisition of tacit knowledge involves either learning-by-doing or intensive face-to-face interaction between the recipient and one who already possesses the know-how. Together, these factors imply that intellectual capital in biotechnology comes from close contact with experts in the field or from being an expert oneself (Owen-Smith and Powell 2004; Stuart et al. 2007).

Consequently, only a small set of people can start biotechnology companies (though clearly they may join teams of others with complementary abilities). One pool of potential founders is found among the faculty and postdoctorates in biotechnology and other closely related fields. They gain the relevant knowledge through learning-by-doing and learning-by-observation in their studies and research (Zucker and Darby 1996; McMullan and Gillin 1998). The other consists of employees at existing biotechnology and pharmaceutical companies (Mitton 1990; Haug 1995; Stuart and Sorenson 2003a). Not only have these individuals usually received training similar to that received by academic entrepreneurs, but also they may have valuable experience in other activities, such as patenting, clinical trials, manufacturing, and building and managing a commercial firm. Universities and existing firms in the biotechnology and pharmaceutical industries therefore serve as the primary sources of biotechnology entrepreneurs.

In this respect also, biotechnology is little different from other settings. Research has found that spin-offs – start-ups by those with prior experience in the industry – account for a large share of start-ups overall and an even larger share of successful ones in manufacturing industries such as automobiles (Klepper 2002), service industries such as law firms (Phillips 2002), and high-technology firms such as semiconductor manufacturers (Brittain and Freeman 1985). One question that naturally arises is, why, if these individuals are gainfully employed in the industry, do they choose to leave their jobs for a risky new venture? One possibility is that employees simply see an opportunity to capture a larger share of the value of their ideas. Another is that they may gain satisfaction from seeing their ideas reach the market. Consistent with both of these explanations, one sees a strong demonstration effect in rates of entrepreneurship (Sorenson and Audia 2000; Stuart and Ding 2006; Fornahl 2007). In other words, people more commonly found firms when they observe others doing so. Or, they may disagree with their employers over the future direction of the field (Klepper and Sleeper 2005). Consistent with this notion, one tends to see spin-offs occur in response to changes in the leadership of existing firms in the industry (Brittain and Freeman 1985; Stuart and Sorenson 2003a).

### 3.3.3 Human Capital

Few entrepreneurs in biotechnology could develop a product or service on their own. It is therefore critical in biotechnology – as in other high-technology industries where the production of intellectual property represents the primary source of value – to enlist able employees. Despite the importance of this resource, little empirical research has investigated how entrepreneurs recruit their first employees and the extent to which these employees affect the success of their businesses. Anecdotal accounts nonetheless suggest that social networks play an important role, as entrepreneurs appear to draw their first employees from friends and family.

To see why social relationships facilitate recruitment, it is useful to consider the problem from the perspective of the potential employee. A vast degree of uncertainty surrounds any new venture. For example, the science underlying the firm's research may prove a dead end. Or, the market may not accept the product. Or, the founder may not have the managerial acumen to run a company effectively. Moreover, the potential employee trying to evaluate these risks must also contend with the fact that the entrepreneur has an incentive to exaggerate the firm's prospects and his own abilities (Amit et al. 1990). If the employee joins the start-up, all of these factors can potentially affect her income and career; she might easily find herself out of a job.

Social relationships can help to mitigate these uncertainties. They do so in at least two ways. First, they allow potential employees to gather private information on the entrepreneur and the probable quality of his venture. They also allow entrepreneurs to locate high-potential job candidates. Since the best people typically already have jobs, they cannot simply advertise positions and expect them to apply (Granovetter 1973). Studies of job search therefore commonly find that people learn about jobs through their social networks (Granovetter 1973; Fernandez et al. 2000). The importance of social relationships to the process undoubtedly becomes even more pronounced among start-ups, where the firms lack human resource policies and personnel, and where employees face even greater uncertainty regarding the characteristics of the job being offered and the quality of the employer.

Social relationships may also play another interesting role in mitigating the doubts of potential employees. Experimental research has shown that people tend to evaluate more positively things that are familiar to them. Both experimental and field studies moreover suggest that this bias can explain why buyers and sellers frequently exchange repeatedly with the same partners (Kollock 1994; Sorenson and Waguespack 2006). Here, prior interactions with the entrepreneur may lead the potential employee to think more highly of the individual (regardless of his true quality), and therefore to feel sufficiently confident in the venture to join it as an employee despite the many obvious risks.

Given that social relationships can facilitate recruitment, potential entrepreneurs will vary in their ability to mobilize human capital on the basis of their positions. Employees in the biotechnology industry tend to come from the same two sources as entrepreneurs themselves. First, as with many high-technology industries, universities provide an important source of labor. Recent graduates serve as a source of bench scientists, running experiments and performing the "grunt work" of biotechnology. Meanwhile, certain faculty members – "star scientists" – provide valuable intellectual leadership and endorsements (Zucker and Darby 1996; Zucker et al. 1998). Second, employees at existing firms in the industry provide a large pool of labor, already steeped in the specific tacit knowledge that comes with experience in the industry (Sorenson and Audia 2000). Once again, those individuals who either have prior employment experience or have lived in close proximity to clusters of existing biotechnology firms typically have the best networks for mobilizing human capital.

### 3.3.4 Financial Capital

Equally important to any new venture, and especially to those in businesses such as biotechnology where firms cannot expect revenue for many years, is the availability of financial capital. As in other high-technology industries, the dominant form of funding in biotechnology has been venture capital (Florida and Kenney 1988; Haug 1995). Few investors other than venture capitalists will accept the risks inherent in investing in firms with uncertain prospects and long time horizons to profitability.[4]

Although important, one might expect financial capital to flow freely across regions, and therefore to have no effect on the location of industry. This expectation, however, ignores one of the key problems facing the venture capitalist (and other investors in private firms): the difficulty of evaluating the quality of the venture. Like potential employees, investors must assess a host of risks surrounding the new venture – the quality of the science, the potential for competition, the managerial ability of the founding team, etc. Social relationships again provide access to the private information necessary to understand these risks better (Sorenson and Stuart 2001). They may also, as with the case of employees,

---

[4] Government research grants, however, do serve as an important source of early stage funding in many countries (see Carsrud, Brännback and Renko, this volume).

bias investors' assessments in favor of the entrepreneur (Sorenson and Waguespack 2006). In fact, venture capitalists rarely invest in entrepreneurs who have not been referred to them by a known party (Fried and Hisrich 1994; Shane and Cable 2002). Since these relationships cluster geographically, venture capitalists primarily invest in firms located in close proximity – within an hour's drive or so – of their offices (Gupta and Sapienza 1992; Sorenson and Stuart 2001; Engel 2002).[5] Hence biotechnology entrepreneurs located near concentrations of venture capital firms have an advantage in finding financial support.

## 3.4 Implications and Evidence

Together, the mechanisms described earlier explain why firms in the biotechnology industry tend to concentrate geographically. Entrepreneurs arise from the ranks of employees in the biotechnology and pharmaceutical industries, and from the research staff of universities. These individuals can see the potential for building a business around some new technology or some underserved market. They also have the scientific and technical skills necessary to start a biotechnology company.

That, by itself, however, cannot explain the geographic concentration of the industry because these entrepreneurs could, in principle, move to any region to begin their commercial ventures (and presumably would, given sufficient potential for financial gain). The importance of social networks to recruiting employees and securing financing, however, binds entrepreneurs to the regions in which they live and work. It is within these regions that they have the connections required for mobilizing the resources necessary to found their firms.

Together, these two factors suggest that biotechnology entrepreneurs will primarily come from and will locate their firms in those regions that already have a significant presence in the field – either in an academic department or via existing firms. These organizations provide entrepreneurs and human capital. A local venture capital community, meanwhile, serves an important complement, providing financial capital. Consistent with these expectations, Stuart and Sorenson (2003b) find that the rate of biotechnology firm formation in a region rises with (1) the number of existing biotechnology firms in the region, (2) the presence of biotechnological research at a local university, and (3) the number of venture capital firms with headquarters in the region. Each university increases the founding rate by more than twice as much as each existing biotechnology firm and more than ten times as much as each venture capital firm. But given that universities tend to be far less numerous than these other two, the most important predictor of entry is the number of biotechnology firms, followed by the number of venture capital firms.

These relationships combine to form a coherent picture of the evolution of biotechnology clusters. They begin when one firm locates in a region, perhaps

---

[5] Research suggests that investors earn higher returns when they invest locally (Coval and Moskovitz 2001).

because a scientist at a local university sees an opportunity to put some of the science she has developed into practice. That firm then becomes the parent for more start-ups, its progeny, that in turn spin off additional firms. At some point, people begin to see the group as a cluster. That story, for example, describes the rise of the biotechnology cluster in San Diego (Mitton 1990). Hybritech formed in 1978 to commercialize science developed by Ivor Royston, a faculty member at University of California – San Diego, and his research assistant Howard Birndorf. It then spawned many progeny when a number of its scientists started their own firms following its acquisition by Eli Lilly in 1986. Similar dynamics have been described as underlying the origins of many high-technology clusters, including Cambridge (Keeble et al. 1999) and Oxford (Cooke 2001) in the United Kingdom, Jena in Germany (Hendry et al. 2000), and Grenoble in France (DeBernardy 1999).

Of course, other theories could explain these patterns of entry, particularly if firms benefited from being located near their rivals. All firms in a region may prosper from locating near one another if they can share some valuable resource (Marshall 1890). If, however, geographic concentration correlated negatively with firm performance, few (if any) explanations – other than the one forwarded here – could account for the geographic concentration of the industry. In fact, Stuart and Sorenson (2003b) find just such an effect: Biotechnology firms perform significantly worse – in terms of their ability to go public and the amount of funds they can raise – when they locate near other biotechnology firms.

Although inconsistent with efficiency-based explanations for agglomeration, such as agglomeration externalities, these negative effects should not surprise us. As competition for a fixed pool of resources rises, prices for these resources should rise and performance should decline (Hannan and Freeman 1989). In biotechnology, firms primarily compete at the local level for human capital. Not only does this drive up the local wage for technicians and bench scientists, but also it can lead to strategic convergence. Sørensen (1999), for example, found that organizations become more similar – and therefore more competitive – on the product market when they hire from the same labor pool. Biotechnology firms may also compete secondarily for financial resources, as most regions have a limited supply of venture capital.

Interestingly, being located near many venture capital firms also corresponds to lower performance. Although this effect may reflect a spurious relationship created by the effect that venture capital has in stimulating entry (and therefore competition), the availability of local financial resources raises another related problem for firms: retaining their most valuable employees. In regions with more abundant venture capital, employees find it easier to leave the firm to start their own ventures. Not only does their exit imply the loss of human capital, but also they may enter a closely related field, thereby competing with their previous employer on a number of dimensions.[6]

---

[6] Non-compete covenants can mitigate this behavior, but many states, such as California, do not enforce these agreements (Stuart and Sorenson 2003a).

Although in general these processes result in a reproduction of the existing geography of industry, two factors can moderate these effects over time and allow the industry to diffuse gradually. On the one hand, as the industry matures, industry associations emerge that serve as foci for connections across regions, easing for example the ability of entrepreneurs to recruit human capital from other regions. On the other hand, as firms within the industry grow, they may expand to new regions. In general, the need for social relationships proves far less constraining to existing firms. These organizations have track records that reduce much of the uncertainty facing potential employees and investors, and they have financial resources that they can bring to bear to substitute for social networks (e.g., by paying someone to relocate to a new region).

## 3.5 Policy Implications

Regional policymakers typically hope to stimulate the development of industry in the region to improve the local economy and expand its tax base. The theory and evidence described here, however, clearly pose a challenge to attempts to develop a biotechnology cluster in regions that do not already have them. One might nonetheless attempt to grow such a cluster through "'seeding."

Two types of seeding policies strike us as potentially sensible and effective. On the one hand, policymakers might seed the industry by trying to attract high-potential academics in the life sciences to local universities. Indeed, Ivor Royston, the founder of Hybritech, had been lured to UC San Diego only a couple of years before he began his company. Although clearly many of these academics may invent nothing of commercial value or show little interest in starting a firm, academics are one of the most geographically mobile segments of the population and regions can attract them with the appropriate incentives (Fornahl and Graf 2003). Some regions have already begun to pursue this strategy. In Canada, for example, Alberta now offers multi-million-dollar start-up grants for "superstar" researchers who move to the province; and Singapore, only 7 years into its bioscience initiative, has had enormous success in convincing prominent researchers to locate there.

On the other hand, policymakers might attempt to lure existing firms from other regions. Empirical evidence suggests that the increased revenues produced by these subsidies more than offset their cost (Greenstone and Moretti 2004). Moreover, to the extent that they bring a "parent' firm to the region that produces many progeny, the progeny contribute fully to the tax-paying industrial base. In terms of selecting such firms, regions probably want to target small- to medium-sized ventures for their subsidies. Not only will they face less competition to attract these firms, but also small firms tend to spin off progeny at a much higher rate than do larger ones (Brittain and Freeman 1985; Sørensen 2007).

But this theory of the geographic concentration of industry raises even more fundamental policy issues. Many policymakers hope to copy the success of other regions by building local economies built around some narrow industrial base (e.g., Sölvell et al. 2003). Given that clustering does not improve firm performance, one might question whether regions wish to promote it at all. Answering that question, however, requires a better understanding not just of how the geographic concentration of an industry affects firm performance, but also how it affects wages. If the colocation of rivals leads to a rise in wages in the industry in the region, then concentration may benefit the region and workers at the expense of the owners of the firm. If, on the other hand, it simply produces a great deal of inefficient entry and exit, then policymakers should consider investing instead in policies to attract a more diverse industrial base.

## 3.6 Summary and Outlook

Many people and policymakers look at regions such as Silicon Valley and San Diego with large numbers of biotechnology firms and presume that this concentration confers benefits to both the region and the firms located there. The empirical evidence does not, however, support such a view. In terms of firm performance, San Diego and Silicon Valley are the two worst possible locations for a biotechnology firm in the United States (Stuart and Sorenson 2003b). Yes, these regions have large numbers of biotechnology firms, but with those numbers come intense competition.

If firms do not profit from locating near their rivals, why do they not move elsewhere? Entrepreneurs require social connections to information and resource holders to identify opportunities and build firms to exploit them. Because these relationships remain largely bounded within regions, they bind entrepreneurs to the communities in which they live and work. In this sense, each entrepreneur maximizes his own expected outcomes; he would do even worse in a region where he could not draw on his social network. However, because entrepreneurs come primarily from the ranks of existing employees in the industry, the geographic pattern of entry tends to mimic that of incumbents, resulting in local overcrowding (and potentially a socially inefficient distribution of production). One would therefore expect industries to concentrate geographically even in the absence of performance benefits or policies designed to encourage clustering.

Although we do not have sufficient evidence to argue that policymakers should actively *discourage* the formation of clusters, the theory and evidence described here raise serious questions about many of the attempts that have been made to replicate the success of Silicon Valley and Route 128. Those tempted to pursue these paths should study history. Compare Chicago and Los Angeles to Akron (tires), Detroit (automobiles), and Pittsburgh (steel). Chicago and Los Angeles never enjoyed the booming success of these smaller cities at the dawn of the twentieth century; however, Chicago and Los Angeles also did not fall into steep decline in the later half of the century in the face of competition from imports. With concentration comes a price of fragility.

# References

Agarwal R, Echambadi R, Franco AM, Sarkar MB (2004) Knowledge transfer through inheritance: spin-out generation, development and survival. Academy of Management Journal 47: 501–522

Amit R, Glosten L, Muller E (1990) Entrepreneurial ability, venture investments and risk sharing. Management Science 36: 1232–1248

Bernal JD (1939) The social foundations of science. Macmillan, New York

Blau PM (1964) Exchange and power in social life. Wiley, New York

Blau PM (1977) Inequality and heterogeneity. Free Press, New York

Bossard JS (1932) Residential propinquity as a factor in marriage selection. American Journal of Sociology 38: 219–224

Brenner T (2004) Local industrial clusters, existence, emergence and evolution. Routledge, London

Brittain JW, Freeman J (1986) Entrepreneurship in the semiconductor industry. Unpublished manuscript, University of California, Berkeley, CA

Burt RS (1992) Structural holes: the social structure of competition. Harvard University Press, Cambridge, MA

Cooke P (2001) Biotechnology clusters in the U.K.: lessons from localisation in the commercialisation of science. Small Business Economics 17: 43–59

Coval J, Moskowitz TJ (2001) The geography of investment: informed trading and asset prices. Journal of Political Economy 109: 811–841

DeBernardy M (1999) Reactive and proactive local territory. Regional Studies 33: 343–352

Engel D (2002) Welche Regionen profitieren von Venture Capital-Aktivitäten? ZEW Discussion Paper No. 02-37, Centre for European Economic Research, Mannheim

Ernst & Young (2002) Neue Chancen – Deutscher Biotechnologie-Report 2002. Ernst & Young

Ernst & Young (2004) Ernst & Young's Global Biotechnology Report 2004. Ernst & Young

Feld SL (1981) The focused organization of social ties. American Journal of Sociology 86: 1015–1035

Fernandez RM, Castilla EJ, Moore P (2000) Social capital at work: networks and employment at a call center. American Journal of Sociology 105: 1288–1356

Festinger L, Schacter S, Back KW (1950) Social pressures in informal groups. Harper, New York

Florida R, Kenney M (1988) Venture capital and high technology entrepreneurship. Journal of Business Venturing 3: 301–319

Fornahl D (2007) Changes in regional firm founding activities – a theoretical explanation and empirical evidence. Routledge, London

Fornahl D, Graf H (2003) Standortfaktoren und Gründungsaktivitäten in Jena. In: Cantner U, Helm R, Meckl R (eds) Strukturen und Strategien in einem Innovationssystem – Das Beispiel Jena. Verlag Wissenschaft und Praxis, Stuttgart, pp 97–123

Fried VH, Hisrich RD (1994) Toward a model of venture capital investment decision making. Financial Management 23: 28–37

Granovetter M (1973) The strength of weak ties. American Journal of Sociology 78: 1360–1380

Greenstone M, Moretti E (2004) Bidding for industrial plants: does winning a 'million dollar plant' increase welfare? Unpublished manuscript, MIT

Gupta AK, Sapienza HJ (1992) Determinants of capital firms' preferences regarding the industry diversity and geographic scope of their investments. Journal of Business Venturing 7: 347–362

Hannan MT, Freeman JH (1989) Organizational ecology. Harvard University Press, Cambridge, MA

Haug P (1995) Formation of biotechnology firms in the greater Seattle region: an empirical investigation of entrepreneurial, financial and educational perspectives. Environment and Planning A 27: 249–267

Hendry C, Brown J, Defillippi R (2000) Regional clustering of high technology-based firms: opto-electronics in three countries. Regional Studies 34: 129–144

Keeble D, Lawson C, Moore B, Wilson F (1999) Collective learning processes, networking, and institutional thickness in the Cambridge region. Regional Studies 33: 319–332

Klepper S (2002) The capabilities of new firms and the evolution of the US automobile industry. Industrial and Corporate Change 11: 645–666

Klepper S, Sleeper S (2005) Entry by spinoffs. Management Science 51: 1291–1306

Knight FH (1921) Risk, uncertainty, and profit. Houghton Mifflin, Boston

Kollock P (1994) The emergence of exchange structures: an experimental study of uncertainty, commitment and trust. American Journal of Sociology 100: 313–345

Lawton Smith H, Mihell D, Kingham D (2000) The biotechnology industry in Oxfordshire. Area 32: 179–188

Lazarsfeld PF, Merton RK (1954) Friendship as a social process: a substantive and methodological analysis. In: Berger M, Abel T, Page CH (eds) Freedom and control in modern society. Van Nostrand, New York, pp 18–66

Lemarié S, Mangematin V, Torre A (2001) Is the creation and development of biotech SMEs localised? Conclusions drawn from the French case. Small Business Economics 17: 61–76

Marshall A (1890) Principles of Economics. MacMillan, London

McMullan WE, Gillin LM (1998) Developing technological start-up entrepreneurs: a case study of a graduate entrepreneurship programme at Swinburne University. Technovation 18: 275–286

McPherson M, Smith-Lovin L, Cook JM (2001) Birds of a feather: homophily in social networks. Annual Review of Sociology 27: 415–444

Merton RK (1942) Science and technology in a democratic order. Journal of Legal and Political Sociology 1: 115–126

Mitton DG (1990) Bring on the clones: a longitudinal study of the proliferation, development, and growth of the biotech industry in San Diego. In: Churchill NC, Bygrave WD, Hornaday JA, Muzyka DF, Vesper KH, Wetzel WE (eds) Frontiers of entrepreneurship research, 1990. Babson College, Wellesley, MA, pp 344–358

Niosi J, Bas TG (2001) The competencies of regions – Canada's clusters in biotechnology. Small Business Economics 17: 31–42

Owen-Smith J, Powell WW (2004) Knowledge networks as channels and conduits: the effects of spillovers in the Boston biotechnology community. Organization Science 15: 5–21

Packard D (1995) The HP way: how Bill Hewlett and I built our company. HarperCollins, New York

Phillips DJ (2002) A genealogical approach to organizational life chances: the parent–progeny transfer among Silicon Valley law firms, 1946–1996. Administrative Science Quarterly 47: 474–506

Rinaldi, A (2006) More than the sum of their parts? EMBO Reports 7: 133–136

Say JB (1821) A treatise on political economy. Sherwood, Neeley and Jones, London

Schumpeter J (1934) Theorie der wirtschaftlichen Entwicklung, 4th edn, Duncker & Humblot, Berlin

Shane S, Cable D (2002) Network ties, reputation, and the financing of new ventures. Management Science 48: 364–381

Sölvell Ö, Lindquist G, Ketels C (2003) The cluster initiative greenbook. Ivory Tower AB. http://www.cluster-research.org/dldocs/GreenbookSep03.pdf (accessed 28 September 2006)

Sørensen JB (1999) Executive migration and interorganizational competition. Social Science Research 28: 289–315

Sørensen JB (2007) Bureaucracy and entrepreneurship. Administrative Science Quarterly (in press)

Sorenson O, Audia PG (2000) The social structure of entrepreneurial activity: geographic concentration of footwear production in the United States, 1940–1989. American Journal of Sociology 106: 424–462

Sorenson O, Fleming L (2004) Science and the diffusion of knowledge. Research Policy 33: 1615–1634

Sorenson O, Rivkin J, Fleming L (2006) Complexity, networks and knowledge flow. Research Policy 35: 994–1017

Sorenson O, Singh J (2007) Science, social networks and spillovers. Industry and Innovation 14: 219–238

Sorenson O, Stuart T (2001) Syndication networks and the spatial distribution of venture capital investments. American Journal of Sociology 106: 1546–1588

Sorenson O, Waguespack DM (2006) Social structure and exchange: self-confirming dynamics in Hollywood. Administrative Science Quarterly 51: 560–589

Stouffer SA (1940) Intervening opportunities: a theory relating mobility and distance. American Journal of Sociology 99: 614–639

Stuart TE, Ding WW (2006) When do scientists become entrepreneurs? The social structural antecedents of commercial activity in the academic life sciences. American Journal of Sociology 112: 97–144

Stuart TE, Ozdemir SZ, Ding WW (2007) Vertical alliance networks: the case of university–biotechnology–pharmaceutical alliance chains. Research Policy 36: 477–498

Stuart TE, Sorenson O (2003a) Liquidity events and the geographic distribution of entrepreneurial activity. Administrative Science Quarterly 48: 175–201

Stuart TE, Sorensen O (2003b) The geography of opportunity: spatial heterogeneity in founding rates and the performance of biotechnology firms. Research Policy 32: 229–253

Zeller C (2001) Clustering biotech: a recipe for success? Spatial patterns of growth of biotechnology in Munich, Rhineland and Hamburg. Small Business Economics 17: 123–141

Zipf GK (1949) Human behavior and the principle of least effort. Addison-Wesley, Reading, MA

Zucker LG, Darby MR (1996) Star scientists and institutional transformation: patterns of invention and innovation in the formation of the biotechnology industry. Proceedings of the National Academy of Sciences 93: 12709–12716

Zucker L, Darby MR, Brewer MB (1998) Intellectual human capital and the birth of the US biotechnology enterprises. American Economic Review 88: 290–306

# 4 Innovation Networks in Biotechnology

Pier Paolo Saviotti[1] and David Catherine[2]

[1] UMR GAEL, Universitè Pierre Mendès – France, B.P. 47, 38040 Grenoble Cedex 9, and GREDEG CNRS, I2C, 250 rue Albert Einstein, 06560 Valbonne, France
[2] Grenoble Ecole de Management, 12 rue Pierre Sémard, B.P. 127, 38003 Grenoble Cedex 01, France

## 4.1 Introduction

The frequency of inter-firm partnerships, alternatively called inter-firm alliances, increased rapidly and unexpectedly during the 1970s. This increase has been particularly fast in fields that are usually called either high-technology or knowledge-intensive, such as biotechnology or ITC. Such fields do not necessarily correspond to industrial sectors, but they are subsets of knowledge. Thus, biotechnology constitutes a very important part of the knowledge base of the pharmaceutical, agrochemical and chemical sectors. The high knowledge intensity of these sectors will turn out to be a very important factor in explaining the diffusion of inter-firm partnerships.

Typically such partnerships include three types of institutional actors: incumbent large diversified firms (LDFs); new technology firms, usually small entrepreneurial outfits often created by researchers, which in the case of biotechnology are called dedicated biotechnology firms (DBFs); and public research institutes (PRIs). In this chapter these examples of inter-firm collaboration will be called innovation networks (INs). LDFs, DBFs and PRIs constitute the nodes and their interactions are the links of the network. Recently the concept of network has acquired a considerable prominence in the scientific literature in several disciplines. The social sciences started investigating this phenomenon and were recently joined by physics. Although we cannot claim that our knowledge of networks is in any sense definitive, an intellectual framework that considerably facilitates our interpretation of empirical developments in this field has been created by the joint efforts of the disciplines previously mentioned. In this chapter the existing evidence about INs will be briefly recalled and interpreted on the basis of recent literature on networks.

H. Patzelt and T. Brenner (eds.), *Handbook of Bioentrepreneurship*,
doi: 10.1007/978-0-387-48345-0_4, © Springer Science + Business Media, LLC 2008

The chapter will focus on a number of key questions.

- *Are INs a temporary or stable form of industrial organization?* When INs first emerged in the late 1970s, many economists were very sceptical about their stability. On the basis of then current theories INs were considered a response to a temporary situation, possibly because of the emergence of new technological paradigms, destined to be superseded by the only stable forms of industrial organization (markets or hierarchical organizations) as soon as the new paradigm had been metabolized by incumbent LDFs. The persistent increase in the number of Ins, which has since taken place in several fields, sheds considerable doubts on this interpretation. However, as it will be seen subsequently, this hypothesis has not been proved completely false.

- *Why did INs become a new form of industrial organization only starting from the 1970s?* Was it the sudden discovery of an inherently better form of industrial organization or had there been a change in the economic environment that started favouring a form of industrial organization that would previously have been unstable? It will be seen that the second answer is much more likely to be correct. In particular it will be seen that there are historical trends in the development of capitalism that induced important changes in industrial organization, of which INs are a part.

- *Statics vs. dynamics.* Understanding the factors determining the emergence and the stability of INs is only part of the problem. What can we expect to happen to industrial organization after the emergence of INs? In other words, what is the expected dynamics of INs? As it will be seen, the answer to this question will help us to provide an answer to the first question. In this context processes of knowledge creation and utilization will turn out to be a particularly important component of the overall explanation of the dynamics of INs.

- *What help can recent network theories give us in the interpretation of INs?* Here reference will be made to concepts such as exponential and scale-free networks, small worlds, and to the evolution of network properties such as the distribution of links around nodes, density, connectivity and centrality. The expected time path and the meaning of these properties will be discussed.

- *What are the specificities of biotechnology INs?* INs are found in a number of sectors, although they seem to be more frequent in knowledge-intensive sectors. Are biotechnology INs different from, for example, ITC networks, and if so in what ways?

- *What is the expected evolution of industrial organization in biotechnology?* An attempt will be made here to foresee the expected future development of industrial organization in biotechnology.

After discussing all these questions, the chapter will provide a synthetic statement of the interpretation of the observed evolution of INs in biotechnology, of the factors and mechanisms determining such evolution and of the expected future developments of this form of industrial organization.

## 4.2 The Nature of Innovation Networks

### 4.2.1 The Entry of New Firms

The creation of INs is closely related to the emergence of a new type of firm, which in biotechnology has been called dedicated biotechnology firm, or DBF. DBFs are start-ups whose main competitive advantage at the beginning was their greater ability to learn and to develop the new biotechnology created in PRIs. On the basis of past experience and on the economic knowledge existing at the time of their emergence, the creation of such firms and even more their subsequent survival seemed very unlikely. Starting from the beginning of the twentieth century, large, vertically integrated corporations had dominated most industrial sectors (Chandler 1962, 1977). Small firms still existed in large numbers, but very rarely they had a dominating influence on any industrial sector. Given this pattern of dominance, the entry of new firms could be expected to face considerable barriers linked to economies of scale and scope and to complementary assets (Teece 1986). Such a dominating form of industrial organization had been explained by means of transaction costs theory (see Sect. 4.2.3). Furthermore, although dominated by large firms, the pharmaceutical industry was not highly concentrated, compared to other industries, such as aircraft (Grabowsky and Vernon 1994). Contrary to these expectations, DBFs not only were created in very large numbers, but in the very early years of the new biotechnology they had much greater capabilities in this new speciality than did incumbent LDFs (Grabowsky and Vernon 1994). The rate of creation of DBFs and even more the role they played in INs constituted a question to which economists did not have any ready answer. While it is true that DBFs could have been created by Schumpeterian entrepreneurs (Schumpeter 1912, 1934), according to Schumpeter the new firms should have replaced the old ones in an example of creative destruction. On the contrary, DBFs played an extremely important role in the sectors based on biotechnology, but co-existed with incumbent LDFs. The reasons for this co-existence will be discussed in the subsequent section on INs, but here it needs to be pointed out that none of the then current theoretical frameworks could easily explain the emergence of DBFs. Although Schumpeter is certainly the economist who came closest to predicting the existence of similar types of firms, the co-existence of DBFs and LDFs seems an unprecedented combination of the view points of the young (1912, 1934) and of the mature (1942) Schumpeter. In his early years Schumpeter stressed the role of the entrepreneur in economic development while later on in his career he moved to emphasize the role of large corporations in the increasingly routinized creation of innovations, two different and somewhat incompatible view points, which have been called Schumpeter Mark 1 and Mark 2 (Freeman and Soete 1997) respectively. The type of industrial organization of which DBFs were both one of the causes and constituting element seems a hybrid between Schumpeter Mark 1 and Mark 2. It has to be pointed out that recently a trend towards vertical disintegration has been observed (Langlois 2003, 2006). Together with a growing role played by entrepreneurial firms

(Audretsch et al. 2006), this emerging pattern of vertical disintegration could represent a transition in the long-term development of industrial capitalism, especially as we move towards a knowledge-based society (Grebel et al. 2006).

An important empirical feature of the creation of DBFs is their location. In the early years of the new biotechnology DBFs were created mainly in the USA. Both in Europe and in other countries long delays were experienced in the creation of DBFs. The number of DBFs in the EU overcame that in the USA only in the second half of the 1990s. In spite of the important progress made by EU biotechnology firms, USA DBFs are still larger and more mature than their EU counterparts, as shown by the much more numerous products in stages of their product pipeline close to the market (Saviotti 2005). This very early emergence of DBFs in the USA is likely to be related to some specific feature of the economic environment of this country. Recently the number of DBFs has been growing not only in the EU but in many other countries, including some emergent or newly industrializing ones (Saviotti 2005).

While the number of DBFs has been growing and their geographical distribution keeps becoming relatively more uniform, the role they play has been changing. Since this role is crucial to the dynamics of INs, it will be discussed in the relevant section.

## 4.2.2 Biotechnology

The development of biotechnology can be divided into three generations. The first generation started very early in historical times and includes the processes used to make yoghurt, cheese, beer etc. The second generation, which started in the nineteenth century, ended with creation of antibiotics and of a series of drugs based on synthetic organic chemistry. The third generation was ushered in by some important discoveries in molecular biology and immunology which occurred during the 1970s, namely recombinant DNA and monoclonal antibodies. Thus, the transition from the second to the third generation of biotechnology involved an important discontinuity in the knowledge base that firms could use to create products from it. Until the 1970s, the knowledge base of pharmaceutical firms, the first which could make use of the new biotechnology, was based on organic chemistry, while with the third generation of biotechnology it shifted to molecular biology and to immunology. Such a knowledge discontinuity had very important implications for incumbent LDFs in the pharmaceutical sector and in other biotechnology-based sectors. In fact, biotechnology is not an industrial sector but a field of technology. However, given the ambiguous use made of the term sector in the literature, biotechnology is sometimes referred to as a sector. Assuming their R&D personnel to be composed mainly by organic chemists, it seems clear that incumbent LDFs had a very low absorption capacity (Cohen and Levinthal 1990) for third generation biotechnology. Of course, a possible strategy to increase their absorptive capacity would have been to hire new R&D personnel with competencies in the new biotechnology. Yet, considering the size of existing LDFs, a complete replacement of their R&D staff would have required considerable time. The problem inherent in changing the KB of incumbent LDFs would have been magnified by the need to integrate the new R&D personnel with the rest of the firm by creating the required interfaces and coordination mechanisms. It seems clear that such a transition was likely to be spread over a considerable period of time (Dominguez-Lacasa et al. 2003). During this transition phase, incumbent LDFs were likely to be at a competitive disadvantage with respect to any firm that could master quickly the new KB of third generation biotechnology. Of course, any other field where a similar knowledge discontinuity occurred was likely to experience a similar transition. To the extent that access to the new knowledge was the crucial step in determining firm competitiveness, we could expect new firms founded by researchers competent in the new biotechnology to be able to replace incumbent LDFs. However, this was not the case. DBFs and LDFs not only co-exist but do so by means of a pattern of collaboration involving PRIs as well.

### 4.2.3 The Changing Role of Universities

Almost simultaneously with the emergence of DBFs, universities started changing their role within society. The modern university system had been created in Germany towards the middle of the nineteenth century (Ben David 1977; Murmann 2003) as part of a long-term process which starting from the industrial revolution is leading towards a knowledge-based society (Mokyr 2002). There for the first time research started to be combined with higher education in what was later called the German or Humboldt University System. Universities in other countries subsequently imitated and sometimes improved the German University System. Notable amongst these was the United States, which by successive improvements, created the most effective university system in the world (Nelson 1988, 1990). Other countries adopted much more slowly and partially the same combination of higher education and research. In the initial version of the university system which followed this transition, universities carried out predominantly fundamental or pure research, which was communicated by scholarly publications and assessed by other scientists or researchers in what was called the peer review system. The selection of publications was based on criteria internal to scientific disciplines and intended to foster knowledge production.

A further and related development emerged towards the end of the nineteenth century. Some industrial firms started creating their internal R&D laboratories (Hounshell and Smith 1988; Reich 2002). Until the Second World War this institutionalization of industrial R&D was a relatively rare phenomenon and it is only since the 1950s that the number of industrial firms performing R&D has grown very rapidly. The institutionalization of industrial R&D can be interpreted as part of the process that gave rise to the vertically integrated corporations which dominated industrialized countries from the beginning of the twentieth century and until the 1970s and which Chandler described as the visible hand (Chandler 1962, 1977). During this period, the organization of R&D in most industrialized countries was based on this form of division of labour between universities (and fundamental research institutes) on the one hand and large industrial firms on the other hand. This organizational form of knowledge production was called Mode 1 by Gibbons et al. (1994). They argued that Mode 1, although not being completely superseded, is now gradually being replaced by a new mode of creation and utilization of knowledge called Mode 2, in which the boundaries between fundamental and applied research become fuzzier than in the past. Universities stretch their competencies into applied research while industrial firms venture with growing frequency into fundamental research. As a consequence the evaluation of research has to be based on hybrid criteria simultaneously emphasizing knowledge production and its industrial applications.

These changes, although not making universities equal to industrial firms, replaced the neat chronological and institutional separation between fundamental and applied research which existed in Mode 1 with a more dynamical and more interactive system in which institutional functions had a greater degree of overlap than in the past. That the chronological separation between fundamental and applied research has been falling is clearly proved by the shortening delay between the creation of a new idea and its industrial application. This delay fell from 32.76 years in 1887–1906 to 3.4 years in 1967–1986 (Agarwal and Gort 2001). This faster rate of knowledge application is likely to have led to a growing overlap between fundamental and applied research. In this more dynamical world industrial firms could not expect to find a ready-made pool of knowledge which had been created a long time in advance of its utilization, whose basic principles were well understood and which only needed to be applied. It became increasingly difficult to perform the exploitation of some type of knowledge of which one could not perform the exploration. As it will be pointed out later (Sect. 4.2.5), both the nature of the new knowledge and its rate of creation contribute to the emergence of DBFs and of INs. However, the growing rate of knowledge production created new opportunities for universities as well.

The trend towards the growing involvement of universities in both applied research and semi-commercial activities began in the USA and could be observed with growing frequency from the 1980s. In reality a number of universities, such as MIT, had since a long time started developing applied research, but this was not considered to be the general mission of universities. The present trend coincided with a hardening of IPRs. The Bayh–Dole act of 1980 is often mentioned as the catalyst that induced universities to start patenting the results of their research even if it was federally funded. In fact it turns out that this act, even leaving aside its negative effects, which some critics contended would have destroyed the ethos of basic research, was just an event in a trend which would have taken place anyway (Mowery et al. 2001). Thus, it was not just universities and firms which needed to adapt to a changing external environment in which knowledge creation was acquiring a growing importance. Governments became increasingly involved because of their sponsorship of fundamental research, to their influence on competition, on intellectual property rights and on the creation of new firms amongst others. That these three spheres of society needed to interact in the transition towards a knowledge-based society was stressed by Etkowitz and Leydesdorff (1997, 2000), who described this phenomenon as the emergence of a

Triple Helix, in which both the internal organization of each of the three spheres and their interactions would undergo a profound transformation. In the process universities and academic institutions would end up playing a more important role than in the past.

## 4.2.4 Theories of Industrial Organization

As previously pointed out, the theories of industrial organization in the early 1980s did not predict that forms of organization different from the market or from hierarchical organization could be stable. The evolution of such theories can be traced back to Coase (1937), for whom the existence of the firm could be justified by the costs incurred in using the market, also called transaction costs. Transactions for which these costs become very high are then carried out in the firm rather than in the market. In his attempt to explain the existence of the firm, Coase did not admit any coordination mechanisms other than the market and the firm. The theory of transactions was further articulated by Williamson (1975, 1985, 1991), who tried to explain the existence of different governance structures by means of the three attributes of transactions, frequency, specificity and uncertainty. Furthermore, Williamson relied heavily on the concepts of opportunism and of limited rationality (Simon 1951). In his early work (1975), Williamson admitted the existence of hybrid forms of governance, but considered their existence only temporary. Later in his career Williamson shifted first (1985) to admitting that 'transactions in the middle' were much more common than he had previously thought, and finally (1991) took into account the existence of three organizational forms, the market, hierarchy and the hybrid form, linked to three levels of specificity. In spite of this considerable evolution in Williamson's work, transaction cost analysis remained confined to the dichotomy 'making or buying'. In other works, it was exclusively concerned with the allocation of existing resources and it did not take into account the creation of new resources. A number of papers during the late 1980s and the 1990s followed a williamsonian approach. Notable examples are Pisano and Teece (1989) and Shan (1990). Other papers follow in a similar line while gradually evolving towards a more e recognition of the existence of 'hybrid' forms. Thorelli (1986) considers networks as an intermediate form in a spectrum of arrangements going from total integration to the market. Aoki (1988) distinguishes firm types A and J, where the latter cooperates with suppliers, giving rise to a hybrid organizational form, which can be stable and allows the generation of an organizational quasi rent (p. 218). However, Aoki's analysis is limited to one type of transaction, the inter-firm hierarchical relationship. Imai and Baba (1989) consider networks as an organizational response to technological or competitive changes in the environment, arising from the systemic character of the technology and from 'hyper' dynamic competition. The firm needs to construct a network context capable of generating continuous interactions and processes of innovation. The boundaries of the firm become changing and evolving. Thus, the literature on industrial organization of the 1980s and 1990s seems to start from a dichotomy market – hierarchies and to move gradually to the recognition of what was then considered a hybrid or intermediate form of industrial organization.

The paper which proved to be the most decisive advance towards the interpretation of INs had in fact been written in advance of their emergence. Richardson (1972) started by considering cooperation and market transactions as alternative modes of coordinating economic activities (p. 887). According to Richardson, existing organizational forms range from market transactions, a minimum cooperative element, to 'intermediate areas in which there are linkages of traditional connection and goodwill … to interlocking clusters, groups and alliances which represent cooperation fully and formally developed'. In addition to the explicit recognition of this range of organizational arrangements, Richardson made several conceptual advances. First, he defined an industry as the set of firms carrying out 'a large number of *activities*, ranging from the discovery and estimation of future wants, to research development and design, to the execution and coordination processes of physical transformation to the marketing of goods and so on'. Second, he stressed the need to include the competencies, capabilities, knowledge and organization of firms amongst the factors required to construct a theory of industrial organization and to provide an explanation of the division of labour between the firm and the market. Third, he distinguished between *similar* and *complementary* activities. Fourth, he distinguished the creation of resources from the exchange of goods already produced, the former being preferentially carried out by inter-firm coordination and the latter by the market. Richardson maintained that there is a strong tendency for similar activities to be grouped preferentially within a firm, while complementary activities need to be coordinated quantitatively and qualitatively (p. 890). The complex networks of interaction exist because of the need to coordinate closely complementary but dissimilar activities (p. 892). Sadly, Richardson's paper was adequately recognized only 20 years after it had been written.

### 4.2.5 Innovation Networks

The gradual evolution of the literature on industrial organization towards a more explicit recognition of hybrid organizational forms described in the previous section was accompanied, during the late 1980s and early 1990s, by a growing number of publications that either documented the increasing frequency of INs or attempted to propose explanations of their existence. Papers of these types include Freeman (1991), Hagedoorn (1993, 1995), Saxenian (1991), Mowery (1989), Powell et al. (1996), Hakansson (1987), Callon (1991). The more theoretical of these papers did not approach the problem of explaining the existence of INs by an extension of existing theories of industrial organization, but used new, network-specific, conceptual tools and methods of analysis.

Any analysis of INs must be preceded by a disclaimer about its exhaustiveness. In fact, the concept of network, even if we limit it to technological alliances, is so broad that it is virtually impossible to provide a description that encompasses all existing types of networks. Just to mention a few examples, networks can be formal or informal (Von Hippel 1989; Steward and Conwey 1996), inter- or intra-organizational (Powell et al. 1996; Oliver and Liebeskind 1998), focusing on individuals or on firms (Liebeskind et al. 1996; Zucker and Darby 1996), inter-penetrated forms of market and organization (Imai and Baba 1989; Freeman 1991), constellations of firms (Justman and Zuscovitch 1995). Although many different network typologies have been proposed (see for example Freeman 1991; Hagedoorn 1995), none has been consensually adopted by scholars working in this area. Thus, as far as biotechnology is concerned, we will have to be content with an implicit definition in which INs are constituted by three types of actors, dedicated biotechnology firms (DBFs), large diversified firms (LDFs) and public research institutes (PRIs), participating in variable proportions and with patterns of interaction changing depending on the degree of maturity of the technology that is being developed and used.

Starting from the earliest papers it was observed that the density of technological alliances was closely related to the R&D intensity or to the technological complexity of the sector studied (Hagedoorn 1993, 1995). This indicates that learning processes are central elements in the formation of INs. According to Powell et al. (1996), the network is the 'locus' of innovation. It is no surprise that biotechnology is the sector characterized by the highest density of strategic alliances (Hagedoorn 1993). It is to be noticed that a slowdown in the rate of creation of INs observed at the beginning of the 1990s (Mytelka 1999) turned out to be temporary and was followed by a subsequent increase.

The most immediate question raised by the existence of INs is, why do they exist? Amongst the potential answers that were given to this question are the following:

- To exploit positive network externalities (Economides 1996; Katz and Shapiro 1985, 1992)
- To reduce R&D costs and uncertainty (Hagedoorn 1993; Dodgson 1992)
- As learning networks (Powell et al. 1996; Eisenhardt and Schoonhoven 1996)
- To access certain types of resources (Pisano 1990)
- To adapt to a growing complexification of innovation (Orsenigo et al. 2001)
- To cope with a growing rate of technological change (Saxenian 1991)
- To provide faster access to technological capabilities (Mowery 1989)
- To assemble complementary resources to create viable products (Rothaermel 2001; Rothaermel and Hill 2005; Teece 1986; Pisano 1990) while simultaneously acquiring core competencies (Prahalad and Hamel 1990)

Two types of factors, knowledge and resources, are underlying these potential explanations. Thus, it seems that the creation of knowledge and the combination complementary resources are two crucial steps required for biotechnology firms to succeed (Rothaermel and Hill 2005). This conclusion is reinforced by the role played in INs by public research institutions, responsible for advancing the frontier of knowledge, and by DBFs, which behave as intermediaries between PRIs and LDFs (Oliver and Liebeskind 1998).

Admitting that the overall objective of INs is either to create new knowledge or to acquire complementary resources, why do firms participate in them? A general answer is that firms join networks of innovation as a means of acquiring competitive advantage and gaining access to capabilities held by other economic actors, thus minimising uncertainty. Existing evidence shows that firms participating in INs (Powell et al. 1996; Shan et al. 1994; Hagedoorn and Schakenraad 1994),

- have a better performance than firms that do it alone as measured by the rate of creation of new products (Rothaermel and Deeds 2004), the rate of growth of sales (Stuart 2000), the rate of growth of R&D and of total employment, by R&D expenditures and by the profit rate (Baum et al. 2000);
- have lower mortality rates (Mitchell and Singh 1996);
- have faster access to the stock market and better initial valuation (Kale et al. 2000); and
- acquire credibility especially as new entrants (Stuart et al. 1999).

The evidence previously described seems to provide some initial answers to the question, why do INs exist? They exist because

- they create new knowledge;
- they help to obtain complementary resources; and
- they provide participating firms with a competitive advantage by improving several dimensions of their performance relative to that of firms not participating in INs.

These answers help to understand the phenomenon of INs but leave substantially untouched the problem of network dynamics. In addition to the very general question asking whether INs are temporary or stable forms of industrial organization, other aspects of INs dynamics need to be explained. For example, how do the various actors (DBFs, LDFs, PRIs) and their interactions change during the evolution of INs?

## Network Dynamics

Although the need to understand the dynamics of network was already evident in the early 1990s (Nohria and Eccles 1992), it took longer to accumulate the observations required to construct proper dynamic models. In this section selected examples of papers dealing with the problem of network dynamics are going to be briefly described in order to present the most general findings available today.

Some aspects of networks structure and behaviour were observed to change according to systematic patterns as the networks aged. It was observed that some networks changed their focus from exploration to exploitation (March 1991) in the course of time (Gilsing and Nooteboom 2006; Gay and Dousset 2006; Rothaermel and Deeds 2004; Koza and Lewin 1998). Exploration-based INs had the objective of discovering new opportunities while exploitation-based INs had the objective of adding value to existing capabilities by using the complementary assets of partners. Closely related conclusions had been reached by Oliver and Liebeskind (1998), who noticed that alliances between universities, or PRIs, and DBFs are preferred in the early phases while alliances between DBFs and LDFs become dominant in the later phases. In the early phases knowledge flows from universities or PRIs to DBFs, thus allowing DBFs to access very advanced knowledge. In the more mature phases alliances are mainly driven by the access to complementary assets, such as capital for product development and for clinical trials, manufacturing capabilities, marketing infrastructure and expertise, and established distribution channels (ibid, p. 90). Thus, INs evolve from the search for new knowledge to the combination of knowledge and complementary assets. The evolution of legal forms was also observed to proceed according to systematic patterns (Cainarca et al. 1992; Gulati 1995), changing from equity alliances in the early phases to non equity alliances in more mature phases. These observations started giving the impression that the typical pattern of evolution of INs was cyclical. However, the cycle of INs was not identical to that of the industry, or industries, in which the participating firms could be classified. Cainarca et al. (1992) noticed that the dominant factor in inducing cyclical behaviour was the technology used rather than the industry. An early confirmation of these predictions came from a study of agricultural biotechnology in which it was found that firms formed mainly R&D alliances in the 'pre-commercial' phase but shifted to market-related alliances in the commercial phase (Kalaitzandonakes and Bjornson 1997).

It soon became evident that even within biotechnology there could be more than one cycle. Thus, Oliver (2001) observed that the number of alliances formed by American DBFs rose during the 1980s, fell in the early 1990s and started rising again in the late 1990s. It subsequently turned out that this time path was due to a shift between two generations of biotechnology. The first generation of INs was linked to recombinant DNA and monoclonal antibodies and the second one to genomics. These two generations were both contained within what was called before third generation biotechnology; that is, they were both the result of progress in molecular biology.

The patterns of development so far described can be explained by different resources that firms need to have access to in different stages of the evolution of the INs in which they participate. Such resources would shift from knowledge in the early, pre-commercial, phases to complementary assets in the more commercial phases. Even the relative advantage of INs with respect to other forms of economic coordination can change during this time path. INs can be relatively more important in the early phases, when no firm has all the resources required to succeed, and in the intermediate ones, when increasing entry and competition push firms to specialise. On the other hand, INs could loose importance in mature phases when product standardization and price competition gradually eliminate the weakest firms (Gemser et al. 1996; Hobday 1994). In these conditions INs could be replaced by hierarchical organizations. An interpretation in terms of resources is attractive but somewhat problematic because of the meaning of the term resources. In particular, the distinction between *given* resources and *creative activities* needs to be taken into account. The former exist in the economic system at a given time and firms can have access to them by investment. The latter lead to the creation of new goods, of new services, and of new knowledge, which can become resources after they have been created. Access to existing resources can be considered a part of economic routines while creative activities are a part of search activities. INs evolve from the creation of new resources in the early phases to the exploitation of existing ones in the later phases.

The previous observations were related to the behaviour of individual firms during the evolution of networks. Other studies analysed network dynamics at the level of the industry. An important aspect of networks at this level is their density, which indicates the generalized intensity of interaction of the participating organizations. Network density was found to grow in the course of time for Toyota's networks with its American suppliers (Dyer and Nobeoka 2000) and for three Italian firms producing packing machinery (Lorenzoni and Lipparini 1999). However, this finding was not confirmed by further studies. Bonaccorsi and Giuri (2001) found that even within the aero-engine industry networks evolved differently depending on the market segment and on the technology adopted by engine producers. Orsenigo et al. (2001) found that while network organization seems to be growing during subsequent technological generations, network density falls as a consequence of the continuous inflow of new entrants. In a recent study of pharmaceutical biotechnology networks covering the period since 1975, Roijakkers and Hagedoorn (2006) find that network density grows in the course of time.

In summary, a number of systematic patterns of evolution have been detected in which INs evolve from exploration to exploitation, from the search for knowledge to that for complementary assets, and the type of alliances from DBFs–PRIs to DBFs–LDFs. These systematic patterns provide evidence for the existence of cycles in the time paths of INs, the main factor leading to cyclical behaviour being technology. In some cases, depending on the industrial sector or on the technology, more than one cycle can occur. For example, in biotechnology a second generation on INs linked to genomics seems to arise during the 1990s. A further variable that can be expected to have an important influence on the dynamics of INs is their density. Here the findings seem to be contradictory and probably sector-dependent, with some studies finding a growing density and others a falling density. This problem will be reconsidered later in this chapter. Now we move on to some theoretical approaches and methods of network analysis.

### Network Theories and Methods

In Sect. 4.2.3 different theories of industrial organization attempting in different ways to justify the existence of hybrid organizational forms were discussed. In this section a number of theories and methods attempting to describe, treat analytically and explain the existence and properties of networks will be discussed. These theories and methods originated in different disciplines ranging from mathematics and physics to sociology and management. They attempt to analyse networks as an object of its own and not as a component of something else (i.e. industrial; organization). While this approach may seem more limited than one analysing networks as a component of a larger class of problems, it can provide us with more specific insights into and analytical capabilities in the study of networks. The concept of networks is in fact a very general one, in principle applicable to any system comprising elements and interactions amongst them. Thus, many types of systems, physical, biological or social, can be analysed by means of networks. In what follows in this section two theoretical approaches of sociological inspiration and an approach developed by physicists will be discussed. Furthermore, the application of graph theory to the analysis of networks will be briefly described.

*Two early conceptual models of networks.* Hakansson (1987) considered networks as a combination of three elements: actors, resources and activities. He used a very wide definition of actors, including firms, research institutes, universities, consulting firms etc. In his view resources can be physical, financial and human. Activities can be of two types, transformation and transaction. Actors play a central role in networks. They control resources either individually or collectively and have an incomplete knowledge of these resources. Actors are involved in activities of which they have an incomplete knowledge. The position of each actor in the network depends on the activities the same actor has carried out in the past. Past activities define and constrain future opportunities for the actor belonging to a network, leading to irreversibilities.

Callon (1991) considered techno-economic networks (TENs) as a coordinated set of heterogeneous actors (public laboratories, technical research centres, firms, financial organizations, public institutions etc.). The environment in which these networks operate comprises three poles, science, techniques and the market, linked by intermediaries. Each of the poles has a different type of human resources, for example, researchers for science, and gives rise to a different type of output, for example, patents and prototypes for techniques. Actors participate in each pole and in the interactions of the various poles. Actors attempt to increase their influence on the network and to make themselves indispensable, thus creating a situation of irreversibility. The dynamics of techno-economic networks is driven by the struggle of different actors. In their attempt to gain influence, actors can lead to a completely rigid and irreversible network. However, even when a given network has become completely rigid and irreversible a different entry strategy is possible. Actors can look for new interactions and new intermediaries in a new space.

*Graph theory and networks.* Graph theory provides us with a graphical representation of networks irrespective of their content. A network is here considered as a collection of nodes, or vertices, and links, or edges (Knole and Kuklinski 1982; Gross and Yellen 1998). Nodes can be any type of interacting entities, ranging from molecules and biological species to individuals and organizations. The links indicate the interactions existing between the entities considered. Depending on the cases, the links can indicate the *presence* of an interaction, the *extent* or *value* of the interaction (valued graphs), and the *direction* of the interaction (Directed graphs). In our case the graph of a network shows us which actors are connected to other actors. In this perspective networks have at least two interesting properties: the *centrality* of actors and the *density* of the network.

The centrality of a given actor tells us how well connected the actor is. A more central actor is expected to have a better access to the knowledge and information held by the other actors to whom he or she is linked. In biotechnology a more central actor can then be expected to play a leading role in the processes of knowledge generation and utilization which are crucial for market success. Unfortunately, it is not easy to define unambiguously a measure of centrality. As a consequence several measures are used.

*Degree centrality* measures simply the total number of *direct* links that a given actor has with other actors in the sale network. It has two shortcomings. First, it depends on the size of the network, thus making it impossible to compare two networks of different sizes. Second, it provides only a *local* measure of centrality. To overcome the first problem, it is possible to normalize the measure dividing the value obtained by the number of nodes existing in the network minus one. The second problem, the local character of the measure, is an intrinsic feature of the concept of degree centrality. A different measure, called *betweenness centrality*, has been developed to capture the global dimension of centrality (Freeman 1979). Betweenness centrality for a given node, say i, is based on the number of *geodesics* crossing i and joining all pairs of nodes in the network to which i is linked directly or indirectly. A geodesic is the shortest path linking a pair of nodes in the network. An actor located on a geodesic joining two other actors i and j can be expected to be able to affect i and j and to take advantage of the knowledge and information originating in any one of them. The ability of an actor to affect the other actors located at the extremes of a geodesic is expected to fall with a growing number of geodesics crossing it. As in the case of degree centrality, betweenness centrality can be normalized to eliminate the effect of network size. Another measure of centrality, called *closeness centrality* (Freeman 1979), provides us with a global measure of centrality. Thus, we have different measures of centrality, giving us the local and global aspects of this variable.

A further and very important property of networks is their *density*. This property tells us what fraction of the links which can potentially be formed between the nodes of a given network is effectively 'occupied'. As it will be seen, such a property is very important in the dynamics of networks.

*Scale fee networks.* It has recently been discovered that a large class of networks possess some common properties for which they are called scale-free (Barabasi et al. 1999; Barabasi 2002; Barabasi and Bonabeau 2003; Reka et al. 2000; Reka and Barabasi 2002). In particular, these networks have a very asymmetrical distribution of links around nodes: few nodes have many links and many nodes have few links. This distribution is very different from that predicted for previously studied networks, called exponential networks, which had a much more egalitarian distribution of links around nodes. Scale-free networks have a power law distribution while exponential networks have a Poisson distribution of links around nodes. As a consequence, scale-free networks have the interesting property of being very resistant to random attack: almost 80% of the links can be cut before a scale-free network is destroyed while the corresponding percentage for an exponential network is less than 20%. However, a targeted attack selectively cutting links around the most central nodes (hubs) destroys the network by cutting less than 20% of the links.

Two conditions are required in order for scale-free networks to exist: (1) growth – the number of nodes must grow; (2) preferential attachment – new links tend to be formed more easily with already linked nodes. These conditions are often present in biotechnology networks. In socio-economic networks the second condition – preferential attachment – depends on sources of increasing returns to adoption. Examples of these sources are reputational structure and various types of resources. Let us take the example of an alliance between an incumbent LDF and a start-up. In its choice of partner the start-up is likely to favour the LDF with the best reputation. If the alliance leads to a further enhancement of the LDF's reputation, other start-ups will continue to favour it with respect to other LDFs. Moreover, if a growing number of alliances raises the resource base of incumbent LDFs, those already having a greater number of alliances will be better able to form further ones than other LDFs. Thus, conditions (1) and (2) can often be found in biotechnology networks. The presence of these two conditions leads to a higher probability of creation of scale-free networks than other types of networks. This condition is at best necessary, but not sufficient, to justify a high concentration of scale-free networks. However, one of the most important findings about this type of networks is their resistance to attack. If we interpret attack as selection, scale-free networks are likely to have a high rate of variation and a low rate of selection whenever conditions (1) and (2) are satisfied. Thus, since conditions (1) and (2) are often present in biotechnology networks, we can expect the scale-free geometry to be quite common in this type of network.

These network properties are obviously interesting and highly relevant for socio-economic networks. However, although research in scale-free networks has concentrated on the distribution of links around nodes, other related network properties are of great importance. For example, the existence of scale-free networks implies an uneven distribution of the degree of centrality of nodes. Few nodes are highly central while others have a low centrality. Furthermore, the distribution of centrality is likely to change dynamically, for example, with the distribution becoming at times more skewed or more even, with the relative centrality of some nodes falling and that of others rising.

Another property the role of which has already been discussed is density. As already pointed out, we can expect network density to measure the extent of interaction existing in a network. Such extent of interaction is likely to vary systematically during the life of a IN as a consequence of a number of phenomena. First, innovations are introduced by Schumpeterian entrepreneurs in a relatively institutionally poor environment. If an innovation is successful we can expect it to be widely imitated and to diffuse gradually in society. To acquire its 'economic weight', an innovation also requires the co-evolution of appropriate institutions (Nelson 1988). The creation of complementary technologies and of appropriate institutions leads to the formation of new links, thus raising the density of the network. For example, the creation of a regulatory institution can be expected to lead to interactions with the firms and the other organizations responsible for the production and use of the new technology. These interactions may be impersonal and simply provide constraint, as it would happen in the case of standard creating institutions, or be more localized and directed, as in the case of a firm producing complementary inputs to the innovation and technology concerned. Examples of these situations for the automobile could be (1) the ministries responsible for issuing driving permits or driving rules, (2) the firms producing and distributing tyres or petrol (Saviotti 2005). In all these cases the new links created reduce the number of degrees of freedom of each node and provide constraint. This progressive increase in density as an innovation and the relative technology mature on the one hand increases the potential market size of the new technology by improving the technology with respect to its initial form, but on the other hand, makes the new technology progressively more rigid, even if more coherent. In this way an increasing connectivity allows a technology to acquire its full 'economic weight' but contributes to the process whereby diminishing returns gradually take over and slow down the rate of improvement of maturing technologies.

Network dynamics at the industry/technology level can be expected to be characterized by low density during the emergence phase and by growing connectivity as the sector matures. At the aggregate level of the whole economic system, increasing diversity or variety means an increasing number of nodes. However, this increase is likely to be unevenly distributed in time and space. The creation of new nodes cannot be expected to be followed immediately by the creation of new links. The emergence of important innovations can be expected to lower connectivity while the subsequent process of diffusion can be expected to raise connectivity. The more radical the innovation, the greater its capacity to disorganize existing network links. Thus, we can expect network density to oscillate, falling when discontinuities in the external environment emerge and rising when the network matures.

## 4.3 Recent Developments in Network Dynamics

In this section a number of recent empirical findings and of models of INs are going to be discussed. Most of the empirical evidence comes from the PhD thesis of Catherine (2007). In this thesis a database of about 7,600 collaborative agreements in biotechnology and covering the period 1973–1999 has been constructed. The INs studied here have three types of nodes – DBFs, LDFs, and PRIs. The agreements belong to two generations, depending on the technologies on which they are based. Agreements of the first generation are based on recombinant DNA and on monoclonal antibodies; agreements of the second generation are based on genomics. Furthermore, within each generation agreements are classified as either R&D- or market based. As it was previously pointed out, both of these generations are contained in what is often called third generation biotechnology. In other words, they are both based on the progress of molecular biology.

Figures 4.1–4.4 show the variation of the number of agreements during the period studied both for the whole set and for each generation. These results provide a confirmation for the existence of a technology-based life cycle for INs. For both generations R&D agreements rise first and then fall. R&D agreements dominate in the early phases of the life cycle and market-based agreements in the more mature ones. The life cycle of the first generation seems to be in decline and very few new R&D agreements are taking place within it. Agreements of the second generation start in the early 1990s and already show signs of saturation. However, when the two generations are combined, the total number of agreements keeps rising for the whole period (Fig. 4.4).

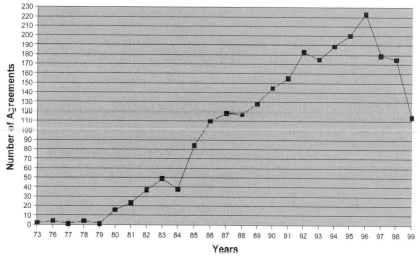

**Fig. 4.1.** Number of agreements in the first generation of biotechnology

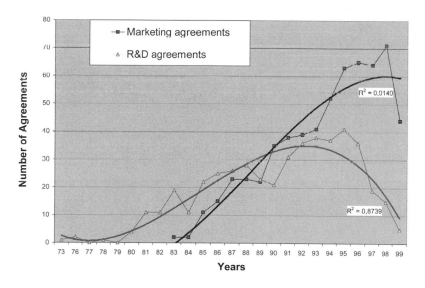

**Fig. 4.2.** R&D and marketing agreements in the first generation of biotechnology

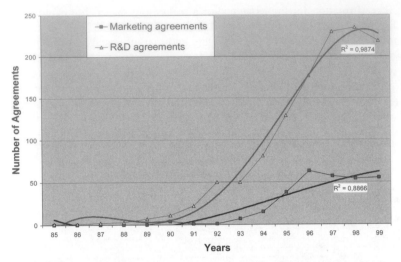

**Fig. 4.3.** R&D and marketing agreements in the second generation of biotechnology

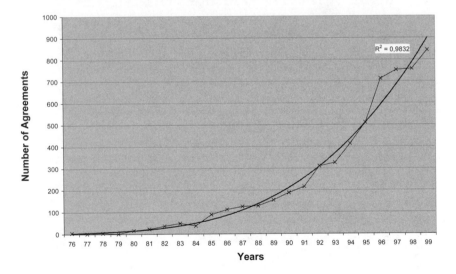

**Fig. 4.4.** Total number of agreements in biotechnology, 1973–1999

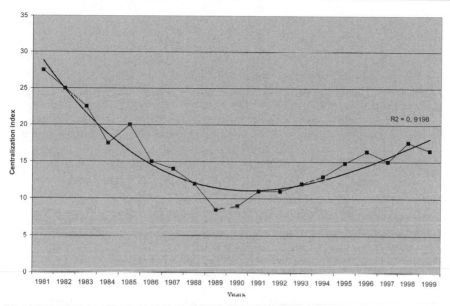

**Fig. 4.5.** Evolution of network density for the first biotechnology generation

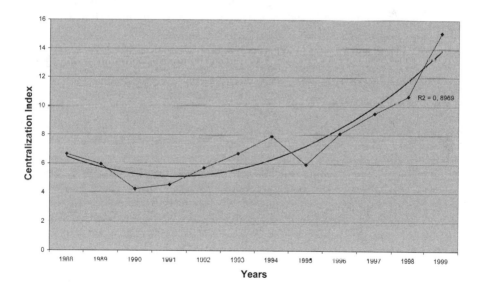

**Fig. 4.6.** Evolution of network density for the second generation of biotechnology

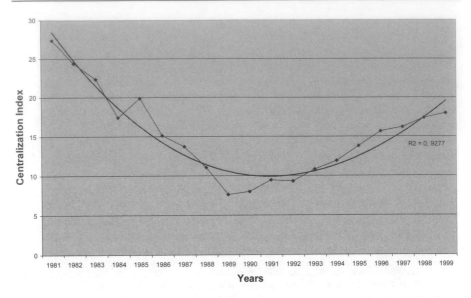

**Fig. 4.7.** Evolution of network density for the two biotechnology generations combined

Figures 4.5–4.7 show the change in the density of the networks for each generation (Figs. 4.5 and 4.6) and for the two generations combined (Fig. 4.7). In all three cases the density falls first and then rises. However, we can notice that the period of fall is much shorter in the second than in the first generation. Our findings here contrast with those of Rojikanners and Hagedoorn (2006), who found that network density has always been rising in the period since 1975, but confirm those of Orsenigo et al. (2001). We cannot immediately our results because the other measures were obtained by means of different techniques. However, we are able to provide an interpretation of the reasons for which density can be expected to behave in the way we observe. This behaviour of network density can be explained by our previous analysis of scale-free networks, according to which density was expected to fall during periods of environmental discontinuity and to rise during the subsequent period of environmental stabilization. Of course, in this context the environment is the socio-economic one and not the purely physical or biological. In the case of biotechnology INs the network dimension which gave rise to the discontinuity is knowledge, and in particular the emergence of molecular biology and of its industrial applications. We can consider molecular biology as a new paradigm, forcing firms in the biotechnology-based sectors (pharmaceuticals, agrochemicals etc) to radically update their knowledge base (Grabowski and Vernon 1994; Saviotti et al. 2003, 2005; Nesta and Saviotti 2005, 2006). According to this view, a rising density should imply that the new paradigm is being absorbed by incumbent firms and that the science/entrepreneurial phase is being followed by a more market-based one. We can notice that the period during which density falls is shorter for the second than for the first generation of biotechnology INs. This seems to imply that the second generation was less of a discontinuity than the first, not an illogical interpretation given that the second generation is based on genomics, which can be considered a refinement of molecular biology, of which it uses the basic conceptual apparatus. Extending our interpretation to other sectors, we can expect density to rise for more mature ones such as automobiles or packing machinery, thus confirming the results of Dyer and Nobeoka (2000) and of Lorenzoni and Lipparini (1999). If our interpretation is correct, network density can be a very important variable, capable of indicating the extent of knowledge discontinuity arising at given times during the evolution of industrial activities, for example, when new technological paradigms emerge. However, such a phenomenon clearly requires further study.

Another important property of INs is the centrality of the different types of actors involved. Tables 4.1 and 4.2 show the evolution of centrality for DBFs, PRIs and LDFs during the period studied. We can see a clear pattern emerging in both generations of INs, with DBFs being the most central actor in the early phases and LDFs becoming the most central actor in the late phases. PRIs have initially a high degree centrality but become very marginal as the technology moves towards maturity. The fall of DBFs and PRIs centrality becomes even more evident when betweenness centrality is used.

**Table 4.1.** Centrality of the different actors (DBFs, LDFs, PRIs) involved in the first generation of biotechnology alliances

| First generation biotechnology | 1976–1984 | | | 1985–1992 | | | 1993–1999 | | |
|---|---|---|---|---|---|---|---|---|---|
| | DBFs | LDFs | PRIs | DBFs | LDFs | PRIs | DBFs | LDFs | PRIs |
| Average number of agreement | 5.67 | 3.20 | 2.63 | 6.20 | 10.79 | 2.61 | 6.12 | 15.50 | 2.05 |
| Average N-degree centrality | 5.84 | 3.30 | 2.71 | 1.71 | 2.97 | 0.72 | 1.41 | 3.58 | 0.47 |
| Median N-degree centrality | 3.09 | 2.06 | 2.06 | 1.10 | 1.38 | 0.55 | 0.92 | 1.73 | 0.23 |
| Average betweenness centrality | 4.95 | 2.82 | 0.85 | 0.71 | 1.38 | 0.20 | 0.40 | 1.40 | 0.10 |
| Median betweenness centrality | 1.17 | 0 | 0 | 0.20 | 0.53 | 0 | 0.07 | 0.18 | 0 |

**Table 4.2.** Centrality of the different actors (DBFs, LDFs, PRIs) involved in the second generation of biotechnology alliances

| Second generation biotechnology | 1985–1992 | | | 1993–1999 | | |
|---|---|---|---|---|---|---|
| | DBFs | LDFs | PRIs | DBFs | LDFs | PRIs |
| Average number of agreement | 5.98 | 5.90 | 5.48 | 12.50 | 25.13 | 9.27 |
| Average N-degree centrality | 2.48 | 2.45 | 2.27 | 1.68 | 3.38 | 1.25 |
| Median N-degree centrality | 2.08 | 1.66 | 1.66 | 1.21 | 1.55 | 0.81 |
| Average betweenness centrality | 2.70 | 2.21 | 2.69 | 0.41 | 0.97 | 0.13 |
| Median betweenness centrality | 1.91 | 1.36 | 2.14 | 0.18 | 0.15 | 0.07 |

In order to interpret adequately these results it is important to establish clearly the meaning of centrality. In general we can expect a more central actor to be more important in a network. The gradual shift of average N-degree centrality from DBFs and PRIs towards LDFs as a technology ages would seem to confirm this interpretation. We expect that as a technology matures exploitation will become more important than exploration. Since LDFs are the only actor in these networks having the resources required for exploitation, it seems logical that they become more central as the technology matures. Likewise, since we expect both DBFs and PRIs to have a competitive advantage in the early phases of a technology life cycle, it is logical for their centrality to be higher in these phases and to fall as the technology moves towards maturity. Incidentally, these results indicate that although recent trends in knowledge production seem to make boundaries of institutions fuzzy and their functions overlap, DBFs, PRIs and LDFs still conserve different roles. However, in spite of this apparent support for the interpretation of centrality as indicator of the relative importance of an organization in its economic environment, this interpretation is limited. For example, it is not clear that in spite of their growing centrality pharmaceutical DBFs are in a good position. Although they have substantially increased their R&D expenditures and participated in INs, large pharmaceutical firms cannot find enough new molecules to sustain their past strategy of identifying blockbusters (Hopkins et al. 2007). Apparently the new biotechnology has introduced radically new concepts but does not seem to be able to provide a lease of life for the blockbuster strategy. Perhaps the strategy itself is doomed and biotechnology is leading to a new strategy for the pharmaceutical industry.

Further doubts about the meaning of centrality arise if we take into account the results of the different measures used, such as N-degree or betweenness centrality. Although all the measures tend to confirm the earlier results, they give absolute and relative values of centrality. Clearly although centrality seems to be an important variable to map the dynamics of INs, further research is required in order to clarify its meaning.

By combining centrality and density measures we can see that periods of falling density tend to coincide with periods in which DBFs and PRIs have a relatively high centrality while periods of growing density tend to coincide with a relatively high centrality of DBFs. This finding seems logical given that both falling network density and a relatively high centrality of DBFs and PRIs are expected to occur immediately after a knowledge discontinuity while a high centrality of LDFs is more likely to occur when a new technology begins to mature.

Some recent models of INs shed light on the impact of knowledge generation and utilization on network dynamics. Gilbert et al. (2001) have developed an agent-based model of INs. Although their model is not specific to biotechnology, it provides several interesting insights about the dynamics of INs. In the model, firms innovate by changing their Kene, an expression which is used to indicate the individual agent knowledge base. The Kene comprises a set of units of knowledge. Each unit is defined by three parameters which represent the scientific, technological or business domain, the ability to perform a given application in this domain and the expertise level with which such applications can be performed. Firms innovate by means of innovation hypotheses, which are derived from a subset of the existing kene. The kene can be transformed into a product by means of a standard mapping function which combines the firm's existing knowledge with an innovation hypothesis. Firms try to improve their overall competitiveness by innovating. They do so by improving their knowledge base through adaptation to user needs, by incremental or radical learning and by cooperation or networking. When they form partnerships, firms can adopt a conservative strategy by choosing a partner having similar capabilities, or a progressive strategy by choosing a partner with a different capability set. In this model networks are 'normal' agents. The network can create innovations in addition to those of its members and it can distribute rewards to the members. The profits for each member will be the sum of individual and of network profits, which would explain the advantage of being in a network as opposed to proceeding alone. Simulations of this model show that INs are a viable form of industrial organization. The model predicts that both the number of actors and the number of networks will increase in the course of time. The model also leads to predictions about the relative merits of progressive and conservative strategies, about the expected network connectivity and about the evolution of industrial concentration.

In a recent paper Pyka and Saviotti (2005) developed a model of INs in biotechnology. The model includes two types of actors, DBFs and LDFs. The former have technological competencies and the latter only so-called economic competencies. Of course, LDFs do have technological competencies, but they are obsolete. The only valuable competencies they are left with initially are other competencies required to produce final products, such as financial, marketing etc. They are in fact complementary assets (Teece 1986). The model starts with the objective of comparing the two strategies of collaboration and of going it alone. Given the starting conditions it predicts that collaboration will be more effective. However, beyond this simple prediction the model gives interesting insights about network dynamics. For example, it predicts that collaboration and the formation of INs will continue in the long run even if by collaborating LDFs learn the new technological competencies. This can occur because of the changing role of DBFs, which shifts from that of *translators* of the new knowledge for LDFs to that of *explorers* of a knowledge space which LDFs can in principle know, but which expands at too fast a pace. Also, the model predicts correctly that while in the initial phases the collaboration will be mainly between DBFs and LDFs, in subsequent phases collaboration between different DBFs will become frequent. The model is oversimplified and it does not contain subsequent generations of biotechnology. Thus, it misses an important source of continued network formation. However, an alternative mechanism of continued network formation is here provided by the extremely high rate of growth and by the increasing complexity of new knowledge, which makes it impossible for any LDFs to explore it all, even when it was in principle capable of doing it. Shifting to the role of explorers allows DBFs to keep entering and giving rise to new INs. In other words, INs could be an advantageous form of industrial organization both due to knowledge discontinuities, that is to the qualitative difference between old and new knowledge, and to the rate at which new knowledge is created, which could exceed the capabilities of LDFs. At this point the relative weight of DBFs entry and of the succession of two generations of biotechnology constitutes an interesting question which requires further work.

## 4.4 Summary and Conclusions

This chapter began by raising a number of fundamental questions about INs. In particular; it asked (1) whether INs are a temporary or stable form of industrial organization, and (2) why they became a new form of industrial organization only starting from the 1980s. These questions were prompted by the reaction of economists to the emergence of INs. Most economists interpreted this phenomenon as temporary response to a shock. They expected that when the shock had been absorbed by the economic system industrial organization would have reverted to the market and to large corporations. The point of view of economists changed gradually by accepting that INs were there to stay. However, up to the present no complete and consensually accepted theory of INs has been created. The research results quoted in this chapter allow us to give an answer to the first question. According to our interpretation of these results, INs are not a temporary phenomenon but their existence has already spanned a period of almost 30 years and seems destined to continue in the foreseeable future. In fact research about the long-term dynamics of capitalism (Langlois 2003, 2006) seems to indicate that INs are a component of the transition of mature post-industrial societies from an economy dominated by large corporations (the visible hand) to an increasingly vertically disintegrated one (the vanishing hand). This transition itself is heavily affected by the growing knowledge intensity of post-industrial economies. Yet the initial answer given by economists was not completely wrong. The stability of INs as a form of industrial organization depends on the presence of multiple technological generations. Within each generation we can expect INs to be superseded by hierarchies as the initial discontinuity disappears and the technology matures. However, the emergence of new generations of technology with which incumbent LDFs are unfamiliar will provide renewed impetus for the entry of DBFs and for the formation of new INs. Sectors with a stable and mature knowledge base are less likely to see the entry of new technology firms and the formation of INs. The persistence of INs is linked to the emergence of subsequent generations of biotechnology, which recreates the asymmetry in capabilities and absorptive capacities between DBFs and LDFs.

As far as question two is concerned, INs became an important form of industrial organization only in the 1980s because of evolution of industrial capitalism. There has been a shift away from conditions favouring the creation of the large corporations described by Chandler and towards some form of vertical disintegration, a transition that has been described by Langlois as the shift from the visible to the vanishing hand. One of the conditions underlying this transition is the shortened delay between the generation of new ideas and their industrial utilization, delay which fell from 32.76 years in 1887–1906 to 3.4 years in 1967–1986 (Agarwal and Gort 2001). In the present, more dynamic environment large corporations do not disappear, but they require the complementary presence of smaller, more flexible firms. Amongst these smaller firms there are the new technology firms (NTFs in general or DBFs in biotechnology), which function as intermediaries between the creation of new knowledge and its subsequent exploitation by LDFs.

It has to be noticed that the answer to the first question (Stability of INs) has been provided by exploring patterns of network dynamics. In this chapter we have provided an explanation for the existence of these patterns. Such an explanation seems in principle applicable not only to biotechnology networks but to all types of networks in which knowledge generation plays an important role. In fact, the pattern we observed is likely to be a *trajectory* in the dynamics of INs. The trajectory could be described in the following way. As a new technology qualitatively different from any of the pre-existing ones emerges,

- the rate of entry on new firms (DBFs or NTFs) is very high;
- the rate of creation of INs is very high;
- the object of INs is predominantly R&D;
- the organizations creating the new knowledge (PRIs) and the firms having a competitive advantage in it (DBFs or NTFs) have a high centrality; and

- network density falls as the rate of creation of new nodes exceeds the rate of creation of new links.

As the new technology starts maturing,

- the rate of entry of new firms falls;
- the rate of creation of INs falls;
- the object of INs shifts from R&D to marketing;
- the centrality of DBFs (or of NTFs) and of PRIs falls while that of LDFs rises; and
- network density rises as the rate of creation of links starts exceeding the rate of creation of nodes.

At the end of this cycle the network ceases to exist unless a new generation of the technology underlying it comes into existence. If such a new generation emerges the network can survive and even grow, although the DBFs (NTFs) of the second generation are unlikely to be the same ones as those of the first generation. Amongst incumbent LDFs those that can absorb and master the new technology by participating in INs can be expected to survive from one generation to the next one. The less cyclical influence of a high and growing rate of creation of new knowledge can be superimposed upon that of the discontinuity. Even when incumbent LDFs can in principle absorb the new knowledge they may not be in a position to increase their R&D budgets proportionally to the rate of growth of new knowledge. The information existing in this moment does not allow us to separate the *discontinuity* from the *rate* effect and the *translator* from the *explorer* role of

DBFs. We hope that our results have contributed to improve the understanding of INs in biotechnology and in general, but realize that we are still very far from having achieved a complete knowledge of such a complex subject. Clearly, further work is still required.

# References

Agarwal R, Gort M (2001) First mover advantage and the speed of competitive entry. Journal of Law and Economics 44: 161–177

Aoki M (1988) Information, incentives, and bargaining in the Japanese economy. Cambridge University Press, New York

Audretsch DB, Keilbach MC, Lehman EE (2006) Entrepreneurship and economic growth. Cambridge University Press, Cambridge

Barabasi A (2002) Linked: the new science of networks. Perseus, Cambridge, MA

Barabasi A, Bonabeau E (2003, May) Scale free networks. Scientific American: 52–59

Barabasi A, Reka A, Jeong H (1999) Mean field theory for scale free random networks. Physica 272: 173–187

Baum JAC, Calabrese T, Silverman B (2000) Don't go it alone: alliance network composition and startups' performance in Canadian biotechnology. Strategic Management Journal 21: 263–294

Ben David J (1977) Centers of learning: Britain, France, Germany. McGraw Hill, New York

Bonaccorsi A, Giuri P (2001) The long-term evolution of vertically-related industries. International Journal of Industrial Organization 19: 1053–1083

Cainarca G, Colombo M, Mariotti S (1992) Agreements between firms and the technological life cycle model: evidence from information technology. Research Policy 21: 45–62

Callon M (1991) Réseaux technico-economiques et irréversibilités. In: Byer R (ed), Les figures de l'irréversibilité en economie. Editions de l'Ecole des Hautes Etudes en Sciences Sociales, Paris

Catherine D (2007) Dynamique de l'organisation industrielle dans le secteur des biotechnologies: une analyse en termes de réseaux. PhD Thesis, Grenoble Ecole de Management, Grenoble

Chandler AD (1962) Strategy and structure. MIT Press, Cambridge

Chandler AD (1977) The visible hand. Harvard University Press, Cambridge

Coase R (1937) The nature of the firm. Economica, traduction dans la Revue Française d'économie II/1 : 133–163

Cohen WM, Levinthal DA (1990) Absorptive capacity, a new perspective of learning and innovation. Administrative Science Quarterly 35: 128–152

Dodgson M (1992) The strategic management of R&D collaboration. Technology Analysis and Strategic Management 4: 227–244

Dominguez-Lacasa I, Grupp H, Schmoch U (2003) Tracing technological change over long periods in Germany in chemicals using patent statistics. Scientometrics 57: 175–195

Dyer JH, Nobeoka K (2000) Creating and managing a high-performance knowledge-sharing network: the Toyota case. Strategic Management Journal 21: 345–367

Economides N (1996) The economics of networks. International Journal of Organization 14: 673–699

Eisenhardt K, Schoonhoven CB (1996) Resource-based view of strategic alliance formation: strategic and social effects in entrepreneurial firms. Organization Science 7: 136–150

Etkowitz H, Leydesdorff L (eds) (1997) Universities in the global economy: a triple helix of university–industry–government relations. Cassell, London

Etkowitz H, Leydesdorff L (2000) The dynamics of innovation: from national systems and "Mode 2" to a triple helix of university–industry–government relations. Research Policy 29: 109–123

Freeman C (1991) Networks of innovators: a synthesis of research issues. Research Policy 20: 499–514

Freeman C, Soete L (1997) The economics of industrial innovation, 3rd edn. Pinter, London

Freeman L (1979) Centrality in social networks: conceptual clarification. Social Networks 1: 215–239

Gay B, Dousset B (2006) Innovation and network structural dynamics: Study of the alliance network of a major sector of the biotechnology industry. Research Policy 35: 1457–1475

Gemser G, Leenders M, Wijnberg N (1996) The dynamics of inter-firm networks in the course of the industry life cycle: the role of appropriability. Technology Analysis and Strategic Management 8: 439–453

Gibbons M, Limoges C, Nowotny H, Schwartzmann S, Scott P, Trow M (1994) The new production of knowledge – the dynamics of science and research in contemporary societies. Sage, London

Gilbert N, Pyka A, Ahrweiler P (2001) Innovation networks, a simulation approach. Journal of Artificial Societies and Social Simulation 4(3). http://www.soc.surrey.ac.uk/JASSS/4/3/8.html

Gilsing V, Nooteboom B (2006) Exploration and exploitation in innovation systems: the case of pharmaceutical biotechnology. Research Policy 35: 1–23

Grabowski H, Vernon J (1994) Innovation and structural change in pharmaceuticals and biotechnology. Industrial and Corporate Change 3: 435–449

Grebel T, Krafft J, Saviotti PP (2006) On the life cycle of knowledge intensive sectors. Revue de l'OFCE, Special issue, 63–85

Gross J, Yellen J (1998) Graph theory and its applications. CRC, Boca Raton, FL

Gulati R (1995) Does familiarity breed trust? The implications of repeated ties for contractual choice in alliances. Academy of Management Journal 38: 85–112

Hagedoorn J (1993) Understanding the rationale of strategic technology partnering: interorganizational modes of cooperation and sectoral differences. Strategic Management Journal 14: 371–385

Hagedoorn J (1995) Strategic technology partnering during the 1980s: trends, networks and corporate patterns in non-core technologies. Research Policy 24: 207–231

Hagedoorn J, Schakenraad, J (1994) The effect of strategic technology alliances on company performance. Strategic Management Journal 15: 291–309

Hakansson H (1987) Industrial technological development. A network approach. Croom Helm, Kent, UK

Hobday M (1994) The limits of Silicon Valley: a critique of network theory. Technology Analysis and Strategic Management 6: 231–244

Hopkins M, Martin P, Nightingale P, Kraft A, Mahdi S (2007) The myth of the biotech revolution: an assessment of technological, clinical and organisational change. Research Policy 36: 566–589

Hounshell D, Smith JK (1988) Science and corporate strategy: Du Pont R&D 1902–1980. Cambridge University Press, Cambridge

Imai K, Baba Y (1989) Systemic innovation and cross border network. OCDE, communication au séminaire international sur la science, la technologie et la croissance économique

Justman M, Zuscovitch E (1995) Networks, sustainable differentiation and economic development. In: Batten D, Casti J, Thord R (eds) Networks in action: communication, economic and human knowledge. Springer, Berlin

Kalaitzandonakes N, Bjornson B (1997) Vertical and horizontal coordination in the agro-biotechnology industry: evidence and implications. Journal of Agricultural and Applied Economics 29: 129–139

Kale P, Singh H, Perlmutter H (2000) Learning and protection of proprietary assets in strategic alliances: building relational capital. Strategic Management Journal 21(Special issue): 217–237

Katz M, Shapiro, C (1985) Network externalities, competition and compatibility. American Economic Review 75: 424–440

Katz M, Shapiro C (1992) Product introduction with network externalities. Journal of Industrial Economics 40: 55–84

Knole R, Kuklinski, JH (1982) Network analysis. Sage, Beverly Hills

Koza MP, Lewin AY (1998) The co-evolution of strategic alliances. Organization Science 9: 255–264

Langlois RN (2003) The vanishing hand: the changing dynamics of industrial capitalism. Industrial and Corporate Change 12: 351–385

Langlois RN (2006) The dynamics of industrial capitalism: Schumpeter, Chandler and the new economy. Routledge, London

Liebeskind JP, Oliver AL, Zucker LG, Brewer M (1996) Social networks, learning and flexibility: sourcing scientific knowledge in biotechnology firms. Organization Science 7(1): 428–443

Lorenzoni G, Lipparini A (1999) The leveraging of interfirm relationships as a distinctive organizational capability: a longitudinal study. Strategic Management Journal 20: 317–338

March JG (1991) Exploration and exploitation in organizational learning. Organization Science 2: 71–87

Mitchell W, Singh K (1996) Survival of businesses using collaborative relationships to commercialize complex goods. Strategic Management Journal 17: 169–195

Mokyr J (2002) The gifts of Athena – historical origins of the knowledge economy. Princeton University Press, Princeton

Mowery D (1989) Collaborative ventures between U.S. and foreign manufacturing firms. Research Policy 18: 19–33

Mowery D, Nelson RR, Sampat BN, Ziedonis A (2001) The growth of patenting and licensing by US universities: an assessment of the effects of the Bayh–Dole act of 1980. Research Policy 30: 99–119

Murmann JP (2003) Knowledge and competitive advantage. Cambridge University Press, Cambridge

Mytelka LK (1999) New trends in biotechnology networking. International Journal of Biotechnology 1: 30–41

Nelson R (1988) Institutions supporting technical change in the US. In: Dosi G, Freeman C, Nelson R, Soete L, Silverberg G (eds) Technical change and economic theory. Pinter, London

Nelson R (1990) Capitalism as an engine of progress. Research Policy 19: 193–214

Nesta LLJ, Saviotti PP (2006) Firm knowledge and market value in biotechnology. Industrial and Corporate Change 15: 625–652

Nesta LJJ, Saviotti PP (2005) Coherence of the knowledge base and the firm's innovative performance: evidence from the US pharmaceutical industry. Journal of Industrial Economics 53: 105–124

Nohria N, Eccles RG (1992) Networks and organizations: structure, form, and action. Harvard Business School Press, Boston

Oliver AL (2001) Strategic alliances and the learning life-cycle of biotechnology firms. Organization Studies 22: 467–489

Oliver AL, Liebeskind JP (1998) Three levels of networking for sourcing intellectual capital in biotechnology. International Studies of Management and Organizations 27(4): 76–103

Orsenigo L, Pammolli F, Riccaboni M (2001) Technological change and network dynamics. Lessons from the pharmaceutical industry. Research Policy 30: 485–508

Pisano G (1990) The R&D boundaries of the firm: an empirical analysis. Administrative Science Quarterly 35: 153–176

Pisano G, Teece D (1989) Collaborative arrangements and global technology strategy: some evidence from the telecommunications equipment industry. In: Rosenbloom RS, Burgelman RA (eds) Research on technological innovation, management and policy, Vol. 4. JAI Press, Greenwich, CT

Powell WW, Koput KW, Smith-Doerr L (1996) Inter-organisational collaboration and the locus of innovation: networks of learning in biotechnology. Administrative Science Quarterly 41: 116–145

Prahalad CK, Hamel G (1990) The core competences of the corporation. Harvard Business Review 68: 79–90

Pyka A, Saviotti P (2005) The evolution of R&D networking in the biotech industries. International Journal of Entrepreneurship and Innovation Management 5: 49–68

Reich L (2002) The making of American industrial research: science and business at GE and Bell, 1876–1926. Cambridge University Press, Cambridge

Reka A, Barabasi A (2002) Statistical mechanics of complex networks. Reviews of Modern Physics 74: 47–97

Reka A, Jeong H, Barabasi A (2000) Error and attack tolerance of complex networks. Nature 406: 378–382

Roijakkers N, Hagedoorn J (2006) Inter-firm partnering in pharmaceutical biotechnology since 1975: trends, patterns and networks. Research Policy 35: 431–446

Rothaermel FT (2001) Incumbent's advantage through exploiting complementary assets via interfirm cooperation. Strategic Management Journal 22: 687–699

Rothaermel FT, Deeds D (2004) Exploration and exploitation alliances in biotechnology: a system of new product development. Strategic Management Journal 25: 201–221

Rothaermel FT, Hill CWL (2005) Technological discontinuities and complementary assets: a longitudinal study of industry and firm performance. Organization Science 16: 52–70

Richardson G (1972) The organisation of industry. Economic Journal 82: 883–896

Saviotti PP (2005) Biotechnology. A report for the key technologies expert group appointed by the European Commission. DG RTD K2 Technology Foresight Unit

Saviotti PP, de Looze MA, Maupertuis MA, Nesta L (2003) Knowledge dynamics and the mergers of firms in the biotechnology based sectors. International Journal of Biotechnology 5: 371–401

Saviotti PP, de Looze MA, Maupertuis MA (2005) Knowledge dynamics and the mergers of firms in the biotechnology based sectors. Economics of Innovation and New Technology 14: 103–124

Saxenian A (1991) The origins and dynamics of production networks in Silicon Valley. Research Policy 20: 423–437

Schumpeter J (1934, original edn 1912) The theory of economic development. Harvard University Press, Cambridge

Schumpeter J (1942, 5th edn 1976) Capitalism, socialism and democracy. George Allen and Unwin, London

Shan W (1990) An empirical analysis of organizational strategies by entrepreneurial high-technology firms. Strategic Management Journal 11: 129–139

Shan W, Walker G, Kogut B (1994) Interfirm cooperation and startup innovation in the biotechnology industry. Strategic Management Journal 15: 387–394

Simon H (1951) A formal theory of the employment relationship. Econometrica 19: 103–110

Steward F, Conwey S (1996) Informal networks in the origination of successful innovations. In: Coombs R, Richards A, Saviotti PP, Walsh V (eds) Edward Elgar, Cheltenham, pp 201–221

Stuart TE (2000) Interorganizational alliances and the performance of firms: a study of growth and innovation rates in a high-technology industry. Strategic Management Journal 21(8): 791–811

Stuart TE, Hoang H, Hybels RC (1999) Inter-organisational endorsements and the performance of entrepreneurial firms. Administrative Science Quarterly 44: 315–349

Teece DJ (1986) Profiting from technological innovation: implications for integration, collaboration, licensing and public policy. Research Policy 15: 285–305

Thorelli HB (1986) Networks: between markets and hierarchies. Strategic Management Journal 7: 37–51

Von Hippel E (1989) Cooperation between rivals: informal know-how trading. In: Carlsson B (ed) Industrial dynamics. Kluwer, Dordrecht

Williamson O (1975) Markets and hierarchies: analysis and antitrust implications. The Free Press, New York

Williamson O (1985) The economic institutions of capitalism. The Free Press, New York

Williamson O (1991) Comparative economic organization: the analysis of discrete structural alternatives. Administrative Science Quarterly 36: 269–296

Zucker L, Darby M (1996) Star scientists and institutional transformation: patterns of invention and innovation in the formation of the biotechnology industry. Proceedings of the National Academy of Science 93: 12709–12716

# 5 Strategy and Strategic Thinking in Biotechnology Entrepreneurship

Alan L. Carsrud, Malin Brännback, and Maija Renko

Eugenio Pino and Family Global Entrepreneurship Center, Florida International University, 11110 Southwest 11th Street, University Park – VII 130, Miami, FL 33199-0001, USA
Department of Business Administration, Åbo Akademi University, Henriksgatan 7, FIN-20500 Åbo, Finland

## 5.1 Introduction

The motivation (and personal *ex-ante* assumption) for this chapter comes from our combined 20 years' experience of research, consulting, operational positions, and ownership of more than 100 innovative, very early stage biotechnology firms in the United States (California and Florida), Finland (countrywide), Australia (New South Wales and Queensland), France (Grenoble), and Chile (countrywide). When we use the term "innovation" we mean something novel, which can be a process or a way of doing something that does not necessarily mean a physical invention.

From a definitional perspective, we do not mean that an innovation is the same as an "invention." An invention is something physical, but it does not necessarily have any commercial value. An innovation is what will be *successfully commercialized*. It should be noted that following intellectual property law in the United States, both an innovation and an invention can be patented and can be the basis of a business. The protection of intellectual property should be of great concern to any biotechnology entrepreneur. We also understand that for most early-stage biotechnology firms, the primary concern is the $R$ in R&D, rather than the $D$. The "science" *is* their business. This reality makes biotechnology very different from other technology-based industrial sectors. For example, in Information and Communications Technology, making a chip that functions is common knowledge among firms, just like in the automobile industry all companies have the knowledge of how to manufacture a technologically advanced and functional car. Businesses in those sectors are, for the most part, involved in the $D$ (for more, see Pisano 2006).

H. Patzelt and T. Brenner (eds.), *Handbook of Bioentrepreneurship*,
doi: 10.1007/978-0-387-48345-0_5, © Springer Science + Business Media, LLC 2008

In this chapter, we describe numerous factors that are essential components of strategic thinking in early-stage biotechnology firms. Even if we will not present primary empirical data, our text is based not only on theoretical insights but also on our extensive combined experiences in researching and consulting early-stage biotechnology firms, as described earlier. Most of these firms were initially university based and most of them were at one time funded by governmental grants. Some had angel investors, others did not. Only a small portion had received formal venture capital. It is these very early stage firms that are often ignored in existing research literature, which tends to study later stage firms that have already gathered some venture capital investments and are thus easier to identify (see for example Pisano 2006). Later in this chapter we will call this early-stage group of firms the *fifth tier*. The goal of this chapter is to explore an interesting set of observations about this fifth tier. Interested academic scholars, but more important, practitioners, can find recommendations to how to enhance their entrepreneurial endeavors.

It is our goal in this chapter to provoke a wide range of research and application questions. We attempt to do this using a structured and logical approach. While we are critical of the industry, we still believe in its long-term potential. But the business of biotechnology is neither as simple as policymakers wish it would be, nor as theoretically straightforward and driven as most academic researchers of the field would like to make one believe (Pisano 2006). Any practitioner (biotechnology entrepreneur) will attest to how difficult it is to make the science work, and even more so, to make a profit from this science.

From our personal experience, and observations globally, these firms are a legion. However, rarely is their situation described or analyzed in academic textbooks or articles, because it is cumbersome to collect and access empirical data about them. While we will present limited direct empirical evidence here, the views and arguments are based on a wide range of empirical studies and nearly a decade of observation, in-depth case studies, and action research by the authors actively helping clusters of these firms (Brännback et al. 2001a, b, 2004, 2007; Renko et al. 2005; Renko 2006; Grundsten 2004). As mentioned earlier, this chapter is based on extensive experience with Finnish-, French-, Australian-, Chilean-, and US-based early-stage biotechnology firms. This is different from most previous work on biotechnology strategy, which is primarily based on US data, obtained from lists of firms provided by venture capitalists or firms who exist in established regional clusters (San Diego or Seattle). There are of course exceptions such as the work of Lynn Zucker and Michael Darby, who have looked at samples of biotechnology entrepreneurs in both the USA and Japan (Zucker and Darby 1997; Zucker et al. 1998, 2002). Some of our observations are longitudinal, covering the *total* population of some 130 biotechnology firms in Finland (Brännback et al. 2001a, b, 2004). We can find no similar research of American or other European nation's total populations.

While we would not claim that this chapter is an exhaustive, in-depth, or rigid scholarly examination of all of the existing academic literature on strategy in young biotechnology firms, we do believe that based on the existing empirical evidence at this point (and our personal experiences) we can present our convictions about strategic orientations in early-stage biotechnology firms. We will present these by describing the relevant theories and some of the existing empirical evidence. Our central claim is that early biotechnology firms generally lack a strategic mindset beyond fund raising and technology development. We will further argue that they are not market-oriented enough at the early stage to survive or to be acquired (Brännback et al. 2007). This reality of early-stage firms gains support from the Colombo and Grilli (2005) study of technology-based firms that did not, however, focus on biotechnology.

In this chapter we argue for a more reflected, proactive, and market-oriented strategy development and implementation in early biotechnology firms. The development of a sustainable strategic business model and a related revenue model has been a matter of debate in the industry for several years. However, this discussion has been limited to a small number of approaches available, primarily focused on how to "cash out" either through licensing technology, being acquired by a larger pharmaceutical company, or by undertaking IPO (Pisano 1996, 2006; Robbins-Roth 2000; Oliver 2000).

The chapter will proceed as follows. In the section following this introduction, we will give the reader a short review of the development of the global biotechnology sector. This will be done with an emphasis on the diversity of the sector; even if the early advances in biotechnology were mostly based on chemistry and biology, today's biotechnology firms base their businesses on a multitude of scientific disciplines and technologies. In Sect. 5.3, we will focus on innovation in biotechnology. This section also provides the basis for Sect. 5.4, where the two complementary views of innovation, the one by Schumpeter and the one by Kirzner, are discussed. After this, we will widen the focus in Sect. 5.5. Section 5.5 introduces ideas from the strategy and entrepreneurship literatures that go beyond innovation management but are still helpful in understanding the strategic thinking in early-stage biotechnology firms. Building on all the previous sections, Sect. 5.6 introduces proactiveness, reactiveness, strategic fit, and traditions as components of strategy in biotechnology start-ups. Finally, Sect. 5.7 provides discussion and conclusions for the chapter. As mentioned earlier, all of this is written from a highly applied orientation, not solely an academic one.

## 5.2 Sector Development Review

The complexity of developing strategy for biotechnology firms is best understood by starting with a brief review of the early days of the modern biotechnology industry. Although the first genetic engineering project might well have been the mule whose commercial value is recognizable, it is commonly agreed that the modern industry started in November 1973, when an article by Stanley Cohen and Herbert Boyer was published. This article reported on the scientific breakthrough of recombinant DNA. Scientific advances in biotechnology in the 1970s led not only to the emergence of a new scientific and technological paradigm (Dosi 1988) but also to structural and strategic changes most visible in intensive new business development activities beginning in the USA in the early 1980s (Zucker and Darby 1997; Zucker et al. 1998, 2002; Deeds and Hill 1996, 1998; Robbins-Roth 2000; Deeds 2001; Oliver 2000; Murray 2002). The commercial break-through followed on October 14, 1980, when Genentech went public and listed their stock on the US stock exchange. The firm, which had been founded a few years earlier, had gone from small-scale protein production for R&D purposes to large-scale production for commercial purposes. What happened that day in 1980 nobody had anticipated. Genentech was going to sell 1 million shares for $35 a piece, an outrageous idea in itself, since the company did not anticipate having a product before 1984; that is, they were selling hope. Hope did sell well. Within 20 min the stock sold at $89, and ended at $70. In 24 h the market capitalization of the firm had doubled (Robbins-Roth 2000).

This was certainly an auspicious start to a new industrial sector and many since have thought this could be replicated provided the right environmental forces and internal resources were combined correctly. However, the biotechnology industry went through at least two setbacks before 1995, when the industry started booming once again, this time all over the world. Now Amgen had become the role model. In 1994 there were only 4 profitable biotechnology firms worldwide; in 1999 there were 17 and in 2000 there were 22 out of a total of less than 5,000 firms worldwide (Amdjadi et al. 2000; Brännback et al. 2001a). The situation has not improved since then, but rather the opposite (Pisano 2006).

Biotechnology business is a cluster of interrelated industries, building upon knowledge-intensive scientific (often basic) research, which is growing because of the dynamic interplay of a wide variety of traditional disciplines and newly emerging ones (Renko 2006). The field of biotechnology is indeed complex and vast. It is a multidisciplinary set of industrial sectors with a variety of distinct industry recipes, company paradigms, and strategy logic. Some sectors of modern biotechnology operate at the intersection of several industries, making it increasingly complex to define markets and identify competitors. In Fig. 5.1, which is a simplified picture of the biotechnology field, these intersections are depicted as circles.

An industry recipe is the common beliefs and assumptions, which are held as consistent and realistic within an industry (Grinyer and Spender 1979; Spender 1989). A company business model or paradigm is how the firm operates and interacts within the industry (Johnson and Scholes 1988). It is obvious from Fig. 5.1 that the choice of appropriate strategies within biotechnology is anything but simple or direct. Strategy logic within a biotechnology firm represents the subjective thinking of key persons in a firm (Näsi et al. 1996). These concepts prove instrumental when comparing performance and creation of firms that operate in the same industry. One would anticipate very different strategies in firms in different groupings, as described in Fig. 5.1.

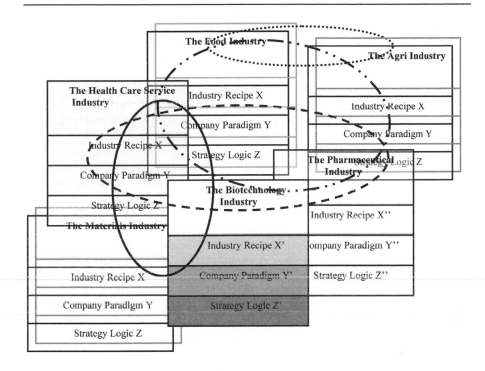

**Fig. 5.1.** The complex business arena of biotechnology (Brännback et al. 2001a)

This diversity of the biotechnology field is also reflected by Wolff (2001), who lists over 30 of the most promising business areas within biotechnology, all of which constitute their own sector, which often is dependent on other sectors.[1] Moreover, those who invest in these fields classify firms not only by the technology the firms are attempting to commercialize, but also by their size and risk profile. Wolff (2001) classifies biotechnology firms in four tiers. Tier 1 firms are those that have established records of earnings and have market evaluations greater than US $5 billion. Clearly these are firms that have met the market challenge and that have succeeded in implementing their strategy. Second tier are those firms that have not yet established a meaningful revenue stream, yet have begun to sell to the marketplace, and have a market capitalization of more than US $2 billion. Third tier are those firms that have a market value of US $800 million or more, but have yet to sell commercially. Firms in this tier have a

---

[1] E.g. therapeutic proteins, monoclonal antibodies, immune system modulators, gene therapy, angiogenesis, anti-angiogenesis, tissue regeneration, armed viruses, stem cell therapy, drug delivery mechanisms, drug delivery systems, curative vaccines, signal transduction, photodynamic therapy, pharmaco-genomics, telomeres, genomics, proteomics, combinatorial and ADMET chemistry, assay development, computer modeling, bio-informatics, gene shuffling, high throughput machinery, biochips, cardiovascular devices, nutraceuticals, biometrics, microrobotics, nanoparticles, biocomputing, and biomedical engineering.

promising near-term pipeline and/or a credible R&D effort for treatment development. Most, if not all of these firms, are publicly traded firms with all of the reporting mechanisms that this status entails. The fourth tier consists of firms with market values less than US $800 million. Firms in tiers 2, 3, and 4 have strategies that appear to function, but that are likely to face considerable strategic challenges. As mentioned earlier, these firms have been the subject of the bulk of existing academic studies as data concerning these firms are more readily available from public sources.

We focus this chapter on what we call the *fifth tier*. Thus, we expand beyond Wolff's focus on larger and more easily studied larger firms. For example, there are some 130 biotechnology firms in Finland – all sectors accounted for – of which only two are publicly traded on the Helsinki Stock Exchange, and two on the London Stock Exchange. Here we have a population of firms that never appears in easily available samples, yet the firms are in business and actually reflect the majority of biotechnology companies in Finland. Many of these firms have market values less than US $25 million. What makes this group of firms very different from the prior four tiers of firms is their lack of readily identifiable market, lack of sales revenues, and a leadership team often bereft of management, finance, and strategic planning skills. However, it is this particular tier of biotechnology entrepreneurs that are the most likely to think that the process of success is merely one of technology. Marketing and market orientation are something only large health-care conglomerates such as Johnson & Johnson (J&J) need worry about as these new ventures do not sell band-aids or established cardiovascular devices as J&J firms do.

The above-mentioned historical description and review of the industry prompts a set of fundamental questions:

• What kind of strategy supports the kind of market and commercial success described earlier?
• Are there really technology-based strategies, or is it *"research hunting for money?"*, and
• What is a sustainable competitive advantage for an early-stage biotechnology firm?

To be blunt, the only sustainable competitive advantage is constant innovation and even that does not guarantee a success, since it occurs everywhere in the world. Moreover, through the entire history, *luck* and *serendipity* have been a major success factors in the pharmaceutical and biotechnology sectors, starting with penicillin (Robbins-Roth 2000; Oliver 2000; Wolff 2001; Pisano 2006).

## 5.3 Innovation in Biotechnology

Product, process, and technology innovations should be the core activities of all small start-up biotechnology firms. An innovation has to be new. It can be an idea, or an invention, but there is an explicit requirement for it to be *a commercialized innovation*, i.e. to have commercial value. Mere commercial *potential* is not sufficient. This view follows Schumpeter's conceptualization of an innovation (Schumpeter 1934). However, the CEOs of modern biotechnology firms that we have encountered over the past years are typically very technology-oriented, often paying little attention to the commercialization side of their innovations. Strategic thinking is often substituted for, and restricted to, what can be described as immediate tactics to raise money in order to continue R&D. These firms have an idea, invention, or innovation looking for an investor, not a market (Brännback and Carsrud 2003). Marketing is often ignored, except for going to research conferences or having booths at industry conferences.

Aside from commercialized ideas and inventions, an innovation can also be defined as an internal capability, which is dynamic (Teece et al. 1997; Deeds et al. 1999), based on an absorptive capacity in the firm and industry. Acording to this view, innovation enables the firm to generate and disseminate new knowledge for the purpose of developing new products (inventions) and ultimately wealth creation (Cohen and Levinthal 1989, 1990; Kogut and Zander 1993, Ensign 1999).

Entrepreneurial orientation provides yet another view to innovativeness in biotechnology. Entrepreneurial orientation in a firm has five dimensions: (1) autonomy, (2) innovativeness, (3) proactiveness, (4) competitive aggressiveness, and (5) risk-taking (Miller 1983). Lumpkin and Dess (2001) argue that while firms are strong in one or two aspects of entrepreneurial orientation, they show surprisingly low levels in the other dimensions. Many biotechnology start-up firms are innovative, if innovativeness means an ability to conduct cutting edge research. However, they are not quite autonomous since they are forced to comply with the increasing dictates of their funders, for example, angel investors or governmental agencies. Having a constant shortage of resources, they end up reactive and fail to develop the competitive aggressiveness they would need. In practical terms they become "grant junkies" often losing even the focus of their research in order to pursue grant dollars. Some of them never advance beyond being a substitute for a university-based R&D laboratory.

For any innovative activity to be commercially successful it requires carefully crafted business strategies (Chesbrough 2005, 2006), not just research strategies. Even beyond biotechnology firms, a sound strategy is a creative process that becomes the backbone, or road map, for navigating the firm towards ultimate success (Carsrud and Brännback 2007). Strategy and strategic thinking becomes the process of purposefully coordinating actions and resources, resources that often are extremely scarce or even nonexistent. For small start-up biotechnology firms the complexity is amplified in two ways. Not only is it necessary for these firms to continue their R&D processes, thereby developing their non-existent products into viably commercializable products, but they also have to develop the venture into a functioning, sustainable organization. Unfortunately, the founders traditionally have a scientific background, but rarely any business knowledge or experience that would be useful for strategic business development (Colombo and Grilli 2005). Thus, the development of a business model and a fully functioning organization tend to be ignored and strategy is reduced to managing the *R* in the

R&D process. This ultimately becomes a major contributor to failure of many of these early-stage ventures.

As mentioned in the introduction, we are focusing our discussion on the strategic thinking in biotechnology on small, early-stage start-ups that are still desperately pursuing a core technology. These firms are not publicly traded and exist because of governmental research grants or with limited private investment. Many have either recently left a physical or virtual incubator, or still reside in one or in university laboratories (Renko 2006). We have also attempted to focus on firms not just located in the "hotbeds" of biotechnology (San Diego, Boston, or Seattle), but to describe the larger phenomena as many areas are attempting to become biotechnology hubs from scratch, such as the Scripps Institute in Florida (Clouser 2007) or BioCity in Singapore.

## 5.4 Theoretical Bases for Entrepreneurial Biotechnology

Many high growth, venture capital backed, technology-based firms seem to embrace the Schumpeterian (Schumpeter 1934) view of entrepreneurship (Brännback et al. 2007). Certainly this is the model that most venture capitalists employ. This is also true for firms and investors in biotechnology. Two schools of thought from entrepreneurship have clearly impacted governmental policy decisions, regulations, and investor expectations about biotechnology firms and thereby also indirectly the strategic thinking within biotechnology firms. First, Schumpeter's (1934) views on entrepreneurship are often cited as mantra by public policymakers trying to create new industrial sectors and jobs based on various technologies. Schumpeter's (1934) entrepreneur is an innovator and developer of frame-breaking technology, which explains why so many governmental officials charged with economic development, venture capitalists, and even biotechnology entrepreneurs cite him as an intellectual father of the field. This occurs because Schumpeter's conceptualization best fits their desires, perceptions, and expectations of the entrepreneurial phenomena.

The second perspective of biotechnology entrepreneurship is based on Kirzner (1973, 1979), who sees the entrepreneur as an actor in the process, very conscious of market demands, exhibiting deliberate behaviors. That is, where Schumpeter's innovator is shifting the costs and revenue curves (through radical innovation) Kirzner's entrepreneur is, through entrepreneurial alertness, able to notice that *the curves have shifted* because of innovation. This means that Schumpeter's entrepreneur is working *outside* the ordinary market processes, whereas Kirzner's entrepreneur is clearly *market-driven*. Both may be true descriptions of very different types of biotechnology entrepreneurs, fundamental views of their entrepreneurial ventures, *and the strategies they develop*. In fact, one might argue that Wolff's (2001) first four tiers are more likely populated with Kirzner-type leaders than Schumpeter's types, although Hagedorn and Roijakkers (2002) argue that the entire sector is Schumpeterian. We disagree with the latter researchers as some larger firms are not doing frame-breaking research but acquiring it from smaller firms and thus extending their pipeline.

Schumpeter's entrepreneur seeks to enter new markets through disruptive innovation. Kirzner's entrepreneur is more likely to exist in market-oriented, later-stage firms, or in firms involved with the incremental development of existing technology. The dominant view in early-stage biotechnology entrepreneurship is Schumpeter's, as the new biotechnology entrepreneur is usually totally technology- and product-oriented. We argue that it is the lack of Kirznerian-type market orientation that is one of the biggest challenges within biotechnology entrepreneurship (Brännback and Carsrud 2003, 2004; Renko et al. 2005; Renko 2006). Kirznerian market orientation is just as important to biotechnology entrepreneurship as is the frame-breaking view of Schumpeter. Knowing that a disease does not have a cure is not the same as being market-conscious or market - oriented. Schumpeterian biotechnology entrepreneur is so preoccupied with his innovation that market considerations have been pushed aside *to a later stage, when time allows.* For those whose products are further along, or whose products are similar to those already on the market, they may view the entrepreneurial venture through Kirznerian lenses, i.e., seeing the innovation primarily through its ability to meet a market need, want, or fear. This really reflects "market pull" rather than "science push" strategies.

Science-based firms typically find that their executives believe in advanced science as a major source of future success for the firm. This is often reflected in CEOs' comments implying that the strengths of firms lie in "communicated science" and technology-related strengths such as "scientific competence," "scientific know-how," "own patented innovation," "advanced and focused research," and "internationally recognized high scientific level." Most early-stage biotechnology entrepreneurs see themselves as contributors to science, or even academic research, rather than as customer-oriented marketers of their firm's technology. Moreover, this focus on *science* is equated with reputation for internationally recognized research and thus a proxy of a sustainable competitive advantage. We seriously doubt that this is a sufficient equivalency. What is scientifically ground-breaking may still lack commercial value.

## 5.5 Strategic Management, Entrepreneurship, and Biotechnology

Traditionally, the field of strategic management has been regarded as the "big brother" to entrepreneurship. Strategic management researchers have primarily been interested in large organizations whereas entrepreneurship has been the discipline about small and medium-sized enterprises. As pointed out by Meyer et al. (2002), the core of strategic management research has been to understand the decision and actions which lead to competitive advantage. It can be argued that this development has its roots in the now classic books *Competitive Strategy* and *Competitive Advantage* written by Porter (1980, 1985). But, it can equally well be accredited to Baumol (1968), who argued that an entrepreneur was a person who practiced *leadership* by locating new ideas and putting them into effect. A manager oversees the efficiency of ongoing processes. The focus of entrepreneurship research has been on understanding how opportunities emerge and are converted into commercializable products or services. Meyer et al. (2002) show that the fields of strategy and entrepreneurship are different, but recent developments are closing the gap. Both fields share two areas of common interest – *firm performance* and *creation* (Meyer et al. 2002).

A rough categorization of strategic management would divide the field into three strategic paradigms (Teece et al. 1997; Meyer et al. 2002): competitive forces championed primarily by Porter (1980, 1985), strategic conflict (Shapiro 1989, Camerer 1991) and the resource-based view (Wernerfelt 1984; Barney 1991). The first and the last appear to have had a prominent presence in entrepreneurship (Grégoire et al. 2006). Later an extension of the resource-based view, the *dynamic capability* stream of strategic management (Teece et al. 1997; Henderson and Mitchell 1997; Teece 2000; Deeds 2001), and closely related contemporary views on organizational knowledge creation and organizational learning (Cohen and Levinthal 1990; Leonard-Barton 1992; Levinthal and March 1993; Kogut and Zander 1992) have emerged and have been used as theoretical frame of reference in studying biotechnology firms. Often this research has focused on R&D and innovation management and has been explicitly linked to knowledge management and organizational learning. Here R&D and innovative activities are seen as complex search, learning, and problem-solving processes, which are as much based on existing knowledge as they are on creating new knowledge (Dosi and Orseniego 1988; Cohen and Levinthal 1990; Levinthal and March 1993; Teece et al. 1997; Koschatzky 1999; Pitt and Clarke 1999; Ensign 1999). Moreover, the role of networks in venture success has also been extensively covered (Deeds and Hill 1996, 1998; Audretsch and Stephan 1996; Coombs and Deeds 2000; Murray 2002; Riccaboni and Pammolli 2002; Zucker and Darby 1997; Zucker et al. 1998, 2002).

Unlike in strategic management research, the concept of industry in entrepreneurship research is an emergent construct as many activities take place before the formation of an industry (Johnson and Van de Ven 2002). In the study of strategic management one assumes that an industry already exists. However, in Schumpeter's view the entrepreneur may actually create a new industry. For example, the industry of biotechnology did not exist before Genentech. Johnson and Van de Ven (2002) suggest four perspectives particularly useful when studying entrepreneurial strategy, which are relevant also in the context of biotechnology (Fig. 5.2).

The detailed model in Fig. 5.2 provides a representation of the issues a new biotechnology firm faces and that must be mastered in order to achieve success. We argue that firms in the first tier (Wolff 2001) master all areas; tier 2, 3, and 4 still face challenges in some instances of the four areas, e.g., standards, cultural norms, resource channels, financing and market creation and demand. Firms in the fifth tier face challenges in all areas. In fact, tier 5 firm may only have the science and technology in some acceptable shape. If not, their failure is almost assured.

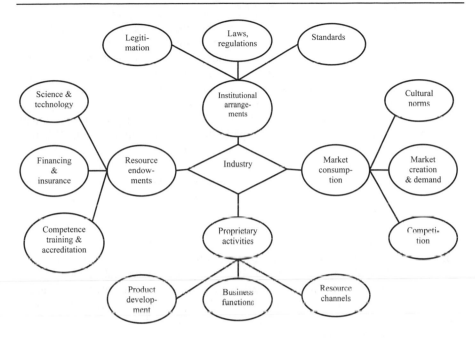

**Fig. 5.2.** An augmented view of an industry (Johnson and Van de Ven 2002, p. 77)

By now we have briefly reviewed the history of biotechnology business, described the central role of innovations in the strategy of biotechnology firms, outlined how entrepreneurship in general and innovations in particular can be viewed through Schumpeterian or Kirznerian lenses, and described how the early-stage biotechnology firms fit within the academic research on strategy and entrepreneurship. On the basis of these perspectives provided so far, we will next present various strategy components that we have observed in the biotechnology firms we have researched and worked with over the past years. Our aim here is not to provide an exclusive, exhaustive typology of strategies in young biotechnology firms. Instead, we want to show how each of the aspects described so far – history, innovation, strategy – is present in the everyday reality of early-stage biotechnology firms.

## 5.6 Strategy Components in Early-Stage Biotechnology Firms

### 5.6.1 Proactiveness

On the basis of previous literature, Sandberg (2005, pp. 53–54) defines market proactiveness as "either acting based on the information gathered about the market before the circumstances have had a direct impact on the firm, or deliberately influencing and creating changes in the market." Any successful strategy has to address the market environment. However, the concept of *a market* or *served market* and the concept of a *customer* are indeed complex especially when discussing an early-stage firm in the biotechnology industry. When is a biotechnology product commercialized? Is it when it receives FDA approval 15 years after a molecule was discovered? Is it when an early-stage biotechnology company sells off a lead compound to another biotechnology company? Is it when a firm licenses off a drug candidate that has passed Phase II clinical trials to a larger pharmaceutical company, who has the resources to complete the Phase III clinical trials. When is *when*? If that question is difficult, we also have to deal with who is *who*? That is, who are the customers or customer groups that have to be reached and that have to buy into the product? These questions are important because depending on how they are answered the forces shown in Fig. 5.2 will be defined differently.

Many early-stage biotechnology firms will argue that they do not have to worry about the patient or the doctors (the consumers in the end market – *demand*) since they are not addressing that end market. They think only patents are critical. In fact, most young firms have a scientific concept that has yet to be transformed into a commercially viable offering of any sort. Many firms have not formed a clear understanding of what the ultimate offering could be, and are unable to even target a market. All these firms really have is *potentially enormous potential*. For example, let us assume that a biomaterials firm developing technology that could become hip replacement products is interested in the market size. A market researcher would analyze the market potential and try to establish a possible target market. Upon closer discussions with this firm, it may be revealed that hip replacements are just one option among other *sketches* of potential outcomes. In fact, the firm may have no real idea what the technology ultimately will become. The firm is, in other words, light years from the ultimate commercialization of a future innovation.

A firm in the abovedescribed case should also worry about issues limiting demand, such as reimbursement systems. Typically these firms argue that they really do not have to worry about a reimbursement system since they are selling their patented replacement parts to medical supply houses or hospitals. Again, given their enormous distance from the end market, such a line of reasoning may make sense. However, it is important, even at this stage, to have an understanding of what forces influence ultimate demand.

As a conclusion, market proactiveness is an essential part of strategic thinking in early-stage biotechnology firms. Proactiveness is also a key quality required from those firms that will be challenging the marketplace through a Schumpeterian-type innovation. The only way to revolutionize the marketplace and to create demand for something inherently novel is through proactive deeds and market foresight.

## 5.6.2 Fit

The emergent strategies of many entrepreneurial biotechnology firms have to be formulated as a result of the interplay between the business environment (including market) and resources available to the firm (Fig. 5.2). One of the enduring assumptions in the strategy formulation literature is that the appropriateness of a firm's strategy can be defined in terms of its fit, i.e., match with the environmental or organizational contingencies facing the firm (Andrews 1971). The pursuit of strategic fit has traditionally been viewed as having desirable performance implications (Miles and Snow 1994). In an ideal situation, the resources of a firm would be aligned with the environment, including market needs. If environmental conditions change through either the emergence of new opportunities or threats, then according to the resource-based view of firms (Wernerfelt 1984; Barney 1991), it is not obvious that an organization should change its strategy to achieve better fit with environmental conditions. This is especially the case if such changes are a clear misfit with established organizational strengths (Zajac et al. 2000). While resource arguments have typically been tested in a large corporation setting, they have been used to explain how entrepreneurs can create competitive advantages (Alvarez and Busenitz 2001; Fiet 2002). In very young ventures, resources act as inducements to experiment, take risks, and make proactive strategic choices. Resources also are deployed as buffers in periods of economic duress. Finding a balance between proactive and risky strategic choices based on technological and scientific resources of a firm on one side, and the changing business environment of the firm on the other is a major strategic challenge for these young firms. The practical aspects of this challenge were highlighted by the hip replacement technology example.

In addition to strategic fit perspective, the environment–resources linkage can be approached from learning perspective. With regard to technological learning, Cohen and Levinthal (1989) suggest that in order for a firm to be able to exploit external knowledge from the environment, it needs to have the internal skills to understand this knowledge and its potential uses. Absorptive capacity concerns a firm's ability to adapt and exploit external scientific and technical knowledge from the environment. With regard to learning about markets, the concept of market orientation has been developed within marketing literature. Market orientation of the firm refers to adapting and exploiting external knowledge concerning customers, competitors, and relevant changes in the market environment (Kohli and Jaworski 1990; Kohli et al. 1993; Jaworski and Kohli 1993). This kind of knowledge acquisition is the prerequisite for Kirznerian-type innovation, which is based on superior understanding of markets and ways to serve those markets. The reluctance (or inability) of highly technology-oriented companies to employ a breath of market knowledge in their strategic decision-making often leads them to introduce products that evolve "naturally" from their current technology base. This can happen without regard to the needs of markets or even end users (Sheth and Ram 1987).

Contrast this with an early-stage start-up that has a high level of market orientation. This is a firm that effectively generates, disseminates, and responds to market intelligence (Kohli and Jaworski 1990). This type of firm can develop an understanding of markets within the whole organization. This, again, has a potential to promote the firm's alertness to relevant market information available in the business environment. If market-oriented thinking is present at all levels and in all functions of an organization through effective dissemination of market intelligence, all the employees, not just the business development managers, can absorb market knowledge from the environment (Renko 2006).

It is evident that for many firms the technology base of the firm has been developed in a proactive manner, while the strategies used to focus the firm on its markets are more reactive. Instead of finding a true strategic fit between the market environment and the firm's technology resources, young technology firms often only try to match their technology with the available opportunities for funding resources. More specifically, the influence of resource availability in the form of governmental research funding, license and royalty streams, as well as venture capital at later stages influence firm strategies with regard to target markets.

### 5.6.3 Reactiveness

Technological and scientific achievements should be behind the establishment of most knowledge-intensive, biotechnology-based ventures. For example, a single drug discovery project, or biotechnology platform process, may give rise to several development candidates for a variety of different medical indications. Companies can select some therapeutic indications for in-house development, and license out others. For example, a firm may keep a human application for in-house development while licensing out animal applications. Decisions such as these are at the heart of the business strategies employed by entrepreneurial biotechnology ventures, who are trying to transition to a revenue model and move up to a higher tier (1, 2, 3, or 4), as described earlier. These strategies are often based on issues of perceived revenues and revenue sources.

As early-stage entrepreneurial biotechnology firms are small and highly R&D-intensive, they typically spend all their financial resources on additional R&D (Oliver 2000). Thus, the dominant strategic concern is the next round of financing to continue research. Consequently, the research undertaken is not always long-term goal directed, but often dictated by the immediate demands of the research fund provider. New firms are highly dependent on research grant or contract dollars (usually governmental or private foundation). The firms often state that they conduct cutting-edge scientific research, which reflects their academic orientation. Sometimes the real goal of the R&D firm is to find sufficient funds to just do research.

The global funding environment for early-stage biotechnology companies has clearly changed over the past decade. To secure financing, many companies have felt compelled to move their technology away from a service model to a focus on a product-based strategy. Early-stage companies have also shifted away from platform technologies to clinical development businesses. Both of these adjustments have been largely triggered by investors, who understand that their exits are driven by late-stage clinical products (Chaya 2005).

### 5.6.4 Traditions and History

The traditional operating strategies of most early-stage biotechnology firms are focused on achieving enough funding through research grants, angel investors, formal venture capital, or initial public offering to enable the firm to develop a drug beyond Phase I or Phase II clinical trials. At this point, the firm might enter into a strategic alliance (to obtain additional research dollars) with a large pharmaceutical company, or license the product to a large pharmaceutical firm. It is the larger firm that would conduct the Phase III clinical trials and ultimately commercialize the product on the world market. Perhaps the early-stage R&D firm will obtain some royalty stream from the development.

This choice of a "standard" or "typical" biotechnology business model that investors seem to be happy to finance creates a number of issues. Drug discovery and development has become a longer and more expensive process. As companies reposition their business, the need for capital has increased considerably. There are significant risks involved, but many management teams see having product candidates in the development pipeline as the only option in the current climate to create a more sustainable long-term business (Chaya 2005). When business models are determined by investors' preferences, and not by the actual fit between a firm's resources and market needs, many potentially good firms fail. Failures cannot always be attributed to technology defects, or the lack of understanding of customers' needs. Many of the failures of new biotechnology firms result from a mismatch between the optimal business model that could fit the company's technology with market needs, and the actual business model required by venture capitalists for the firm to gain financing.

A proactive market management approach is not always at odds with fulfilment of short-term goals of a biotechnology firm, namely, finding access to funding. If venture capitalists place high value on market aspects in their investment decision-making, then these requirements are directly reflected on the potential investment targets. In the venture capitalists' view, the expectation of high financial returns from a biotechnology investment is mainly correlated with the size and growth of markets targeted by the firm, and the radical nature of its innovations (Tyebjee and Bruno 1984). A firm's market orientation should have a positive effect on external investors' willingness to invest in the firm. A consistent finding from previous research is that venture capitalists and business angels place importance on the abilities and characteristic of firm management when making investment decisions (Shepherd and Zacharakis 1999; Muzyka et al. 1996). Additional criteria in investment decision-making include product characteristics (proprietary features, competitive advantage, potential to achieve strong market position), market characteristics (size, growth, limited competition), and returns (potential for high returns, clear exit opportunity) (Fried and Hisrich 1994; Sweeting 1991). A market-oriented firm should be knowledgeable of its market characteristics. By providing good communication of positive market characteristics the new firm can have a positive effect on investors' willingness to invest in the firm (Renko 2006).

## 5.7 Discussion and Conclusions

In this chapter, we have highlighted a myriad of factors that are essential components of strategic thinking in early-stage biotechnology firms. Even if we have not presented primary empirical data, our text is based not only on theoretical insights but also on our extensive combined experiences in researching and consulting early-stage biotechnology firms.

To summarize, three categories of topics have been discussed here. First, the history of the field of biotechnology and the traditional business models that have been used by companies and funded by investors have a bearing on the strategic options available for firms today. Second, we have reflected the field of biotechnology entrepreneurship through the lenses provided in contemporary strategy- and entrepreneurship research. Especially, the strategic fit between the firm's environment and its resources is important for the early-stage biotechnology firms. Third, and most important, this chapter has introduced multiple concepts to highlight the importance of the technology–market balance in biotechnology start-ups. We complemented the traditional Schumpeterian view of entrepreneurship and innovation with the Kirznerian view, which emphasizes the role of market knowledge in discovering business opportunities and acting upon them. We also employed the concept of market orientation from the marketing literature to illustrate the importance of learning about markets. Finally, the general terms of "proactiveness" and "reactiveness" were used throughout the chapter to emphasize not only the role of technological foresight but also market foresight in successful biotechnology strategies.

We are not alone with our argument that even the early-stage, science-driven biotechnology firms should strive for a balance between technological knowledge and market knowledge. As mentioned earlier, biotechnology entrepreneurship is typically viewed through a Schumpeterian (1934) perspective where the entrepreneur revolutionizes the marketplace with a technology-based innovation. The keys to this revolution are typically technological knowledge because of its "valuable, rare, and imperfectly imitable" characteristics (Wernerfelt 1984; Barney 1991). This resource-based view of the firm (Wernerfelt 1984; Barney 1991) and that of the dynamic capabilities approach (Teece et al. 1997), and the knowledge-based view (Kogut and Zander 1992) all explicitly state, or imply, that a firm's technological capability can be a source of competitive advantage and above-normal performance (Coombs and Bierly 2001). However, evidence from the new product development (NPD) literature suggests that the process of NPD should not be characterized as being a dichotomy between a technology-led or customer-led. Rather, successful new innovations result from the interplay between actors, typically technology developers (or manufacturers) and customers (Slater and Narver 1995; Gatignon and Xuereb 1995, 1997). Integration of customers' needs to product development has been studied extensively in NPD literature, and extant research in NPD supports the claim that NPD projects, which rely on carefully defined customer needs, are more likely to succeed than those that are "only" based on new technological opportunities (Holt et al. 1984). Adopting a resource-based view, Hult and Ketchen (2001) have actually proposed that market orientation, entrepreneurship, innovation, and organizational learning do not constitute unique resources independently, but rather that they can collectively contribute to the creation of a unique resource. We believe that those biotechnology entrepreneurs who are best able to balance between adopting a simultaneous market orientation and technology orientation are the ones with best chances to create sustainable competitive advantages in the marketplace.

A sustainable competitive advantage in entrepreneurial biotechnology firms is not an outcome of some secret formula. Neither is the field that different from other fields of economic activity, even though practitioners in biotechnology often want to describe biotechnology entrepreneurship as something fundamentally different from entrepreneurship in other fields. Differences in firms' competitive advantages and performance can be explained in terms of their distinctive resource sets (Wernerfelt 1984). In the resource-based view valuable, rare, and imperfectly imitable resources form the basis for competitive advantage and may thus lead to positive abnormal returns (Barney 1991). We hope that this chapter has served as a reminder that even if biotechnology is a science-driven field, market orientation is the other key resource that should be fostered (Renko 2006; Hunt and Lambe 2000; Hult and Ketchen 2001). Finding a strategic fit between a firm's resources and the business environment is critical for sustainable competitive advantage in biotechnology as it is in any other business sector.

# References

Alvarez SA, Busenitz LW (2001) The entrepreneurship of resource-based theory. Journal of Management 27(6): 755–775

Amdjadi K, Herold CD, Patel SK, Razvi ES (2000) The top 10 merger and acquisition deals in the biotechnology and pharmaceutical industries. Drug & Market Development Publications, Westborough, MA

Andrews KR (1971) The concept of corporate strategy. Dow Jones Irwin, Homewood, IL

Audretsch DB, Stephan P (1996) Company-scientists location links: The case of biotechnology. The American Economic Review 86(3): 641–652

Barney JB (1991) Firm resources and sustained competitive advantage. Journal of Management 17: 99–120

Baumol WJ (1968) Entrepreneurship and economic theory. The American Economic Review 58(2): 64–71

Brännback M, Carsrud A (2003) Market management in biotechnology or how to avoid being a mule. Screening 4(6): 22–24

Brännback M, Näsi J, Renko M (2001a) Technological, structural, and strategic change in the global pharmaceutical industry – The Finnish biotechnology industry. Innomarket Research Reports No. 8, Turku School of Economics, Finland. http://www.tukkk.fi/innomarket/Reports/9736.pdf

Brännback M, Hyvönen P, Raunio H, Renko M, Sutinen R (2001b) Finnish pharma cluster – Vision 2010. Target Programme initiated by the Finnish Pharma Cluster. TEKES Technology Review 112: 65

Brännback M, Jalkanen M, Kurkela K, Soppi E (2004) Securing pharma development in Finland today and in 2015. TEKES Technology Review No. 163, Helsinki

Brännback M, Carsrud A, Renko M (2007) Born or grow global: Exploring the concept of born global in the biotechnology context. Journal of Enterprising Culture 15(1): 79–100

Camerer CF (1991) Does strategy research need game theory? Strategic Management Journal 12 (Special Issue): 137–152

Carsrud AL, Brännback M (2007) Entrepreneurship. Greenwood, Westport, CT

Chaya D (2005) Survival strategies for start-ups. Journal of Commercial Biotechnology 11(2): 130–135

Chesbrough H (2005) Open innovation. Harvard Business School Press, Boston, MA

Chesbrough H (2006) Open business models. Harvard Business School Press, Boston, MA

Clouser MR (2007) Scripps.edu: Triple helix power deal in the sunshine state. Babson College Entrepreneurship Research Conference, June 2007

Cohen WM, Levinthal DA (1989) Innovation and learning: The two faces of R&D. The Economic Journal 99(397): 569–596

Cohen WM, Levinthal DA (1990) Absorptive capacity: A new perspective on learning and innovation. Administrative Science Quarterly 35(1): 128–152

Colombo MG, Grilli L (2005) Founders' human capital and the growth of new technology-based firms: A competence-based view. Research Policy 34(6): 795–816

Coombs JE, Bierly PE (2001) Looking through the kaleidoscope: Measuring technological capability and performance. Academy of Management Proceedings 2001, B1–B7

Coombs JE, Deeds DL (2000) International alliances as sources of capital: Evidence from the biotechnology industry. Journal of High Technology Management Research 11(2): 235–253

Deeds DL (2001) The role of R&D intensity, technical development and absorptive capacity in creating entrepreneurial wealth in high technology start-ups. Journal of Engineering and Technology Management 18(1): 29–47

Deeds DL, Hill CW (1996) Strategic alliances and the rate of new product development: An empirical study of entrepreneurial biotechnology firms. Journal of Business Venturing 11(1): 41–55

Deeds DL, Hill CW (1998) An examination of opportunistic action within research alliances: Evidence from the biotechnology industry. Journal of Business Venturing 14(2): 141–163

Deeds DL, DeCarolis D, Coombs J (1999) Dynamic capabilities and new product development in high technology ventures: An empirical analysis of new biotechnology firms. Journal of Business Venturing 15(3): 211–229

Dosi G (1988) Sources, procedures, and microeconomic effects of innovations. Journal of Economic Literature 26(3): 1120–1171

Dosi G, Orseniego L (1988) Coordination and transformation: An overview of structures, behaviours and changes in evolutionary environments. In: Dosi G, Freeman C, Nelson R, Silverberg G, Soete L (eds) Technical change and economic theory. Pinter, London, pp. 13–37

Ensign PC (1999) Innovation in the multinational firm with globally dispersed R&D: Technological knowledge utilization and accumulation. Journal of High Technology Management Research 10(2): 203–221

Fiet JO (2002) The systematic search for entrepreneurial discoveries. Quorum Books, Westport

Fried VH, Hisrich R (1994) Toward a model of venture capital investment decision making. Financial Management 23(3): 28–37

Gatignon H, Xuereb J-M (1995, June) Strategic orientation of the firm and new product performance. INSEAD Working Paper Series, 95/60/MKT, Fontainebleau, France

Gatignon H, Xuereb J-M (1997) Strategic orientation of the firm and new product performance. Journal of Marketing Research 36: 77–90

Grégoire DA, Noël MX, Déry R, Béchard J-P (2006) Is there conceptual convergence in entrepreneurship research? A co-citation analysis of frontiers of entrepreneurship research, 1981–2004. Entrepreneurship Theory and Practice 30(3): 333–374

Grinyer PH, Spender J-C (1979) Recipes, crises, and adoption in mature industries. International Studies of Management and Organization 9(3): 113–133

Grundsten H (2004) Entrepreneurial intentions and the entrepreneurial environment: A study of technology-based new venture creation. Doctoral dissertation, Helsinki University of Technology, Espoo

Hagedorn J, Roijakkers N (2002) Small entrepreneurial firms and large companies in inter-firm R&D networks – The international biotechnology industry. In: Hitt MA, Ireland RD, Camp SM, Sexton DL (eds) Strategic entrepreneurship: Creating a new mindset. Blackwell, Malden, MA, pp. 223–252

Henderson R, Mitchell W (1997) The interaction of organizational and competitive influence on strategy and performance. Strategic Management Journal 18 (Special Issue): 5–14

Holt K, Geschka H, Peterlongo G (1984) Need assessment, a key to user-oriented product innovation. Wiley, Chichester

Hult GTM, Ketchen DJ (2001) Research notes and commentaries: Does market orientation matter? A test of the relationship between positional advantage and performance. Strategic Management Journal 22: 899–906

Hunt SD, Lambe CJ (2000) Marketing's contribution to business strategy: Market orientation, relationship marketing and resource advantage theory. International Journal of Management Reviews 2(1): 17–43

Jaworski BJ, Kohli AK (1993) Market orientation: Antecedents and consequences. Journal of Marketing 57: 53–70

Johnson G, Scholes K (1988) Exploring corporate strategy. Prentice Hall, London

Johnson S, Van de Ven AH (2002) A framework for entrepreneurial strategy. In: Hitt MA, Ireland RD, Camp SM, Sexton DL (eds) Strategic entrepreneurship: Creating a new mindset. Blackwell, Malden, MA, pp. 66–86

Kirzner IM (1973) Competition and entrepreneurship. University of Chicago Press, Chicago, IL

Kirzner IM (1979) Perception, opportunity, and profit. University of Chicago Press, Chicago, IL

Kogut B, Zander U (1992) Knowledge of the firm, combinative capabilities, and the replication of technology. Organization Science 3(3): 383–397

Kogut B, Zander U (1993) Knowledge of the firm and the evolutionary theory of the multinational corporation. Journal of International Business Studies 24(4): 625–645

Kohli AK, Jaworski BJ (1990) Market orientation: The construct, research propositions, and managerial implications. Journal of Marketing 54(2): 1–18

Kohli AK, Jaworski BJ, Kumar A (1993) MARKOR: A measure of market orientation. Journal of Marketing Research 30: 467–477

Koschatzky K (1999) Innovation networks of industry and business-related services – Relations between innovation intensity of firms and regional inter-firm cooperation. European Planning Studies 7(6): 737–757

Leonard-Barton D (1992) Core capabilities and core rigidities: A paradox in managing new product development. Strategic Management Journal 13 (Special Issue): 111–126

Levinthal DA, March JG (1993) The myopia of learning. Strategic Management Journal 14 (Special Issue): 95–112

Lumpkin GT, Dess GG (2001) Linking two dimensions of entrepreneurial orientation to firm performance: The moderating role of environment and industry life cycle. Journal of Business Venturing 16: 429–451

Meyer GD, Neck HM, Meeks MD (2002) The entrepreneurship–strategic management interface. In: Hitt MA, Ireland RD, Camp SM, Sexton DL (eds) Strategic entrepreneurship: Creating a new mindset. Blackwell, Malden, MA, pp. 19–44

Miles RE, Snow CC (1994) Fit, failure and the hall of fame. Macmillan, New York
Miller D (1983) The correlates of entrepreneurship in three types of firms. Management
    Science 29: 770–791
Murray F (2002) Innovation as co-evolution of scientific and technological networks:
    Exploring tissue engineering. Research Policy 31(8/9): 1389–1403
Muzyka D, Birley S, Leleux B (1996) Trade-offs in the investment decisions of European
    venture capitalists. Journal of Business Venturing 11: 273–287
Näsi J, Laine P, Laine J (1996) Strategy logic in a mega leader company. University of
    Jyväskylä Department of Economics and Management, Reprint Series, No. 43, Finland
Oliver RW (2000) The coming of the biotech age. McGraw Hill, New York
Pisano GP (1996) The development factory: Unlocking the potential of process innovation.
    Harvard Business School Press, Boston, MA
Pisano GP (2006) Science business. Harvard Business School Press, Boston, MA
Pitt M, Clarke K (1999) Competing on competence: A knowledge perspective on the
    management of strategic innovations. Technology Analysis and Strategic Management
    11(3): 301–317
Porter ME (1980) Competitive strategy. Free Press, New York
Porter ME (1985) Competitive advantage. Free Press, New York
Renko M (2006) Market orientation in markets for technology –Evidence from
    biotechnology ventures. Doctoral dissertation, Turku School of Economics, Turku
Renko M, Carsrud A, Brännback M, Jalkanen J (2005) Building market orientation in
    biotechnology SMEs: Balancing scientific advances. International Journal of
    Biotechnology 7(4): 250–268
Riccaboni M, Pammolli F (2002) On firm growth in networks. Research Policy 31(8/9):
    1405–1416
Robbins-Roth C (2000) From alchemy to IPO. Perseus, Cambridge, MA
Sandberg B (2005) The hidden market – Even for those who create it? Customer-related
    proactiveness in developing radical innovations. Doctoral dissertation, Turku School
    of Economics, Turku, Finland
Schumpeter JA (1934) The theory of economic development. Oxford University Press,
    Oxford
Shapiro C (1989) The theory of business strategy. Rand Journal of Economics 20(1): 125–137
Shepherd DA, Zacharakis AL (1999) Conjoint analysis: A new methodological approach
    for researching the decision policies of venture capitalists. Venture Capital: An
    International Journal of Entrepreneurial Finance 1(3): 197–217
Sheth JN, Ram S (1987) Bringing innovation to market. How to break corporate and
    customer barriers. Wiley, New York
Slater S, Narver J (1995) Market orientation and the learning organization. Journal of
    Marketing 59(3): 63–74
Spender J-C (1989) Industry recipe – An enquiry into the nature and sources of managerial
    judgement. Basil Blackwell, New York
Sweeting RC (1991) UK venture capital funds and the funding of new technology based
    businesses: Process and relationships. Journal of Management Studies 28(6): 601–622
Teece DJ (2000) Strategies for managing knowledge assets: The role of firm structure and
    industrial context. Long Range Planning 33(1): 35–54
Teece DJ, Pisano G, Shuen A (1997) Dynamic capabilities and strategic management.
    Strategic Management Journal 18(7): 509–533
Tyebjee TT, Bruno AV (1984) A model of venture capitalist investment activity.
    Management Science 30(9): 1051–1066
Wernerfelt B (1984) A resource-based view of the firm. Strategic Management Journal 5:
    171–180

Wolff G (2001) The biotech investor's bible. Wiley, New York

Zajac E, Kraatz M, Bresser RKF (2000) Modeling the dynamics of strategic fit: A normative approach to strategic change. Strategic Management Journal 21(4): 429–453

Zucker LG, Darby MR (1997) Present at the biotechnological revolution: Transformation of technological identity for a large incumbent pharmaceutical firm. Research Policy 26(4/5): 429–446

Zucker LG, Darby MR, Brewer MB (1998) Intellectual human capital and the birth of US biotechnology enterprises. American Economic Review 88(1): 290–305

Zucker LG, Darby MR, Armstrong JS (2002) Commercializing knowledge: University science, knowledge capture, and firm performance in biotechnology. Management Science 48(1): 138–153

# 6 Research on Strategic Alliances in Biotechnology: An Assessment and Review

Maxim Sytch[1] and Philipp Bubenzer[2]

[1]Kellogg School of Management, Northwestern University, 2001 Sheridan Road, Leverone 395, Evanston, IL 60201, USA
[2]WHU – Otto Beisheim School of Management, Burgplatz 2, 56179 Vallendar, Germany

## 6.1 Introduction

Since the late 1980s, the rate of interorganizational alliances, or voluntary agreements between firms involving exchange, sharing, or codevelopment of products, technologies, or services, has accelerated in multiple industries (Gulati 2007). Subsequently, scholars have grown interested in issues around the formation of strategic alliances and selection of partners (e.g., Chung et al. 2000; Gulati 1995b; Hagedoorn 1993; Walker et al. 1997), governance of alliances (e.g., Casciaro 2003; Reuer et al. 2002), as well as understanding the implications of strategic alliances for the behavior and performance of firms (e.g., Ahuja 2000a; Chan et al. 1997; Doz 1996). These issues have been examined both in more traditional industries, such as global airline industry (Gimeno 2004), automotive (Dyer 1996), steel (Koka and Prescott 2002; Rowley et al. 2000), chemical (Ahuja 2000b), and packaging machine manufacturing (Lorenzoni and Lipparini 1999), as well as in more technology-oriented fields such as cellular services (Rosenkopf et al. 2001), computers (Gulati et al. 2007), semiconductors (Rowley et al. 2000; Stuart 1998), software (Lavie and Rosenkopf 2006; Singh and Mitchell 1996), and biotechnology (Powell et al. 1996; Rothaermel and Deeds 2004).

H. Patzelt and T. Brenner (eds.), *Handbook of Bioentrepreneurship*,
doi: 10.1007/978-0-387-48345-0_6, © Springer Science + Business Media, LLC 2008

Among these industries, biotechnology[1] stands out because interorganizational collaborations have played a crucial role in the industry since its inception. In fact, the first true biotechnology firms, Genentech and Biogen, founded in 1976 and 1978, respectively,[2] realized initial successes largely through ties with organizations including research laboratories and pharmaceutical incumbents. Other newly founded biotechnology companies followed suit. One decade later, more than 70% of US biotechnology companies were engaged in strategic alliances, with an average of ten alliances per firm (Ernst & Young 1988). These trends position biotechnology among the industries with the highest alliance formation rates (Hagedoorn 1993, 2002).

This proliferation of alliances in biotechnology is in part due to their tremendous importance for biotechnology firms' survival and performance. Emerging from the confluence of many disciplines, biotechnology has evolved to represent a complex value chain. In the therapeutics area of biotechnology, for example, early discovery research platforms generate product candidates, which move through preclinical stages of development, testing in human trials, the FDA approval process, commercial-scale manufacturing and, ultimately, marketing and distribution to consumers. Many biotechnology firms lack the knowledge, resources, and required legitimacy in the eyes of other market constituents to effectively go through this value chain on their own. Thus biotechnology firms form alliances at each stage of the value creation cycle: Research and development partnerships, formed in the early stages of the value chain, typically focus on discovery research and codevelopment of technologies or products, comprising collaborations with universities, government research laboratories, hospitals, and peer biotechnology firms. Such alliances usually focus on exploration of new knowledge and technology and entail identification and validation of new molecular targets and new chemical and biological entities, as well as screening compounds for commercially viable drug candidates. Biotechnology firms enter alliances also in the later stages of the value chain, that aim at exploitation of existing technology, by partnering with organizations that are closer to the market, such as pharmaceutical companies, clinical research organizations, or large-scale manufacturers. These alliances often focus on ensuring the safety and efficacy of

---

[1] The biotechnology industry comprises various sectors, such as health care, agricultural and industrial biotechnology (Burrill 2007). Alliances have mostly, if not exclusively, been studied within the health-care sector, since the other sectors are characterized by a smaller number of firms with comparatively little alliance activity. Within the health-care sector, only a handful of studies have distinguished among its different subfields, such as therapeutics and diagnostics, in order to account for their respective differences (e.g., Folta 1998; Santoro and McGill 2005). In accordance with the existing studies, our discussion remains inclusive of different health-care subfields when developing theoretical arguments.

[2] Cetus Corp. was founded earlier, in 1971, but its original technology could be characterized as biological engineering rather than recombinant genetic engineering, which formed the basis of the biotechnology industry.

the product through complex clinical trials, gaining FDA approval for it, and marketing it to customers (Baum et al. 2000; Higgins and Gulati 2006; Rothaermel and Deeds 2004).

Considering the criticality of these alliances for the success of biotechnology firms, it becomes of paramount importance to understand biotechnology enterprises' as well as their partners' motivations for entering these partnerships, the determinants of these partnerships' efficient governance, and the precise benefits and costs for biotechnology firms of participating in strategic alliances. This chapter reviews the research evidence accumulated over the last 20 years on the alliances involving biotechnology firms and the networks which they create. We demonstrate the importance of considering a biotechnology firm's individual alliances as well as its position in the broader social structure of the industry, a structure created by the interconnectedness of firms through strategic partnerships.

Although our primary focus is on the drivers and implications of strategic alliances for biotechnology firms, we also highlight some concomitant ramifications for other types of organizations that partner with biotechnology firms. We first discuss the motives underlying alliance formation in biotechnology; in this discussion we highlight firms' pursuit of knowledge and other complementary resources, as well as their quest for legitimacy. In addressing these motives, we also consider factors that determine how biotechnology firms choose alliance partners. Next we review the factors and conditions determining the initial governance form of biotechnology alliances, as well as their ongoing governance dynamics. Third, we highlight the performance consequences of strategic alliances and biotechnology firms' resulting positions in the industry's social structure, outlining both the benefits and the constraints associated with these. Finally, we draw attention to some of the lacunae in extant research in this area, and suggest promising avenues for future studies.

## 6.2 Why and with Whom Do Biotechnology Firms Form Alliances?

The high frequency of alliance formation in biotechnology has drawn significant scholarly interest (e.g., Powell 1996; Powell et al. 2005). Many of the motives underlying alliance formation in biotechnology mirror those observed in other industries. For instance, given that product development in biotechnology is costly and associated with highly uncertain returns,[3] firms seek to share their costs and risks of innovation through strategic partnerships. Developing a product jointly with an alliance partner may ease the resource burden on the firm and grant it a

---

[3] In therapeutics, by some estimates, it may take more than 15 years for an experimental drug to progress from the laboratory to market. Further, for every 10,000 compounds screened, only five will enter clinical testing and only one will receive FDA approval, representing the likelihood of 0.01 for turning a newly discovered molecule into a revenue-generating product (Rothaermel and Deeds 2004: 208–209).

certain degree of flexibility to alter its resource commitments should environmental conditions change (cf. Eisenhardt and Schoonhoven 1996). Additionally, biotechnology firms may seek strategic alliances with established rivals so that they can avoid direct competition with them in the product market (Gans et al. 2002).

Although it would be difficult to present a comprehensive inventory of the motives underlying biotechnology alliances, we suggest that there are two key drivers of alliance formation that are particularly characteristic of this industry: (1) the pursuit of knowledge and other complementary resources and (2) the quest for legitimacy.

## 6.2.1 Access to Knowledge and Other Complementary Resources

Scholars have long proposed that firms are best described as open-system structures, whose survival depends on the effective exchange of resources with multiple elements of their environments, such as suppliers, buyers, and competitors (Pfeffer and Salancik 1978; Thompson 1967). In biotechnology, a biotech's pursuit of knowledge and complementary resources stems largely from the monumental challenge of new product development and commercialization process, which is highly resource-intensive. Many biotechnology firms lack the resources to execute a full product development cycle, and their existing resources are further squeezed by intense competition (Gambardella 1995: 146–161; Shan 1990). Thus accessing much-needed resources through strategic alliances is crucial to boosting the firm's viability. Research shows that firms often seek contractual partners when they perceive their resource base as either fully utilized or inferior to that of the partner (Odagiri 2003). By partnering with pharmaceutical companies, for example, biotechnology firms gain access to production facilities, distribution channels, and expertise regarding clinical development and government approval of new products (Dalpe 2003; Kogut et al. 1992). Biotechnology companies in general lack these downstream resources and capabilities and therefore have to reach out to potential partners (Rothaermel and Boeker 2007).

Of the resources that biotechnology companies seek, knowledge deserves special attention. Because many of the firms in this field have no product sales for years, proprietary knowledge often constitutes their core competitive advantage and becomes central to their survival. Further, the knowledge required to develop a new chemical or biological molecular entity is complex and multifaceted, spanning disciplines, including molecular biology, immunology, genetics, physiology, analytical and medicinal chemistry, and bioinformatics (Henderson and Cockburn 1994; Sorensen and Stuart 2000). Adequately developing this broad and deep knowledge base exceeds the capacity of a single firm. As a result, the locus of innovation in biotechnology has moved beyond a single firm's boundaries and into the network of collaborations, spanning the entire industry to access a widely dispersed pool of knowledge (Liebeskind et al. 1996; Powell and Brantley 1992; Powell et al. 1996). The resulting knowledge-driven collaborations typically target upstream segments of the value chain, or the research and development components of the product development cycle, and include partnerships with research laboratories, universities, and peer biotechnology firms, among others. For instance, biotechnology firms' reliance on knowledge contributed by university molecular biology departments has been particularly strong (Argyres and Liebeskind 1998; Kenney 1986).

Thus, through partnerships, firms strive to gain access to the wide pool of knowledge of the biotechnology industrial and scientific community. Some may simply seek membership in a biotechnology community to access knowledge spillovers (Owen-Smith and Powell 2004). But because the complex knowledge typical of this field requires rich and deep interactions for successful transfer and absorption (Rothaermel 2001; Zucker et al. 1998), many firms aim for a central position in the network of partnerships, which would position them on the intersection of knowledge flows (Powell et al. 1996).This is further reflected in how biotechnology firms pursue network expansion, connecting to one another through multiple independent paths, thereby increasing the number and diversity of accessible actors (Powell et al. 2005). Evidence confirms that many biotechnology firms pursue a diverse network, spanning different types of partners (e.g., pharmaceutical firms, hospitals, research laboratories), to access a broader knowledge base and ultimately position themselves for higher innovation rates (Baum et al. 2000).

In sum, many biotechnology firms enter strategic alliances in pursuit of knowledge and other complementary resources for research and development or commercialization purposes. As further support for these general motives, studies show that alliance formation patterns for firms in biotechnology are age-dependent and nonlinear, peaking around 4 years after founding, then declining until the 10-year mark, after which they rise again (Oliver 2001). This nonlinear trend roughly corresponds to the needs associated with the biotechnology product development process, which requires access to research and development expertise early on, followed by commercialization capabilities later in a firm's life. Companies can obtain some complementary resources through dyadic relationships with more resourceful partners. The choice of partners, therefore, is atomistic and is largely made in the narrow context of the potential relationship. The pursuit of knowledge, however, especially as related to early stages of the drug development process, requires a biotechnology firm to seek a central position in the broader network structure of the market, to better access industry-wide knowledge flows and pool of innovations (Powell et al. 1996).

## 6.2.2 Pursuit of Legitimacy

In addition to being embedded in a technical environment, where a firm's survival is largely driven by access to resources and its reliance on the related production efficiencies, firms are also situated in normative environments where their survival hinges on conforming to the social standards of the market (Dacin et al. 2007; DiMaggio and Powell 1983; Scott 1995). While nimble and innovation-driven, many new biotechnology firms lack the necessary underpinnings of legitimacy, which can be defined as social justification or public endorsement (Dacin et al. 2007). Because of their relative newness, most biotechnology firms do not have the validation associated with stable exchange relations with important market constituencies and with significant experience delivering a product or service to market (cf. Stinchcombe 1965). In fact, many biotechnology companies lack a product to show, owning instead the rights to a set of ideas with ambiguous commercial viability. Building legitimacy, therefore, is critical for biotechnology ventures, particularly young ones, because market participants – on whom they depend for physical, financial, and reputational capital – face extremely high levels of uncertainty with respect to the quality of the biotechnology product or service. Securing public validation and reducing the level of uncertainty associated with the biotechnology firm can subsequently yield significant economic and competitive benefits (Dacin et al. 2007; Higgins and Gulati 2006; Kim and Higgins 2008).

Strategic alliances with prominent partners are one of the most promising routes to legitimacy for biotechnology firms (Baum and Silverman 2004; Stuart et al. 1999). Indeed, one of the fundamental precepts of sociological theory is that interorganizational relations and the resulting networks of connections are not merely pipes carrying resources and information, but also prisms of the market, reflecting and inducing differentiation among market participants (Podolny 2001). Thus, forging alliances with prominent market participants may confer an aura of legitimacy to a biotechnology firm, which in turn facilitates the acquisition of other resources. Note that the legitimacy enhancement effect could be bidirectional: not only do biotechnology firms benefit from endorsements, but so do some of their endorsing partners. Nicholls-Nixon and Woo (2003), for instance, demonstrate that by forming more R&D contracts and licensing agreements in biotechnology, pharmaceutical companies enhance their expertise in biotechnology, as perceived by peer firms.

### 6.2.3 Choosing Partners

Given the importance of accessing knowledge, complementary resources, and legitimacy for biotechnology firms, they would be expected to favor alliance partners who can offer better resource and knowledge endowments, as well as superior legitimacy benefits (Baum et al. 2000; Powell et al. 2005; Rothaermel and Boeker 2007). These rather calculative motives, however, represent only a subset of those underlying biotechnology firms' choices of alliance partners. Many studies point to the strong influence of homophily, wherein similarities among firms foster mutual trust and co-identification (cf. Gulati and Sytch 2008; Lazarsfeld and Merton 1954; McPherson and Smith-Lovin 1987), increasing the likelihood of their partnership. In a study on the formation of research and development partnerships in biotechnology, Baldi et al. (2007) found that firms are more likely to collaborate if their founders have graduated from the same educational institution. This effect does not necessarily reflect a direct social tie between scientists (e.g., they often have graduated from different professional schools and in different years), but rather their sense of shared identity. Along similar lines, Powell et al. (2005) show that biotechnology firms, particularly new entrants, tend to choose partners based on the allies' similarity to previous partners; Kim and Higgins (2008) find additional evidence for the influential role of homophily, such that firms occupying similar positions in the market's social structure inherit similar obligations and expectations, which draw them toward each other. More specifically, they find that firms gravitate toward potential partners that employ upper echelon members with matching affiliations. The presence of a downstream affiliation, one example of which would be having a biotechnology executive previously employed at a firm like Pfizer, increases the chance of attracting a downstream alliance partner by 40%. While biotechnology firms generally gravitate to similar partners, studies also find that it is largely the firms that are underperforming with respect to their historical performance aspirations and their peer reference group, that venture outside of their comfort zone and search for foreign partners (Ener and Hoang 2007).

Note that any episode of alliance formation requires a bilateral choice, wherein both the focal biotechnology firm and the partner must be motivated to enter the alliance. The extant research often overlooks this seemingly intuitive concept (for a thoughtful discussion of this issue, see Ahuja 2000b). The ability to attract a partner is critical, since biotechnology firms face vigorous competition for the attention of prominent and valuable potential allies. Several factors are instrumental in this respect. Kim and Higgins (2008) find that a firm's upper echelon affiliations with prominent players facilitate partnerships with such allies. The affiliations grant biotechnology firms an aura of legitimacy, thus mitigating prominent partner's concerns regarding loss of status over allying with a lower status firm. Stern and Dukerich (2007) further demonstrate that firms founded by more prominent scientists with stronger publication records are more likely than others to attract commercial partners early in the product development cycle, when uncertainty regarding a start-up's commercial potential is particularly high. The legitimacy stemming from higher academic reputation of a founding scientist helps deflect possible reservations of financing entities over partnering with the biotechnology firm holding unclear commercial promise.

Overall, although it is difficult to explicate all the factors firms may consider when choosing alliance partners, the multifaceted nature of this choice is clear. Motives include those of a more or less calculative nature and address both the needs of biotechnology firms as well as their ability to attract desirable partners.

## 6.3 Governance of Alliances

Representing a hybrid governance form of market and hierarchy, strategic alliances are associated with a variety of governance forms, ranging from more market-like contractual arrangements to more hierarchical equity-based alliances and joint ventures. Several studies have investigated the antecedents of variations in alliance governance.[4] Many of these investigations have approached this issue through the lens of transaction cost economics (e.g., Williamson 1975, 1985), highlighting the role of transaction costs in the choice of governance form. At the heart of this theoretical perspective is the idea of discriminatory alignment or the belief that certain governance structures are better suited for certain transactions. The preferred governance mode of a transaction, in turn, is the one that minimizes transaction costs, which may be loosely classified into the ex ante costs of search and contracting and ex post costs of monitoring and enforcement (Williamson 1985). The ex post transaction costs can be particularly high, as humans are viewed as inherently prone to opportunistic behavior (Simon 1985; Williamson 1975: 26–37; 1985: 46–52) and limited in their rationality (Simon 1957: xxiv).[5] Such bounded rationality, in turn, prevents organizational agents from writing complete contracts that would cover all possible contingencies and therefore diminish opportunistic pursuits in the form of ex post haggling. The expected costs of such postcontractual haggling are especially high at increased levels of behavioral and task uncertainty. While behavioral uncertainty refers to the unpredictability of a partner's behavior, task uncertainty relates to highly complex tasks where monitoring and evaluating a partner's behavior and contributions is not easy and hence costly. When uncertainty is high, firms tend to prefer more hierarchically organized exchanges, since common ownership may decrease partners' opportunistic advances and managerial fiat could provide tighter control and speed the resolution of conflicts (Williamson 1981).

Some evidence derived from studies of biotechnology alliances supports the key propositions of transaction cost economics. Higher partner and task uncertainties lead biotechnology firms to adopt a more hierarchical governance form for their alliances (Santoro and McGill 2005). Further attesting to the firms' desire to avoid the hazard of opportunistic haggling in their alliances, Pisano (1989) finds that if there are fewer partners available with a specific expertise, pharmaceutical firms are more likely to have equity participation in the biotechnology alliance rather than develop it through a contractual partnering agreement. A more hierarchical governance arrangement in this instance may help alleviate the risk of an opportunistic contract renegotiation, which could be provoked by the small-numbers hazard.[6]

---

[4] Another intriguing line of inquiry has looked at factors driving the choice of alliance governance form vs. arm's length and fully internalized transactions, as well as the performance of alliances relative to these alternative forms of governance (Dyer 1996; Gulati et al. 2005).

[5] Some of these assumptions are debated in the literature (Ghoshal and Moran 1996). This debate, though an important discourse in organizational science, is beyond the scope of this chapter.

[6] Competitive considerations also may drive taking a major equity stake in the partner. For instance, by taking significant ownership in a biotechnology company, a pharmaceutical firm may attempt to prevent competitors from accessing the resources and capabilities of the biotechnology firm. Pharmaceutical firms' willingness to lock out competitors from

It is further essential to note that collaborations in biotechnology, particularly those including an R&D component, are filled with behavioral and task uncertainties. Many biotechnology firms enter partnerships with no meaningful organizational history and no prior collaborative experience, bringing extreme levels of behavioral uncertainty to the arrangements. High task uncertainty emanates from extreme complexity of biotechnological knowledge, which spans a wide array of disciplines and thus transcends the capabilities of a single firm (Powell et al. 1996; Sorensen and Stuart 2000). Moreover, many biotechnology collaborations include a broad scope of activities, further increasing the concomitant task uncertainty (Pisano 1990). Complicating matters further for R&D collaborations, there are usually few substitute partners available for a particular line of business, creating an increased risk of self-seeking haggling. Beyond that, the nature of many R&D activities in biotechnology is significantly complex and entails high levels of asset-specific investments, which are tailored to the current relationship and thus cannot be redeployed to other transactions without a significant loss in value.[7] Taken together, these conditions – particularly when applied to R&D collaborations in biotechnology – should create high expectations of opportunistic behavior and thus motivate firms to adopt a more hierarchical governance form for partnerships,[8] as manifested in the distinct preference for equity-based alliances over simple contractual arrangements. So it is remarkable that the tendency to use less hierarchical contractual R&D collaborations is exceptionally strong in biotechnology and pharmaceuticals, compared to other industries (Hagedoorn 2002).

One way to shed some light on this empirical conundrum is to consider an additional factor that shapes alliance governance choice: firms' desire to maintain strategic flexibility. The pursuit of strategic flexibility – often invoked under the rubric of "real options" – suggests that firms frequently form alliances with a strong expectation that these partnerships will evolve in response to the shifting strategic and environmental demands and that their inherent value to the firm may change. Maintaining initial flexibility becomes particularly crucial in situations marked by high technological uncertainty, when the value of many technological developments is unclear. Specifically, when operating under these conditions, firms may opt for more flexible and less hierarchical governance arrangements to

---

valuable biotechnology expertise is particularly high when there are few biotechnology firms with comparable capabilities. As an example, consider Roche's pursuing Genentech's unique expertise and product pipeline in monoclonal antibodies by taking a 60% stake in the company in 1990, subsequently securing exclusive non-US marketing rights for all of Genentech's products through a licensing deal in 1995.

[7] In the reasoning of transaction cost economics, the condition of asset specificity is critical for the uncertainty argument to hold: Uncertainty increases costs associated with ex post haggling only at nontrivial levels of asset specificity (David and Han 2004; Williamson 1985).

[8] This expectation is in line with extant research, which generally suggests that R&D transactions will entail higher transaction costs and, subsequently, will have more hierarchical forms of governance (Gulati 1995a).

avoid making irreversible commitments to a lost cause (e.g., Folta 1998; Santoro and McGill 2005).

Evidence from biotechnology partnerships supports the importance of maintaining strategic flexibility as related to the choice of alliance governance form. For instance, partnerships involving technological applications in the field of therapeutics are considered highly technologically uncertain and tend to involve more flexible governance arrangements (Santoro and McGill 2005). This initial flexibility gives firms the opportunity to alter the governance form later and ramp up their commitment to more promising partnerships as their potential becomes more fulfilled. Folta and Miller (2002) report that biotechnology firms tend to purchase additional equity stakes in their partners when the partners' market valuations are increasing, which lends further support to this hypothesis.[9]

Scholars of strategy and organizations also have gained valuable insights by investigating postformation changes in alliance governance structures. Reuer et al. (2002) found that roughly 44% of alliances in their sample experienced a governance change as the alliance evolved. These changes included contractual alterations, major changes in the committee or board overseeing the alliance, and the introduction or formalization of monitoring mechanisms. Taking a deeper look into why such postformation governance changes may transpire, they found that prior partner-specific experience facilitates ex post adjustments in alliances by fostering interorganizational routines specific to the collaboration. These routines equip partners to better understand shifts in the partnership, discuss possible courses of actions more openly, and eventually implement governance change more smoothly.

In a related line of inquiry Lerner et al. (2003) explored the initial allocation of control rights in an alliance, as well as subsequent changes in this allocation. The authors suggest that the imbalance of bargaining power between larger pharmaceutical companies and smaller biotechnology firms may lead to the initially skewed allocation of control rights in the alliance (see also Lerner and Merges 1998).[10] Such skewed allocation manifests in the pharmaceutical firm's obtaining a lion's share of control over management of clinical trials, the manufacturing process before and after product approval, choice of sales

---

[9] Evidence also suggests that a rather strict, when compared to other industries, intellectual property protection regime in biotechnology may further contribute to the formation of less hierarchical contractual alliances by stimulating licensing agreements. In the presence of strong intellectual property protection, firms are generally more open to licensing partnerships as there is less threat that the licensee will invent around the licensed innovation and renege on the terms of the agreement (Anand and Khanna 2000b).

[10] This study provides further evidence that relative bargaining power of the partners matters in gaining control rights in R&D agreements. Using a sample of 200 research and product development agreements in biotechnology, Lerner and Merges (1998) find that the financial status of R&D firms affects their ability to retain control rights in R&D agreements. More specifically, a one standard deviation increase in shareholders' equity leads to an 11% drop in the predicted number of control rights assigned to the financing firm.

categories (by region and indication), and even issues related to marketing exclusivity. The bargaining imbalance and the resulting skewed allocation of control rights is particularly acute when the public financial markets are unavailable to a given biotechnology firm, depriving it of alternative sources of financing and, ultimately, some measure of bargaining power. However, Lerner et al. (2003) also show that agreements that are disadvantageous to R&D firms are significantly more likely to be renegotiated as the firms' public financing potential improves and their bargaining power in the alliance increases.

In sum, existing research clearly identifies a set of predictors of governance choice in biotechnology alliances. While behavioral and task uncertainties in biotechnology alliances motivate firms to adopt more hierarchical governance forms, the need to maintain strategic flexibility due to high technological uncertainty promotes looser, quasi-market alliance structures. Building on early research that focused on the choice of initial governance form, a promising stream of work has sought to unpack factors driving changes in the governance form of the alliance as the partnership evolves.

## 6.4 Consequences of Alliances

As highlighted earlier, biotechnology firms pursue alliances to secure access to knowledge and other complementary resources, and to gain legitimacy. Therefore, upon entering alliances, firms can be expected to develop a more effective resource base, as well as to show more promise to potential partners and to the market in general. These consequences can manifest in several positive organizational outcomes. Specifically, firms that engage more actively in alliance formation have been shown to have higher rates of innovation (Shan et al. 1994), product development and commercialization (Rothaermel and Deeds 2004), growth (Baum et al. 2000; Niosi 2003; Powell and Brantley 1992; Powell et al. 1996), IPO success (Stuart et al. 1999), and survival (Oliver 2001).

In reviewing studies on the consequences of alliances for biotechnology firms, we first focus on those that have explicated firms' access to knowledge and other complementary resources, along with the benefits stemming from that access. These benefits emanate from individual alliance linkages and access to the resources of current alliance partners, as well as from the firm's position in the broader network of alliances. Next we examine how alliance formation leads to tangible benefits by reducing uncertainty with respect to a biotechnology firm's overall quality. Finally, we illuminate a promising yet underdeveloped line of inquiry: the costs and constraints associated with alliances. Specifically, we discuss evidence that alliances do not generate uniformly positive effects across all types of partners and relationships, and the resulting structural positions of the firm in the web of alliance linkages. In some instances, the effects of alliances can be neutral, hinting at less effective use of a firm's resources or the existence of factors that cause performance trade-offs; in others, the effects of alliances and the concomitant structural position of the firm can be outright detrimental, possibly reducing the entire enterprise's viability. We thus review and conceptualize extant research on the possible role of alliances as a "relational liability," suggesting that the pursuit of complementary resources, knowledge, and legitimacy may come at a price.

## 6.4.1 Consequences of Accessing Knowledge and Other Complementary Resources

From its outset, research on the role and impact of strategic alliances in biotechnology focused on the benefits of a firm's assembling portfolios of complementary resources through access to partners' resource endowments. In an early study, Shan et al. (1994) argued that forming commercial ties allows a biotechnology company to reduce its resource and attention inputs into commercialization, freeing it to focus more effectively on innovation, especially new product discovery and development. Analyzing alliance formation patterns in the first decade of the industry, Shan et al. (1994) show that the number of commercial agreements a biotechnology start-up holds is positively related to its innovation rate, as measured by granted patents. Subsequent research shed further light on how alliances can also contribute to a firm's commercialization rates by bringing it complementary resources. Using a sample of 325 biotechnology firms and their 2,565 alliances from 1973 to 1997, Rothaermel and Deeds (2004) show that a firm's downstream alliances – those focused on clinical trials, the FDA regulatory process, or marketing and sales – afford it access to pharmaceutical companies' expertise in regulatory compliance, large-scale product manufacturing, marketing and sales, and, certainly not least of all, their capital reserves. These complementary resources and expertise boost the biotech's commercialization rates, increasing the number of products it has on the market.

Downstream alliances, as suggested earlier, are certainly important, but the ability of a firm to access biotechnology-specific knowledge through upstream or exploration-focused alliances is no less critical (Rothaermel 2001). Evidence suggests that a firm's upstream alliances, which are focused on early discovery research and preclinical development, are associated with greater levels of knowledge creation and internalization for the firm. This effect may be stronger for more similar partners, since they can avail themselves of smoother knowledge transfer and absorption. Specifically, having basic knowledge pools, compensation practices, and commercial objectives comparable to those of a partner increases a firm's ability to value, assimilate, and commercialize the partner's knowledge (Lane and Lubatkin 1998). While both downstream and upstream alliances can benefit the firm directly by channeling knowledge and other resources, they can also offer indirect benefits by limiting access to these resources for the firm's rivals. Silverman and Baum (2002) found that upstream partnerships of firms with government laboratories and research institutes, as well as their downstream marketing partnerships, can deprive rivals of comparable access and thus threaten competitors' survival.

In the process of pursuing knowledge and other complementary resources through alliances, firms tend to develop a relational capability, or an ability to transfer and internalize knowledge adeptly, as well as to effectively manage alliance relationships (cf. Dyer and Singh 1998; Kale et al. 2002). Greater relational capability can lead to superior performance outcomes for firms participating in alliances for several reasons.[11] First and foremost, as a firm's experience in alliance formation and its resulting relational capability grow, it gains an edge in regard to its level of receptivity toward and ability to absorb knowledge generated in the alliance and to the exclusive knowledge brought to the alliance by its partner (Cohen and Levinthal 1990; Hamel 1991). Externally acquired knowledge often entails an unfamiliar set of heuristics; thus a firm's relational capability, which represents an accumulation of experience dealing with various heuristics, positions it to better process, interpret, and understand the information this knowledge carries (Zahra and George 2002). Second, having a formal support structure in place and informal organizational processes for expediting knowledge transfer is likely to amplify the firm's intent to learn and acquire knowledge (Hamel 1991). The resulting high motivation and effort regarding knowledge internalization are likely to enhance a firm's already superior capacity to absorb knowledge. A similar boost is likely to be demonstrated for alliance management skills. As firms go through alliance formation repeatedly, they develop organizational routines that enable them to select the most effective type of agreement for a particular alliance. As firms gain experience with alliances and develop relational capability, they also improve their ability to respond to contingencies that could not be specified in formal contracts and to manage collaboration activities in general (Anand and Khanna 2000a; Mayer and Argyres 2004; Vanneste and Puranam 2007).

The development of biotechnology firms' relational capability and its resulting performance benefits have been thoroughly documented. For instance, in one of the earlier studies on the subject, Zollo et al. (2002) showed that familiarity through prior partnership experience leads to improved alliance performance when biotechnology and pharmaceutical firms partner. Along similar lines, Katila and Mang (2003) show that biotechnology firms that have prior collaborative experience with a focal partner as well as with other firms strike deals earlier in the technology development process. This timing carries tremendous performance implications for biotechnology firms, since it enables them to capitalize on a technological opportunity early, before others move in or before the opportunity loses its appeal in a high-velocity technological environment. Finally, in a comprehensive study of 292 drug development projects between biotechnology and pharmaceutical firms between 1980 and 2000, Hoang and Rothaermel (2005) found a positive association between a biotechnology firm's level of general collaborative experience – accumulated through prior alliances with firms other than the focal alliance partner – and the alliance's performance. This manifests in

---

[11] See Wang and Zajac (2008) for the exploration of how experiential learning from alliance formation may transfer to mergers and acquisitions as well as how experience with mergers and acquisitions may translate into benefits in the alliance formation arena.

the higher probability of FDA and European Medicines Evaluation Agency approval for a jointly developed drug. This effect is curvilinear, and thus exhibits diminishing marginal returns of collaborative experience, which is possibly due to companies' exploiting their most promising opportunities first or relying excessively on certain technological competencies.

The discussion thus far has focused on the benefits firms extract from individual alliance linkages by effectively accessing the knowledge and other resources of immediate partners. The numerous alliance linkages among firms also cumulate into the broader social structure of the market; this network, in turn, serves as a conduit of knowledge and other valuable information. For example, a firm's position in the larger social structure shapes the quality of its leads and referrals regarding alliance and technological opportunities, as well as its access to the industry-wide pool of knowledge (Gulati 2007). Thus, the implications of alliances transcend a given relationship, with their magnitude dependent on a firm's position with regard to the industry's pipes of knowledge and information flows. This is particularly important in biotechnology, a field marked by sophisticated and increasingly complex technologies. As such, the innovative efforts of individual firms have clear limits, and the locus of innovation has shifted to the broader network of relationships (Powell and Brantley 1992; Powell et al. 1996). Preferential access to this network enables firms to garner timely knowledge about available partners and their resource endowments, developmental trends in the industry, and the most promising technological opportunities. Specifically, a biotechnology firm's position on the high-traffic intersection of R&D-related knowledge flows enables it to develop a portfolio of diverse relationships, move toward an even more central and advantageous network position, and ultimately enjoy greater rates of growth (Powell et al. 1996).

Contributing to the research into a firm's access to knowledge through its superior position in the network structure, subsequent work involved structural and geographical mapping of firms and their partners in the web of alliance linkages. Specifically, this research looked into the different ways by which alliances with collocated partners generate value, relative to those in which partners belong to different geographical clusters. For instance, Zaheer and George (2004) suggest that while alliances with both collocated and noncollocated partners create value for firms, resulting in their higher market valuations, they do so in different ways. Alliances within a geographical cluster due to a firm's proximity to the sources of knowledge contribute to the firm's ability to transfer complex and tacit knowledge and to access information spillovers. In contrast, alliances that span different clusters allow a firm to access a more diverse pool of knowledge and hence create value by fostering heterogeneity in its knowledge base.

In the setting of biotechnology, the potential ability of a firm to use alliances as an entrée to the research community and to subsequently access knowledge spillovers within that community constitutes a particularly intriguing research question. This is because knowledge in biotechnology is viewed as so complex and difficult to transfer that it guarantees its "natural excludability" (Zucker et al. 1998). Such natural excludability makes knowledge in biotechnology relatively immune to absorption from spillovers. Accordingly, Zaheer and George (2004) found that merely belonging to an alliance cluster or a geographic cluster through a single alliance linkage does not benefit a firm's performance. In other words, spillovers are not of much consequence, and to benefit from industry-wide knowledge, a firm has to link more strongly to knowledge pools through the information-transferring pipes of alliance ties (cf. Podolny 2001).

Other studies extend this debate, suggesting that understanding the role of a firm's structural position in benefiting from spillovers should not be limited to considering how well firms can absorb those spillovers. In addition to looking at absorption efficiency, these studies concentrate on spillover availability, the key predecessor to benefits associated with spillovers (Owen-Smith and Powell 2004). The availability of spillovers, in turn, may be contingent on the nature of the specific organizations that anchor the network of the geographical cluster. On the basis of these ideas, Owen-Smith and Powell (2004) established the presence of knowledge spillovers in the Boston biotechnology community, demonstrating that a simple alliance membership in the Boston cluster boosts a firm's innovation rates. The key to this effect is that the Boston biotechnology network is anchored by public research organizations, which are more committed to open information-sharing and public disclosure. Because of these norms, significant knowledge leaks through organizational boundaries, allowing biotechnology firms to internalize some of it.[12] This internalization is attained simply through membership in the research community or having at least one tie to an existing member.[13] If, however, a firm is situated in a more diverse network of firms – one outside the Boston cluster, for example – where attitudes toward open knowledge-sharing may vary, the effect of simple membership subsides. Thus of more importance is not a firm's simple access to the knowledge community through a peripheral alliance tie, but rather the centrality of its position in the network of alliances, which places the firm at the intersection of different network ties and the knowledge flows they represent (Owen-Smith and Powell 2004). The importance of the central position in the industry knowledge network further manifests in that biotechnology firms may pursue and benefit from alliances with their rivals, by securing advantages from rivals' structural positions in the industry network (Silverman and Baum 2002).

---

[12] While not focusing on the issue of collocation or industry-wide norms of knowledge sharing, Silverman and Baum (2002) provide additional evidence that spillovers matter. They show that rivals' upstream alliances with universities can benefit the focal firm by generating a larger pool of knowledge, of which at least a part becomes available to the firm.

[13] More precisely, Owen-Smith and Powell (2004: 13) look at the presence of at least one connection to the largest weakly connected component within the network, which indicates the largest segment of the overall network, where each firm is connected to every other firm by least one path.

## 6.4.2 Consequences of Enhancing Legitimacy

In addition to enabling a firm to access the complementary resources and knowledge of its partners and those of the broader network community, the firm's alliances play a crucial role in enhancing its legitimacy. By providing a firm with the endorsements of established partners, alliances send a strong signal with respect to the firm's reputation, reliability, and commercial promise, thereby alleviating the uncertainty various market stakeholders may perceive regarding the firm. Reduced uncertainty may in turn lead to increased support of the firm by venture capitalists, underwriters, and public investors, as well by as prominent alliance partners. While venture capitalists, for instance, sometimes invest in biotechnology firms with less obvious potential, they are generally keen on investing in clear winners with tangible market potential (Baum and Silverman 2004). Thus Baum and Silverman (2004) suggest that signaling a clear capacity for success to the VC community through the alliance capital of downstream and horizontal alliances is critically important. Specifically, they find that start-ups with greater alliance capital obtain significantly more VC financing than those without it. Along similar lines, Higgins and Gulati (2003) provide some evidence that companies with a larger alliance portfolio can secure a more prestigious underwriter because the ties reduce uncertainty regarding their commercial potential. The benefits stemming from a biotechnology firm's enhanced legitimacy are particularly important in situations when uncertainty about the biotechnology firm's commercial promise is high, such as in earlier stages of the firm's life.[14]

By focusing on the impact of a firm's alliances with commercially and technologically prominent partners, other extant research suggests that such prestigious affiliations are even more instrumental than general ties in alleviating uncertainty regarding a firm. Here, market participants not only rely on the ability of prominent partners to discern the quality of the firm, but also consider the established partners' reputational concerns over affiliating themselves with low-quality firms (Stuart et al. 1999). Indeed, a partnership with a "lemon" can certainly damage the social standing of a prominent firm, motivating it to conduct especially thorough due diligence of potential allies. The expectation of this strict scrutiny, in turn, endows market participants with greater confidence in the signaling quality of the endorsement, and legitimizes the firm even further. These outcomes, with time, translate into tangible financial gains by helping young

---

[14] It is essential to note one methodological difficulty in exploring the role of alliances as legitimizing endorsements and their subsequent impact on firm's performance. It is possible that the unobserved dimension of the firm quality both attracts the more prestigious alliance partners and triggers the observed performance outcomes. Thus, the observed performance outcomes may be independent of and have only a spurious correlation with endorsement. In the absence of a controlled experiment, scholars need to employ a rigorous set of controls for the quality of the firm, try to instrument out the omitted-variable endogeneity, and invoke qualitative research to shed additional light on the nature of the observed relationship.

biotechnology firms make their IPOs more quickly and ensuring superior IPO returns (Stuart et al. 1999).

### 6.4.3 Taking Off the Rose-Colored Glasses: Alliances as Relational Liability

It is fair to say that existing research on alliances in biotechnology, much like work in other industrial settings, has approached interfirm linkages with strong positive predispositions. In other words, the primary focus has been on the benefits companies can reap through strategic partnerships. There is evidence, however, that under certain conditions alliances may generate neutral or even negative consequences for participating firms (e.g., Deeds and Hill 1996; Baum et al. 2000; Baum and Silverman 2004). In other words, the resources and social capital emanating from the firm's alliance linkages and its position in the structure of network ties may turn into liabilities. An interesting and yet underdeveloped line of inquiry, then, involves the analysis of possible costs and other constraining effects of alliances and firms' positions in the network of strategic partnerships.

We identify several sources of such constraining effects. First, with respect to alliances providing access to knowledge and complementary resources, some partners and types of relationships may severely constrain firms' performance by triggering resource misallocations and by bringing out competitive rather than cooperative motivations in some partners. We also show that a firm's structural position in the network may trigger relational and structural lock-in, preventing a firm from pursuing a more efficient set of relations by confining it to a disadvantageous competitive pool, where it may be mismatched on its ability to create and internalize knowledge. Second, regarding alliances that legitimize a firm, we highlight that access to well-established partners is not cost-free and that the costs of entering and maintaining such partnerships may outweigh the benefits.

Some alliances may lead biotechnology firms to over-allocate resources to some activities at the expense of other important ones. For instance, in contrast to studies suggesting that a firm's commercial ties may free significant resources for innovative research and development projects (Shan et al. 1994), some research indicates that such alliances may in fact slow down a biotech's innovation rate by diverting its resources exclusively into commercialization (Baum and Silverman 2004). There is also evidence that a start-up biotechnology firm's alliances with government laboratories significantly slow its revenue growth (Baum et al. 2000). While, as Baum and colleagues suggest, this effect may reflect a selection bias, due to the higher commercial uncertainty of projects brought to government laboratories, it may also indicate an inefficient resource lock-in in a relatively unproductive relationship. Furthermore, upstream alliances of biotechnology firms with universities frequently involve flows of scientists into commerce and therefore pose a high risk of legal disputes over the ownership of intellectual property, which can further consume valuable resources of a biotechnology firm (Rothaermel and Deeds 2004). One influential example includes the dispute between the University of California and Genentech over misappropriation of intellectual property rights on genetically engineered human growth hormones,[15] which later triggered a patent infringement lawsuit,[16] leading Genentech to settle the case for $200 million in 1999. Finally, evidence also suggests that – regardless of the kind of partnerships – excessive alliance formation may result in diminishing returns to accessing and leveraging complementary resources as well as stretch the managerial capacity of the firm. The resulting burden can outweigh the benefits generated by alliances and put a strain on the firm's product development and innovation efforts (Deeds and Hill 1996).

Of critical importance, some alliance partners may have their competitive or value appropriation motivations dominate their cooperative or value creation motives (Amburgey et al. 1996). Take, for example, a typical downstream alliance situation in which a cash-starved biotechnology firm cannot afford to divert its management's attention for the several months often required to raise additional venture financing. In this circumstance, a financially strong pharmaceutical partner can use its relative bargaining power to demand control rights far beyond what the biotechnology firm would be prepared to cede under less pressing conditions. Studies suggest that such situations do occur and that they often lead to an inefficient allocation of control rights, lowering the success rate of the project (Lerner and Merges 1998; Lerner et al. 2003).

Horizontal alliances among peer biotechnology firms, which are aimed at joint product development, also may entail such motivation imbalance. The source of the problem is that while peer biotechnology firms may be willing to cooperate on a particular project, they may be competing fiercely in other lines of business. That is why when it comes to research-driven collaborations, biotechnology firms have to balance their aspirations of access to new knowledge with their need to guard against misappropriation of that knowledge (Liebeskind et al. 1996). A possible negative outcome of such competitive tension is the unwillingness of biotechnology firm partners to share information. In partnering with competitors, biotechnology firms can thus be overly protective with respect to knowledge-sharing, hurting joint knowledge creation and decreasing the total value generated by the alliance. Alternatively, partnerships with competitors may be characterized by learning races wherein each firm strives to maximize its own learning and the application of that learning outside the scope of the alliance – without regard for the partner's learning (Amburgey et al. 2000; Khanna et al. 1998). It is not surprising, then, that a biotechnology firm's participation in horizontal alliances, which often entails partnering with competing firms, has been linked to decreased revenues and reduced innovation levels (Baum et al. 2000; Baum and Silverman 2004).

Pursuits of relational capability through repeat partnering with the same set of partners may lead to another peril for biotechnology firms: the relational lock-in. The relational lock-in denotes parties' attempts to perfect a suboptimal exchange relationship or, at the extreme, their unwillingness and inability to disengage from

---

[15] The case was settled in 1980 with Genentech's agreeing to pay up to $2 million in royalties.

[16] Genentech Inc. v Regents of University of California, 939 F. Supp. 639 (S.D. Ind. 1996).

clearly dysfunctional partnerships. Maurer and Ebers (2006) suggest that the desire to honor the norms of reciprocal exchange may lock biotechnology allies into such dysfunctional ties. Additional evidence comes from Hoang and Rothaermel (2005), who found that prior partner-specific collaborative experience has no positive impact on alliance performance with the partner and, at high levels, can even be detrimental. These findings hint at the presence of inertia or relational lock-in in interorganizational partnering, wherein firms engage in repeated alliance formation because of the comfort partnering with familiar firms, rather than clear performance benefits (Li and Rowley 2002). Such relational lock-ins are particularly hazardous in light of evidence that more successful biotechnology firms reshape and restructure their alliance portfolios as the firms mature and face new objectives. For biotechnology firms, in particular, while many young start-ups embed themselves into cohesive partnership networks early on (Walker et al. 1997), successful companies evolve to develop a diverse portfolio of links to other players in the market, gaining access to the information and other resources these partners hold (Maurer and Ebers 2006). This evidence resonates with a larger body of literature suggesting that, particularly in high-velocity and uncertain technological environments, the performance of firms could be substantially impeded by maintaining alliance linkages to a set of familiar partners because it limits the ability of the firms to access novel and nonredundant information (e.g., Goerzen 2007; Rowley et al. 2000).

Just as with individual ties, a firm's network position may be a source of both opportunity and constraint. Owen-Smith and Powell (2004), for instance, found that a weak connection or a simple membership in the noncollocated network has either neutral or negative implications for a firm's innovation levels. They suggest that, given the unavailability of localized knowledge spillovers, a weak structural network position would be akin to "a competent minor leaguer attempting to play in the majors while lacking the necessary skills" (Owen-Smith and Powell 2004: 16). In other words, a firm's structural position locks it into a disadvantageous competitive pool where it is likely grossly mismatched on its ability to generate and internalize knowledge.

As discussed earlier, the detriments of alliances and a firm's structural position in the web of partnerships have to do with the access to knowledge and other complementary resources alliances provide. It appears, however, that the legitimizing effect of alliances is also not uniformly positive. Some research, for instance, finds no impact of downstream alliances with prominent pharmaceutical and health-care organizations on the IPO success of biotechnology firms (Gulati and Higgins 2003). Thus the key to unpacking these observed relationships is scrutinizing not only the benefits but also the costs of such endorsements. It is no secret that affiliations with highly prestigious partners generally entail asymmetric terms of exchange (Hsu 2004; Podolny 1993). A young biotechnology firm unknown to the market community may be forced to pay a hefty premium for an affiliation with a prestigious alliance partner. This premium may manifest, for instance, in the biotech's having to transfer to the partner a disproportionate share of control rights to intellectual property or to revenue streams from commercialized products (Lerner and Merges 1998). In other instances, to gain access to a prestigious pharmaceutical firm, a biotechnology firm may have to compromise its learning and business development objectives, tailoring the alliance exclusively to the needs of the partner. But when and under what circumstances the benefits of endorsement by prestigious partners may outweigh related costs remain to be explored.

## 6.5 Future Research

Over the past 20 years, management scholars have collected illuminating insights about the motives underlying alliance formation and choice of partners by biotechnology firms, the governance structure of these alliances, and the implications of partnerships for the performance of firms. In addition to enhancing the current state of the art, extant research also reveals several promising avenues for future research. We outline three intriguing directions: (a) detailed investigations of firms' dual cooperative and competitive motivation in biotechnology alliances; this naturally extends to the multifaceted effects of the firm's position in the networks of alliances, which could influence both cooperative and competitive behaviors; (b) studies of dynamics of power and dependence in strategic alliances and their effects on the processes of value creation and appropriation; and (c) the application of a richer, multilevel lens of analysis spanning individual relationships, portfolios of alliances, and entire networks of interorganizational linkages.

First, scholars can pay closer attention to the symbiosis of cooperative and competitive aspects of strategic alliances among biotechnology firms. We need further insights into when biotechnology firms tend to maximize their individual learning in the alliance at the expense of joint value creation. Another fruitful line of inquiry could unpack when firms' concerns about knowledge misappropriation thwart knowledge-sharing in alliances. Additionally, scholars have to take a deeper look at certain kinds of partnerships with respect to the underlying motivations of the firms involved. For instance, licensing deals, which many scholars classify as cooperative ties, sometimes result from settlements of intellectual property disputes, and thus may have strong underpinnings of conflict and rivalry. There is also a sizable opportunity to use insights from studies on the structure of cooperative relations in biotechnology to gain a deeper understanding of competitive trends in the industry. Indeed, cooperative ties provide differential access to resources, information flows, and status, and may therefore impact firms' ability and motivation to engage in competitive behavior (Gnyawali and Madhavan 2001).

Second, based on the need to consider both cooperative and competitive aspects of strategic alliances in biotechnology, research could delve more deeply into dynamics of power and dependence in interorganizational alliances, especially as related to value creation and value appropriation. Gulati and Sytch (2007), for instance, reveal that value-capturing advances of partners may destroy value-creation trends in an alliance. Other work suggests that biotechnology firms often exchange knowledge with pharmaceutical firms for money on disadvantageously asymmetric terms (Barley et al. 1992; Lerner and Merges 1998), and that when allocation of control rights is skewed toward a funding company, it may be detrimental to biotechnology alliances (Lerner et al. 2003). Scholars could take a more detailed look at the behavioral dynamics of such partnerships and unpack their implications for the performance of the ventures.

Finally, while existing research has examined strategic alliances in biotechnology using several distinct units of analysis, ranging from individual alliance linkages to the networks of alliances, there are more opportunities to cut across different levels of analysis (cf. Rothaermel and Hess 2007). We will identify three of these. First, it is essential to consider that while many aspects of interorganizational relations become institutionalized at the level of an organization, they are still largely based on interpersonal interactions (cf. Gulati and Sytch 2008). Alliance research would benefit from taking a more fine-grained look at the interpersonal dynamics between boundary-spanning organizational agents and other employees involved in managing strategic partnerships. The implications could be informative and valuable. For instance, positive implications of interpartner familiarity and prior partnerships can be downplayed by frequent personnel turnover or tender relationships between organizational boundary-spanners. Also, much existing research on the development and implications of relational capabilities has implicitly assumed that organizational experience with alliances smoothly diffuses throughout the firm, making it a better overall partner. Studying interpersonal networks within organizations with respect to alliance formation activity could shed light on organizational knowledge diffusion, accumulation, and internalization, leading to more precise inferences with respect to organization-level outcomes.

Second, while there is quite a bit of research focused on individual alliances, there is ample room to consider the origins and implications of a firm's entire alliance portfolio. There is evidence, for example, suggesting that firms in different stages of an evolutionary cycle and facing different market demands may require distinct alliance portfolio configurations (Maurer and Ebers 2006). Future research can unpack this in greater detail, looking at behavioral and performance implications of alliance portfolios that differ on the dimensions of partner diversity, relationship scope, strength, duration, and others. Finally, recent theoretical and methodological advances in studies of complex systems (e.g., Guimera and Amaral 2005; Gulati et al. 2007; Newman 2004) offer a tremendous opportunity for analyzing networks of biotechnology alliances in a new light.[17]

---

[17] The authors thank Sekou Bermiss, Ranjay Gulati, Jeff Reuer, Frank Rothaermel, Ithai Stern, Sharmi Surianarain, and Bart Vanneste for their helpful comments and discussions on the chapter.

# References

Ahuja G (2000a) Collaboration networks, structural holes, and innovation: A longitudinal study. Administrative Science Quarterly 45: 425–455

Ahuja G (2000b) The duality of collaboration: Inducements and opportunities in the formation of interfirm linkages. Strategic Management Journal 21: 317–343

Amburgey TL, Dacin MT, Singh JV (1996) Learning races, patent races, and capital races: Strategic interaction and embeddedness within organizational fields. In: Shrivastava P, Baum JAC, Dutton JM (eds), Advances in Strategic Management, Vol. 13, JAI, Greenwich, CT, pp. 303–322

Amburgey TL, Dacin MT, Singh JV (2000) Learning races and dynamic capabilities. Unpublished manuscript

Anand BN, Khanna T (2000a) Do firms learn to create value? The case of alliances. Strategic Management Journal 21: 295–315

Anand BN, Khanna T (2000b) The structure of licensing contracts. Journal of Industrial Economics 48: 103–135

Argyres NS, Liebeskind JP (1998) Privatizing the intellectual commons: Universities and the commercialization of biotechnology. Journal of Economic Behavior and Organization 35: 427–454

Baldi C, Stern I, Dukerich J (2007) Mascot love: Common educational background and alliance formation. Working Paper

Barley SR, Freeman J, Hybels RC (1992) Strategic alliances in commercial biotechnology. In: Nohria N, Eccles RG (eds), Networks and organization. Harvard Business School Press, Cambridge

Baum JAC, Silverman B (2004) Picking winners or building them? Alliance, intellectual, and human capital as selection criteria in venture financing and performance of biotechnology startups. Journal of Business Venturing 19: 411–436

Baum JAC, Calabrese T, Silverman BS (2000) Don't go it alone: Alliance network composition and startups' performance in Canadian biotechnology. Strategic Management Journal 21: 267–294

Burrill GS (2007) BIOTECH 2007 Life sciences: A global transformation. Burrill & Comp., San Francisco, CA

Casciaro T (2003) The determinants of governance structures in alliances: The role of strategic, task, and partner uncertainties. Industrial and Corporate Change 12: 1223–1251

Chan SH, Kensinger JW, Keown AJ, Martin JD (1997) Do strategic alliances create value? Journal of Financial Economics 46: 199–221

Chung S, Singh H, Lee K (2000) Complementarity, status similarity and social capital as drivers of alliance formation. Strategic Management Journal 21: 1–22

Cohen WM, Levinthal DA (1990) Absorptive capacity: A new perspective on learning and innovation. Administrative Science Quarterly 35: 128–153

Dacin MT, Oliver C, Roy J-P (2007) The legitimacy of strategic alliances: An institutional perspective. Strategic Management Journal 28: 169–187

Dalpe R (2003) Interaction between public research organizations and industry in biotechnology. Managerial and Decision Economics 24: 171–185

David RJ, Han S-K (2004) A systematic assessment of the empirical support for transaction cost economics. Strategic Management Journal 25: 39–58

Deeds DL, Hill CWL (1996) Strategic alliances and the rate of new product development: An empirical study of entrepreneurial biotechnology. Journal of Business Venturing 11: 41–55

DiMaggio PJ, Powell WW (1983) The iron cage revisited: Institutional isomorphism and collective rationality in organizational fields. American Sociological Review 48: 147–160

Doz YL (1996) The evolution of cooperation in strategic alliances: Initial conditions or learning processes? Strategic Management Journal 17: 55–83

Dyer JH (1996) Does governance matter? Keiretsu alliances and asset specificity as sources of Japanese competitive advantage. Organization Science 7: 649–666

Dyer JH, Singh H (1998) The relational view: Cooperative strategy and sources of interorganizational competitive advantage. Academy of Management Review 23: 660–679

Eisenhardt KM, Schoonhoven CB (1996) Resource-based view of strategic alliance formation: Strategic and social effects in entrepreneurial firms. Organization Science 7: 136–150

Ener H, Hoang H (2007) Organizational search behavior as a driver of international alliances. Working Paper

Ernst & Young (1988) Biotech 89: Commercialization. Ernst & Young, San Francisco, CA

Folta TB (1998) Governance and uncertainty: The trade-off between administrative control and commitment. Strategic Management Journal 19: 1007–1028

Folta TB, Miller KD (2002) Real options in equity partnerships. Strategic Management Journal 23: 77–88

Gambardella A (1995) Science and Innovation. Cambridge University Press, Cambridge

Gans JS, Hsu DH, Stern S (2002) When does start-up innovation spur the gale of creative destruction? Rand Journal of Economics 33: 571–586

Ghoshal S, Moran P (1996) Bad for practice: A critique of the transaction cost theory. Academy of Management Review 21: 13–47

Gimeno J (2004) Competition within and between networks: The contingent effect of competitive embeddedness on alliance formation. Academy of Management Journal 47: 820–842

Gnyawali DR, Madhavan R (2001) Cooperative networks and competitive dynamics: A structural embeddedness perspective. Academy of Management Review 26: 431–445

Goerzen A (2007) Alliance networks and firm performance: The impact of repeated partnerships. Strategic Management Journal 28: 487–509

Guimera R, Amaral L (2005) Functional cartography of complex metabolic networks. Nature 433: 895–900

Gulati R (1995a) Does familiarity breed trust? The implications of repeated ties for contractual choice in alliances. Academy of Management Journal 38: 85–112

Gulati R (1995b) Social structure and alliance formation patterns: A longitudinal analysis. Administrative Science Quarterly 40: 619–652

Gulati R (2007) Managing network resources: Alliances, affiliations, and other relational assets. Oxford University Press, Oxford

Gulati R, Higgins MC (2003) Which ties matter when? The contingent effects of interorganizational partnerships on IPO success. Strategic Management Journal 24: 127–144

Gulati R, Sytch M (2007) Dependence asymmetry and joint dependence in interorganizational relationships: Effects of embeddedness on exchange performance. Administrative Science Quarterly 52: 32–69

Gulati R, Sytch M (2008) Does familiarity breed trust? Revisiting the antecedents of trust. Managerial Decision and Economics 29: 165–190

Gulati R, Lawrence PR, Puranam P (2005) Adaptation in vertical relationships: Beyond incentive conflict. Strategic Management Journal 26: 415–440

Gulati R, Sytch M, Tatarynowicz A (2007) The rise and fall of small worlds. Working Paper

Hagedoorn J (1993) Understanding the rationale of strategic technology partnering: Interorganizational modes of cooperation and sectoral differences. Strategic Management Journal 14: 371–385

Hagedoorn J (2002) Inter-firm R&D partnerships: An overview of major trends and patterns since 1960. Research Policy 31: 477–492

Hamel G (1991) Competition for competence and inter-partner learning within international strategic alliances. Strategic Management Journal 12: 83–103

Henderson R, Cockburn I (1994) Measuring competence? Exploring firm effects in pharmaceutical research. Strategic Management Journal 15: 63–84

Higgins MC, Gulati R (2003) Getting off to a good start: The effects of upper echelon affiliations on underwriter prestige. Organization Science 14: 244–263

Higgins MC, Gulati R (2006) Stacking the deck: The effects of top management backgrounds on investor decisions. Strategic Management Journal 27: 1–25

Hoang H, Rothaermel FT (2005) The effect of general and partner-specific alliance experience on joint R&D project performance. Academy of Management Journal 48: 332–345

Hsu D (2004) What do entrepreneurs pay for venture capital affiliation? Journal of Finance 59: 1805–1844

Kale P, Dyer JH, Singh H (2002) Alliance capability, stock market response, and long-term alliance success: The role of the alliance function. Strategic Management Journal 23: 747–767

Katila R, Mang PY (2003) Exploiting technological opportunities: The timing of collaborations. Research Policy 32: 317–332

Kenney M (1986) Biotechnology: The university–industrial complex. Yale University Press, New Haven

Khanna T, Gulati R, Nohria N (1998) The dynamics of learning alliances: Competition, cooperation, and relative scope. Strategic Management Journal 19: 193–210

Kim JW, Higgins MC (2007) Where do alliances come from? The effects of upper echelons on alliance formation. Research Policy 36: 499–514

Kogut B, Shan W, Walker G (1992) The make-or-cooperate decision in the context of an industry network. In: Nohria N, Eccles RG (eds), Networks and organization. Harvard Business School Press, Cambridge, MA, pp. 348–365

Koka BR, Prescott JE (2002) Strategic alliances as social capital: A multidimensional view. Strategic Management Journal 23: 795–816

Lane PJ, Lubatkin M (1998) Relative absorptive capacity and interorganizational learning. Strategic Management Journal 19: 461–477

Lavie D, Rosenkopf L (2006) Balancing exploration and exploitation in alliance formation. Academy of Management Journal 49: 797–818

Lazarsfeld PF, Merton RK (1954) Friendship as a social process: A substantive and methodological analysis. In: Berger M, Abel T, Page CH (eds), Freedom and control in modern society. Van Nostrand, Toronto, pp. 18–66

Lerner J, Merges RP (1998) The control of technology alliances: An empirical analysis of the biotechnology industry. Journal of Industrial Economics 46: 125–156

Lerner J, Shane H, Tsai A (2003) Do equity financing cycles matter? Evidence from biotechnology alliances. Journal of Financial Economics 67: 411–445

Li SX, Rowley TJ (2002) Inertia and evaluation mechanisms in interorganizational partner selection: Syndicate formation among U.S. investment banks. Academy of Management Journal 45: 1104–1118

Liebeskind JP, Oliver AL, Zucker L, Brewer M (1996) Social networks, learning, and flexibility: Sourcing scientific knowledge in new biotechnology firms. Organization Science 7: 418–443

Lorenzoni G, Lipparini A (1999) The leveraging of interfirm relationships as a distinctive organizational capability: A longitudinal study. Strategic Management Journal 20: 317–338

Maurer I, Ebers M (2006) Dynamics of social capital and their performance implications: Lessons from biotechnology start-ups. Administrative Science Quarterly 51: 262–292

Mayer KJ, Argyres NS (2004) Learning to contract: Evidence from the personal computer industry. Organization Science 15: 394–410

McPherson JM, Smith-Lovin L (1987) Homophily in voluntary organizations. American Sociological Review 52: 370–379

Newman ME (2004) Fast algorithm for detecting community structure in networks. Physical Review E 69: 066133

Nicholls-Nixon CL, Woo CY (2003) Technology sourcing and output of established firms in a regime encompassing technological change. Strategic Management Journal 24: 651–666

Niosi J (2003) Alliances are not enough explaining rapid growth in biotechnology firms. Research Policy 32: 737–750

Odagiri H (2003) Transaction costs and capabilities as determinants of the R&D boundaries of the firm: A case study of the ten largest pharmaceutical firms in Japan. Managerial & Decision Economics 24: 187–211

Oliver AL (2001) Strategic alliances and the learning life-cycle of biotechnology firms. Organization Studies 22: 467–489

Owen-Smith J, Powell WW (2004) Knowledge networks in the Boston biotechnology community. Organization Science 15: 5–21

Pfeffer J, Salancik G (1978) The external control of organizations. Harper and Row, New York

Pisano GP (1989) Using equity participation to support exchange: Evidence from the biotechnology industry. Journal of Law, Economics, and Organization 5: 109–126

Pisano GP (1990) The R&D boundaries of the firm: An empirical analysis. Administrative Science Quarterly 35: 153–176

Podolny JM (1993) A status-based model of market competition. American Journal of Sociology 98: 829–872

Podolny JM (2001) Networks as the pipes and prisms of the market. American Journal of Sociology 107: 33–60

Powell WW (1996) Interorganizational collaboration in the biotechnology industry. Journal of Institutional and Theoretical Economics 152: 197–215

Powell WW, Brantley P (1992) Competitive cooperation in biotechnology. In: Nohria N, Eccles RG (eds), Networks and organization. Harvard Business School Press, Cambridge

Powell WW, Koput KW, Smith-Doerr L (1996) Interorganizational collaboration and the locus of innovation: Networks of learning in biotechnology. Administrative Science Quarterly 41: 116–145

Powell WW, White DR, Koput KW, Owen-Smith J (2005) Network dynamics and field evolution: The growth of interorganizational collaboration in the life sciences. American Journal of Sociology 110: 1132–1205

Reuer JJ, Zollo M, Singh H (2002) Post-formation dynamics in strategic alliances. Strategic Management Journal 23: 135–151

Rosenkopf L, Metiu A, George VP (2001) From the bottom up? Technical committee activity and alliance formation. Administrative Science Quarterly 46: 748–772

Rothaermel FT (2001) Incumbant's advantage through exploiting complementary assets via interfirm cooperation. Strategic Management Journal 22: 687–699

Rothaermel FT, Boeker W (2007) Old technology meets new technology: Complementarities, similarities, and alliance formation. Strategic Management Journal 28

Rothaermel FT, Deeds DL (2004) Exploration and exploitation alliances in biotechnology: A system of new product development. Strategic Management Journal 25: 201–221

Rothaermel FT, Hess AM (2007) Building dynamic capabilities: Innovation driven by individual, firm, and network level effects. Organization Science 18

Rowley T, Behrens D, Krackhardt D (2000) Redundant governance structures: An analysis of structural and relational embeddedness in the steel and semiconductor industries. Strategic Management Journal 21: 369–386

Santoro MD, McGill JP (2005) The effect of uncertainty and asset co-specialization on governance in biotechnology alliances. Strategic Management Journal 26: 1261–1269

Scott RW (1995) Institutions and Organizations. Sage, Thousand Oaks, CA

Shan W (1990) An empirical analysis of organizational strategies by entrepreneurial high-technology firms. Strategic Management Journal 11: 129–139

Shan W, Walker G, Kogut B (1994) Interfirm cooperation and startup innovation in the biotechnology industry. Strategic Management Journal 15: 387–394

Silverman BS, Baum JAC (2002) Alliance-based competitive dynamics. Academy of Management Journal 45: 791–806

Simon HA (1957) Administrative behavior, 2nd edn. Macmillan, New York

Simon HA (1985) Human nature in politics: A Dialogue of psychology with political science. American Political Science Review 79: 293–304

Singh K, Mitchell W (1996) Precarious collaboration: Business survival after partners shut down or form new partnerships. Strategic Management Journal 17: 99–115

Sorensen J, Stuart TE (2000) Aging, obsolescence and organizational innovation. Administrative Science Quarterly 45: 81–112

Stern I, Dukerich J (2007) All that glitters is not gold: Scientists' academic status attributes and alliance formation between pharmaceutical and biotechnology firms. Working Paper

Stinchcombe AL (1965) Social structure and organizations. In: March JG (ed), Handbook of organizations. Rand McNally, Chicago, pp. 142–193

Stuart TE (1998) Network positions and propensities to collaborate: An investigation of strategic alliance formation in a high-technology industry. Administrative Science Quarterly 43: 668–698

Stuart TE, Hoang H, Hybels RC (1999) Interorganizational endorsements and the performance of entrepreneurial ventures. Administrative Science Quarterly 44: 315–349

Thompson JD (1967) Organizations in action. McGraw-Hill, New York

Vanneste BS, Puranam P (2007) Repeated interactions and contractual detail: When does learning dominate trust? Working Paper

Walker G, Kogut B, Shan W (1997) Social capital, structural holes, and the formation of an industry network. Organization Science 8: 109–125

Wang L, Zajac E (2007) Acquisition or alliance? A dyadic perspective on interfirm resource combinations. Strategic Management Journal 28: 1291–1317

Williamson OE (1975) Markets and hierarchies: Analysis and antitrust implications. Free Press, New York

Williamson OE (1981) The economics of organization: The transaction cost approach. American Journal of Sociology 87: 548–577

Williamson OE (1985) The economic institutions of capitalism: Firms, markets, relational contracting. Free Press/Collier Macmillan, New York

Zaheer A, George VP (2004) Reach out or reach within? Performance implications of alliances and location in biotechnology. Managerial and Decision Economics 25: 437–452

Zahra SA, George G (2002) Absorptive capacity: A review, reconceptualization, and extension. The Academy of Management Review 27: 185–203

Zollo M, Reuer JJ, Singh H (2002) Interorganizational routines and performance in strategic alliances. Organization Science 13: 701–713

Zucker LG, Darby MR, Armstrong JS (1998) Geographically localized knowledge: Spillovers or markets. Economic Inquiry 36: 65–86

# 7 Mergers and Acquisitions in the Biotechnology Industry

Lars Schweizer[1] and Dodo zu Knyphausen-Aufsess[2]

[1]Johann Wolfgang Goethe University Frankfurt am Main, USB-Stiftungsprofessur Betriebswirtschaftlehre, Mertonstr. 17, 60325 Frankfurt am Main, Germany
[2]Chair of Human Resources and Organization, Otto-Friedrich University of Bamberg, Feldkirchenstr. 21, 96045 Bamberg, Germany

## 7.1 Introduction

This chapter deals with mergers and acquisitions (M&As) involving biotechnology companies, the number of which has increased steadily since the beginning of the 1990s. Basically, M&As – regardless of motive – are among the most dramatic and visible manifestations of strategy at the corporate level, and they are driven by various motives (Steiner 1975; Trautwein 1990). In the biotechnology industry, M&A deals are an essential element of the "business development" activities of a company (Kind and zu Knyphausen-Aufsess 2007).

This chapter proceeds in the following manner. First, we briefly describe the development of the biotechnology industry from scientific, organizational, and financial perspectives. This analysis leads to the conclusion that a strategic consolidation resulting in fewer but stronger, larger, more market-capitalized, and, thus, more financeable biotechnology companies is only a question of time.

Second, we distinguish between two different layers of M&A activities. The first layer deals with M&A activities between biotechnology companies, while the second layer concerns M&A activities between pharmaceutical and biotechnology companies. For each of these layers we are going to discuss the following questions: What are the motives for the respective M&A activities? What different M&A strategies are applied by biotechnology and pharmaceutical companies? Are there any peculiarities of these M&A deals?

Finally, on the basis of the above-mentioned analysis, we summarize the major issues and identify future research questions.

H. Patzelt and T. Brenner (eds.), *Handbook of Bioentrepreneurship*,
doi: 10.1007/978-0-387-48345-0_7, © Springer Science + Business Media, LLC 2008

## 7.2 Development of the Biotechnology Industry and the Need for M&A

In this section, we analyze the development of the biotechnology industry from scientific, organizational, and financial perspectives. These perspectives reveal the need for a strategic consolidation in the biotechnology industry.

### 7.2.1 The Development of the Biotechnology Industry from a Scientific Perspective

Broadly considered, biotechnology includes techniques as old as Western civilization itself: e.g., the cultivation of microorganisms for brewing and the intentional cross-breeding of plants and animals. Thus, the roots of modern biotechnology, the so-called first generation of biotechnology, lie in the fermentation of foods and drinks, industries spanning almost every society and evolving over centuries (Sharp 1991; Kenney 1986).

"Second-generation biotechnology" developed as an outgrowth of traditional fermentation in the late nineteenth and early twentieth centuries and depicted the greater understanding about microorganisms. The discovery of penicillin by the British bacteriologist Alexander Fleming in 1928 and the subsequent development of the antibiotic industry is one of the major milestones of the twentieth century.

"Third-generation biotechnology," also called "new" or "modern" biotechnology, resulted from the discovery in the early 1970s of the method by which genes could be cut and spliced. It includes the use of recombinant DNA and cell fusion techniques as well as bioprocessing technology to make or modify products.

The development of "new biotechnology" has been characterized by Wirth (1994) in four phases; however, in this chapter we are adding a fifth phase. The *first phase*, the so-called research phase, lasted from 1970 to 1980 and was dominated by two path-breaking discoveries that revolutionized molecular biology. First, in 1973, Herbert Boyer of Stanford University and Stanley Cohen of the University of California at San Francisco reported the discovery of recombinant DNA. Second, in 1975, Cesar Milstein and Georges Kohler of the British Medical Research Council discovered monoclonal antibodies by fusing cells from a mouse myeloma with cells derived from mouse B lymphocytes to create a "hybridoma." In this phase, universities and research institutes played a critical role in biotech's emergence, not only as the places where young scientists were educated, but, particularly, as the sources of breakthrough discoveries and techniques that fostered scientific and technological innovations (Powell 1996). Hence, most biotechnology firms have been started by scientists with the help of venture capitalists, specialized law firms, or ex-pharmaceutical executives, while pharmaceutical companies have applied a "wait-and-see approach" and remained on the sideline.

The *second phase*, from 1980 to 1985, is considered as being the pioneering phase. The first product of a biotechnology company made by recombinant DNA, human insulin, was launched in 1982 and was soon gaining significant market penetration. In 1983, first experiments with genetically modified microorganisms were allowed to be carried out in the USA, and in 1985 the first genetically produced hepatitis B viral antigens were introduced.

The *third phase*, from 1984 to 1990, is regarded as being the first prosperous phase of biotechnology, because there had been strong indications that the real "take-off" point for the large corporations came in the years 1984–1985. Big-firm investment in commercial biotechnology in the USA increased markedly (Office of Technology Assessment 1988).

The *fourth phase*, from 1990 to 1996, is perceived as the real prosperous phase of biotechnology leading to new opportunities. In 1990, the first experiment to treat ADA deficiency genetically took place, and in 1992 the US Trade Office had worked out new rules for biotechnology as well as genetic engineering according to which genetically developed products are to be treated equally as conventional products. In this same period, the market share of drugs and diagnostic methods based on biotechnology increased steadily. By the end of 1994, more than two dozen biotech drugs and vaccines had been approved by the FDA, more than 200 medicines were in various stages of clinical testing, and approximately two dozen drugs awaited FDA approval (Powell 1996).

The *fifth phase*, which began in 1997 and continues to the time of publication of this chapter, is characterized by the discussion about necessary consolidation activities and the future "dream" about the never-ending benefits of biotechnology. On the one hand, biotechnology companies are considered as being the "innovative engine" for the pharmaceutical and biotechnology industry. On the other, however, institutional investors are not motivated by biotechnology's past performance and are looking for new areas to invest (Purcell 1998). Moreover, with the launch of the Human Genome Project in 1990, there was a growing perception that drug discovery was to undergo radical changes. First, the number of possible targets relevant to diseases was about to rocket. Second, new technologies such as high-throughput screening and new bioinformatics tools related to combinatorial chemistry made it possible to test a large number of potential drug targets against an even larger number of chemical entities. Third, the growing awareness of the innovation deficit at pharmaceutical companies makes them look for alternatives: biotechnology. Overall, the convergence of genomics and informatics not only heralds a new era of biomedical research, but will also foster M&A activities in the biotechnology sector.

## 7.2.2 The Development of the Biotechnology Industry from an Organizational Perspective

University laboratories have played a critical role in developing the scientific fundamentals of biotechnology during the first phase of the development of the new biotechnology. However, it was the dedicated biotechnology firms that commercially exploited the results of the research. The scientific breakthroughs of biotechnology constituted a radical change from previously dominant technologies in the pharmaceutical sector. Hence, "biotechnology is a dramatic case of a competence-destroying innovation" (Powell and Brantley 1992: 368). This particular radical technological change builds on a scientific basis (immunology and molecular biology) that differs significantly from the knowledge base (organic chemistry and its clinical application) of the established pharmaceutical industry (Powell 1993).

Internally, biotechnology firms are organized flexibly in overlapping interdisciplinary project teams with minimal hierarchy in order to create a lean and effective organization for drug discovery and commercial development (Powell 1996). Small biotechnology firms require large financial support and regulatory knowledge, while larger pharmaceutical companies desire access to the research capabilities of smaller companies. It is usually the case that the full range of relevant skills needed to develop therapeutic drugs is not readily available under a single roof. The necessary basic and research skills to create a new product are found in universities, research institutes, or small biotechnology companies, whereas the cash needed for product development, clinical trials, and worldwide marketing is located in large pharmaceutical companies. Hence, the players in this field have turned to numerous forms of collaboration such as joint ventures, research agreements, or licensing agreements. Overall, the biotechnology industry is placed in an extremely challenging, hypercompetitive environment, compounded by appropriation problems, high levels of uncertainty, and critical resource immobility (Liebeskind et al. 1996).

The biotechnology industry is characterized by a social network structure that ensures the reliability of scientific information due to well defined and socially enforced norms, reciprocity, respect for individuals' intellectual property rights, and honesty in research (Blau 1973; Crane 1972; Merton 1973). A better environment for efficient organizational learning and enhanced flexibility for responding to unpredictable changes is provided by firms that organize themselves to maximize the benefits of this social network structure. A prerequisite for success is a shift from coordinating the internal activities of the firm through a command and control structure to providing organizational support for internal as well as external exchanges.

The pattern of interfirm collaboration in biotechnology is probably more extensive than in any other industry (Arora and Gambardella 1990; Barley and Freeman 1992; Powell 1993; Powell and Brantley 1992). Greis et al. (1995) distinguish four different types of partnership agreements: (1) research contracts or minority investments for the purpose of gaining a window on new technologies, (2) licensing and marketing agreements to obtain the use of a particular technology, (3) corporate alliances such as joint ventures with or without the transfer of equity, and (4) mergers and acquisitions. Interestingly, M&As are referred to as types of "partnership" agreements reflecting the specific context of the biotechnology industry and its social network structure.

### 7.2.3 The Development of the Biotechnology Industry from a Financial Perspective

Financing a biotechnology company or venture is the result of interactions between entrepreneurs, venture capitalists, management teams, investment bankers, research analysts, and institutional investors (Hurwitz 1999). The role and influence of each player depend on which stage the company is in. The biotechnology industry has enjoyed more funding by governments, pharmaceutical companies, the equity capital markets, and the venture capital community than has virtually any other high-growth sector in the worldwide economy.

Teitelman (1989) describes Wall Street's initial attitude toward biotechnology as "biomania." In 1980/1981 biotechnology investments in the USA were attracting nearly $100 million of venture capital. However, Wall Street's overall relationship with biotechnology has been extremely variable, being hot and cold on a number of occasions. In its early enthusiasm for the technology, Wall Street ensured that many new biotechnology firms enjoyed substantial funding. Large, established pharmaceutical companies have generally been slow to become involved in biotechnology, but, over time, have been devoting considerable resources to it and many also have acquired biotechnology firms.

The restructuring and reorganization within the two primary sources of biotechnology funding – pharmaceutical companies and the institutional investment community – now pose a threat for the continued growth of the industry. On the one hand, the short-term earnings pressure on pharmaceutical companies to maintain their valuations will probably result in a reduction of discretionary dollars traditionally used for biotechnology funding. On the other, the bull markets that institutional investors have enjoyed, combined with the inconsistent market performance of biotechnology investments, have reduced their interests in future investments. From the point of view of the institutional investor, Coyler (1999) stresses that investors' caution in the biotechnology sector is rooted in its historical return, which means that the additional risk assumed by biotechnology investors has not been rewarded within a reasonable time. Investors in the average biotech IPO in 1993 have enjoyed on average only an 8% return through 1998, whereas the return to investors in the average US pharmaceutical company over the same period averages 36%.

The restructuring of pharmaceutical industry and the institutional investment community will ultimately provide a dilemma for biotechnology companies. For example, Saviotti et al. (2005) described how Hoechst and Rhône-Poulenc attempted to transform themselves into life sciences companies during the 1990s before their merger to form Aventis. The drug companies who still believe in the promise of biotechnology no longer have excess discretionary dollars to spend, and the institutional investors with discretionary dollars to spend are not "true believers." The short-term strategic answer is to find ways to give both kinds of investors what they need. First, biotechnology companies have to become as financially innovative in their interactions with pharmaceutical partners as they are scientifically innovative by using creative financing structures such as off-balance sheet or product debenture financing. Second, they have to develop a critical mass – through organic growth, consolidation, or collaborative agreements – in order to meet the needs of the pharmaceutical industry as well as the institutional investment community. This may lead to an increase in M&A activities between biotechnology companies, on the one hand, as well as more acquisitions of biotechnology firms by pharmaceutical companies, on the other.

The development of the biotechnology industry has been described from three different perspectives: (1) scientific, (2) organizational, and (3) financial. We can conclude that a strategic consolidation resulting in fewer but stronger, larger, more market capitalized, and, thus, more financeable biotechnology companies is only a question of time because most biotechnology companies desperately need money in order to ensure their future growth and survival. Basically, biotechnology companies can choose between two approaches in order to solve this problem: a biotech-to-biotech deal or a pharma-to-biotech solution.

## 7.3 Layers of M&A Activities

The previous section contained a short description of the development and challenges of the biotechnology industry. We argued that this industry is undergoing radical changes and that it faces many difficulties, thus making M&A a very likely strategic option.

### 7.3.1 M&A Activities Among Biotechnology Companies

Start-up companies in research-intensive high-technology industries such as biotechnology face a high risk of failure during the first few years of their existence. It is a challenging task for start-up company managers to build up a valuable resource platform in order to gain competitive advantage because the development of complex new technologies requires not only substantial financial resources but also competencies in different scientific and technological fields (Jones et al. 2001). Although at least 50–100 M&A transactions are announced on average in the biotechnology industry every year (BioCentury 2003), with 75 biotechnology acquisitions in 2006 (BioCentury 2007), there is only very little scientific research devoted to M&A activities between biotechnology firms (Patzelt et al. 2007).

Analyzing the one scientific article on biotechnology M&A activities (Patzelt et al. 2007), along with several business articles and reports (e.g., Arnold et al. 1999; BioCentury 2003; Van Brunt 2005; Webber 1999), the following reasons and motives for M&A activities in the biotechnology industry can be identified:

- IPOs become more and more difficult because the window of IPO financing has been shut for the last years, reflecting the unfavorable or hostile financing climate.

- Some venture capitalists are simply not ready to wait any longer to cash in their investments, so that they use their networks to facilitate M&As.
- Venture capitalists concentrate on their existing portfolio and make no further investments. And if they make further investments, they put their money into companies with clinical products already in the pipeline, rather than into those still working on discovery.
- M&As can add revenue and profit to the newly combined biotechnology firm.
- Too many biotechnology stocks have greatly underperformed.
- There are many young biotechnology companies who desperately need money.
- There is a necessity to increase market capitalization by achieving a critical mass in order to gain access to new investors.
- High-profile clinical trial failures or difficulties are making investors wary of limited pipeline companies
- Larger biotechnology companies might be interested in the acquisition of manufacturing facilities.
- Some biotechnology companies acquire others in order to position themselves as integrated product developers, thus becoming a more fully integrated drug discovery company, or service providers.
- The access to products and sales distribution channels is a further reason for consolidation.
- Through M&A activities a completion of the existing intellectual property portfolio may be reached, so that the company is able to establish a leading position in a certain technology.
- The acquisition of a biotechnology company can provide access to local or regional networks.
- A merger between two biotechnology companies can provide access to necessary management skills as biotechnology companies are often faced with a lack of experienced management.

All these reasons and motives appear to be in place for a major increase in M&As among biotechnology companies over the coming years. Taking a closer look at the two major reasons for M&A activities in the biotechnology sector, one can first identify the financial necessities from the point of view of the biotechnology companies. The financing environment for biotechnology offerings was not robust in the last years, and most of the companies are only in early-stage development of products and will face significant challenges to stay solvent. Thus, one biotechnology company may acquire another merely for its fat bank account in order to ensure their future survival. Second, biotechnology acquisitions are driven by the desire to get access to promising drug candidates (i.e., fill up the pipeline), enabling technologies, or intellectual property in order to achieve a critical mass and improve their competitive position.

Hence, it is possible to identify two different M&A strategies among biotechnology firms: financing acquisitions are driven by the acquired firm's need for cash, whereas strategic acquisitions aim at improving the current competitive position of the acquiring biotechnology company.

Bernstein (2003) points out five key questions to analyze whether to carry out a biotechnology acquisition or not:

- Does the acquisition strengthen the balance sheet?
- Does the acquisition strengthen the intellectual property?
- Does the acquisition fill the pipeline?
- Does the acquisition provide any technological synergies?
- Does the acquisition add key people?

These key questions correspond also to the main benefits Patzelt et al. (2007) identify in their empirical study concerning the acquisition of German biotechnology companies. In a first step, they show that M&As provide an important opportunity for biotechnology start-ups to acquire financial resources as they give a clear signal to investors that the companies are willing to reduce costs and to restructure their project portfolio. Moreover, a merger with a foreign company may be a possibility for biotechnology start-ups to escape the hostile financing environment of their home country. Second, Patzelt et al. (2007) demonstrate that M&As are an opportunity for biotechnology start-ups to expand their pipeline of clinical products and that the integration of new technologies can save time and costs in comparison to building up the resources internally. Third, they display that managerial benefits can be achieved through M&As, if one company is lacking management experience that the other company offers.

However, according to Ernst & Young (2004) and the findings of Patzelt et al. (2007), there might be hurdles that prevent successful M&A activities between biotechnology companies. These hurdles have their roots in the attitudes of the investors and the management. With regard to investors, they may not be willing to sell or merge their companies cheaply in hostile financing environments, when valuations of private companies are low. Besides the egos of biotechnology CEOs, brokering an agreement among all parties to an M&A transaction is a major hurdle that is often complicated by a lack of relevant M&A experience vis-à-vis both management and investors.

Zu Knyphausen-Aufsess et al. (2006) analyze the M&A and diversification strategies of venture capital firms and their portfolio companies in the biotechnology sector. They argue that in an economic downturn there should be a rationale for venture capital firms to merge some of their portfolio companies in order to make the best of their biotechnology investments. They refer to this approach as "flagship strategy." There are several obstacles to successfully implementing a flagship strategy. First, the younger the companies are, the lesser the cost reduction potential will be. Second, the management teams may have reservations in a "downside merger" because it is not clear beforehand who will take the leading positions in the merged company. Third, given the different interests of the participating venture capitalists, valuation problems usually arise. Fourth, there exists a negative notion that a merged company "burns even more money" than each of the companies did on their own. Fifth, the newly created companies that are supposed to grow rapidly often require additional financing.

Moreover, zu Knyphausen-Aufsess et al. (2006) observe that biotechnology companies founded and managed by scientists have a lower tendency to consider M&As as a possible mode of strategic business development. In contrast to this, biotechnology companies with management teams who are not the scientific founders exhibit a higher likelihood of using M&As as a part of risk diversification and growth strategy.

Haeussler (2007) analyzed firm characteristics and external firm linkages as determinants of M&A activities in the biotechnology industry. She found that firms with interfirm collaborations are generally more likely to engage in M&A activities than firms that lack such connections. Moreover, the results of her study surprisingly do not support that financial distress is a factor that influences the propensity to engage in M&As. On the basis of this finding, she concludes that M&As in the biotechnology industry are proactively carried out rather than reactively enforced.

To sum up, in a hostile financing environment, M&A activities between biotechnology companies, or the acquisition by a pharmaceutical company, provide a viable solution to get access to new capital, so that an increasing number of painful insolvencies of biotechnology companies can be prevented. Nonetheless, products are considered as the primary motive for M&A deals in the biotechnology sector because every company needs to fill up its pipeline.

## 7.3.2 M&A Activities Between Pharmaceutical and Biotechnology Companies

The desire to obtain valuable resources, including know-how, technologies, and capabilities possessed by target firms has always been a driver of M&A activities (Ahuja and Katila 2001; Chaudhuri and Tabrizi 1999). It seems that this motive has increased in importance in the most recent wave of acquisition activity (Bower 2001) because in industries characterized by rapid innovation, technological complexity, and highly specialized skills and know-how, the pace and magnitude of technological change may not allow firms to internally develop all the necessary technologies and capabilities to remain competitive. The number of acquisitions during the 1990s rose dramatically in high-technology sectors such as telecommunications and biotechnology (BioCentury 2007; Goldman Sachs 2001; Inkpen et al. 2000). Although, there is a very notable trend in increasing M&A activities during the last years concerning big pharma acquisitions of biotechnology firms (Van Brunt 2006), there is very little scholarly research in this field (Bower 2001; Schweizer 2005).

In recent years, pharmaceutical companies have conceded the need to maintain earnings growth through product line expansion as opposed to an increase in drug prices. This has put an almost unbearable burden on internal R&D. Thus, pharmaceutical companies have had to gain access to novel drugs and technologies coming out of biotechnology companies. Although the majority of the access will take the form of collaboration ranging from R&D agreements to joint ventures, acquisitions have become a more attractive alternative. Further reasons and motives for the acquisition of biotechnology companies are as follows:

- Pharmaceutical companies might realize economies of scale and the possibility to exploit hidden values.
- Many biotechnology companies are still cheap because they have not yet enjoyed enough positive attention from investors.
- Patent expiration in the pharmaceutical industry will result in a dramatic drop in sales revenues.
- Megamergers between large pharmaceutical companies have often not been successful in terms of generating innovations and developing new blockbusters.
- Pharmaceutical companies face the need to acquire knowledge in order to remain competitive in the future by having enough promising lead compounds.
- M&A is a possible strategy for overcoming lack of biotechnology knowledge, reducing R&D costs, increasing the number of potential products in a pipeline, and closing an earnings gap (Ahuja and Katila 2001; Higgins and Rodriguez 2003; Ranft and Lord 2002).
- By internalizing a whole body of laboratory or product development capabilities, pharmaceutical companies try to create internally a research environment that fosters the kind of innovation and discovery necessary to survive in the long run (Powell and Brantley 1992; Powell 1993).

Major pharmaceutical companies have always had a big interest in biotechnology companies, primarily to secure access to new technologies and products. However, these companies have more commonly operated through licensing agreements rather than outright takeovers. In the meantime, the valuations of biotechnology firms have been adjusted downwards, making acquisitions more attractive and cheaper. Consequently, large biotechnology acquisitions have multiplied in the last years. Pharmaceutical companies are now looking at the possibility to acquire broad-based technologies (1) cheaper than they could have acquired them before and (2) cheaper than they can build internally. In line with this argumentation, the total valuations of M&As which involved biotechnology companies have increased steadily from $3.3 billion in 1997, to more than $8.9 billion in 1998 and $13.7 billion in 1999, and up to $19.0 billion in 2000. Apart from that, the average valuation attached to the acquisition of a biotechnology company has also increased from $129 million in 1998 to more than $191 million in 1999 and up to $202 million in 2000 (Goldman Sachs 2001). However, Bower (2001: 99–100) pointed out that "many of the pharmaceuticals' R&D acquisitions are yet to pay off" because biotechnology products and technologies are organic and far more difficult to integrate than are computer or chip components. Intangible assets such as know-how and intellectual property do not passively translate into tangible revenue.

Schweizer (2005) showed in his study that biotechnology acquisitions are driven by multiple motives. The motives behind the biotechnology acquisitions were very similar: they were a desire to fill up the R&D pipeline, to gain access to potential blockbusters, and to acquire valuable biotechnology know-how and technologies that would enhance the acquirer's growth strategy. Moreover, these motives turned out to be divided between short- and long-term motives. Although the long-term rationale behind the acquisitions was largely identical in the analyzed acquisitions (support of the pharmaceutical firms' growth strategy by acquiring valuable biotechnology know-how and technologies), some of the short-term drivers for the acquisitions differed substantially (e.g., improvement of market position; getting a blockbuster and filling up R&D pipelines; acquire patent rights; increase efficiency).

When acquiring biotechnology companies, pharmaceutical companies face the need to make hybrid organizational arrangements (Borys and Jemison 1989) in order to integrate biotechnology companies in some way and, at the same time, to preserve the autonomy of the latter so as not to endanger the future existence of the desired capabilities. Schweizer (2005) develops a postacquisition integration framework that calls for a hybrid integration approach with simultaneous short- and long-term orientations and segmentation across different functions and value chain components. The integration of acquired biotechnology firms requires the simultaneous application of two distinct integration approaches concerning R&D and non-R&D-related portions. The reason for this is that pharmaceutical companies pursue different motives, which in turn require different integration approaches depending on the know-how and competencies of the acquired biotechnology firms.

For a successful postacquisition integration of acquired biotechnology companies it is necessary to protect the acquired firms' competencies by applying a slow preservation approach concerning R&D-related areas, granting the acquired biotechnology companies a high degree of autonomy (Datta and Grant 1990). Highly specific know-how such as that in the biotechnology context (Powell 1993) is hard to transmit because fewer parties other than the innovator can benefit from its application (Henderson and Cockburn 1994; McEvily and Chakravarthy 2002). However, as far as clinical trials, regulatory affairs, and sales and marketing are concerned, a rapid integration is possible as they belong to the core competencies of the pharmaceutical company.

The acquisition and subsequent integration of biotechnology companies is a multidimensional and multifaceted phenomenon (Javidan et al. 2004) driven by different motives (Bower 2001; Steiner 1975). This is due to the fact that pharmaceutical companies pursue different motives, especially the desire to acquire specific technological know-how and technologies (Ahuja and Katila 2001). Thus, pharmaceutical companies usually pursue a hybrid acquisition strategy when approaching biotechnology companies. On the one hand, they pursue the short-term strategy of improving their market positions by filling their R&D pipelines and gaining potential blockbusters. On the other, they pursue the long-term strategy of supporting their overall growth strategies by accessing biotechnology know-how and technologies.

## 7.4 Summary and Future Research

The biotechnology and pharmaceutical industries have witnessed a continuous increase in M&A activities since the beginning of the new millennium. In biotech-to-biotech deals, first, the key is whether a transaction can be leveraged to put the merged entity on a new growth curve. In an industry context where developing a successful product is no guarantee that it will ever happen again, companies will frequently have to look outside for new products in order to fill up their pipeline. Second, drug discovery and development is about getting the right teams of people with the necessary skills, know-how as well as capabilities together, and it is often cheaper and more effective to buy these teams than to build them internally. However, the acquiring company needs to make sure that these people and teams also stay within the company and that they do not decide to leave. Third, even if a deal seems to put the merged entity on a new growth curve, it will take a lot of time to finally realize the intended synergies because the development cycles in biotechnology companies are very long. This makes it especially difficult to measure the success of such a biotechnology merger because M&As in the biotechnology sector work in the long run, whereas some investors tend to have a short-term focus. The following major research questions that may guide research for M&As in the biotechnology sector can be derived:

- When do biotechnology companies need to look for acquisition or merger partners?
- How do biotechnology firms compare M&As with other strategic options such as alliances or licensing agreements?
- What criteria do they use in making such comparisons?
- What criteria do biotechnology firms use in evaluating the target firm in terms of their technology, and also their management and research teams?
- How and by what means can the acquiring company ensure that the key know-how and knowledge holders of the acquired firm remain with the new entity?
- Do prior ties and relationships with the potential target or partner play a role in the implementation and success of the deal?
- How do biotechnology firms calculate the expected synergies of the deal?
- How is success defined and measured in biotech-to-biotech M&As?
- Given the long development cycles in the biotechnology industry, is it possible to isolate the long-term effects of M&As?
- What differences exist between public and private M&A deals?

Pharmaceutical companies have three potential strategies (Hagedoorn and Duysters 2002) to seek access to biotechnological know-how in order to fill up their R&D pipeline and to remain competitive in the long run: organic growth, in which pharmaceutical companies build this know-how on their own, strategic alliances with biotechnology firms, and M&A to integrate companies with know-how and capabilities. In the field of biotechnology, the technological frontier is advanced with a knowledge, skill, and competence base fundamentally different from prior know-how (Powell 1993), so that it is not enough for an acquirer to simply "buy" a technology, because, to create value, this technology must be nurtured and integrated throughout the postacquisition integration process (Larsson and Finkelstein 1999). However, considering the big differences in culture and organizational styles between pharmaceutical and biotechnology companies, the challenge of gaining access to the desired capabilities becomes even more obvious and highlights the importance of the "absorptive capabilities" (Cohen and Levinthal 1990) as well as the importance of keeping the top R&D people of the acquired biotechnology company. Thus, future research of M&A activities between pharmaceutical and biotechnology companies might focus on the following questions:

- How can a pharmaceutical company evaluate a patent or technology during the due diligence phase when it is lacking an in-depth understanding of the new area?
- How is it possible for a pharmaceutical company to retain the top R&D people or teams of the acquired biotechnology company?
- Do pharmaceutical companies profit from experience of previous biotechnology acquisitions?
- How can a pharmaceutical company keep up the innovative and research culture of the acquired biotechnology firm in the long run?
- What is the importance of speed in the postacquisition integration process?
- How can pharmaceutical companies measure the long-term success of biotechnology acquisition?

In these sections, we have identified key questions that may provide some guidance for future research concerning M&A activities in the biotechnology and pharmaceutical sectors. We encourage researchers to keep these questions in mind as they pursue future studies.

# References

Ahuja G, Katila R (2001) Technological acquisitions and the innovation performance of acquiring firms. Strategic Management Journal 22: 197–220

Arnold R, Grindley J, Smart S (1999) Honorable disposals as planned exit route. Nature Biotechnology 17(suppl): BE6–BE7

Arora A, Gambardella A (1990) Complementarity and external linkages. The strategies of large firms in biotechnology. Journal of Industrial Economics 38(4): 361–379

Barley S, Freeman J (1992) Strategic alliances in commercial biotechnology. In: Nohria N, Eccles R (eds), Networks and organizations. Harvard Business School Press, Boston, MA, pp. 311–347

Bernstein K (2003) Modeling deals. BioCentury 11(38): A19

BioCentury (2003) Back-to-school issue. The M&A game. BioCentury 11(38): A1–A18

BioCentury (2007) M&A upside. BioCentury 15(1): A1–A7

Blau P (1973) The organization of academic work. Wiley, New York

Borys B, Jemison DB (1989) Hybrid arrangements as strategic alliances: Theoretical issues in organizational combinations. Academy of Management Review 14: 234–249

Bower JL (2001) Not all M&As are alike – And that matters. Harvard Business Review 79(2): 93–101

Chaudhuri S, Tabrizi B (1999) Capturing the real value in high-tech acquisitions. Harvard Business Review 77(5): 123–130

Cohen W, Levinthal D (1990) Absorptive capacity: A new perspective on learning and innovation. Administrative Science Quarterly 35: 128–152

Coyler A (1999) Financing as a driver for mergers and acquisitions. Nature Biotechnology 17 (suppl): BE13

Crane D (1972) Invisible college: Diffusion of knowledge in scientific communities. University of Chicago Press, Chicago

Datta DK, Grant JH (1990) Relationships between type of acquisitions, the autonomy given to the acquired firm, and acquisition success: An empirical analysis. Journal of Management 16: 29–44

Ernst & Young (2004) Per Aspera Ad Astra. "Der steinige Weg zu den Sternen". Deutscher Biotechnologie-Report 2004 [The stony way to the stars. German biotechnology reports 2004]. Mannheim

Goldman Sachs (2001) Strategic alliances in biotechnology. Goldman Sachs, New York

Greis N, Dibner M, Bean A (1995) External partnering as a response to innovation barriers and global competition in biotechnology. Research Policy 24: 609–630

Haeussler C (2007) Proactive versus reactive M&A activities in the biotechnology industry. Journal of High Technology Management Research 17(2): 109–123

Hagedoorn J, Duysters G (2002) External sources of innovative capabilities: The preference for strategic alliances or mergers and acquisitions. Journal of Management Studies 39: 167–188

Henderson R, Cockburn I (1994) Measuring competence? Exploring firm effects in pharmaceutical research. Strategic Management Journal 15: 63–84

Higgins MJ, Rodriguez D (2003) The outsourcing of R&D through acquisitions in the pharmaceutical industry. Emory Economics Paper Series, 0324

Hurwitz EM (1999) Biotech finance. A family affair. Nature Biotechnology 17 (suppl): BE35–BE37

Inkpen AC, Sundaram AK, Rockwood K (2000) Cross-border acquisitions of U.S. technology assets. California Management Review 42(3): 50–71

Javidan M, Pablo A, Singh H, Hitt M, Jemison D (2004) Where we've been and where we're going. In: Pablo A, Javidan M (eds), Mergers and acquisitions: Creating integrative knowledge. Blackwell, Oxford, UK, pp. 245–261

Jones GK, Lanctot A, Teegen HJ (2001) Determinants and performance of external technology acquisition. Journal of Business Venturing 16(3): 255–283

Kenney M (1986) Biotechnology. The university–industrial complex. Yale University Press, New Haven, CT

Kind S, zu Knyphausen-Aufsess D (2007) What is 'business development'? The case of biotechnology. Schmalenbach Business Review 59(4): 176–198

Larsson R, Finkelstein S (1999) Integrating strategic, organizational, and human resource perspectives on mergers and acquisitions: A case survey of synergy realization. Organization Science 10: 1–26

Liebeskind J, Oliver A, Zucker L, Brewer M (1996) Social networks, learning, and flexibility: Sourcing scientific knowledge in new biotechnology firms. Organization Science 7(4): 428–443

McEvily S, Chakravarthy B (2002) The persistence of knowledge-based advantage: An empirical test for product performance and technological knowledge. Strategic Management Journal 23: 285–305

Merton R (1973) The sociology of science. University of Chicago Press, Chicago

Office of Technology Assessment (1988) New developments in biotechnology: U.S. investment in biotechnology – Special Report OTA-BA-360. U.S. Government Printing Office, Washington, DC

Patzelt H, Schweizer L, zu Knyphausen-Aufsess D (2007) Mergers and acquisitions of German biotechnology startups. International Journal of Biotechnology 9(1): 1–22

Powell W (1993) The social construction of an organizational field: The case of biotechnology [Working paper]. Department of Sociology, University of Arizona, Tucson

Powell W (1996) Inter-organizational collaboration in the biotechnology industry. Journal of Institutional and Theoretical Economics 152(1): 197–215

Powell W, Brantley P (1992) Competitive cooperation in biotechnology: Learning through networks? In: Nohria N, Eccles R (eds), Networks and organizations. Harvard Business School Press, Boston, pp. 366–394

Purcell DJ (1998) Navigating biotechnology's new fiscal opportunities. Nature Biotechnology 16 (suppl): 51

Ranft AL, Lord MD (2002) Acquiring new technologies and capabilities: A grounded model of acquisition implementation. Organization Science 13: 420–441

Saviotti P, de Looze M-A, Maupertuis MA (2005) Knowledge dynamics, firm strategy, mergers and acquisitions in the biotechnology based sectors. Economics of Innovation and New Technology 14(1/2): 103–124

Schweizer L (2005) Organizational integration of acquired biotechnology companies into pharmaceutical companies: The need for a hybrid approach. Academy of Management Journal 48(6): 1051–1074

Sharp M (1991) Technological trajectories and the corporate strategies in the diffusion of biotechnology. In: Deiaco E, Hornell E, Vickery G (eds), Technology and investment: Crucial issues for the 1990s. Pinter, London, pp. 93–114

Steiner PO (1975) Mergers: Motives, effects, policies. University of Michigan Press, Ann Arbor

Teitelman R (1989) Gene dreams: Wall Street, academia, and the rise of biotechnology. Basic Books, New York

Trautwein F (1990) Merger motives and merger prescriptions. Strategic Management Journal 11: 283–295

Van Brunt J (2005) Biotech's old soldiers. Signals Magazine, May 10. http://www.signalsmag.com

Van Brunt J (2006) M&As were hot in 2005. Signals Magazine, March 15. http://www.signalsmag.com

Webber D (1999) Economic Darwinism versus financial tooth fairies. Nature Biotechnology 17 (suppl): BE14–BE15

Wirth P (1994) Biotechnologie/Biomedizin – Stand und Perspektiven [Biotechnology/ Biomedicine – State of the art and perspectives]. In: Hollenberg CP, Hempel V (eds), Biotec: Technologieforum [Biotech: Technology forum]. Rudolf Stehle, Düsseldorf, Germany, pp. 53–65 zu Knyphausen-Aufsess D, Zaby A, Kind S (2006) M&A and diversification strategies of VC-backed firms in the biotechnology industry – Towards understanding the perspectives of venture capitalists and their portfolio companies. In: Butler J (ed), Venture capital and entrepreneurship. Information Age Publishing, Greenwich, CT

# 8 Synergy, Strategy, and Serendipity: Kirin Brewery's Entry into Biopharmaceuticals

Michael J. Lynskey

Institute of Innovation Research, Hitotsubashi University, 2-1 Naka, Kunitachi, Tokyo 186-8603, Japan

## 8.1 Introduction

Contemporary business literature has examined the biotechnology industry from various theoretical and empirical perspectives. A broad range of issues have been addressed, including strategic alliances, venture capital funding, and academic–industry relations. In analyzing such topics, scholars have focused invariably on one, or all, of the actors that constitute the industry's "locus of innovation": small, new, dedicated biotechnology firms; large, well-established pharmaceutical companies; and universities or research institutes (McKelvey 1996; Powell et al. 1996). Few accounts, if any, however, consider another actor in the biotechnology industry: the large, established firm that entered biotechnology from another sector or with other core competences, and successfully commercialized bio-pharmaceutical products.

One such "new entrant" firm was the Kirin Brewery Company of Japan. In moving from "old" to "new" biotechnology, it was a surprisingly early user of the techniques ushered in by the biotechnology revolution of the 1970s, and it has survived longer than many other firms. It entered the field when there was enormous enthusiasm in Japan about the potential of biotechnology, which prompted US concern about potential rivalry. In 1984, a seminal report on biotechnology by the Office of Technology Assessment (OTA) of the US Congress concluded, "Japan is likely to be the leading competitor of the United States (in biotechnology)" (OTA 1984, p. 7).

Kirin's entry was the result of managerial intention to diversify and to capitalise on *synergy*, but its subsequent development of new technological competences owed much to *serendipity*, in terms of fortuitous incidents of "entrepreneurial

H. Patzelt and T. Brenner (eds.), *Handbook of Bioentrepreneurship*,
doi: 10.1007/978-0-387-48345-0_8, © Springer Science + Business Media, LLC 2008

alertness" and "opportunity recognition" by individuals throughout the firm.[1] This underlines that *strategy* may not always come about in a clear and planned fashion, but may be emergent and "realized" without the explicit attention of managers. Indeed, Kirin's history in biopharmaceuticals illustrates the role of individual entrepreneurship within a large company setting. This factor is often obscured or is omitted in treatments on entrepreneurship and innovation. One reason for this neglect may be the difficulty of locating entrepreneurship in the complexities of large firms. Where is the entrepreneur in the large company? Is he or she the CEO, or the director of R&D? Or does entrepreneurship manifest itself elsewhere in the organization? The answer to this conundrum is not obvious.

## 8.2 The Locus of Entrepreneurship

Writing early in the twentieth century, Schumpeter (1912, 1934) emphasized the centrality of entrepreneurship and innovation in understanding the dynamics of industrial and economic change. He extolled the virtues of the individual entrepreneur as the sole agent of economic change and as one who introduces new combinations, or innovation. Schumpeter (1934) viewed the entrepreneur as being, among other things, a rare individual; and he also drew a sharp distinction between entrepreneurs and managers, who, by his definition, were not entrepreneur-innovators.

In a later work, presenting his prognosis of the demise of capitalism, Schumpeter (1942) altered fundamentally his analysis of the sources of innovation in the economy. He argued that the distinctive role of individual entrepreneurs has become obsolete because the task of innovation is now increasingly routinized in big business, and individual entrepreneurs are no longer necessary to overcome resistance to change in such organizations. Hence, "the perfectly bureaucratized giant industrial unit ... ousts the entrepreneur" (Schumpeter 1942, p. 134). Instead, teams of trained specialists in research and development (R&D) departments replace the functions of the individual innovator on the one hand, and a bureaucracy of salaried managers assumes the role once played by individual entrepreneurial leaders on the other. The necessity of entrepreneurial attitudes and behavior is forgotten, for in this world of automatic progress and routinized innovation they are obsolete.

A major question mark for Schumpeter's (1942) later work concerns the actual nature and managerial content of its central concept, the notion of routinized innovation. Schumpeter (1942) uses this term without ever going into detail what it means precisely. One might well ask: How is innovation routinized? What are the general strategies and operational procedures involved? Moreover, is it true to

---

[1] "Entrepreneurial alertness" and "opportunity recognition" are themes in the literature on entrepreneurship. For example, see Kirzner (1982a, b, 1985), Santarelli and Pesciarelli (1990), and Stevenson and Jarillo (1990).

say that in today's world innovation is reduced to routine, so that entrepreneurial alertness is entirely absent?

Schumpeter's general approach was subsequently developed by the neo-Schumpeterian evolutionary economists (Nelson and Winter 1977, 1982). They viewed firms as stores of knowledge that were instilled via "regular and predictable behavior patterns," which they labeled "organizational routines." They introduced the concept of "search," referring to all the organizational activities of the firm that are involved in the evaluation, modification, and/or suspension or replacement of current routines. In this evolutionary approach, routines may be viewed as "genes," and search activities as stochastic procedures for the creation of "mutations" (i.e., innovation). Management engages in "organizational routines" that may change as a result of the firm's "search" (innovation) activities. Large organizations, in particular, tend to develop such elaborate routines to assist managers in their decision-making function.

The neo-Schumpeterian approach provides a useful theoretical framework for examining economic change at the levels of intraindustry competition and the macroeconomy, but it does not clearly articulate how firms search (i.e., innovate), and it provides little guidance on the organizational processes involved. Another drawback in the neo-Schumpeterian treatment reflects a shortcoming in Schumpeter's (1942) later work, namely, that entrepreneurship disappears from view. Management engages in "routines," and even changes them as a result of "search" activities, but this seems to be viewed in a somewhat mechanistic light, expunged of any element of entrepreneurial alertness or creativity (Lynskey 2002).

There is perhaps something of an Achilles' heel in such universal, theoretical approaches to entrepreneurship that can be attributed to the reluctance of economists to draw upon detailed case studies and inductive analyses of entrepreneurship and innovation at the level of the specific firm, the individual entrepreneur, and the actual innovation (Livesay 1977). Although this may be defended in terms of a philosophy of science of the nominalist variety (e.g., Friedman 1953), it is not without potential weaknesses. Specifically, there is a risk in the traditional methodological approach of economics that historical sources and the accounts of those who perform entrepreneurship may be neglected. A theoretical, nominalist approach may be adequate for the needs of economics qua science, but it can appear rather abstract and reveal little about entrepreneurship in practice.

## 8.3 Background

The Kirin Brewery Company is the oldest brewing company in Japan. Its origins date back to 1870, when Norwegian American William Copeland established Japan's first brewery, Spring Valley Brewery, above a high-quality spring near Tokyo. Partnership problems ensued, however, and the brewery fell into disuse. In 1885, Thomas Glover, a Scottish merchant, and several other foreigners renovated the brewery from the remnants and established the Japan Brewing Company.

British engineers built the new brewery, and expert brewers were brought in from Germany. In 1888, the company launched a new beer, which Glover named after the *Kirin*, a mythological winged creature that symbolizes good fortune. Subsequently, the Japan Brewing Company was acquired by what became known as the Kirin Brewery Company, which was established in 1907 with financial support and management from the emerging Mitsubishi *zaibatsu*.

Shortly after the Second World War there were three breweries in Japan (Nakajo and Kono 1989). Kirin was the largest for much of the remaining half-century, until intense rivalry with Asahi Brewery for the premier position meant that each firm vied for 36–39% of the market. Kirin, however, produced a more comprehensive list of alcohol beverages, and it dominated the beer business throughout Asia and Oceania. In 1996, Kirin and Anheuser-Busch – the world's largest brewer and maker of *Budweiser* – established Kirin Brewery of America as a joint venture, in which both companies brewed, marketed, and distributed each other's products in their respective countries. Kirin's sales revenue of $12,799 million in 2000 made it the 12th largest food-and-beverage company in the world; and it was the 80th largest company in Japan in terms of market capitalization (Higgins 2001, 2002). Kirin has about 6,500 employees organized into five business groupings: food and beverages, biotechnology, information systems, engineering, and service. The biotechnology grouping comprises three divisions: the pharmaceutical division, the yeast-related business development department, and the agri-bio division.

Kirin's commercial focus was alcohol and other beverages, which represent 68% and 17%, respectively, of its 2005 revenues. Although its core business was based on the traditional biotechnology of fermentation, in 1982 the company's policy "changed dramatically" when it diversified into modern biotechnology.[2] Kirin took this step despite its position as the top income earner, for the seventh year in succession, among companies submitting their annual corporation tax returns in January 1982.

## 8.4 Synergy

Why did Kirin decide to enter new biotechnology? After all, it was the market leader in its core business and was not presented with a threat of substitution by a major product innovation. The decision can be seen as part of the firm's strategy of diversification, which Kirin formulated in the late 1970s, when it attained the largest historic share in the Japanese beer market, and it was difficult to foresee further significant growth. Kirin's share peaked at 63.8% in 1976. By 1981, as the

---

[2] Interview with Jun-ichi Koumegawa, 16 Feb. 2000. It is instructive to compare what was happening in the USA at this time. In October 1982, human insulin became biotechnology's first product, as developed by Herbert Boyer's fledgling company, Genentech, after it received approval from the US Food and Drug Administration to market genetically engineered human insulin. Kirin, therefore, was an early entrant to the newly emerging field of modern biotechnology.

company was on the verge of entering modern biotechnology, it was 62.7%. The share of beer in the total alcohol market culminated at 67% in 1982. Thereafter, increases in alcohol duties, coupled with changing demographics, resulted in a fall in alcohol consumption. According to Shuji Konishi, the company president at the time, Kirin decided to invest in pharmaceutical research and development in anticipation of a future slowdown in growth. Jun Kojima, of Kirin's pharmaceutical division, noted that the firm was looking to diversify in the 1980s. While optimistic about its prospects, the management understood that there were risks involved.

The firm's strategy of diversification was also influenced by macroeconomic concerns. Owing to the two oil shocks of the 1970s, Japan experienced an economic downturn after a period of sustained expansion from 1955 to 1970, and the country entered a term of slower growth. Sales of beer, which had risen during the high-growth period, also suffered as a result. Consequently, in 1981, the company formulated a long-term vision whose central theme was, according to Kojima, "diversification into businesses somewhat related to our core business or competence."

This "relatedness" is significant. Kirin's entry into new biotechnology was an example of diversification into products and markets that, at face value, bore no logical relationship to its existing ones. Nevertheless, there was a desire to use excess cash, and the directors hoped the company could benefit from synergy: the gains that can accrue from linking two or more activities. The extent of a firm's familiarity with the technology and market being addressed explains much of the success, or failure, of new business-development strategies. The technological diversification of large, established firms should not be a "miscellaneous collection" of technologies from many fields, but, rather, diversification within a widely defined area of specialization (Penrose 1959). According to Shigeru Morotomi, deputy manager of its pharmaceutical division, Kirin was seeking something new that it could do using its brewing technology, and it entered the pharmaceutical domain with the aim of making drugs "the second pillar" of its business after beer.

Kirin intended to leverage its existing expertise at a time when the techniques of new biotechnology had not yet been widely adopted, "due to the conservatism of the large Japanese pharmaceutical firms" (OIA 1992, p. 31). For many pharmaceutical companies, adopting these techniques involved a transition from the practice of "random screening" of compounds to "guided" or "rational" drug design (see Bevan et al. 1995; Galambos and Sturchio 1998; Henderson et al. 1999). Koichiro Aramaki, of Kirin's pharmaceutical division, recalled, "[At the time, the big Japanese pharmaceutical companies] had not yet tried research in the new area. We thought if we could use biotechnology as a competitive edge, we could take a leading position, at least in Japan."

In fact, the standing of Japan's pharmaceutical companies was intriguing. By the mid-1980s, the market value of pharmaceuticals in Japan represented ~15% of the worldwide market, second only to that of the USA at 28% (Inaba 1987, p. 50). Despite this position, Japanese companies were relatively minor players, as exemplified by the following data:

- In 1985, 54 of the 100 top-selling pharmaceutical products in Japan were based on foreign technology or licenses; only 46 were purely domestic products.
- Overseas sales represented only 10% for most Japanese producers, as opposed to 22–98% for major European and US providers.
- In 1985, only the largest of the Japanese producers, Takeda, had total sales exceeding $1 billion, a level that was surpassed by 11 US pharmaceutical companies (Dibner 1985, p. 1231).

Moreover, contemporaneous estimates for the potential of the biotechnology market were promising. The 1987 market in Japan for genetic engineering and cell-fusion products was estimated at $240 million, up 44 % from 1986 (Miyata 1987, p. 17). A 1985 survey by the Bioindustry Development Center (BIDEC) in Japan concluded that the market for products based on such technology to reach $21 billion by the turn of the century, or an increase of 88-fold over 15 years (Dibner and White 1989, p. 8). A subsequent survey predicted a market of $375 billion worldwide for all products of biotechnology by 2000.

Besides these factors bearing on Kirin's decision, there was parallel activity by Japanese government ministries and private firms. In 1981, the Ministry of International Trade and Industry (MITI) turned its attention to biotechnology, reflecting the industry's strategic importance and MITI's customary role in promoting the competitiveness of industries under its jurisdiction (Fransman and Tanaka 1995a, b). MITI recognized that from a long-range point of view these were the industries where income elasticity of demand was high (OECD 1986, p. 9). In the same year, MITI invited 14 companies to participate in the biotechnology part of its Programme on Basic Technologies for Future Industries (*Jisedai sangyo kiban gijutsu kenkyu kaihatsu seido*). In 1982, MITI established a special Bio-industry Office and began subsidizing companies and research institutions involved in biotechnology research. MITI's activity encouraged more than 150 companies, especially from the pharmaceutical, chemical, and food industries, to invest in research, with the expectation of future growth in the market for biotechnology-related products.

Thereafter, other ministries and government agencies began to promote the biotechnology industry. They often established their own biotechnology research projects and assigned them to consortia of private companies, with the support of various subsidies. In doing so, different ministries competed with one another to extend their policies to sectors outside their jurisdiction, a trait that has been qualified as "bureau pluralism" (Aoki 1988; Okazaki 2001). This attempt by competing state agencies to compartmentalize biotechnology and the lack of policy coordination were criticized by industry (Tanaka 1991). Nevertheless, this intragovernmental pluralism may have helped to stimulate private enterprise and to promote the biotechnology industry during what has been called Japan's first *bio-boom* (Miyata 1994).

## 8.4.1 Opportunity Recognition

Against such a backdrop, Kirin recognized an opportunity to enter this strategic industry through corporate entrepreneurship. The suggestion was made by a senior managing director, Dr Tomoo Itoga, in the late 1970s, and supported by other senior executives. Several targets for diversification were proposed, such as agri-biotechnology and genetically modified organisms. Masaharu Ishikawa, product development manager in Kirin's Pharmaceutical Division, recollected that the firm first thought of various medical uses for fermentation products while recognizing that microorganisms that are fermented to make beer are different from those that are cultivated to fight cancer.

Kirin's decision to enter the field of new biotechnology became part of its long-term vision, articulated in 1980, which declared the goal of becoming a company that "contributes to life and health around the world." In the words of Jun-ichi Koumegawa, the step was taken by the firm as part of a natural progression because of Kirin's accumulated fermentation, biochemical, and engineering expertise. Furthermore, in Jun Kojima's view, the opportunity arose at an auspicious moment, when genetic engineering was just beginning. He commented, "Japan was not a global player, so we were aware that, in order to compete with existing pharmaceutical companies, it was necessary to use new technology."

Once the decision to diversify was made, the next questions that occupied Kirin concerned implementation: What entry strategy should it use? What target should be chosen? How would it develop the necessary competences? Akihiro Shimosaka, of Kirin's pharmaceutical division, recalled that three entry strategies were proposed: to procure an embryonic product to develop by themselves, to undertake research and discovery, or to acquire a company. The company chose R&D, but then had to decide what the target would be.

## 8.4.2 Early Efforts with Erythropoietin

Kirin's initial target was interferon, an antiviral protein produced in the body in response to infection by viruses, which was just becoming known as a promising anticancer agent. But interferon was a popular choice for other big companies, including Toray and Sumitomo Chemical, which had already decided to pursue its development. Kirin therefore selected a niche segment.

Kirin's decision to play on a less crowded therapeutic field led it to explore opportunities in nephrology, the treatment of kidney disease. It focused on developing a genetically engineered growth factor to replace erythropoietin (EPO), a naturally produced protein hormone that acts on stem cells in bone marrow to stimulate the production of red blood cells. According to a report in the US journal *Science*, Kirin's researchers "were intrigued by the prospect of treating anemia in patients undergoing dialysis—patients whose failed kidneys couldn't make the hormone on their own" (Kinoshita 1993, p. 596).

Kirin's researchers began studying how to isolate the human gene that produces EPO, clone it into cells, and mass-produce those cells, using a process that could be likened to an "extension" of fermentation technology. They soon encountered difficulties, though, because the gap between their expertise and that required to produce a purified version of EPO needed for research was too great.

### 8.4.3 Importance of Tacit Knowledge

In deciding to "focus on kidney disease" and in trying to "clone or to identify EPO from the human body," Kirin initially attempted to replicate the published results of Takaji Miyake, of Kumamoto University, who had first succeeded in producing human erythropoietin with colleagues at the University of Chicago in 1977.[3] But this proved impossible for two reasons. First, while the results of a project are usually unambiguous, the ways in which they are obtained are usually not disclosed in detail in scientific publications. Scientists are often prone to secrecy, and seldom does a research paper reveal all that is needed to replicate an experiment (Collins 1982). Second, the scientific process involves a degree of technical know-how and implicit knowledge that is difficult to convey in a paper.[4]

The purification of erythropoietin described by Miyake and his colleagues involved a seven-step procedure, which included ion exchange chromatography, ethanol precipitation, gel filtration, and adsorption chromatography. Thus, although Kirin had recognized a "productive opportunity" (Penrose 1959, pp. 31–32) and was willing to act upon it, the company faced impediments that restricted its ability to respond to that opportunity. To pursue EPO development, specific scientific knowledge and skills were required.

Kirin needed to ascertain whether it should accumulate the knowledge and skills it required via in-house research, or whether it should rely on external sources of knowledge. Accepting the latter, however, would have meant confronting a conundrum or "innovation dilemma": in order to assimilate and utilize complex knowledge required for innovation, a firm must already possess some underlying prior knowledge. This is a firm's "absorptive capacity," defined as "the ability of a firm to recognize the value of new, external information, assimilate it, and apply it to commercial ends" (Cohen and Levinthal 1990, p. 128). But since some of the knowledge needed is tacit, this is difficult and costly to acquire, if not impossible. These complications may increase a firm's incentive to develop the necessary knowledge internally. On the other hand, Japanese firms have historically been considered particularly effective and rapid users of external technology.

---

[3] Interview with Isao Ishida, 15 Feb. 2002. In 1973, the work of Miyake became known to the famous American biochemist, Professor Eugene Goldwasser, of the University of Chicago, who was searching for the causal agent in blood that signals bone marrow to replace red blood cells. Goldwasser arranged for Miyake to go to the USA under an NIH grant to work with him. As a result, erythropoietin (EPO) was the first hematopoietic growth factor to be identified, in 1977. See Miyake et al. (1977) and Goozner (2004).

[4] Interview with Jun Kojima, 27 May 2002. Kojima confirmed: "In other words, there was a tacit part and we were unable to produce EPO simply in accordance with the papers. We could not easily replicate Dr. Miyake's results."

But how easy was it for Kirin to acquire the necessary expertise? In practice, it transpired that Kirin did both: it developed its in-house capabilities *and* it relied on external sources of knowledge.

## 8.4.4 Scientific Gatekeepers and Academic Collaboration

Kirin needed to accumulate in-house expertise in specific aspects of new biotechnology. This was achieved by three means: recruiting science graduates from the best universities, hiring senior researchers from academic institutes and other firms, and seconding staff to universities to participate in collaborative research projects.

The majority of Kirin's researchers were "recruited directly from universities."[5] Tadashi Sado, general manager of Kirin's pharmaceutical research laboratory, explained: "We were looking for good people from universities, and we employed them after [they had completed their] masters' courses, especially from pharmaceutical and agricultural departments." Their expertise lay in several fields: "chemistry, pharmacology, microbiology, genetics, protein chemistry, and molecular biology."[6] Kirin, like other major firms, recruited talented new hires en masse from leading universities each spring. The laboratories of university professors functioned in effect as information clearing-houses, whereby professors played decisive roles in allocating new graduates among leading firms (Aoki 1988, p. 252; Coleman 1999).

For example, Jun-ichi Koumegawa, general manager of the product development department in Kirin's pharmaceutical division, read microbiology at the University of Tokyo. When he entered Kirin in 1971, it was a decade before the company established its pharmaceutical division. He spent the first 3 years in the company's brewing plant, before transferring to its central research laboratory, where he focused on the fermentation and brewing fields. He later undertook research in urology.

Kirin also hired many people from pharmaceutical and chemical companies, as well as postdoctoral researchers and assistant professors from universities and public research institutes, as a mechanism for breaking routines in R&D and introducing novel ideas (see Nelson and Winter 1982).[7] The practice of recruiting from other firms was unusual, given the lifetime employment system that prevailed in Japan at the time and which had evolved to protect companies' investments in training their employees. Nonetheless, as Akihiro Shimosaka confirmed, "the pharmaceutical business had to be operated completely differently from the beer business," and hence there was the need to recruit experienced people. Some were recruited from the established pharmaceutical companies,

---

[5] Interview with Jun-ichi Koumegawa, 16 Feb. 2000.
[6] Interview with Tadashi Sudo, 1 Mar. 2000.
[7] Interview with Jun-ichi Koumegawa, 16 Feb. 2000.

especially for the toxicology study group, while members of the organic synthesis group came from Tokyo University or Kyoto University.[8]

These key personnel facilitated the translation of scientific knowledge into skills that could be more directly exploited for industrial and commercial objectives, and they performed this role by being connected to an academic or professional network in which knowledge circulates. They can be thought of as the "scientific gatekeepers" who enabled Kirin to develop new competences. Technological gatekeepers have been discussed in the literature (Allen 1971, 1984). They span boundaries, bridging the knowledge gap between two parties, and they can be either part of the organizational structure of producers or else internal to the users of new technologies (Cross and Prusak 2002). In biotechnology, which is based to a large extent on *scientific* knowledge, "scientific gatekeepers" enable "the connections between basic scientific knowledge and possible industrial applications, as well as, more generally, between industry and scientific institutions" (Buratti et al. 1993). Accordingly, despite Japan's reputation at the time for having an inflexible labor market, Kirin recruited such scientific gatekeepers.

One such scientific gatekeeper was Isao Ishida, director of Kirin's pharmaceutical business department and senior manager and team leader of its human antibody project. Ishida had earned his PhD in molecular biology from the University of Tokyo. Prior to joining Kirin, he worked for 8 years at the Tokyo Metropolitan Institute for Neuroscience. He also undertook 2 years' postdoctoral research in molecular immunology on T-cell receptor $\gamma\delta$, under the supervision of Nobel laureate and immunologist Susumu Tonegawa at the Massachusetts Institute of Technology's Center for Cancer Research. Tonegawa was awarded the Nobel Prize in medicine in 1987 for his discovery of the genetic principle for the generation of antibody diversity. Ishida was attracted to immunology, and Tonegawa was very interested in neurobiology. When Ishida returned to Japan in 1990, he joined Kirin and worked in the Central Laboratories for Key Technology (CLKT), which had opened in February 1987 outside Yokohama. The CLKT undertook basic research in biotechnology, genetic engineering, protein engineering, and cell technology. Ishida specialized in chromosome engineering and acquired a reputation for the development of human antibody medicines for patients with immunity deficiencies suffering from cancer or infectious diseases. He had decided to join Kirin instead of a mainstream pharmaceutical company, because it offered the prospect of applying his knowledge to a broader field. As he put it: "In Kirin, my knowledge of molecular biology was diversified to plant science and also medical science. I was doing basic research in all areas for Kirin: beer- and yeast-related, and also pharmaceuticals."[9]

In addition to employing scientific gatekeepers, Kirin cultivated academic links through collaborative research projects with many universities, such as Tokyo,

---

[8] Interview with Akihiro Shimosaka, 15 July 2002.
[9] Interview with Isao Ishida, 15 Feb. 2002.

Kyoto, and Keio Universities.[10] Most of these projects lasted from 1 year to about 5 years.[11] Shimosaka reported that the pharmaceutical division sent its researchers to leading universities, including Tokyo University, the Microbiology Department of which was known for the discovery of anticancer drugs. Researchers were also dispatched to *Bikaken* (the Microbial Chemistry Research Foundation) in Tokyo. Researchers interested in the hematopoietic growth factor were sent to Fumimaro Takaku's laboratory at Tokyo University.[12]

In conclusion, the recruitment of capable science graduates, the connections established by its in-house scientific gatekeepers, and its active participation in projects with academia all facilitated Kirin's transition to the new biotechnology. These were instances of search activities designed to change or replace Kirin's existing behavior patterns, as depicted in the neo-Schumpeterian model.

## 8.5 Serendipity

Another search outcome that facilitated Kirin's transition to new biotechnology was a landmark joint venture that it established in early 1984. Strategic alliances for the acquisition of new competences were prevalent among Japanese firms, which benefited from such knowledge links when commissioning research or establishing licensing agreements (see Badaracco 1991). The alliance in this case was with the new – and still small – US biotechnology firm Amgen.[13] Japan at the time had no start-up biotechnology firms that were comparable to those in the USA (Lynskey 2003, 2004a–d, 2006).

By the end of 1983, Kirin had amassed information on EPO gene cloning and had identified two new American biotechnology firms – Amgen and Genetics Institute – as having the EPO gene as recombinant technology. Amgen had just made a significant breakthrough in its research into the treatment of renal anemia. Fu-Kuen Lin, an Amgen molecular biologist, had succeeded in cloning EPO in

---

[10] Interview with Jun-ichi Koumegawa, 16 Feb. 2000. For example, in its research on transchromosomic mice and human immunoglobulin genes, Kirin worked with Mitsuo Oshimura in the Faculty of Medicine, Tottori University. For its human antibody project, Kirin worked with Kazunori Hanaoka in the Laboratory of Molecular Embryology, Kitasato University. Kirin also collaborated with research institutes, e.g., with Michio Oishi at the Helix DNA Research Institute in Chiba.

[11] Interview with Tadashi Sudo, 1 Mar. 2000.

[12] Interview with Akihiro Shimosaka, 15 July 2002. Takaku was an expert in hematopoietic growth factor and also belonged to the National Hospital Center.

[13] Amgen was founded in April 1980, by venture capitalists Sam Wohlsteadter and William Bowes, with a UCLA molecular biologist, Winston Salser, and about $200,000 in seed money. They persuaded a senior scientific executive, George Rathmann, from Abbott Laboratories, to join the company. In February 1981, they attracted additional capital by selling shares privately for $18.8 million, at the time one of the largest private placements ever for a biotechnology business. Amgen became the largest biotechnology company in the world, with an annual turnover exceeding the entire British biotechnology industry.

October 1983, the first time that any company except Genentech had cloned a human protein. Kirin's scientists read Amgen's December 1983 announcement that it had produced the EPO hormone by splicing the human gene into bacteria, yeast, and mammalian cells. Akihiro Shimosaka recalled, "During the course of our erythropoietin research, we were aware that some competitors were interested in this molecule [EPO]. For example, we knew that Biogen had a contract with Schering-Plough for erythropoietin research. Then we found this news [about Amgen] when it was released in early 1984, in the January issue [of *Experimental Hematology*]."[14]

Collaboration between entrepreneurial, advanced-technology firms and large, capital-rich companies offers "the possibility of reasonably quick market impact and profitability, for it seeks to build on competitive strengths already in place" (Roberts 1980). But Kirin was certainly not the first – or, indeed, the most obvious – choice of partner for Amgen. Fortunately, though, there was serendipity on its side, and the entrepreneurial alertness and opportunity recognition of a Kirin manager proved timely. According to Shimosaka, Kirin had set up a monitoring group to ascertain which companies were doing research in the field, and it learned of Amgen's success in December 1983. Kirin then contacted the small start-up directly, only to discover that Amgen had already been approached by several other companies.[15] It had made a deal with Schering-Plough that excluded the Japanese market; for this market, it had been approached by Toyobo. However, according to Shimosaka, other Kirin managers failed to notice the significance of the report of Amgen's announcement of its research findings. "We were very lucky we could have access to Amgen. We already had the phone number and telex number and we called them directly. Amgen was very small ... fewer than 90 employees. They said they had already been contacted by several companies. This report [about Amgen producing EPO] was ignored by other managers in Kirin. It was found by my wife, ... who reported it to her management in Kirin. But it was not well understood. She told me this information, and I made a few phone calls."[16]

## 8.5.1 Origins of the Alliance with Amgen

Early in February 1984, Dr George B. Rathmann, the president of Amgen, received a telephone call from a Kirin representative who enquired why Rathmann was not answering the numerous telex messages that Kirin had sent him. It

---

[14] Interview with Akihiro Shimosaka, 15 July 2002.

[15] Jun-ichi Koumegawa said, "When we established the agreement with Amgen, it was a very small company; maybe the total number of employees was about 120." Interview with Jun-ichi Koumegawa, 16 Feb. 2000. At the end of 1981, Amgen's staff numbered 42, expanding to 100 in 1982. See Rathmann (1999).

[16] Interview with Akihiro Shimosaka, 15 July 2002. According to Kirzner (1982b, p. 273), "Entrepreneurial profit opportunities exist where people do not know what they do not know, and do not know that they do not know it. The entrepreneurial function is to notice what people have overlooked."

transpired that Kirin had used the wrong telex number, but the caller nevertheless wished to arrange an appointment the following week to discuss licensing rights to EPO. This was an 11th hour appeal, according to Jun Kojima: "At the time, many Japanese companies had already embarked on negotiations with Amgen. If we were any later in entering into negotiations, we would have been too late."[17]

The lead negotiator from Kirin was Dr Shimosaka. He displayed entrepreneurial "alertness" (Kirzner 1982a, b) by recognizing the opportunity that collaboration with Amgen would provide. Shimosaka recalled the first meeting with Amgen in the United States, held in February 1984, at which he explained to Amgen that although Kirin had competences in research, it was not yet able to purify EPO and clone the gene. He pointed out that, although there were several new biotechnology firms such as Amgen that were able to license their technology to other companies, technology in isolation is insufficient, and a technological lead cannot be sustained for too long because of innovations from other firms. Shimosaka suggested to Amgen that the key to the pharmaceutical industry was marketing. With the R&D function alone, a firm may have profits, but not for long. But with the marketing function, a firm can survive. Hence, the question for Amgen was whether it wanted to survive as a pharmaceutical company or purely as a biotechnology venture.[18]

Although Amgen had several potential suitors, many pharmaceutical companies were uninterested in EPO at the time. There were several reasons for this, which seem surprising in retrospect because of the product's subsequent success. First, even after the protein was cloned, there was uncertainty about whether EPO would be efficacious and free of side effects. Second, the economic feasibility of producing an effective dosage at a price that would represent a saving over the blood transfusions that EPO treatment would replace was another uncertainty. Third, EPO was an injectable product, and few pharmaceutical products that were limited to a subcutaneous delivery system had achieved prominent success. Finally, EPO represented a significant change in therapeutic approach, and it was difficult to ascertain a priori the potential size of the market, because there were no competing products at the time.

According to Shimosaka, Amgen's president understood the importance of marketing and the need to grow from being a small biotechnology venture firm. The next question for Amgen was how development expenditures in the United States would be financed. Kirin proposed a joint venture, to be called Kirin–Amgen, in which both parties would have equal rights.[19] This was to be a holding company, which would license to Amgen or to Kirin in their respective territories. It would cover all the development costs in the United States and Japan, and Kirin would fund the company based on estimates for these costs.

The agreement was brokered remarkably quickly, despite some initial hesitation from Tokyo. Unlike most negotiations involving the terms and conditions of international strategic alliances, this deal to commercialize a genetically engineered

---

[17] Interview with Jun Kojima, 27 May 2002.
[18] Interview with Akihiro Shimosaka, 15 July 2002.
[19] Interview with Akihiro Shimosaka, 15 July 2002.

substance for treating kidney disease was struck in just 3 days. This was extra-ordinary, particularly when one considers the longevity of the arrangement (cf. Prevezer and Toker 1996).

Rathmann met Kirin's representatives in Japan in March 1984, when the concept for the partnership was decided. Amgen first suggested, without citing specific figures, an exclusive Japanese license for Kirin in exchange for a front-end payment and a significant royalty. Kirin, however, insisted on more than marketing rights in Japan. The negotiations might have ended there, but Amgen agreed that EPO be developed and marketed in a joint venture. Rathmann acknowledged that Amgen's primary market was the United States, but he conceded that international posture was an important strategy that would be furthered by having Kirin make and market EPO in Japan. A license and its accompanying royalty rate would have assumed something about market size and profit margins. In contrast, the advantage of a joint venture was that risk and return sharing would be self-compensating for unknowns on both the downside and the upside. In a 50–50 joint venture, the partners would share equally in the costs, if it proved to be more expensive than expected to take EPO though clinical trials, and would likewise share the benefits if sales exceeded expectations. Philip Whitcome, director of strategic planning at Amgen, expressed satisfaction with the arrangement, commenting on Kirin's positive attitude during the negotiations.

### 8.5.2 Structure of the Joint Venture

The Kirin–Amgen joint venture was managed by a board comprising three representatives from each company. The post of president and CEO was held by Amgen, and that of chairman was controlled by Kirin. Rathmann served as the first president and CEO of Kirin–Amgen until 1988. The venture was capitalized at $24 million, with a cash infusion of $12 million from Kirin and an investment by Amgen of $4 million, plus proprietary gene-splicing techniques required to manufacture EPO, and valued at $8 million.

The main function of the joint venture was to manage technical exchange and product development between Kirin and Amgen. Since both the partners undertook the R&D themselves in exchange for a fee charged to the joint venture, in practice Kirin–Amgen assumed a largely planning and monitoring role. The principal concern at the outset was whether the manufacturing of EPO from host cells could be refined to the point where it would be economically feasible. It was agreed that Amgen would spend its $4 million contribution on bringing the production method to the point of economic feasibility within 18 months. If this could not be accomplished within the specified resource constraints, Kirin would have the option of taking its $12 million and relinquishing the alliance. Amgen passed this milestone within several months, and the level of feasibility achieved was about 50 times the level of efficiency that existed at the time of the preliminary agreement in spring 1984. The transfer of the methods for producing host cells and for using the cells to manufacture EPO – using roller bottling technology and manufacturing scale-up techniques developed by Kirin – was accomplished in late 1984, and Kirin committed its initial $12 million.

Technology – or, more precisely, "knowledge" – transfer (Lynskey 1999) was accomplished mainly through visits of Kirin representatives to Amgen. When contact between both parties was most extensive, four Kirin researchers at any one time were assigned to Amgen, with some staying as long as 3 years. Much of the exchange of know-how related to the gene-splicing technique used to produce EPO and the treatment of host cells in order to maximize production. Most biotechnology firms at that time were involved in some type of relationship that resulted in technology transfer to Japan.

Originally, Kirin–Amgen owned all the rights to EPO, and a 5% royalty on all sales of EPO by the partners and their licensees went to the joint venture. It was later decided, however, that only dialysis sales in the USA and Japan would deliver royalties to Kirin–Amgen, and that EPO marketed for other indications would not be royalty-bearing.

### 8.5.3 Kirin's Contributions and Manufacturing Scale-Up

In addition to its financial input and skills in mass-cultivation techniques using microorganisms, Kirin made several important contributions to the venture. First, the collaboration during clinical trials brought substantial benefits. Kirin handled all the clinical trials in Japan for EPO (and for the subsequent product, G-CSF), including animal tests.[20] Second, it was important to the process of regulatory approval for the manufacturing techniques to be translatable between the partners. This is because EPO has five isoforms, and it was critical that the partners were able to show regulators that the proportions were standardized for the purpose of evaluating efficacy and side effects. When firms are working to improve the efficiency of a manufacturing process, there may be a failure to record all the knowledge accumulated. That the joint venture was able to prevent loss of codified and tacit knowledge and to meet regulatory standards was the result of the effectiveness of its technology transfer procedures and of Kirin's absorptive capacity.

Kirin also demonstrated entrepreneurial alertness and opportunity recognition when it made an unexpected technical contribution to the design of the partners' manufacturing facilities for EPO. Manufacturing the active ingredient of a compound involves scaling up from the laboratory bench to a commercial level. Amgen had initially wanted to use a manufacturing process in which roller bottles washed nutrients over the living, gene-spliced host cells that produce the EPO protein, but experts contended that it would never be able to scale up roller bottles into a production technology. However, a few Kirin engineers believed that the roller-bottle process could be automated, and, with the help of one of the

---

[20] Kirin's second hematology product, G-CSF (granulocyte colony stimulating factor), was a protein that stimulates the production of neutrophils, the white blood cells used in the creation of antibodies to help prevent bacterial infections.

company's suppliers, they were able to produce such a machine.[21] Development involved physiological and biochemical research on mammalian cells and microorganisms, and adapting the bottle-handling technology utilized in the beer brewing industry to mammalian cell culture. An Amgen employee visited Japan for about a month to learn the specifics of running the automated roller bottle-handling machine, which allowed production to be increased simply by increasing the number of bottles. The automated process was subsequently used at Kirin, Amgen, and more than 70% of the companies worldwide that were granted manufacturing and marketing rights for EPO (see Oda 2001).

### 8.5.4 Outcome of the Joint Venture

In 1989, recombinant EPO was approved, along with the manufacturing process developed by Kirin based on roller-bottle cell culture. Amgen's initial estimate of the worldwide market for EPO was $100 million a year, but this figure was later revised to $350 million (Chase 1984). EPO sales increased sharply on a quarter-to-quarter basis throughout its introductory period. Sales was $97 million in 1989, $276 million in 1990, and $409 million in 1991. Worldwide sales through all licensees were more than $600 million in 1991. EPO became the world's fastest-selling drug in terms of annual sales, with global sales of more than $7.8 billion in 2002. The trade name used by Amgen for marketing the product was Epogen®, while Kirin branded it under the name Espo® in Japan and China.

Several benefits accrued to Kirin as a result of its relationship with Amgen:

- Kirin entered the pharmaceutical market in Japan with two successful products. After abandoning its work on interferon, Kirin initiated development of EPO with Amgen in June 1984 and began clinical trials in May 1985. Kirin commenced marketing Espo (recombinant α-EPO) in Japan on 23 April 1990, and by the end of 1991, sales of EPO in Japan was running at ¥40 billion annually – more than that for interferon. Kirin's second pharmaceutical product, Gran® (recombinant G-CSF), was launched in December 1991 and quickly dominated its category.
- Kirin achieved its stated goal of leveraging technology to become a successful domestic competitor. In 1992, sales of *Espo* and *Gran* were ¥18.6 billion, an increase of 84.5% on 1991. Kirin gained 38% of the EPO market in Japan and 54% of the G-CSF market. Kirin thus drew ahead of its main rival, Chugai Pharmaceutical Company, in the sales of similar products. Although pharmaceutical products accounted for less than 3% of Kirin's 1992 sales of ¥1.64 trillion, this was expected to grow. In the same year, Kirin was ranked the 28th largest company in Japan, in terms of income. The Japanese market for

---

[21] The core engineers were Ken Suzuki, vice president, pharmaceutical research laboratory, Kirin Brewery, Takahashi, Gunma; Hajime Ichihashi, plant manager, pharmaceutical production plant, Kirin Brewery, Takahashi, Gunma; and Atsuo Odagawa, production manager, pharmaceutical production plant, Kirin Brewery, Takahashi, Gunma.

EPO products in 2000 was about ¥110 billion, of which Espo held a 40% share. In the same year, the domestic market for G-CSF products was ¥45 billion, of which Gran had a share of 45%. Espo, accounting for 70% of Kirin's pharmaceutical business, achieved sales of ¥45 billion in 2000.

- Kirin expanded the development and sales of its pharmaceutical products in the Far East – the fastest-growing market for pharmaceutical products. It established a wholly owned subsidiary in Taiwan, and entered into a joint venture in South Korea. In China, Kirin and Amgen agreed to cooperate on sales of EPO and G-CSF.
- Building on its experience with Amgen, Kirin founded the La Jolla Institute for Allergy and Immunology in San Diego in November 1988 and provided the center with several million dollars in research funding annually. This research center was located in a rich biotechnology cluster, close to the University of California at San Diego, the Salk Institute, and the Scripps Research Institute. The institute opened with a staff of around 40–50 Japanese and American scientists. Its first scientific director was Kimishige Ishizaka, an immunologist who had been at Johns Hopkins University in Baltimore, and was known for his discovery of immunoglobulin-E antibodies in 1966. From its location in a US biotechnology cluster, the institute was in a position to provide an exemplar of excellence for Kirin's researchers in Japan.
- Kirin and Amgen augmented their relationship, first with an agreement in 1994 to jointly develop thrombopoietin (TPO); and then with one in 1996 to collaborate in developing a new molecule, novel erythropoiesis-stimulating protein, whose properties in anemia treatment were superior to those of EPO.

## 8.5.5 Key Success Factors

What made the Kirin–Amgen joint venture successful? How did it manage to achieve longevity, facilitate exchange of know-how, and help to build independent businesses, when managerial folklore suggests that many similar alliances are prone to failure (Jones and Shill 1993)? One pharmaceutical analyst commented that Kirin's strategy was unique, with the result that it was the only one among Japanese food and beverage companies that invested in biotechnology to be successful.[22] Although early negotiations owed much to serendipity, hinged on entrepreneurial alertness and persistence, and led to an agreement that was hastily arranged, the outcome was successful for several reasons:

- Kirin was patient and took a long-term view of its investment, despite the fact that it cost $80 million to secure approval from the US Food and Drug Administration for EPO at a time when the joint venture brought in no income. Lowell Sears, senior vice president of Amgen, described the relationship with Kirin as follows: "We talked to just about everybody that moved. ... They

---

[22] Shigero Mishima, Pharmaceuticals Analyst, S. G. Warburg (Japan), quoted in Hamilton (1993a, p. 1; 1993b, p. B3) .

[Kirin] weren't a logical choice – they weren't in pharmaceuticals, they had no background. But they had done their homework. … Of all our corporate partners, Kirin has been the most flexible and the most understanding. If it had been an American company, it wouldn't have worked, because most American companies lack the patience and flexibility."

- Kirin's prime intention was not to harvest valuable research, but to use the joint venture as a platform from which to learn how US biotechnology firms translated research into commercially viable products. Since there were no biotechnology venture firms in Japan at the time (Lynskey 2006), Kirin was unable to learn from a domestic venture. Moreover, despite its market size and the technical expertise of its scientists, Japan generally perceived itself as trailing other nations such as the USA in the commercialization of bio-technology (Science and Technology Agency 1997). Koichiro Aramaki, the head of Kirin's pharmaceutical division, observed that academic research in the United States was more advanced and energetic than scientific study in Japanese universities.

- The complementary resources and contributions of each partner brought synergy to the joint venture. The merits of the alliance were acknowledged by Rathmann, who explained that Kirin provided the funding needed to bring Amgen's product to market. In describing the value of the deal to his company, he pointed out that small biotechnology companies have two goals: to establish their long-term viability as a business and to raise the necessary cash for developing their products over the short term. Few deals were considered as useful in meeting these goals. According to one research analyst, "Japanese companies were strong in antibiotic-screening and fermentation technologies," especially when it came to scaling up to industrial production levels.[23] Kirin–Amgen commenced development of EPO in June 1984 and Kirin started clinical trials in May 1985, an interval which is indicative of Kirin's existing familiarity with the underlying biotechnology. Kirin's complementary resources – such as its manufacturing expertise and distribution presence in Asian markets – helped Amgen increase its revenues from $44 million in 1987 to $1 billion-plus in 1992, an extraordinary rate of 90% a year (Torres 1999). Amgen's Epogen had worldwide sales of $4 billion in 2000. Amgen subse-quently became the world's largest independent biotechnology company. It was also ranked as the 54th largest company in the world in 2002, surpassing several well-known American and European pharmaceutical companies (e.g., Pharmacia, Aventis, Schering-Plough), and Japan's largest pharmaceutical company, Takeda (ranked 110th-largest company in the world).[24]

Kirin maintained this relationship with Amgen, and developed a network of similar ties with other firms that involved licensing and R&D cooperation in several therapeutic fields. By 2005 pharmaceuticals represented Kirin's third

---

[23] Hidemaru Yamaguchi, biotechnology research analyst, Nomura Research Institute, Tokyo, quoted in Dambrot (1992, p. 44).

[24] Amgen's annual turnover exceeded that of the entire British biotechnology industry in 2003. See Financial Times (2002).

business pillar – after alcohol and soft drinks – and accounted for 4% of sales and 13% of its operating income.[25]

## 8.6 Strategy

Rather than grow too quickly or cover widely different therapeutic fields, Kirin chose to strengthen what it saw as its unique technology in specific areas, adopting a so-called smart, focused strategy concentrated on niche areas and specific technology.[26] Isao Ishida, director of Kirin's pharmaceutical business department, emphasized that while the large pharmaceutical companies had grown larger through successive bouts of mergers and acquisitions during the 1990s (see Schweizer and zu Knyphausen-Aufsess in this volume), they also needed a blockbuster drug. He suggested that, although Kirin's pharmaceutical business did not need a blockbuster, as a small company with only 1,000 employees, it did need a special technology to develop its own products. Thus, Kirin engaged in research that the giant companies avoided because it needed only one core technology.[27] This sentiment was echoed by Ken Yamazumi, Kirin's director of corporate planning for pharmaceuticals, who described the company's goal as "surviving in a niche as a maker with special characteristics."

### 8.6.1 Targeting Niche Therapeutic Fields

Kirin targeted four therapeutic areas: hematology, oncology, nephrology, and allergy and immunology. Looking merely at the first of these fields, Kirin's joint venture with Amgen led early-on to the development of Espo (EPO) and Gran (G-CSF), both of which involved gene-splicing techniques using recombinant DNA technology.

Also in hematology, Kirin researchers pioneered the cloning of TPO, a protein hormone that stimulates the production of platelets in the blood. It is used in the treatment of thrombocytopenia, which occurs as a complication of chemotherapy in cancer treatment. In June 1994, Kirin was one of four companies to announce that they had independently discovered MGDF (megakaryocyte growth and development factor), also called platelet growth factor or thrombopoietin, and had applied for patents. Amgen published its findings in the US journal *Cell*, on 1 July 1994. Its rivals, Genentech and ZymoGenetics, published their findings in the British journal *Nature*, on 16 June 1994, and another US company, Immunex, also described its work on the compound.

---

[25] In 2005, Kirin's pharmaceutical sales increased 7.8% to ¥67.6 billion and operating income increased 17.3% to ¥14.2 billion, representing 13% of a record consolidated operating income of ¥111.7 billion.

[26] Interview with Jun-ichi Koumegawa, 16 Feb. 2000.

[27] Interview with Isao Ishida, 15 Feb. 2002.

Although the existence of TPO had been suspected for 30 years, no one had previously been able to detect it, because it is an extremely rare substance. Amgen and Genentech had used a chemical receptor to help purify the hormone from blood. ZymoGenetics adopted the converse technique, called expression cloning, which involved looking for the activity and then trying to isolate the material, rather than attempting to isolate the material and then seeing whether it would cause the activity (Metcalf 1994). Kirin, to everyone's astonishment, had independently isolated the platelet-stimulating protein by chemical purification through a process of ever more refinement and purification of blood to isolate the platelet growth factor and determine whether it caused the activity.

Kirin and Amgen immediately decided to expand their existing joint venture to develop and market the product, as they had done with the earlier compounds, EPO and G-CSF. The agreement was negotiated quickly: "In a single morning, we had a deal," Kevin Sharer, Amgen's president remarked, while Gordon Binder, Amgen's CEO, referred to Kirin as "an excellent partner."

Not only was this the third Kirin–Amgen development project to be settled quickly, but it was also seen as an appropriate match, since the collaboration was able to wield two patents as weapons in any legal wrangling that might have ensued. Additionally, the experience of Kirin–Amgen in guiding EPO and G-CSF through development and clinical trials to market launch was seen as an indication of prospects for the successful commercialization of TPO.

In August 1995, Kirin and Amgen acquired from ZymoGenetics and its parent, Novo Nordisk (Denmark), the rights to their TPO, thereby eliminating a competitor. These licensing rights brought Kirin–Amgen useful technology, strengthened its patent position, and complemented the development of MGDF, the novel platelet growth factor that Amgen and Kirin were codeveloping. The arrangement was also seen as a swift means to commercialization. Novo Nordisk's chief scientific officer remarked that teaming up with Amgen and Kirin, both of which had experience in oncology, would be "the best and fastest way to develop and get TPO on the market and to ensure a strong competitive position." The arrangement was seen also as a logical choice for Kirin, as the company had established good relations with doctors specializing in diseases caused by blood problems.

### 8.6.2 Cell Therapy and Stem Cell Research

Besides its research activities in four main therapeutic areas (hematology, oncology, nephrology, and allergy and immunology), Kirin also conducted research into stem cells and cell therapy. This involved attempts to isolate blood cells that attack cancer cells in order to reproduce them in large quantity for injection into patients. There were great expectations for this research. According to one Kirin official, if through this method they could replace cancer-control agents as a means to treat cancer, they could expect the market to rise to ¥100 billion a year in Japan alone. Katsuhiko Asano, president of Kirin's pharmaceutical division, predicted that these technologies "will change the business structure of pharmaceutical companies."

Kirin's research in these fields derived from its work in hematology and immunology, particularly EPO and G-CSF, as well as its hemotopoietic growth factors and other compounds that could potentiate an immune response. The emphasis, however, was on cell therapy instead of drug therapy, although the techniques could be used to develop new drugs. Yasunori Yamaguchi, a scientist in Kirin, explained the firm's motivation for entering the field of cell therapy: "ost medical products just target one molecule or one cell type, but the cell itself can do a lot to treat patients. This is a new therapy, especially for refractory diseases such as cancers, which cannot be cured by drug therapy." Yamaguchi pointed out that the field was strategically related to the firm's established business in hematology.[28]

Kirin's researchers developed considerable knowledge of blood cell biology and identified two types of cell on which to focus their research activities: the CD34 stem cell and the dendritic cell for cancer immunotherapy. In the case of the latter, they collaborated with Rockefeller University in New York.[29] Having ascertained that cell therapy held promise in the treatment of cancer, chronic infectious diseases, and autoimmune diseases, Kirin established alliances in December 1998 with two pioneers in the field: AmCell, a biotechnology venture firm based in Cologne, Germany, to work on CD34 stem-cell research; and Dendreon, a biotechnology firm based in Seattle, to collaborate in dendritic cells research. Prospects for the development of dendritic cell-based immunotherapies appeared promising.[30] Similarly, the CEO of Dendreon observed that his firm was looking forward to developing a new class of dendritic-cell-based therapeutics with Kirin.

These relationships were subsequently cemented, and clinical trials were conducted. The alliance with Dendreon, for example, evolved from a collaborative licensing agreement into a joint research and clinical development agreement that also culminated in the regulatory support needed to gain marketing approval. Thus, it took in a range of different functions in the business value chain.

## 8.6.3 Monoclonal Antibodies and the Transgenic Mouse

Another niche area in which Kirin pursued research was human monoclonal antibodies. Although monoclonal antibodies had the potential of being highly targeted drugs – and hence had been dubbed "magic bullets" – until the late 1990s, they had not delivered the benefits that their discovery promised. This was

---

[28] Interview with Yasunori Yamaguchi, 1 Mar. 2000.

[29] For example, Yasunori Yamaguchi spent 2 years, from 1992 to 1994, doing postdoctoral research with Dr Ralph Steinmann, the discoverer of dendritic cells, at Rockefeller University.

[30] Koichiro Aramaki, president, Kirin Pharmaceutical Division, quoted in "Dendreon and Kirin to Develop and Commercialize Dendritic Cell Therapies," *Business Wire*, 10 Dec. 1998.

because the antibodies, which were manufactured in mice, provoked an immune response in humans that made them unusable as pharmaceuticals. The race to rectify this early defect generated ferocious competition among biotechnology firms.

A number of researchers responded to the early setbacks with mouse antibodies by creating "transgenic mice." These produced antibodies that were mostly human, but they still retained a rodent component. Ideally, however, a transgenic mouse bearing genes for an entire human antibody would produce a fully human monoclonal. The antibody-making cell could then be isolated to generate an unlimited supply of antibodies.

Kirin was a surprisingly early entrant into this new field. In 1992, it initiated a project to produce a transgenic mouse containing human immunoglobulin. The decision to do so, and the resulting technological breakthrough achieved, again owed much to serendipity. The idea to enter this field stemmed from the postdoctoral research of Isao Ishida on transgenic mice in Susumu Tonegawa's laboratory at MIT in 1989. Ishida described how he started the project in 1992 while conducting unrelated research on GMOs at the Central Laboratories for Key Technology.[31]

Ishida's research was spurred by entrepreneurial alertness and opportunity recognition. He was aware of developments at two US biotechnology firms – GenPharm (later called Medarex) and Cell Genesys (later called Abgenix) – and of the problems they were encountering in producing strains of mice that had been genetically altered to produce human disease-fighting antibodies. Both firms published papers in 1994 on their attempts to create a human antibody mouse and announced their intention to commercialize such mice. They were ahead of Kirin, but were using conventional transgenic technology in an effort to insert the human antibody into a mouse. Ishida read the results in *Nature* and *Nature Genetics* and realized that, although Kirin's competitors were making progress, their technology had limitations. "They couldn't put the whole antibody gene into the mouse because of the size limitation for the transgenesis. They could only produce antibodies that retained some of the properties of the mouse."[32]

Ishida realized that it was necessary to come up with a way to put the whole human immunoglobulin gene into a mouse, and started to develop human chromosome technology. He recognized that a mouse producing fully human antibodies would be a huge advance, because it would hasten the development of new medicines and reduce the possibility of a patient's immune system rejecting the drugs, which was possible with part-mice antibodies. Drugs based on human antibodies would prove more effective than laboratory-developed drugs, because they harness the body's naturally powerful antibodies to fight disease.

Ishida had only one colleague working with him on the project at the time, and he was also involved in plant biology GMO research. Thus, he and his partner devoted just half of their time to the mouse project.[33] They worked to overcome

---

[31] Interview with Isao Ishida, 15 Feb. 2002.
[32] Interview with Isao Ishida, 18 Sept. 2001.
[33] Interview with Isao Ishida, 15 Feb. 2002.

several technical challenges: inactivating the key genes the mouse uses to produce its own antibodies and then inserting human genes. They could only hope that the transplanted human antibody genes, which differ from those of the mouse, would succeed in initiating the maturation cycle that leads to antibodies capable of binding tightly enough to antigens to prove effective.

In recounting his experiments, Ishida said that whereas GenPharm and Cell Genesys had to clone the whole chromosome into the plasmid or vector, a difficult and time-consuming task, he simply selected the human chromosome and put it into the mouse. He did not expect this to work, because the mouse's cell would then have one extra chromosome, which might have led to chromosome abnormality, similar to Down's syndrome in humans. Ishida also pointed out that he had taken the unconventional approach of picking the chromosome from human-derived skin fibroblasts. Since the skin does not normally express antibodies, the chromosome, or antibody locus, was transcriptionally silent. When this chromosome was put into the mouse, the mouse accepted it and there were no abnormalities. The result was a breakthrough. Although there was no guarantee that the differences between mouse and human genes would not have severe consequences, Ishida was prepared to try. The research worked remarkably well, and he succeeded in creating for the first time ever a mouse that produced fully human antibodies with high affinities for a target.

Kirin's TransChromosome Mouse (TC Mouse) was a genetically engineered mouse containing the full complement of human genes for producing antibodies.[34] That is, the mouse genes relating to antibodies were functionally replaced by the entire human chromosomal loci responsible for making human antibodies. Ishida published his results in *Nature Genetics* in 1997 and in subsequent papers (e.g. Tomizuka et al. 1997). The news was also reported in the media, including the *New York Times* and the *Washington Post*. NHK (Japan Broadcasting Corporation) also reported the event in a broadcast. This experimental animal was recognized as "a valuable means of gaining insight into in vivo functions of human genes, for studying human genetic disorders and for developing new ways of making antibodies."[35]

Both of the pioneering US biotechnology firms – Medarex and Abgenix – contacted Kirin after the innovation became known. As a result, Kirin entered into an alliance with Medarex in January 2000 to commercialize technology for creating fully human monoclonal antibodies. This alliance promised synergy by combining complementary assets. Medarex's HuMAb-Mouse technology had strong patent protection in the important US market, but it was incomplete, and the firm was in need of funding. Kirin had the technological competence to improve on the Medarex mouse and could provide the necessary funds. Kirin

---

[34] Whereas the existing technology at the time allowed scientists to insert about 0.5–2 million base pairs of DNA into cells and into mice, the chromosome that Ishida and colleagues at Kirin could insert represented about 20 million base pairs of DNA.

[35] Roger Reeves, associate professor of physiology, Center for Medical Genetics, Johns Hopkins University School of Medicine, Baltimore, USA, on *Talk of the Nation*, National Public Radio (6 June 1997).

invested $12 million in the alliance and obtained a US patent. The alliance also complemented Kirin's patents covering transchromosome technology in Japan and the USA. According to Kazuma Tomizuka of Kirin, "Medarex's patent application described the original concept of the human antibody from a mouse, but Kirin's patent covered a mouse containing the whole immunoglobulin locus. Thus the two companies complemented each other in this field."[36] More broadly, the business benefits of the alliance were recognized by both partners. Donald Drakeman, the CEO and president of Medarex, stated, "We are very pleased to be forming a global alliance with a strong Asian partner like Kirin." Another Medarex executive, Michael Appelbaum, announced, "This alliance gives Medarex a broad platform on which we can provide human antibodies to our partners." Koichiro Aramaki, the president of Kirin's pharmaceutical division, remarked, "We look forward to working with Medarex to bring the HuMAb and TC mice to pharmaceutical and biotechnology companies around the world." Drakeman summed up the benefits of the alliance in this way: "Kirin and Medarex together have the world's most advanced genetically engineered tools for drug development. They [Kirin] have a mouse that has a human chromosome in it that allows those mice to make completely human antibodies, any kind of antibody you'd want to make. … We can help pharmaceutical companies and biotech companies around the world develop new drugs and really participate in the revolution in medicine that's taking place right now."

Kirin and Medarex combined their technologies to create a new crossbred mouse, the Kirin–Medarex Mouse (KM Mouse), which retained the capability to produce all human-antibody isotypes with a robust immune response previously unseen in any human-antibody-producing mouse system. This was the world's most productive mouse in the creation of human antibodies. To support its antibody pharmaceutical operations, Kirin also committed itself to the full-scale production of proteins that are used for the target antibodies. By 2001, the KM Mouse had been supplied to 15 countries across the world to help develop novel therapeutic products for the treatment of cancer, heart disease, infectious diseases, autoimmune disease, and other serious conditions.

## 8.7 Conclusions

In the history of Kirin's endeavors to develop new competences in bio-pharmaceuticals, one occasionally glimpses the entrepreneur, a figure who, curiously, is often absent from the literature on large firms. Perhaps this absence is not surprising. In his later work, Schumpeter (1942, p. 133) lamented the demise of the entrepreneur in the large corporation as innovation became "depersonalized and automatized." This trend was carried over into the neo-Schumpeterian approach to entrepreneurship, to be replaced by organizational routines and search. Later treatments of innovation, such as knowledge creation, also have little to say about

---

[36] Interview with Kazuma Tomizuka, 1 Mar. 2000.

entrepreneurship. For example, Nonaka and Takeuchi (1995, pp. 135–140) mention it only briefly in their discussion of "bottom-up" management in a large firm.

This omission may be due to the difficulty of locating the entrepreneur in the labyrinth of the large, diversified firm. When Schumpeter (1934) published his early treatise on economic development, there were many solo entrepreneurs (as there still are today), but where is the entrepreneur in the large company? Some suggest that the locus of entrepreneurship resides in the marketing department because of its focus on new products and their market potential (e.g. Murray 1981). Although this proposition appears reasonable, because marketing clearly necessitates the creation of "new combinations," can one not say the same of R&D, for example? It may be misleading, then, to state categorically that entrepreneurship resides in just one function. In principle, Kirznerian entrepreneurial alertness could emerge from a variety of functions and levels in a firm.

A more robust, if subtle, response is provided by the notion of "diffused entrepreneurship," which was coined by the business historian B. W. E. Alford and subsequently developed by others (see Cole 1959; Alford 1976; Minkes and Foxall 1980; Minkes 1987). This posits that although a firm may be led by one (or several) dominant individual(s) – some of whom may exhibit entrepreneurial alertness, too – entrepreneurship is commonly dispersed throughout a modern business, and may be found in all major functional areas. Indeed, there is no unequivocal evidence to suggest that the marketing department is the sole location of such activity (Foxall and Minkes 1996). Clearly, this was the case in Kirin, where entrepreneurship – characterized by "new combinations," or innovation – was evident in the licensing department, in manufacturing, and in a research laboratory.

Kirin's diversification into biopharmaceuticals in the early 1980s was a consequence of opportunity recognition by a senior executive, at a time when many of the established pharmaceutical companies in Japan had yet to adopt the techniques of new biotechnology. It was acted upon by Kirin's board of directors, in whom one might expect the entrepreneurial function to reside. However, Kirin's subsequent development of competences relied to some extent on serendipity and instances of entrepreneurship throughout the firm. This was exemplified by the chance relaying of apparently inconsequential information by a Kirin employee and the realization of its significance by a licensing manager, Akihiro Shimosaka. The entrepreneurial alertness and persistence of Shimosaka ensured appropriate recognition of a scientific advance by Amgen and the opportunity that an alliance with the US firm would afford. Similarly, in manufacturing, several engineers recognized an opportunity to improve production of EPO by a roller-bottle process, which benefited the Kirin–Amgen joint venture. Finally, the entrepreneurial alertness of a scientific gatekeeper, Isao Ishida, to external developments in transgenic technology prompted his research – stemming from his postdoctoral work in the USA – and led him to chance upon a scientific breakthrough in antibodies.

In conclusion, the specific case of Kirin's biopharmaceutical history has some general implications. In his early work, Schumpeter (1934) categorically –

contradicting the view of Marshall (1930) – distinguished between the notion of the "entrepreneur" and the "manager." Certainly, it is possible to do this at the conceptual level: management, conceived of as an efficient administration in the sense of Weberian bureaucracy, is distinguishable from the idea of entrepreneurial alertness to opportunities as yet unforeseen by others.[37] However, perhaps this conceptual distinction misses an important point, especially for large, innovative companies. The solution is to combine the two, so that entrepreneurial attitude is seen as suffused throughout the entire organization of the firm. If this is the case, then one should perhaps reconsider the early Schumpeterian distinction between the entrepreneur and the manager – and indeed his later exclusion of the entrepreneur in large firms – and see them as coalescing in the figure of the "entrepreneurial manager" (Minkes 1987). The existence of diffused entrepreneurship and the presence of the entrepreneurial manager in various functions – for example, the "entrepreneurial scientist" in R&D or the "entrepreneurial engineer" in production – are likely to ensure that emerging opportunities are recognized and acted upon. In addition, the case illustrates that serendipity often plays a crucial role in innovation.[38]

# References

Alford BWE (1976) The Chandler thesis: Some general observations. In: Hannah L (ed), Management strategy and business development. Macmillan, London

Allen T (1971) Communications, technology transfer, and the role of technical gatekeepers. R&D Management 1: 14–21

Allen T (1984) Managing the flow of technology: Technology transfer and the dissemination of technological information within the R&D organization. MIT Press, Cambridge, MA

---

[37] Weber (1947) saw the "rational-legal" type of organization, or "bureaucracy" as the dominant institution of modern society, and described it as being like a machine.

[38] A version of this paper, entitled "The Locus of Corporate Entrepreneurship: Kirin Brewery's Diversification into Biopharmaceuticals," appeared in Business History Review 80(4): 689–723, published by Harvard Business School. This chapter draws on interviews with Dr Isao Ishida, director of the Pharmaceutical Business Department and senior manager and team leader of the Human Antibody Project, Kirin Brewery Company Limited, Tokyo; Jun Kojima, manager of the General Affairs Department, Pharmaceutical Division, Kirin Brewery Company Limited, Tokyo; Jun-ichi Koumegawa, general manager of the Product Development Department, Pharmaceutical Division, Kirin Brewery Company Limited, Tokyo; Dr Akihiro Shimosaka, vice president of the Licensing Department, Pharmaceutical Division, Kirin Brewery Company Limited, Tokyo; Dr Tadashi Sudo, general manager of the Pharmaceutical Research Laboratory, Kirin Brewery Company Limited, Takahashi, Gunma; Dr Kazuma Tomizuka, manager of the Human Antibody Business Development Group, Product Development Department, Pharmaceutical Division, Kirin Brewery Company Limited, Takahashi, Gunma; Dr Yasunori Yamaguchi, senior scientist and manager of the Pharmaceutical Research Laboratory, Kirin Brewery Company Limited, Takahashi, Gunma.

Aoki M (1988) Information, incentives, and bargaining in the Japanese economy. Cambridge University Press, Cambridge

Badaracco J (1991) The knowledge link: How firms compete through strategic alliances. Harvard Business School Press, Boston, MA

Bevan P, Ryder H, Shaw I (1995) Identifying small-molecule lead compounds: The screening approach to drug discovery. Trends in Biotechnology 13(3): 115–121

Buratti N, Gambardella A, Orsenigo L (1993) Scientific gatekeepers and industrial development in biotechnology. Biotechnology Review 1 – The management and economic potential of biotechnology (A special publication of the International Journal of Technology Management): 59–75

Chase M (1984, 14 May) Amgen, Japan Brewery form venture to make synthetic hormone. The Wall Street Journal, Eastern Edition, 1

Cohen WM, Levinthal DA (1990) Absorptive capacity: A new perspective on learning and innovation Administrative Science Quarterly 35: 128–152

Cole AH (1959) Business enterprise in its social setting. Harvard University Press, Cambridge, MA

Coleman S (1999) Japanese science: View from the inside. Routledge, London

Collins HM (1982) Tacit knowledge and scientific networks. In: Barnes B, Edge D (eds), Science in context. MIT Press, Cambridge, MA

Cross R, Prusak L (2002) The people who make organizations go – or stop. Harvard Business Review 80(6): 104 112

Dambrot S (1992, 8 April) Strength in fine chemicals: Japan moves toward international biotech market. Chemical Week

Dibner MD (1985, 20 September) Biotechnology in pharmaceuticals: The Japanese challenge. Science: 1231

Dibner MD, White RS (1989) Biotechnology in Japan. McGraw-Hill, New York

Financial Times (2002, 10 May) Financial Times Global 500 List of the world's largest companies

Foxall GR, Minkes AL (1996) Beyond marketing: The diffusion of entrepreneurship in the modern corporation. Journal of Strategic Marketing 4(2): 71–93

Fransman M, Tanaka S (1995a) Government, globalisation, and universities in Japanese biotechnology. Research Policy 24: 13–49

Fransman M, Tanaka S (1995b) The strengths and weaknesses of the Japanese innovation system in biotechnology. In: Fransman M, Juune G, Roobeck A (eds), The biotechnology revolution? Blackwell, Oxford

Friedman M (1953) Essays in positive economics. University of Chicago Press, Chicago

Galambos L, Sturchio JL (1998) Pharmaceutical firms and the transition to biotechnology: A study in strategic innovation. Business History Review 72: 250–278

Goozner M (2004) The $800 million pill: The truth behind the cost of new drugs. University of California Press, Berkeley

Hamilton DP (1993a, 14 January) Suds and drugs: Japan's Kirin brews success in biotechnology venture. The Asian Wall Street Journal, p. 1

Hamilton DP (1993b, 25 January) Kirin Brewery's plunge into biotechnology pays off – Ten years later, Japan concern's sales of two top drugs surpass rivals. The Wall Street Journal, p. B3

Henderson R, Orsenigo L, Pisano GP (1999) The pharmaceutical industry and the revolution in molecular biology: Interactions among scientific, institutional, and organizational change. In: Mowery DC, Nelson RR (eds), Sources of industrial leadership: Studies of seven industries. Cambridge University Press, Cambridge, pp. 267–311

Higgins KT (2001) How the top firms stack up. Food Engineering 73(10): 40–48

Higgins KT (2002) The world's top 100 food and beverage companies. Food Engineering 74(10): 32–43

Inaba Y (1987, June) Multinationals take to the offensive. Tokyo Business Today, p. 50

Jones KK, Shill WE (1993) Japan: Allying for advantage. In: Bleeke J, Ernst D (eds), Collaborating to compete: Using strategic alliances and acquisitions in the global marketplace. Wiley, New York, pp. 115–144

Kinoshita J (1993, 29 January) Is Japan a boon or a burden to U.S. industry's leadership? (Biotechnology Industry). Science, p. 596

Kirzner IM (1982a) Uncertainty, discovery, and human action: A study of the entrepreneurial profile in the Misesian system. In: Kirzner IM (ed), Method, process and Austrian economics: Essays in honour of Ludwig von Mises. L D. C. Heath, Lexington, MA

Kirzner IM (1982b) The theory of entrepreneurship in economic growth. In: Kent CA, Sexton DL, Vesper KH (eds), Encyclopedia of entrepreneurship. Prentice-Hall, Englewood Cliffs, NJ

Kirzner IM (1985) Discovery and the capitalist process. University of Chicago Press, Chicago

Livesay HC (1977) Entrepreneurial persistence through the bureaucratic age. Business History Review 51: 415–443

Lynskey MJ (1999) The transfer of resources and competencies for developing technological capabilities: The case of Fujitsu-ICL. Technology Analysis and Strategic Management 11(3): 317–336

Lynskey MJ (2002) Introduction. In: Lynskey MJ, Yonekura S (eds), Entrepreneurship and organization: The role of the entrepreneur in organizational innovation. Oxford University Press, Oxford, pp. 1–57

Lynskey MJ (2003) A profile of biotechnology and information technology venture firms in Japan: Firm-level and managerial characteristics. International Journal of Biotechnology 5(2): 155–185

Lynskey MJ (2004a) The commercialisation of biotechnology in Japan: Bio-ventures as a mechanism of knowledge transfer from universities. International Journal of Biotechnology 6(2/3): 105–124

Lynskey MJ (2004b) Determinants of innovative activity in Japanese technology-based start-up firms. International Small Business Journal 22: 159–196

Lynskey MJ (2004c) Bioentrepreneurship in Japan: Institutional transformation and the growth of bioventures. Journal of Commercial Biotechnology 11: 9–37

Lynskey MJ (2004d) Knowledge, finance and human capital: The role of social institutional variables on entrepreneurship in Japan. Industry and Innovation 11: 373–405

Lynskey MJ (2006) Transformative technology and institutional transformation: Coevolution of biotechnology venture firms and the institutional framework in Japan. Research Policy 35: 1389–1422

Marshall A (1930) Principles of economics. Macmillan, London. (First published in 1890)

McKelvey M (1996) Evolutionary innovations: The business of biotechnology. Oxford University Press, Oxford

Metcalf D (1994) Thrombopoietin – at last. Nature 369 (6481): 519–520

Minkes AL (1987) The entrepreneurial manager: Decisions, goals and business ideas. Penguin, Harmondsworth, Middlesex

Minkes AL, Foxall GR (1980) Entrepreneurship, strategy, and organization: Individual and organization in the behavior of the firm. Strategic Management Journal 1(4): 295–301

Miyake T, Kung CK-H, Goldwasser E (1977) Purification of human erythropoietin. Journal of Biological Chemistry 252(15): 5558–5564

Miyata M (ed) (1987) Nikkei Baioteku Nenkan 87/88 [Nikkei Biotechnology Annual Review 87/88]. Nikkei, Tokyo. (In Japanese)

Miyata M (1994) Toward a new era in biotechnology. Science and Technology in Japan 50: 10–13

Murray JA (1981) Marketing is home for the entrepreneurial process. Industrial Marketing Management 10(2): 93–99

Nakajo T, Kono T (1989) Success through culture change in a Japanese brewery. Long Range Planning 22(6): 29–37

Nelson RR, Winter SG (1977) In search of a useful theory of innovation. Research Policy 6(1): 36–77

Nelson RR, Winter SG (1982) An evolutionary theory of economic change. Harvard University Press, Cambridge, MA

Nonaka I, Takeuchi H (1995) The knowledge-creating company. Oxford University Press, New York

Oda S (2001, September) Zouketsu Horumon Seizai de 'Baioiyaku no Kirin' e [Following Hematosis Hormone products: A shift towards Kirin Biopharmaceuticals]. Nikkei Biotechnology and Business: 106–109 (in Japanese)

Office of International Affairs (OIA) (1992) U.S. Japan technology linkages in biotechnology: Challenges for the 1990s. U.S. Government Printing Office, Washington, DC

Office of Technology Assessment (OTA) (1984) Commercial biotechnology: An international assessment. U.S. Government Printing Office, Washington, DC

Okazaki T (2001) The government–firm relationship in postwar Japan: The success and failure of bureau pluralism. In: Stiglitz JE, Yusuf S (eds), Rethinking the East Asian miracle. Oxford University Press, Oxford, pp. 323–342

Organisation for Economic Co-operation and Development (OECD) (1986) The industrial policy in Japan. In: McCraw TK (ed), America versus Japan: A comparative study of business–government relations. Harvard Business School Press, Boston, MA

Penrose ET (1959) The theory of the growth of the firm. Basil Blackwell, Oxford

Powell WW, Koput KW, Smith-Doerr L (1996) Interorganizational collaboration and the locus of innovation: Networks of learning in the biotechnology. Administrative Science Quarterly 41(1): 116–145

Prevezer M, Toker S (1996) The degree of integration in strategic alliances in biotechnology. Technology Analysis and Strategic Management 8(2): 117–133

Rathmann GB (1999) Biotechnology startups. In: Moses V, Cape RE, Springham DG (eds), Biotechnology: The science and the business. Harwood Academic, Amsterdam, pp. 47–58

Roberts EB (1980) New ventures for corporate growth. Harvard Business Review 58(4): 134–142

Santarelli E, Pesciarelli E (1990) The emergence of a vision: The development of Schumpeter's theory of entrepreneurship. History of Political Economy 22. 677–696

Schumpeter JA (1912) Theorie der Wirtschaftlichen Entwicklung. Denckner & Humblot, Leipzig

Schumpeter JA (1934) The theory of economic development. Harvard University Press, Cambridge, MA. (Originally published in 1912 as Theorie der Wirtschaftlichen Entwicklung. Denckner & Humblot, Leipzig)

Schumpeter JA (1942). Capitalism, socialism and democracy. Harper and Row, New York

Schweizer D, zu Knyphausen-Aufsess D (2008) Mergers and Acquisitions in the Bio-technology Industry. In: Patzelt H, Brenner T (eds), Handbook of Bioentrepreneurship. Springer, New York, pp. 133–148

Science and Technology Agency (STA) (1997) White paper on science and technology. STA, Tokyo

Stevenson HH, Jarillo JC (1990) A paradigm of entrepreneurship: Entrepreneurial management. Strategic Management Journal 11: 17–27

Tanaka M (1991) Government policy and biotechnology in Japan: The pattern and impact of rivalry among ministries. In: Wilks S, Wright E (eds), The promotion and regulation of industry in Japan. Palgrave Macmillan, London

Tomizuka K, Yoshida H, Uejima H, Kugoh H, Sato K, Ohguma A, Hayasaka M, Hanaoka K, Oshimura M, Ishida I (1997) Functional expression and germline transmission of a human chromosome fragment in chimeaeric mice. Nature Genetics 16: 133–143

Torres A (1999) Unlocking the value of intellectual assets. McKinsey Quarterly 4: 28–37

Weber M (1947) The theory of social and economic organization. Oxford University Press, Oxford

# 9 A Survey Review of University Biotechnology and Entrepreneurship Commercialization

David B. Audretsch[1], T. Taylor Aldridge[1], and Marcus Perry[2]

[1]Max Planck Institute of Economics, Kahlaische Str. 10, 07745 Jena, Germany
[2]School of Public and Environmental Affairs, Indiana University, Bloomington, IL, USA

It is a wonder that Columbus discovered America. It would have been an even greater wonder had America never been discovered.

Mark Twain

## 9.1 Introduction

Interest in entrepreneurship as a key force in economics and management has recently exploded, and management and economics scholars have responded with an explosion of academic research. Entrepreneurship may play an even more important role in the science-based knowledge industries driving economic growth and competitiveness in a globalized economy, such as biotechnology. However, the exact role of entrepreneurship in industries such as biotechnology has generally eluded the analytical lens of scholars. As Michael Crichton observes in the opening pages of his epic, *Jurassic Park*, which was memorialized on the screen by Steven Spielberg, "The late twentieth century has witnessed a scientific gold rush of astonishing proportions: the headlong and furious haste to commercialize genetic engineering. This enterprise has proceeded so rapidly – with so little outside commentary – that its dimensions and implications are hardly understood at all."

The purpose of this chapter is to shed some light on the role of entrepreneurship in biotechnology, and in particular, how scientists engaged in biotechnology research at universities become entrepreneurs. By entrepreneurship, we mean in the context of this paper, the process leading to the start-up of a new biotechnology company, which is consistent with the definition posited by Gartner and Carter (2003) in the 2003 edition of the *Handbook of Entrepreneurship Research*, "Entrepreneurial behavior involves the activities of individuals who are

H. Patzelt and T. Brenner (eds.), *Handbook of Bioentrepreneurship*,
doi: 10.1007/978-0-387-48345-0_9, © Springer Science + Business Media, LLC 2008

associated with creating new organizations rather than the activities of individuals who are involved with maintaining or changing the operations of ongoing established organizations." This definition of entrepreneurship is in contrast to the more general and organization context free definition provided by Sarasvathy, Dew, Velamuri, and Venkataraman, in the 2003 edition of the *Handbook of Entrepreneurship Research*, "An entrepreneurial opportunity consists of a set of ideas, beliefs, and actions that enable the creation of future goods and services in the absence of current markets for them."

We first link entrepreneurial behavior to scientists and researchers in biotechnology. We then relate scientist commercialization to more general theories and models of entrepreneurial choice. Previous studies analyzing scientist comercialization and entrepreneurship are reviewed in the second section. This literature enables us to infer several main hypotheses predicting scientist entrepreneurship. In particular, by examining why some scientists commercialize their scientific research through entrepreneurship while others do not, this chapter is able to identify that, at least in the case of biotechnology, entrepreneurial opportunities are shaped by the context within which the scientist works as well as the characteristics specific to the scientist. Thus, the evidence suggests that the extent and nature of scientist commercialization in biotechnology are shaped by the particular mode of commercialization pursued by the individual scientist.

## 9.2 Commercialization of Science and Entrepreneurial Choice

Why do some biotechnology scientists choose to commercialize their research and, at least in some cases, do it through entrepreneurship by starting a new biotechnology company? It is a virtual consensus that entrepreneurship revolves around the recognition of opportunities and the pursuit of those opportunities (Shane and Eckhardt 2003). Much of the more contemporary thinking about entrepreneurship has focused on the cognitive process by which individuals reach the decision to start a new firm. But where do entrepreneurial opportunities come from? This question has been at the heart of the entrepreneurship literature and holds for scientists and researchers in biotechnology as well as more generally. On the one hand is the view associated with Kirzner that entrepreneurial opportunities are actually exogenous or independent from the entrepreneur. Thus, the central entrepreneurial function, or activity, is to discover such exogenous entrepreneurial opportunities. For example, Stevenson and Jarillo (1990) assume that entrepreneurship is an orientation towards opportunity recognition. Central to the discovery research agenda are the questions "How do entrepreneurs perceive opportunities and how do these opportunities manifest themselves as being credible vs. being an illusion?"

By contrast, the earlier Schumpeterian (1942) tradition has a greater focus on the harnessing of entrepreneurial opportunities by the entrepreneur. The chief function of the entrepreneur is to innovate by combining resources in a novel manner, which creates opportunities that previously did not exist. In the creationist tradition, the entrepreneur does not merely discover entrepreneurial opportunities; rather, she creates them.

Why and how do some scientists become an entrepreneur, while others abstain? The answer to this question, which is at the heart of entrepreneurship theory, has generally revolved around the perception of opportunity and the means and willingness to act upon that opportunity.[1] But what is the source of such entrepreneurial opportunities? The view taken by the contemporary literature on entrepreneurship is no different. On the one hand is a prevalent view suggesting that entrepreneurship revolves around the recognition of opportunities and the pursuit of those opportunities (Venkataraman 1997). But the existence of those opportunities is, in fact, taken as given. The focus has been on the cognitive process by which individuals reach the decision to start a new firm. This has resulted in a methodology focusing on differences across individuals in analyzing the entrepreneurial decision (Stevenson and Jarillo 1990).

Krueger (2003, p. 105) has pointed out that "the heart of entrepreneurship is an orientation toward seeing opportunities," which frames the research questions "What is the nature of entrepreneurial thinking and what cognitive phenomena are associated with seeing and acting on opportunities?" This research agenda has triggered a debate as to whether entrepreneurs are simply born or can be "made." In either case, the discovery literature leaves the focus of the entrepreneurial decision clearly on individual-specific characteristics.

Thus, the discovery approach to entrepreneurship essentially holds the opportunities constant and then asks how the cognitive process inherent in the entrepreneurial decision varies across different individual characteristics and attributes (McClelland 1961). Shane and Eckhardt (2003, p. 187) summarize this literature in introducing the individual–opportunity nexus, "We discussed the process of opportunity discovery and explained why some actors are more likely to discover a given opportunity than others." Some of these differences involve the willingness to incur risk; others involve the preference for autonomy and self-direction, while still others involve differential access to scarce and expensive resources, such as financial-, human-, social-, and experiential capital.

Similarly, Kruger (2003) examines the nature of entrepreneurial thinking and the cognitive process associated with opportunity identification and the decision to undertake entrepreneurial action. The focal point of this research is on the cognitive process identifying the entrepreneurial opportunity which triggers the decision to start a new firm. Thus, a perceived opportunity and intent to pursue that opportunity are the necessary and sufficient conditions for entrepreneurial activity to take place. The perception of an opportunity is shaped by a sense of the

---

[1] In fact, the entrepreneurship literature has generally been sharply divided with respect to this question. Hebert and Link (1989) have identified three distinct intellectual traditions in the development of the entrepreneurship literature. These three traditions can be characterized as the German Tradition, based on von Thuenen and Schumpeter, the Chicago Tradition, based on Knight and Schultz, and the Austrian Tradition, based on von Mises, Kirzner and Shackle.

anticipated rewards accruing from and costs of becoming an entrepreneur. Some of the research focuses on the role of personal attitudes and characteristics, such as self-efficacy (the individual's sense of competence), collective efficacy, and social norms. Shane (2001a, b) has identified how prior experience and the ability to apply specific skills influence the perception of future opportunities.

The concept of the entrepreneurial decision resulting from the cognitive processes of opportunity recognition and ensuing action is introduced by Shane and Eckhardt (2003) and Shane and Venkataraman (2001). They suggest that an equilibrium view of entrepreneurship stems from the assumption of perfect information. By contrast, imperfect information generates divergences in perceived opportunities across different people. The sources of heterogeneity across individuals include different access to information, as well as cognitive abilities, psychological differences, and access to financial and social capital.

This approach focusing on individual cognition in the entrepreneurial process has generated a number of important and valuable insights, such as the contribution made by social networks, education and training, and familial influence. The literature certainly leaves the impression that entrepreneurship is a personal matter largely determined by DNA, familial status, and access to crucial resources. For example, Sarasvathy et al. (2003, p. 142) explain the role of entrepreneurial opportunity in the literature: "An entrepreurial opportunity consists of a set of ideas, beliefs and actions that enable the creation of future goods and services in the absence of current markets for them." Sarasvathy et al. (2003) provide a typology of entrepreneurial opportunities as consisting of opportunity recognition, opportunity discovery, and opportunity creation.

Still, the view of Sarasvathy et al. (2003) is that the entrepreneurial opportunity is exogenous from the cognitive process by which an individual weighs the decision to become an entrepreneur. By contrast, the Schumpeterian (1942) view suggests that economic agents make decisions that can create innovative activity. According to this view, the role of entrepreneurship is to create new opportunities by exploiting new knowledge from inventors. The most predominant theory of innovation, the resource-base view (Barney 1986; Alvarez 2003; Alvarez and Barney 2004), does not assume that opportunities are exogenous. Rather, innovative opportunities are the result of systematic effort by firms and the result of purposeful efforts to create knowledge and new ideas, and subsequently to appropriate the returns of those investments through commercialization of such investments (Cohen and Levinthal 1990; Griliches 1979). In what Griliches formalized as the model of the knowledge production function, incumbent firms engage in the pursuit of new economic knowledge as an input into the process of generating the output of innovative activity. Such efforts to create opportunities involve investments in research and development (R&D) and the enhancement of human capital through training and education. By analogy, scientists investing in their human capital through education, training, and research are essentially investing in their capacity to create new opportunities.

Thus, according to the Schumpeterian tradition, opportunities are endogenously created by purposeful and dedicated investments and efforts to create new knowledge. This is a stark contrast to the discovery tradition in the entrepreneurship literature where opportunities are taken as being exogenous and the chief entrepreneurial function is discovery.

As an alternative to the two polar cases of the discovery and creationist views, we instead suggest that the entrepreneurial opportunity, or the knowledge upon which the entrepreneurial decision is made, is in fact shaped by the context of the individual. In particular, the literature linking such entrepreneurial opportunities to the decision to become an entrepreneur has identified a broad spectrum of external settings. We distinguish among three main contexts – workers in firms, users of technologies, and scientists at universities, to focus on how the source of the entrepreneurial opportunity, or knowledge, shapes the actual entrepreneurial decision. Such a distinction across knowledge contexts may be important in that it sheds light on some of the great debates raging in the entrepreneurship, such as "Are entrepreneurs born or made?" The answer may be less about the former or the latter but more conditioned upon the context of the entrepreneurial opportunity, especially in the context of entrepreneurship in biotechnology.

## 9.3 Scientist Biotech Entrepreneurship

A context generating entrepreneurial knowledge involves scientists and other researchers in the academic or university setting, particularly in the field of life sciences research. A growing literature has tried to identify why some scientists enter into entrepreneurship, at least in the form of commercialization but more specifically by starting a new firm, while other scientists abstain. Some of these studies focus on the individual scientist in biotechnology as the unit of analysis (Zucker et al. 1998; Louis et al. 1989; Berkovitz and Feldman 2004; Audretsch and Stephan 1996). Thursby et al. (2001), and Jensen and Thursby (2001, 2004) identify both patents and the licensing of patents as important modes of scientist commercialization. In particular, Jensen and Thursby (2004, p. 1) employ a principal–agent framework in which the university administration is the principal and the faculty scientist is the agent, and identify that "whether or not the researcher remains in the university, and if so her choice of the amount of time to spend on basic and applied research, is complicated by the fact that she earns license income and prestige both inside and outside the university." Louis et al. (1989) identify the role of individual characteristics and attitudes, along with the norms of scientific peer groups, as an important factor in influencing the scientists' decision to commercialize their research in the form of a new-firm startup. Similarly, Shane (2004) and Lockett et al. (2005) focus on the scientist as the unit of observation in making the decision to become an entrepreneur.

Other studies focus on the new venture (implicitly or explicitly started by the scientist) (Nekar and Shane 2003; Audretsch and Lehmann 2005), or the university, which provides the institutional and cultural context (Lockett and Wright 2005; O'Shea et al. 2005; Di Gregorio and Shane 2003). However, what all of these approaches have in common is that they address the question "What leads a scientist to start a new firm?" The different units of analysis suggest a different focus on searching for an answer to this question, which may reflect a different underlying theory triggering a different source of entrepreneurial opportunity. Studies analyzing the unit of analysis of the scientist have been able to focus on scientist-specific characteristics, such as age, experience, citations, and publications. Studies based on the university as the analytical unit of observations have generally been unable to analyze the impact of scientist-specific characteristics, but instead have contributed a focus on the role of university-specific factors, such as the type of university and the role of the technology transfer office in shaping the decision of scientists to become entrepreneurs. By contrast, studies focusing on the new venture as the unit of analysis are able to shed more light on firm-specific strategies and characteristics, such as age, size, financial sources, and participation in strategic alliances, and link them to competitiveness or performance.

In virtually every study the nature of the entrepreneurial opportunity involves the commercialization of science. The meaning of commercialization varies across studies. The unanimity of the entrepreneurial opportunity reflects the singular activity of scientists engaged in research. Still, the question remains as to why some scientists choose to commercialize their scientific knowledge emerging from their research.

A large amount of literature has emerged focusing on what has become known as the appropriability problem (Cohen and Levinthal 1990). The underlying issue revolves around how firms that invest in the creation of new knowledge can best appropriate the economic returns from that knowledge (Arrow 1962). When the lens is shifted away from the firm to scientist as the relevant unit of analysis, the appropriability issue remains, but the question becomes: How can scientists with a given endowment of new knowledge best appropriate the returns from that knowledge? Stephan (1996) and Levin and Stephan (1991) suggest that the answer is "It depends" – it depends on both the career trajectory as well as the stage of the life cycle of the scientist.

The university or academic career trajectory encourages and rewards the production of new scientific knowledge. Thus, the goal of the scientist in the university context is to establish *priority*. This is done most efficiently through publication in scientific journals (Audretsch and Stephan 1996, 1999). By contrast, with a career trajectory in the private sector, scientists are rewarded for the production of new economic knowledge, or knowledge that has been commercialized in the market, but not necessarily new scientific knowledge per se. In fact, scientists working in industry are often discouraged from sharing knowledge externally with the scientific community through publication. As a result of these differential incentive structures, industrial and academic scientists develop distinct career trajectories.

The appropriability question confronting academic scientists can be considered in the context of the model of scientist human capital over the life cycle. Scientist life-cycle models suggest that early in their careers scientists invest heavily in human capital in order to build a scientific reputation (Levin and Stephan 1991). In the later stages of their career, the scientists trade or *cash in* this reputation for economic return. Thus, early in their career, the scientists invest in the creation of scientific knowledge in order to establish a reputation that signals the value of that knowledge to the scientific community.

With maturity, scientists seek ways to appropriate the economic value of the new knowledge. Thus, academic scientists may seek to commercialize their scientific research within a life-cycle context. The life-cycle model of the scientist implies that, *ceteris paribus*, personal characteristics of the scientist such as age should play a role in the decision to become an entrepreneur. In the early stages of her career, a scientist will tend to invest in her scientific reputation. As she evolves towards maturity and the marginal productivity of her scientific research starts to hit diminishing returns, the incentive for cashing in through entrepreneurship becomes greater.

Scientists working in the private sector are arguably more fully compensated for the economic value of their knowledge. This will not be the case for academic scientists, unless they cash out, in terms of Dasgupta and David (1994), by commercializing their scientific knowledge. This suggests that academic scientists become entrepreneurs within a life-cycle context.

An implication of the resource theory is that those scientists with a greater research and scientific prowess have the capacity for generating a greater scientific output. But how does scientific capability translate into observable characteristics that can promote or impede commercialization efforts? Because the commercialization of scientific research is particularly risky and uncertain (Audretsch and Stephan 1999), a strong scientific reputation, as evidenced through vigorous publication and formidable citations, provides a greatly valued signal of scientific credibility and capability to any anticipated commercialized venture or project.

This life-cycle context presents two distinct hypotheses: both age and scientific reputation, which reflect and signal the underlying scientific human capital of the scientist, should influence the decision of a university scientist to engage in commercialization activities.

Thus, a number of studies have tried to link the propensity of a university-based scientist, with a particular focus in biotechnology, to start a new firm, or become involved with a start-up, to scientist-specific characteristics, such as age, experience, and gender. In particular, Audretsch and Stephan (1996, 1999) find that the propensity for university scientists to start a new biotechnology company is lower for younger scientists and higher for more mature scientists. By contrast, scientist spin-offs from pharmaceutical corporations exhibit less of an age effect. The mean age of scientists starting a new biotechnology startup is considerably lower when the scientist had been employed by a pharmaceutical corporation than at a university. This is consistent with the scientist life-cycle theory of academic scientist commercialization behavior.

Similarly, several studies have linked scientist reputation to the propensity to start a new biotechnology firm. Zucker et al. (1998) find that a reputation as a star scientist, as measured by citations, increases the likelihood of a university scientist starting a biotechnology firm. Zucker et al. (2002) found similar results using the commercialization measure of patents. Similarly, Audretsch and Stephan (1996, 1999) link the propensity for a university scientist to work with a new biotechnology start-up or start a new firm herself to three different measures of reputation – publications, citations, and recipient of a Nobel prize. All three reputation measures are positively related to the likelihood of a scientist becoming an entrepreneur. Studies linking scientific-specific characteristics, such as age, citations, and publications, have been generally restricted to those analyzing the unit of observation of the individual scientist. There is compelling evidence that not only scientific reputation, as measured by citations and publications, but also being the recipient of a Nobel prize is complementary to and not a substitute for entrepreneurial activity. However, as Levin and Stephan (1991) point out, these relationships are not neutral with respect to the stage of a scientist's career but may tend to happen sequentially.

Scientist location can influence the decision to commercialize for two reasons. First, as Jaffe (1989), Jaffe et al. (1993), Almeida and Kogut (1997), and others show, knowledge tends to spill over within geographically bounded regions. This implies that scientists working in regions with a high level of investments in new knowledge can more easily access and generate new scientific ideas. This suggests that scientists working in knowledge clusters should tend to be more productive than their counterparts who are geographically isolated. A number of studies confirm that the geographic location of a scientist influences the propensity to become an entrepreneur (Zucker et al. 1998, 2002; Audretsch and Stephan 1996, 1999). In particular, the studies of both Audretsch and Stephan (1996, 1999) and Zucker et al. (2002) found that location plays a crucial role in influencing the entrepreneurial decision to start a new company in biotechnology.

A second component of externalities involves not the technological knowledge, but rather social capital. A large and robust literature has emerged attempting to link social capital to entrepreneurship (Aldrich and Martinez 2003; Thorton and Flynn 2003; Powell et al. 1996; Sorenson and Audia 2000; Sorenson and Stuart 2001). According to this literature, entrepreneurial activity should be enhanced where investments in social capital are greater. Interactions and linkages, such as working together with industry, are posited as conduits not just of knowledge spillovers but also for the demonstration effect providing a flow of information across scientists about how scientific research can be commercialized (Thursby and Thursby 2004). As Bercovitz and Feldman (2004) show in a study based on the commercialization activities of scientists at Johns Hopkins and Duke University, the likelihood of a scientist engaging in commercialization activity, which is measured as disclosing an invention, is shaped based on the commercialization behavior of the doctoral supervisor in the institution where the scientist was trained, as well as the commercialization behavior and attitudes exhibited by the chair and peers at the relevant department.

Similarly, Audretsch et al. (2006) examine the propensity for university scientists to commercialize by analyzing new databases consisting of the top scientists involved in biotechnology research. Three distinct measures of social capital are linked to the likelihood of a scientist starting a new venture, copatenting with other academic scientists, copublishing with industry scientists, and serving on an industry board of directors or a scientific advisory board. All three measures of social capital found to have a positive impact on the likelihood of a scientist becoming an entrepreneur.

The university context has also been found to shape scientist entrepreneurial knowledge. On the basis of a study of 778 faculty members from 40 universities, Louis et al. (1989) find that it is the local norms of behaviour and attitudes towards commercialization that shape the likelihood of an individual university scientist to engage in commercialization activity, in their case by starting a new firm. This would suggest that university-specific rules, norms, and culture, especially in terms of local behaviour and attitudes, help to shape scientist entrepreneurial knowledge.

Di Gregorio and Shane (2003) use the data from the Association of University Technology Managers database to analyze 503 start-ups spun out from 101 universities. Di Gregorio and Shane (2003) identify two university-specific factors that are conducive to university spin-offs. The first involves the quality of the faculty. The second is the institutional ability enabling both the university and the scientist to take an equity stake in the new venture in lieu of licensing fees. Similarly, O'Shea et al. (2005) identify that the past success of a university in transferring technology creates path dependence in generating scientific entrepreneurial opportunities. Franklin et al. (2001) identify the differential impact of the older, more traditional British universities from the newer ones. They find that while the more traditional universities are stronger in terms of academic research, the newer British universities have an entrepreneurial advantage. In a subsequent study, Lockett et al. (2003) link university strategy to the number of entrepreneurial spin-outs from the university.

Other studies have focused on that role of university-specific institutions, such as the technology transfer office (TTO), in influencing scientist entrepreneurial knowledge. Lockett and Wright (2005) link characteristics of the TTO to university spin-off activity. Using the resource-base view, they find that universities investing more in intellectual property protection capabilities and the business capabilities of the TTO generate a higher number of spin-offs.

Markman et al. (2005) examine the relationship between university spin-off activity and university-based incubators, as intermediated via the TTO. Similarly, Markman et al. (2004a, b) link university spin-offs to a broad spectrum of TTO-specific characteristics, such as speed in processing the technology transfer, involvement of faculty, competency in identifying licensing, and TTO resources.

Most of the studies identified above are typical of a growing literature that has emerged trying to gauge and analyze the extent to which university research spills over into commercial activity. Much, if not most, of this previous research has been restricted to focusing on the activities emanating from TTOs, which have provided systematic and consistent documentation of their efforts over a fairly long period of time. Analyses of these data have typically led to conclusions suggesting that while patents and licenses from university research have increased over time, the typical TTO does not generate significant commercialization of university research. However, an important qualification is that by restricting themselves to TTO-generated data, such studies are not able to consider any commercialization activities not emanating from the TTOs.

In their 2006 study, Audretsch et al. take a different approach examining the determinants of entrepreneurship in the biotechnology context. Rather than focus on what the TTOs do, their study focuses on what university scientists engaged in biotechnology research do. Thus, the findings about the commercialization of university research are based on actual university scientists and not the TTOs. The results are revealing. In particular, while all modes of commercialization are important, scientist entrepreneurship in biotechnology emerges as an important and prevalent mode of commercialization of university research. More than one in four patenting NCI scientists has started a new firm. This is a remarkably high rate of entrepreneurship for any group of people, let alone university scientists. Thus, the extent to which university research is being commercialized and entering the market may be significantly greater than might have been inferred from studies restricted only to the commercialization activities of the TTO. They suggest that scientist entrepreneurship may prove to be the sleeping giant of university commercialization.

Second, the mode of commercialization is apparently not independent on the commercialization route for biotechnology scientists. Nearly one third of patenting biotechnology scientists rely on the entrepreneurial commercialization route, in that they do not assign all of their patents to the university. These scientists exhibit a higher likelihood of starting a new firm but a lower propensity to license. By contrast, biotechnology scientists choosing the TTO commercialization route exhibit a higher propensity to license but a lower likelihood to start a new firm.

## 9.4 Conclusions

The theories and empirical evidence examining the sources of entrepreneurial knowledge suggest something of a mixture between the two dichotomous discovery and creationist views. On the one hand, as the theories and empirical evidence highlighting the role that scientist human capital plays in the entrepreneurial decision suggest, those scientists creating more scientific knowledge have a higher likelihood of becoming entrepreneurs as well. This would suggest that such highly productive scientists are not passive vehicles in which the entrepreneurial opportunity falls like "manna from heaven." On the other hand, the theories and empirical evidence linking social capital, and locational and institutional factors to scientist entrepreneurship suggest that there are numerous mechanisms facilitating the discovery process of an existing entrepreneurial opportunity. Thus, when it comes to entrepreneurial knowledge for scientists, neither the extreme Kirznerian nor the Schumpeterian view fully accounts for the source of entrepreneurial opportunities. Rather, the source of entrepreneurial knowledge for scientists is something of a hybrid – part creation and part discovery. Still, compared to entrepreneurial opportunities for workers and users, such entrepreneurial knowledge has a greater component of being created by scientists rather than discovered.

This would suggest that future research designed to guide public policy should not be limited to those modes of biotechnology commercialization that are publicly available and can be relatively and easily accessed at low cost. Scientist patent activity and participation in the SBIR program are certainly important modes of commercialization in biotechnology, but their ease of access should not lead to the conclusion that they are even the most important and prevalent forms of commercialization. Rather, other modes of commercialization for which no systematic comprehensive public sources of data exist, such as scientist new-firm startups, may also be a highly prevalent and important form of scientist commercialization in biotechnology. Future research needs to explore other modes of commercialization and undertake the painstaking data collection to provide systematic measurement and analysis of commercialization conduits such as the start-up of new firms.

It is imperative that comprehensive and systematic new sources of measurement be created by directly interacting with the scientists themselves to gauge the extent, nature, determinants, and impact of scientist commercialization of research. If the commercialization of science, particularly in fields such as biotechnology, represents one of the missing links of economic growth, job creation and competitiveness in global markets, undertaking the painstaking measurement and analysis is essential to guide public policy in both understanding and promoting this important source of economic growth.

# References

Aldrich H, Martinez M (2003) Entrepreneurship as a social construction: A multi-level evolutionary approach. In: Acs Z, Audretsch D (eds), International handbook of entrepreneurship. Springer, Berlin

Almeida P, Kogut B (1997) The exploration of technological diversity and the geographic localization of innovation. Small Business Economics 9: 21–31

Alvarez S (2003) Resources and hierarchies: Intersections between entrepreneurship and strategy. In: Acs Z, Audretsch D (eds), The handbook of entrepreneurship research. Springer, Berlin

Alvarez S, Barney J (2004) Organizing rent generation and appropriation: Toward a theory of the entrepreneurial firm. Journal of Business Venturing 19: 621–635

Arrow K (1962) The economic implications of learning by doing. Review of Economic Studies 29: 153–173

Audretsch D, Stephan P (1996) Company-scientist locational links: The case of biotechnology. American Economic Review 86: 641–652

Audretsch D, Stephan P (1999) Knowledge spillovers in biotechnology: Sources and incentives. Journal of Evolutionary Economics 19: 97–107

Audretsch D, Aldridge T, Oettl A (2006) The knowledge filter and economic growth: The role of scientist entrepreneurship. Max Planck Discussion Papers

Audretsch DB, Lehmann EE (2005) Mansfield's missing link: The impact of knowledge spillovers on firm growth. Journal of Technology Transfer 30: 207–210

Barney J (1986) Strategic factor markets: Expectations, luck and business strategy. Management Science 42: 1231–1241

Berkovitz J, Feldman M (2004) Academic entrepreneurs: Social learning and participation in university technology transfer. Mimeo, University of Toronto, Toronto

Cohen W, Levinthal D (1990) Absorptive capacity: A new perspective on learning and innovation. Administrative Science Quarterly 35: 128–152

Dasgupta P, David P (1994) Toward a new economics of science. Research Policy 23: 487–521

Di Gregorio D, Shane S (2003) Why do some universities generate more start-ups than others? Research Policy 32: 209–228

Franklin S, Wright M, Lockett A (2001) Academic and surrogate entrepreneurs in university spin-out companies. Journal of Technology Transfer 26: 127–141

Gartner W, Carter N (2003) Entrepreneurial behaviour and firm organizing processes. In: Acs Z, Audretsch D (eds), International handbook of entrepreneurship. Springer, Berlin

Griliches Z (1979) Issues in assessing the contribution of research and development to productivity growth. Bell Journal of Economics 10: 92–116

Hebert R, Link A (1989) In search of the meaning of entrepreneurship. Small Business Economics 1: 39–49

Jaffe A (1989) Real effects of academic research. American Economic Review 79: 957–970

Jaffe A, Trajtenberg M, Henderson R (1993) Geographic localization of knowledge spillovers as evidenced by patent citations. Quarterly Journal of Economics 63: 577–598

Jensen R, Thursby M (2001) Proofs and prototypes for sale: The licensing of university inventions. American Economic Review 91: 240–259

Jensen R, Thursby M (2004) Patent licensing and the research university. NBER Working Papers

Krueger N (2003) The cognitive psychology of entrepreneurship. In: Acs Z, Audretsch D (eds), Handbook of entrepreneurship research. Springer, Berlin, pp. 105–140

Levin SG, Stephan PE (1991) Research productivity over the life cycle: Evidence for academic scientists. American Economic Review 81: 114–132

Lockett A, Wright M (2005) Resources, capabilities, risk capital and the creation of university spin-out companies. Research Policy 34: 1043–1057

Lockett A, Wright M, Franklin S (2003) Technology transfer and universities' spin-out strategies. Small Business Economics 20: 185–200

Lockett A, Siegel D, Wright M, Ensley M (2005) The creation of spin-off firms at public research institutions: Managerial and policy implications. Research Policy 34: 981–993

Louis KS, Blumenthal D, Gluck ME, Soto MA (1989) Entrepreneurs in academe: An exploration of behaviours among life scientists. Administrative Science Quarterly 34: 110–131

Markman GD, Espina, MI, Phan PH (2004a) Patents as surrogates for inimitable and non-substitutable resources. Journal of Management 30: 529–544

Markman GD, Gianiodis PT, Phan PH, Balkin DB (2004b) Entrepreneurship from the ivory tower: Do incentive systems matter? Journal of Technology Transfer 29: 353–364

Markman GD, Gianiodis PT, Phan PH, Balkin DB (2005) Innovation speed: Transferring university technology to market. Research Policy 34: 1058–1075

McClelland D (1961) The achieving society. Van Nostrand, Princeton, NJ

Nekar A, Shane S (2003) When do start-ups that exploit patented academic knowledge survive? International Journal of Industrial Organization 21: 1391–1410

O'Shea RP, Allen TJ, Chevalier A, Roche F (2005) Entrepreneurial orientation, technology transfer and spinoff performance of U.S. universities. Research Policy 34: 994–1009

Powell W, Koput K, Smith-Doerr L (1996) Interorganizational collaboration and the locus of innovation: Networks of learning in biotechnology. Administrative Science Quarterly 42: 116–145

Sarasvathy S, Nicholas D, Ramakrishna V, Venkataraman S (2003) Three views of entrepreneurial opportunity. In: Acs Z, Audretsch D (eds), The handbook of entrepreneurship research. Kluwer, Boston, pp. 141–160

Schumpeter J (1942) Capitalism, socialism and democracy. Harper and Brothers, New York

Shane S (2001a) Technological opportunities and new firm creation. Management Science 47: 205–220

Shane S (2001b) Technology regimes and new firm formation. Management Science 47: 1173–1190

Shane S (2004) Academic entrepreneurship. Edward Elgar, Cheltenham, UK

Shane S, Eckhardt J (2003) The individual-opportunity nexus. In: Acs Z, Audretsch D (eds), The handbook of entrepreneurship research. Kluwer, Dordrecht

Shane S, Venkataraman S (2001) Entrepreneurship as a field of research: A response to Zahra and Dess, Singh and Erickson. Academy of Management Review 26: 13–17

Sorenson O, Audia P (2000) The social structure of entrepreneurial activity: Geographic concentration of footwear production in the United States, 1940–1989. American Journal of Sociology 106: 424–462

Sorenson O, Stuart T (2001) Syndication networks and the spatial distribution of venture capital investments. American Journal of Sociology 106: 1546–1588

Stephan P (1996) The economics of science. Journal of Economic Literature 34: 1199 1235

Stevenson H, Jarillo J (1990) A paradigm of entrepreneurship: Entrepreneurial management. Strategic Management Journal 11: 17–27

Thornton PH, Flynn KH (2003) Entrepreneurship, networks, and geographies. In: Acs Z, Audretsch D (eds), International handbook of entrepreneurship. Springer, Berlin

Thursby J, Jensen R, Thursby M (2001) Objectives, characteristics and outcomes of university licensing: A survey of major U.S. universities. Journal of Technology Transfer 26: 59–72

Thursby JG, Thursby JC (2004) Are faculty critical? Their role in university-industry licensing. Contemporary Economic Policy 22: 162–178

Venkataraman S (1997) The distinctive domain of entrepreneurship research. In: Katz J, Brockhaus R (eds), Advances in entrepreneurship, firm emergence and growth. JAI, Greenwich

Zucker L, Darby M, Brewer M (1998) Intellectual human capital and the birth of U.S. biotechnology enterprises. American Economic Review 88: 290–306

Zucker L, Darby M, Armstrong JS (2002) Commercializing knowledge: University science, knowledge capture, and firm performance in biotechnology. Management Science 48: 138 153

# 10 University-Based Biotechnology Spin-Offs

Amalya L. Oliver

Department of Sociology and Anthropology, The Hebrew University of Jerusalem, Mt. Scopus, Jerusalem 91905, Israel

## 10.1 Introduction

Advanced economies can only hope to stay competitive and preserve their living standard if they further develop their intellectual resources and turn them into marketable products and high value-added jobs. There are various venues for achieving this goal, but this chapter will focus on a relatively recent phenomenon –university-based spin-offs (UBSOs). The chapter is composed of five sections. The chapter will start with introducing the contextually important features of the biotechnology industry and providing a literature review on entrepreneurial science and entrepreneurial universities. Then, I will review the literature of scientific entrepreneurship, highlighting the various complexities associated with this phenomenon. Next, the main characteristics of university spin-offs (USOs) in general will be introduced, focusing on the individual, network, and institutional aspects of this new organizational phenomenon. The following section will contextualize UBSOs within the framework of the specific characteristics of the biotechnology industry. The chapter will end with highlighting some of the complexities of spin-offs, and related concepts, and suggesting directions for future research.

### 10.1.1 The Context of the Biotechnology Industry

University–industry technology transfer in biotechnology has been shown to be crucial in the biotechnology industry (Kenney 1986; Oliver and Liebeskind 1998; Zucker and Darby 1996) both in terms of firm founding and in terms of firms' technological and scientific success.

H. Patzelt and T. Brenner (eds.), *Handbook of Bioentrepreneurship*,
doi: 10.1007/978-0-387-48345-0_10, © Springer Science + Business Media, LLC 2008

In general, three general contextual features characterize the biotechnology industry:

- Basic academic research is the leading force in industrial innovativeness (Liebeskind et al. 1996; Oliver and Liebeskind 2006; Powell et al. 1996), and this knowledge is considered as a highly valuable intellectual property (IP) by universities and biotechnology firms as well as by the State as the institutional environment (Oliver and Liebeskind 2006).
- There is a dense structure of academic–industry collaborations in the industry (Liebeskind et al. 1996; Oliver 2004). Alliances are crucial for knowledge acquisition and it is important for firms to enhance learning through alliances (Powell et al. 1996, 2005; Zaheer and George 2004).
- Universities and academic scientists have become aware of the economic potential of their discoveries, and technology-transfer offices are keen at protecting university IP (Etzkowitz et al. 2005; Oliver and Liebeskind 1998; Oliver 2004). On the other hand, there are active and scientifically sophisticated venture capitalists that facilitate academic scientific entrepreneurship (Oliver and Liebeskind 2006). These features lead to a highly enriching environment that amplifies the "scientific-entrepreneurship" phenomena (Kenney 1986; Zucker and Darby 1996).

These central elements that characterize the biotechnology industry context are, in my view, the antecedents that lead to a relatively high rate of USOs in general and UBSO in particular for biotechnology-related innovations. The importance of the involvement of the inventor-scientist in the development and commercialization process coupled with the needs of universities to provide support for their entrepreneurial and star scientists and retain them within academia constitute a strong motivation for establishing USBOs.

## 10.1.2 Entrepreneurial Universities

Universities have undergone some major transitions in which the entrepreneurial university replaced the traditional research university as new missions of economic and social development on top of the previous missions of knowledge creation, teaching, and research (Etzkowitz 2003). These changes reflect upon changes in inner dynamics within universities as well as the establishment of important linkages with the external industrial environment. The entrepreneurial university is defined by Etzkowitz as having "the ability to generate a focused strategic direction both in formulating academic goals and in translating knowledge produced within the university into economic and social utilities … thus has interface capabilities such as liaison and transfer offices and incubator facilities to manage and market knowledge produced in the university at several levels, from specific pieces or protected intellectual property to technology embodied in a firm and propelled by an entrepreneur" (2003: pp. 112–113).

Universities can perpetuate sites of innovation since they encompass a high through flow of quality human capital. This form of capital includes the students who can become future inventors, and who through their natural incubator structure can team in research groups while establishing innovative interdisciplinary science (Etzkowitz 2003). Under such structure, research groups in universities can be considered "quasi firms" who can establish transfers of knowledge with the industry, or develop research collaborations. At the extreme mode of the entrepreneurial universities, UBSOs can be established by the university technology-transfer office on site to exploit and capitalize on the economic value of the scientific discoveries of the university scientists.

The entrepreneurial academic paradigm is based on normative and analytical components. The normative characteristics are based on the sociological assumptions as to how science is conducted in universities in general and to what degree these normative elements are in line or in conflict within the entrepreneurial university paradigm. The analytical components refer to the structural elements associated with the entrepreneurial university. Etzkowitz et al. (2000) suggest the following components that are associated with the transformation of universities to the entrepreneurial mode:

- Internal transformation in which new functions emerge, such as incorporating teaching with internship in firms facilitated by the professors. In this transformation, knowledge is capitalized rather than being disseminated.
- Trans-institutional impact in which a new equilibrium of overlapping institutional spheres (industrial–government and academic spheres) is established. This change can result in stabilization and adjustments of institutional systems to allow for customary formats of collaborative arrangements, and through doing so, networking arrangements can be easily negotiated.
- Interface processes in which the entrepreneurial university establishes capabilities for intelligence, monitoring, and negotiation with other institutional spheres. These capabilities give the university the ability to identify confluence of interest between external organizations and university research teams and negotiate contracts for collaborations. These changes result in establishing new roles of technical personnel to assist faculty members in assessing commercial potential of research findings and facilitate the establishment of research and commercial collaborations.
- Recursive effects in which the university established capabilities to facilitate the creation of new knowledge-based firms based upon academic research. This can result in cross-organizational and cross-institutional entities of various forms such as specialized research centers, joint ventures with industry, university–industry and university–university consortia, and other forms of collaborations.

These changes are associated with the legitimation basis of universities. The classic legitimation model in which universities research was to contribute openly to the society is still active as long as the university will retain its original educational mission (Etzkowitz et al. 2000). Yet, the question is whether the new line of legitimation based on capitalization of knowledge and aim for economic development will hold as universities are encompassing the earlier-described transformations.

## 10.2 Scientific Entrepreneurship

Governments, universities, and research centers are keen to foster scientific entrepreneurship because it is an important driving force for innovation, growth, and competitiveness (Arzeni 1997; Butler 1998). However, if one wishes to further these causes, and invest one's resources wisely, it seems important to understand when and how exactly scientific entrepreneurship can best achieve these ends.

The task of building economic advantage based on intellectual resources was commonly taken by venture capitalists, entrepreneurs, or industrial actors rather than by universities and academic scientists. The entrepreneurship literature views entrepreneurs as economic actors, who from the outset are executing their idea with an eye on the market, and within the institutional context of a business and the market place. Scientists, by contrast, are socialized into, and operate within, a research community whose values are very different from that of the commercial world. For university scientists, becoming entrepreneurs let alone successfully launching and managing a venture requires basic changes in attitudes, thinking, and relationships. Conversely, it seems difficult for economic entrepreneurs to turn into scientific entrepreneurs to exploit research innovations. This is because they lack the scientific know-how and networks that would assist them in evaluating the prospects of the entrepreneurial venture and to push forward the realization, of specific scientific ventures.

### 10.2.1 Changes in Academic Science

A recent body of research (Etzkowitz 1998, 2003; Etzkowitz et al. 2000) has demonstrated that academic science is undergoing a second "revolution" in which economic benefits are incorporated with academic research in the form of "capitalized knowledge." While the first academic revolution incorporated research into the academic domain, in addition to teaching, which was the initial domain, the second academic revolution, takes new and different forms in which university-based knowledge is exploited by universities for economic returns. To decipher the new structure, Etzkowitz and Leydesdorff (2000) suggested a "triple helix" model that encompasses the university–industry–government relations. This model "attempts to account for a new configuration of institutional forces emerging within innovation systems, weather through the decline of the total state or the opening of the insular corporation" (Etzkowitz et al. 2000, p. 314). The previous model was based on the assumptions that the economy or the policy predominated while the knowledge sector played a subsidiary role, while the significant addition of the new model is the incorporation of knowledge and science as key players in innovation systems.

The classic role of universities was to produce knowledge as "pure science" in the form of "open science" – as it is expected to be universal, skeptical, and most important, openly disseminated to the public for the benefits of public good (Merton 1973). However, in recent years, universities became knowledge producers in the form that provides important source of industrial innovation. University-based knowledge is disseminated into industrial innovation, especially in the biotechnology industry (Liebeskind et al. 1996; Powell et al. 1996; Zucker and Darby 1996).

In recent years we have witnessed a significant growth of the phenomenon of "scientific entrepreneurship" in which academic scientists become entrepreneurs to exploit the economic potential of their scientific discoveries. This phenomenon, although not new (Oliver 2005) and not unique to one industry, has been shown to be central in the biotechnology industry (Kenney 1986; Oliver and Liebeskind 1998; Powell et al. 2005; Zucker and Darby 1996). In the opening paragraph, I have suggested that the three main characteristics of the biotechnology industry are relevant features that facilitate the growth of scientific entrepreneurship. These included the role of basic science in industrial innovation, dense university–industry networks of collaborations and technology transfer, and the changes in the awareness of universities and scientists regarding economic returns of scientific research.

These features jointly led to an institutional change that promotes and supports academic scientific entrepreneurship and entrepreneurial actions of many universities. Such entrepreneurship is not single faceted. The most prominent form occurs when academic scientists themselves are founding new entrepreneurial organizations, taking the role of the scientist-manager in these organizations. Another, less discrete, form of scientific entrepreneurship is when academic scientists engage in various modes of university–industry technology transfer, which facilitate the commercialization of their own scientific discoveries (Etzkowitz 2002).

One such type of "entrepreneurial scientist" is the university "star" scientist, in biotechnology-related areas of research, who is a highly productive university researcher and who works collaboratively with firm scientists in the commercialization of his or her research (Zucker et al. 2002). Such stars can be defined as "facilitation" entrepreneurs, since Zucker et al. found that the joint publications these scientists had with firm scientists increased the number and citation rate for the firm's patents and contributed to its commercial success. These findings corroborate the assertion that the innovation in the biotechnology industry is embedded in the context of academic research and its associated institutions.

## 10.3 University Spin-Offs and University-Based Spin-Offs

USOs are newly developing organizational phenomena in which universities are involved in establishing start-ups that are based on scientific discoveries of their own scientists. There are various definitions for such spin-offs. Nicolaou and Birley (2003) define USOs as the transfer of core technology from an academic institution into a new company, where the founding member(s) may include the academic(s) who may or may not be currently affiliated with the academic institution. This is a wide definition that allows for various degrees of involvement by the inventing scientist, and the role of the university is not specified.

Another definition of USOs focuses on the exploitation of knowledge element: "New firms created to exploit commercially some knowledge, technology or research results developed within a university" (Pirany et al. 2003, p. 355). Since the knowledge component is crucial here, and academic research involves a great deal of tacit knowledge (pieces of personal knowledge accumulated by the scientists through his or her academic activities), the degree to which the scientist is involved in the spin-off is crucial for its success, leading to the emerging phenomena of "entrepreneurial scientists."

The increasing entrepreneurial spirit in academic research is one of the forces that motivate universities to establish spin-offs (UBSO). Aside from the perceived economic potential for revenues to the university, the explanatory logic is based on two elements:

- The proximity to the professor's laboratory and the direct involvement of the scientist can be crucial for the success of the scientific-technological venture.
- Providing promising scientists with an in-house opportunity for developing the process form research idea into the market place can not only motivate these scientists to stay content in the academic setting, but also enhance the entrepreneurial signals of the university for potentially entering scientists.

Based on the distinction between scientific and economic entrepreneurs that was suggested in Sect. 10.2, theoretical frameworks that apply to economic entrepreneurs are incomplete when it comes to understanding scientific entrepreneurship. My overall aim is to draw on the entrepreneurship literature and to ground this literature in a set of theories that are better suited for discerning the specifics of scientific entrepreneurship.

Generally speaking, in this form the entrepreneurial firms offer complementary outlets for academic IP to the traditional university–industry technology transfer, in which universities license to biotechnology or pharmaceutical firms the rights to conduct R&D based on the scientific discoveries of the university scientists. Another entrepreneurial form is based on contractual arrangements specifying research collaborations between the scientist's laboratory at the university and the biotechnology firm in which ongoing academic research and the work of graduate students are funded by the industry. In both forms of contractual arrangement, the university is risking either loosing possible future rents or loosing their invested funds. Yet, such choices made by the university also reduce the risks associated with the failure of the scientific venture due to the involvement of the inventing scientist. Thus, on the level of the university, the research question aims at understanding the conditions under which universities prefer to invest in founding an in-house entrepreneurial spin-off over various sorts of contractual arrangements with biotechnology firms.

In spite of the importance of understanding the institutional shifts on the individual scientist and the entrepreneurial university levels, not much research has been conducted on this front. Owen-Smith and Powell (2003) have studied the decisions made by universities regarding patenting. Pirany et al. (2003) have constructed a typology of USOs, and Etzkowitz (2002) introduced the notion of the triple helix (focusing on the interrelations of universities–industry and government as the engine for innovation as described earlier). UBSOs are considered an important subset of start-up firms because they are an economically powerful set of high-tech companies (Shane and Stuart 2002; O'Shea et al. 2005).

### 10.3.1 University-Based Spin-Offs as a New Organizational Form

Despite the growing body of research on USOs, very few studies focus on university-based spin-offs as a new organizational form and on the complexities embedded in this form (Kirby 2006). UBSOs represent a unique subset of USOs, which differs in characteristics and complexities from the "parent general form" of USOs. USBOs are defined as "An entrepreneurial organizational form that is established by universities    mostly technology-transfer offices – in order to exploit the economic potential in academic discoveries of university scientists." This form differs from other forms of technology-transfer and spin-off ventures in that it represents an economic venture of a university and it assigns a significant and central role for the scientist-entrepreneur. Thus, the university is acting under a composite role of a venture capitalist, an entrepreneur and a general and scientific manager. This is done usually to provide an "in-house" incubator for the university venture, aimed at up-bringing the venture to the stage in which the market potential is exhibited. In UBSOs the specialized technology-transfer officers lead the initial phases of the venture in full collaboration with the entrepreneurial scientist. Once market potential has been exhibited, the venture can be sold to an industrial firm wishing to bring the product into the market.

As suggested in the previous section, explaining scientific entrepreneurship and UBSOs suggests a multilevel theoretical integration, since this phenomenon involves processes that operate at the individual, network, and institutional levels. The ultimate aim of this project is to develop a model that can articulate the linkages that exist among these different levels. This task is complex. Fortunately, there are strong building blocks made up by existing research in each of these levels of analysis.

## 10.3.2 Levels of Analysis of USOs and USBOs

To offer a holistic model, explaining scientific entrepreneurship calls for multi-level theoretical treatment. This is because we are dealing with a phenolmenon that weaves together processes at the individual, network, and institutional levels.

### Individual Characteristics of the Scientific Entrepreneur

The literature of entrepreneurship has made considerable progress in identifying individual characteristics of entrepreneurs (see for example, Kets de Vries 1996; Miner 1997; Morris 1998) and entrepreneurial practices (Lumpkin and Dess 1996). By comparison, we know little about what it takes to be a scientific entrepreneur. On the basis of the sociological literature (Merton 1973; Hall 1996; Oliver 2004), the following three questions on the level of the individual traits, capabilities, and scientific background are crucial for understanding UBSOs:

- What motivates academic scientists to become entrepreneurs?
- Which personal values, traits, skills, capabilities and scientific background make it more likely that a scientist establishes an entrepreneurial venture, and which represent constraints and liabilities?
- What management competencies and leadership qualities are needed for an academic entrepreneur?

The literature offers various answers to these questions:

- The motivation of scientists to become entrepreneurs varies. In an exploratory study of MIT, Shane (2004) suggests a few motivational characteristics of the academics involved in the entrepreneurial venture. These include the desire to bring technology into practice, the desire for wealth, and the desire for independence. The academic interests are also acknowledged by Zucker et al. (1998), who found that scientific "stars" collaborating with firms had significantly more citations than did pure academic stars.
- The literature on the background characteristics of the scientific entrepreneurs is rather limited. Oliver (2004) found that scientific entrepreneurs who are defined as having many collaborations, both with academia and industry, are those who have a larger laboratory that includes also postdoctoral students. Another issue associated with scientific entrepreneurship is expressed in the potential conflict between publications in journals (a form of conducting "open science" activities) and patenting behavior (a form of appropriation of knowledge established in scientific research, thus "close science" activities). Since academic scientists in biotechnology are involved both in publications and in patenting, the arising sociological question is whether the increasing entrepreneurial spirit of scientists causes these activities to be conflicting, reinforcing, or coexisting. Recent findings by Van Looy et al. (2006) suggest that inventors publish significantly more than noninventors, and thus patenting and publications seem to be coexisting or may actually reinforce each other.

- Regarding the needed competencies of scientific entrepreneurs, a recent study of the role of the founder in the growth of new technology-based firms (Colombo and Grilli 2005) looks at the relations between the human capital of the founder and the growth of the firm in Italian firms. The study teases out the effects of wealth and capabilities of human capital, and the findings show that the education and the prior work experience of the founder have a significant influence of firm growth. The educational effect, however, has a stronger impact when it is in economic and managerial fields and less so when it is in scientific and technical fields. Similarly, prior work experience within the same industry is positively associated, while previous work experience in another industry does not have an affect. Synergistic gains were found from the founder's combination of the capabilities associated with economic-managerial with scientific education and technical and commercial industry-specific work experience.

### Network Effects

Recent organizational literature has established a strong relationship between participating in collaborative networks and the success of individual organizations (Baum et al. 2000; Gnyawali and Madhavan 2001; Gulati 1998; Oliver 2001).[1] In addition, earlier research has shown that the successful development of high-technology entrepreneurial firms hinges on strong university–industry linkages (Liebeskind et al. 1996; Oliver and Liebeskind 1998).

While this general insight of the importance of network relations in new ventures is well established, research on university-based entrepreneurial spin-offs is only beginning to address it. What is needed is to test empirically the more specific questions regarding the characteristics of an actor's network are particularly conducive to the successful exploitation of his or her social, scientific, and industrial networks. Factors such as the characteristics of the networks (communication content of exchanges, intensity of past exchanges; dimensions of networks (range and variation of "social capital" – namely "the sum of resources, actual or virtual, that accrue to an individual or a group by virtue of possession a durable network or more or less institutionalized relationships of mutual acquaintances and recognition" (Bourdieu and Wacquant 1992, p. 119)); the ability to occupy "structural holes" positions (Burt 1997); and entrepreneurial networking abilities (such as the ability to reach beyond existing contacts into new contacts, exploiting the advantages of social capital) are important. These characteristics facilitate the spread of racecourses and information, and enhance network diversity, factors that are accounted as crucial for entrepreneurs (Aldrich and Zimmer 1990). It is expected that academic scientific entrepreneurs will have and utilize wide and diverse networks within the scientific and economic communities in order to gain the necessary information and resources for

---

[1] It should be noted that it is unclear, whether participating in collaborative network causes the success of individual organization really. Probably, projects with higher probability of success are accepted by research partner for collaborative work.

establishing their ventures. In addition, such entrepreneurs need to participate in learning and exchange networks that are vital to the success of the new venture. The proposed research will therefore combine a social network perspective with the perspective that focuses on the content of the exchange and the learning perspective (Nonaka and Takeuchi 1995).

The learning networks can facilitate the scientific entrepreneur in acquiring important resources such as information, advice, contacts, and managerial resources that are crucial for the early stages of the firms (Nowak and Grantham 2000). These networks can deliver also capabilities, knowledge, incentives, important contact information, and joint services (Oliver and Ebers 1998; Oliver and Liebeskind 1998). Adding the learning perspective is highly important in the specific context, since academic entrepreneurs need to enhance both their scientific networks and their industrial and venture capital networks in order to establish and operate a successful new venture. These networks are different in terms of norms, content, access, frequency, and reachability, and thus require high flexibility and learning qualities of the academic entrepreneur.

The social and professional networks of academic inventors are an important factor that contributes to the success of the entrepreneurial firm. A study on biotechnology firms and their academic inventors (Murray 2004) argued that the social capital of academic scientists is critical to firms because it can be transformed into scientific networks that embed the firm in the scientific community. In addition, an academic inventor's career plays an important role in shaping the social capital, thus the scientific career has a mediating effect on the relations between scientist and his networks. The social capital of an inventor can emerge his laboratory life (e.g. students, colleagues, clinicians) as well as from his general network of collaborators, colleagues, or competitors. Thus, the scientific careers of inventor-scientists are important is shaping the social capital of the scientists, and thus his scientific networks of the entrepreneurial firm.

Geographical proximity has been conceived to be important for knowledge transfer. The degree to which proximity facilitates knowledge transfer has been one of the important arguments in favor of establishing science parks next to universities. Lindelöf and Löfsten (2004) found that technology-based firms that worked with the proximate universities achieve certain advantage. The advantage resulted from the promoted exchange of ideas through both formal and informal networks. Thus, being geographically close to the academic network is important for firm success. Another study (Link and Scott 2005), focused on USO companies within the university's research park, found that USOs are of greater proportion of the companies in older parks and are associated with richer university research environments. They also found that USOs are a larger proportion of companies in parks that are geographically closer to their universities and in parks that have a biotechnology focus, thus following the proximity advantage argument and the close association of biotechnology industrial research with university research.

## The Institutional Level

The institutional level of analysis focuses on the importance of the university's formal economic and declarative support in spin-off's activities on the one hand, and the characteristics of the institutional environment that can enhance or hinder the founding and success of spin-offs. I will relay to these two important elements.

Differences between universities can be associated with the founding and success of UBSOs. Some universities, such as Oxford University in the UK, operate a technology-transfer office as a vehicle to support the creation of spin-off companies (O'Shea et al. 2004). The technology-transfer office plays a key role in supporting academic entrepreneurship. This can be achieved by the ability to offer synergistic networks between academic scientists, venture capitalists, and managers, who provide the resource-based expertise for establishing a UBSO, while the TT people evaluate the potential markets, write business plans, raise venture capital, and obtain space and equipment.

Beyond the technical and capability-based support of the technology-transfer office, universities that have cultures that support commercialization activities will have higher rates of spin-off activities. By contrast, universities that do not encourage entrepreneurship will inhibit spin-off activity (O'Shea et al. 2004). Entrepreneurial universities have been acknowledged to have an important role in local economic development (Feldman 2001), but spin-off activities are also important for pleasing academics within universities. Feldman found that spin-off activities are established for satisfying frustrated scientists, creating the basis for moving research faster, for applying broad-based platform technology for new products, to retain "star" graduate students and to keep research groups small and focused.

The effects of the wider institutional environment are important here as well. Research on entrepreneurial behavior has mostly assumed an under-contextualized research approach in which firms were studied in relative isolation from their institutional environment (Autio 1997). Recent organizational research has pointed out, however, the important impact that institutional embeddedness can have on firm founding, conduct, and performance (Uzzi 1996). In the context of scientific entrepreneurship, Oliver and Liebeskind (2006) have shown how differences in institutional environments regarding IP rights can impact the commercialization of academic research. In a comparison case study of the invention process and the diffusion-related activities of two leading academic inventions in biotechnology, they show how both commercialization and future scientific development of these key inventions are dependent critically on the institutional environment and the property rights regimes.

Institutions play an important role on the life of academic researchers and thus we need to understand the impact of the institutional environment such as the university (as the key actor in the founding process of UBSOs), governments, and property rights regimes have on the founding and success of scientific entrepreneurial spin-offs.

Indeed, from a sociological point of view, the milieu of scientific innovation comprises a set of interlocking institutions: universities, national research institutes, academic journals, research conferences, laws and regulations, funding sources, government initiatives and policies, etc. Among the institutional forces that affect the propensity of scientists to become entrepreneurs, and the likelihood that they will be successful, are the pertinent regulations adopted by the employers of the scientists (in this case, universities) (Argyres and Liebeskind 1996; Liebeskind et al. 1996; Zucker and Darby 1996). Some universities have extremely open regimes, allowing and even facilitating their scientists to find and manage entrepreneurial firms while retaining university positions. University rules and regulations can inhibit scientists' motivation and the ability to develop and commercialize their own know-how.

A recent study (O'Shea et al. 2004) asks why some universities are more successful than others at generating technology-based spin-off companies. By adopting a resource base perspective they test whether resources and capabilities, institutional, financial, commercial, and human capital resources are attributed to spin-off outcomes. They find that history of successful technology transfer as well as faculty quality, size and orientation of science and engineering funding, and commercial activities are predictors of USO activities.

The legal protection and the ease of transfer of IP rights represent a further important institutional-level influence factor on the founding of successful university-based entrepreneurial spin-offs. Scientific entrepreneurs operate under highly uncertain conditions that require significant managerial attention to legal aspects of "know how" and IP rights. Yet, protection of IP rights on the one hand while facilitating the founding of an entrepreneurial venture on the other hand are somewhat contradicting forces that need to be handled by sensitive and experienced managerial vision.

The research that focuses on the emergence of the entrepreneurial university and associated shifts in IP regimes was noted already in this chapter (Etzkowitz et al. 2005). Etzkowitz et al. argue that concomitant variation between IP and academic regimes is part of a broader transition from the dual helices of university–industry and government–industry relations to an innovation system based on university–industry–government interactions. Thus, entrepreneurial universities are resting on four pillars: legal control over academic resources for research; organizational capacity to transfer technology through patenting, licensing, and incubation; facilitating the entrepreneurial ethos among scientists and administrators; and enhancing academic and managerial leadership to formulate and implement strategic vision for establishing university-based entrepreneurial spin-offs.

The institutional difference in scientists' entrepreneurship corporate involvement was termed "nested embeddedness" by Kenney and Goe (2004). In their study they explain why scientists at the electronic engineering and computer sciences at Stanford and University of California at Berkeley expressed different levels of entrepreneurship. The level of corporate involvement, including founding of start-ups, was higher at Stanford. This suggests that the degree to which the university supports the entrepreneurial activities of its scientists is associated with scientific entrepreneurship.

There are also external institutional factors associated with the founding and success of USOs. O'Shea et al. (2004) suggest three broad factors that have an impact on USO activities. These include access to venture capital, the legal assignment of inventions (especially acts such as the Bayh–Dole act in the USA (also see Mowery and Sampat 2005)), and the knowledge infrastructure in the region.

In the context of biotechnology, Lowe (2005) (who reviews the operation of the Institute of Biotechnology in Cambridge, which aims at creating spin-offs) argues that to be successful, a multidimensional environment is needed. This multidimensionality includes crossing traditional boundaries between disciplines, and integrating other businesses, teaching, and training activities into the entrepreneurial culture that embraces integration with the industry.

### 10.3.3 A Life Cycle Approach to USOs

Since USOs in all forms represent a relatively new phenomenon, we have limited research that offers a longitudinal perspective on this complex organizational form. A life cycle approach to USO forms (Vohora et al. 2004) suggests that there are a number of distinct phases of development, and each venture must pass through the previous phase in order to progress to the next one. These phases include research, opportunity framing, pre organization, re-orientation, and sustainability. However, each phase involves an iterative nonlinear process of development in which information needs to be gathered as the needed resources are searched for. In addition, at the interstices between the phases, the ventures face "critical junctures" in terms of the resources and capabilities needed for moving to the following stage. The critical junctures are identified as (1) opportunity recognition; (2) entrepreneurial commitment; (3) venture credibility; and (4) venture sustainability and returns. Thus, we learn from this study that the evolutionary growth path of USBOs is complex and modular and how social capital, resources and internal capabilities are acquired in order to enable the venture to generate revenues and compete effectively.

## 10.4 Integration, Complexities and New Research Directions

I have already listed the trends that led to an increasing motivation for founding USOs or UBSOs, especially in biotechnology-related research. However, the literature already found that USOs confront some unique difficulties in achieving sustainability, capabilities, and financial profits. These difficulties are due to two major elements (Vohara et al. 2004). The first relates to the fact that they emerge out of an idea in a noncommercial environment, aiming at becoming a commercial competitive firm. In addition and in contrast to none academic start-ups, these ventures suffer from conflicting objectives of central key holders such as the university, the academic entrepreneur, the venture's management team, and suppliers of finance. These difficulties are not surprising, since they are associated with effort to hybrid two distinct institutional environments – the one of academic research and the commercialization processes.

Another complexity is associated with the policies adopted by universities. As mentioned earlier, the role of university policies is important in the success and growth of the ventures (Degroof and Roberts 2004). Not all universities generate spin-offs and not all academic disciplines equally generate new firms, and they are mostly in biotechnology and information technology. Universities can be classified by the support they offer UBSOs and the selectivity they apply in the process (Degroof and Roberts 2004, p. 329). In their effort to characterize spin-offs, they classify four central archetypes and distinguish between policies of universities. The first archetype, which characterized nonentrepreneurial policies, includes universities with an absence of proactive spin-off policies in which scientists derive the entrepreneurial process, and the business project is generally modest. The second archetype includes minimalist support and selectivity policies. There was no proactive technology search, and the identification of opportunities relied on the scientists, and the entrepreneurial environment was weak. IP assessment emerged slowly, and the university provided limited assistance in writing business plans. Selectivity of projects was minimalist and seed funds were provided, but many times, the scientists were left on their own, isolated from the entrepreneurial community. The third archetype is the one that provides intermediate support and selectivity. It involved a proactive technology-transfer policy, in which the technology-transfer office had more independence and resources. More support was provided for the concept testing phase before the venture was funded, and this was aimed at pushing founders to target ambitious opportunities. The university was involved in creating a network among the nascent high-tech community. The forth archetype was based on high support and selectivity policy that was carried out by research institutes outside of the university. These institutes had a strong emphasis on technology transfer and developed proactive procedure for technology opportunity search and of research with commercial potential. This was gained by strong IP capabilities to evaluate the potential of commercialization of academic research. The concept testing was conducted during the incubation stage, while the business side was delegated by managers with industry or policy experience. The start-up support phase was carried over by the management team. There are several implications that result from this study and that are noteworthy: first, when the entrepreneurial environment is weak, universities need to apply spin-off policies that involve high selectivity and high support. In this context, academic institutions need to consider alternative strategies such as partnering with other firms and need to select spin-offs with high growth potential. Second, academic institutions need to develop not only financial resources for spin-offs but also networks in the scientific and business communities. Finally, if resources are constraints, universities need to decide what policies are possible to implement prior to establishing spin-offs.

As a point of closure and a direction for future research, we must note that there is a great heterogeneity of TTO missions and IP as university endowment and mission may differ. Some universities do not engage in university startups and exclusively license, even if they are leaders in biotechnology research. In addition, IP policies differ across the university system and can play a critical role in the commercialization process. If the IP exclusively belongs to the university, it may create less than optimal outcomes for university-based startups.

In summary, these new organizational forms and changes in the academic institutional environment call for future important research that would enhance our understanding of these emerging patterns. New research directions should examine:

- The effect of university policies regarding IP on the proliferation of UBSO
- The recursive effect of UBSO on entrepreneurial science within universities and the changes they may have on the scientific communities and university structures
- The effect of the entry of VC in funding USOs on processes of university decision-making and further academic and research activities
- The internal features of the new organizational forms of USOs and UBSOs and changes in them over time
- Direct and indirect success or failure factors of USOs and UBSOs

# References

Aldrich H, Zimmer C (1990) Entrepreneurship through social networks. California Management Review 33 (1): 3–23

Argyres N, Liebeskind J (1996) Privatizing the intellectual commons: Universities and the commercialization of biotechnology. Journal of Economic Behavior and Organization 35: 427–454

Arzeni S (1997) Entrepreneurship. The OECD Observer 209, December 1997/January 1998: 18–20

Autio E (1997) 'Atomistic' and 'systemic' approaches to research on new, technology-based firms: A literature study. Small Business Economics 9: 195–209

Baum JAC, Calabrese T, Silverman BS (2000) Don't do it alone: Alliance network composition and the startups' performance in Canadian biotechnology. Strategic Management Journal 21 (Special issue): 267–294

Bourdieu P, Wacquant L (1992) An invitation to reflexive sociology, University of Chicago Press, Chicago, IL

Burt R (1997) The contingent value of social capital. Administrative Science Quarterly 42: 339–365

Butler D (1998) France seeks scientific entrepreneurs. Nature 393 (6682): 203

Colombo MG, Grilli L (2005) Founder's human capital and the growth of new technology-based firms: A competence-based view. Research Policy 34: 795–816

Degroof JJ, Roberts EB (2004) Overcoming weak entrepreneurial infrastructure for academic spin-offs ventures. Journal of Technology Transfer 29: 327–352

Etzkowitz H (1998) The norms of entrepreneurial science: Cognitive effects of the new university–industry linkages. Research Policy 27: 823–833

Etzkowitz H (2002) Incubation of incubators: Innovation as a triple helix of university–industry–government networks. Science and Public Policy 29: 115–128

Etzkowitz H (2003) Research groups as 'quasi-firms': The invention of the entrepreneurial university. Research Policy 32: 109–121

Etzkowitz H, Leydesdorff L (2000) The dynamics of innovation: From National Systems and 'Mode 2' to a triple helix of university-industry-government relations. Research Policy 29: 109–123

Etzkowitz H, Webster A, Gebhardt C, Terra BRC (2000) The future of the university and the university of the future: Evolution of ivory tower to entrepreneurial paradigm. Research Policy 29: 313–330

Etzkowitz H, Benner L, Guaranys A, Maculan M, Kneller R (2005) Managed capitalism: Intellectual property and the rise of the entrepreneurial university in the US, Sweden, Brazil and Japan. Paper presented at Druid Summer conference, Denmark.

Feldman PM (2001) Where science comes to life: University bioscience, commercial spin-offs, and regional economic development. Journal of Comparative Policy Analysis 2: 345–361

Gnyawali DR, Madhavan R (2001) Corporative networks and competitive dynamics: A structural embeddedness perspective. Academy of Management Review 26: 431–445

Gulati R (1998) Alliances and networks. Strategic Management Journal 19: 293–317

Hall DT (ed) (1996) The career is dead – long live the career: A relational approach to careers. Jossey-Bass, San Francisco

Kenney M (1986) Biotechnology: The university–industry complex. Yale University Press, New Haven

Kenney M, Goe WR (2004) The role of social embeddedness in professional entrepreneurship: A comparison of electrical engineering and computer science at UC Berkeley and Stanford. Research Policy 33: 691–707

Kets de Vries MFR (1996) The anatomy of the entrepreneur: Clinical observations. Human Relations 49: 853–884

Kirby D (2006) Creating entrepreneurial universities in the UK: Applying entrepreneurship theory to practice. Journal of Technology Transfer 31 (5): 599–603

Liebeskind JP, Oliver AL, Zucker L, Brewer M (1996) Social networks, learning and flexibility: Sourcing scientific knowledge in new biotechnology firms. Organization Science 7: 428–443

Lindelöf P, Löfsten H (2004) Proximity as a resource base for competitive advantage: University–industry links for technology transfer. Journal of Technology Transfer 29 (3/4): 311–326

Link AN, Scott JT (2005) Opening the ivory tower's door: An analysis of the determinants of the formation of US university spin-offs companies. Research Policy 34: 1106–1112

Lowe CR (2005) Commercialization and spin-out activities of the Institute of Biotechnology. Journal of Commercial Biotechnology 11 (4): 305–317

Lumpkin GT, Dess GG (1996) Clarifying the entrepreneurial orientation construct and linking it to performance. Academy of Management Review 21: 135–172

Merton R (1973) The sociology of science. University of Chicago Press, Chicago

Miner JB (1997) A psychological typology of successful entrepreneurs. Quorum Books, Westport, CT

Morris MH (1998) Entrepreneurial intensity: Sustainable advantages for individuals, organizations, and societies. Quorum, Westport, CT

Mowery DC, Sampat BN (2005) The Bayh–Dole Act of 1980 and university–industry technology transfer: A model for other OECD governments? Journal of Technology Transfer 30 (1/2): 115–127

Murray F (2004) The role of academic inventors in entrepreneurial firms: Sharing the laboratory life. Research Policy 33: 643–659

Nicolaou N, Birley S (2003) Academic networks in a trichotomous categorization of university spinouts. Journal of Business Venturing 18: 333–359

Nonaka I, Takeuchi H (1995) The knowledge creating company. Oxford University Press, Oxford

Nowak MJ, Grantham CE (2000) The virtual incubator: Managing human capital in the software industry. Research Policy 29: 125–134

Oliver AL (2001) Strategic alliances and the learning life-cycle of biotechnology firms. Organization Studies 22: 467–489

Oliver AL (2004) Biotechnology entrepreneurial scientists and their collaborations. Research Policy 33: 583–597

Oliver AL (2005) University–industry collaborations: Contrasting metaphors of linear and chaotic networking processes. Working Paper, Department of Sociology, Hebrew University, Jerusalem

Oliver AL, Ebers M (1998) Networking network studies    An analysis of conceptual configurations in the study of inter-organizational relations. Organization Studies 19: 549–583

Oliver AL, Liebeskind JP (1998) Three levels for networking for intellectual capital in biotechnology: Implications for studying interorganizational networks. International Studies of Management and Organization 27 (4): 76–103

Oliver AL, Liebeskind JP (2006) Public research and intellectual property rights: A tale of two inventions. Working paper, Department of Sociology, The Hebrew University, Jerusalem

O'Shea R, Allen TJ, O'Gorman C, Roche F (2004) Universities and technology transfer: A review of academic entrepreneurship literature. Irish Journal of Management 25: 11–29

O'Shea R, Allen TJ, Chevalier A, Roche F (2005) Entrepreneurial orientation, technology transfer, and spinoff performance of U.S. universities. Research Policy 34: 994–1009

Owen-Smith J, Powell WW (2003) The expanding role of university patenting in the life sciences: Assessing the importance of experience and connectivity. Research Policy 32 (9): 1695–1711

Powell WW, Koput KW, Smith-Doerr L (1996) Interorganizational collaboration and the locus of innovation: Networks of learning in biotechnology. Administrative Science Quarterly 41: 116–145

Powell WW, White DR, Kupot KW, Owen-Smith J (2005) Network dynamics and field evolution: The growth of interorganizational collaborations in the life sciences. American Journal of Sociology 110: 1132–1205

Shane S (2004) Academic entrepreneurship: University spin-offs and wealth creation. Edward Elgar, Cheltenham, UK

Shane S, Stuart T (2002) Organizational endowment and the performance of university start-ups. Management Science 48 (1): 154–171

Uzzi B (1996) The sources and consequences of embeddedness for the economic performance of organizations: The network effect. American Sociological Review 61: 674–698

Van Looy B, Callaert J, Debackere K (2006) Publication and patent behavior of academic researchers: Conflicting, reinforcing or merely co-existing? Research Policy 35: 596–608

Vohora A, Wright M, Lockett A (2004) Critical junctures in the development of university high-tech spinout companies. Research Policy 33: 147–175

Zaheer A, George VP (2004) Reach out or reach within? Performance implications of alliance and location in biotechnology. Managerial and Decision Economics 25: 437–452

Zucker LG, Darby MR (1996) Star scientists and institutional transformation: Patterns of invention and innovation in the formation of the biotechnology industry. Proceedings of the National Academy of Science 93: 12709–12916

Zucker LG, Darby MR, Brewer MB (1998) Intellectual human capital and the birth of U.S. biotechnology enterprises. The American Economic Review 88: 290–306

Zucker LG, Darby MR, Armstrong J (2002) Commercializing knowledge: University science, knowledge capture, and firm performance in biotechnology. Management Science 48: 138–153

# 11 Patenting Biotechnology

Saradindu Bhaduri

Centre for Studies in Science Policy, Jawaharlal Nehru University, New Delhi, India

## 11.1 Introduction

While individual rights on physical properties are now well accepted, at least in 'modern' societies, individual rights on intellectual property (IPRs) remains a controversial issue. Theoretical explanations and empirical evidence, both for and against IPR, have only increased in recent years and no reversal of this trend is in sight. Patent, in particular, has been at the centre stage of this debate. In the words of Abraham Lincoln, patents were supposed to promote entrepreneurship and industrial development by adding a 'fuel of incentives' to the 'fire of genius' (creativity of individual scientists). At the same time, patent laws have, often, been accused of promoting monopolies (Machlup 1958, pp. 10–12) and 'corporatisation' of R&D, wherein the rate and the direction of innovations are largely guided by commercial motives, devoid of much 'fire of genius' (Noble 1977, Chap. 6).[1] Clearly, this was conflict with the stated objective of patents to promote creativity of individuals. Therefore, questions were raised on the appropriateness of granting patents, in particular, to the outcomes of large-scale 'routinised' R&D, without any substantive individual fire (Kingston 2005). This matter is now largely settled, where patents to 'routinised' R&D outcomes are no longer questioned. The boundaries of debates surrounding benefits and costs of patenting, however, continue shifting with the inclusion of newer issues. In particular, costs and benefits of strategic patenting, the role of patents in technological catch up, technology transfer and economic development are some of the issues being subsequently discussed threadbare, along with the core issue of whether patents indeed provide incentives to innovate.

[1] According to Alexanderson (1972), the patent system, thus, protects 'the institutions which favour invention' instead of protecting the 'lone inventor'.

H. Patzelt and T. Brenner (eds.), *Handbook of Bioentrepreneurship*, 211
doi: 10.1007/978-0-387-48345-0_11, © Springer Science + Business Media, LLC 2008

The invention of genetic engineering technology and the consequent growth of the modern biotechnology industry have added new dimensions to these debates. Going by the Nobel Prize lecture of Edward Tatum in 1958, the basic purpose of genetic engineering seems to control and regulate the functions of genes in order 'not only to *avoid* structural and metabolic errors in the developing organisms but also to *produce* better organisms' (Tatum 1959, p. 1714). Evidently, the prospects for a widespread use of genetic engineering to develop medicines and to enhance nutritional levels of foods were realised in no time (Kuenning and Makundi 2000). Also, the prospect of modifying genes of plants for better pest resistance provided a ray of hope to rescue agriculture from the crippling co-evolution of pests and (chemical) pesticides in industrialised countries (Goodman et al. 1987).[2] Such prospects for commercial applications can, perhaps, explain the current widespread attempts to privately appropriate new inventions in biotechnology. Indeed, the biotechnological industry has witnessed one of the highest growth rates of patents in recent times. Khan and Dernis (2006, p. 44) report that biotechnology patents have grown at an annual rate of 8.3% a year, surpassing the overall growth rate of patents in European Patent Office (5.7%).

With this increasing rate of patents, arrays of concerns worthy of scholarly attention have surfaced. This chapter is an attempt to provide an overview of these issues as well as to analyse how academic researchers, largely, but not exclusively, in economics, have responded to them. I will, however, restrict myself mainly to studies and issues, which have larger theoretical implications.

There are at least six issues, which warrant attention in any discussion on patenting biotechnology. Most important of them is, perhaps, the issues surrounding appropriation of life forms (Kodish 1997; Caulfield 1999; Caulfield and Gold 2000; Gold 2001; Yamana 2001; UNCTAD-ICTSD 2005). However, one has to very carefully distinguish between the set of issues pertaining to 'patenting' life forms, and the more general set of issues related to 'modifying' life forms through biotechnology.[3] I concentrate only on issues concerning patenting of life forms. In doing so, I will also touch upon a related issue, which analyses the appropriateness of patenting life forms based on a framework, which was originally designed to protect mechanical inventions (Ko 1992; Thurow 1997; Gold et al. 2002; Farnley et al. 2004).

The second issue is the issue of academic entrepreneurs in the context of biotechnology. The progress of biotechnology has reportedly been associated with a spurt in new start ups, where academic scientists are starting new ventures to commercialise the technologies they have developed. It is argued that patents have helped them retain their rights on innovation and enabled them to commercialise these technologies in a major way (Zucker et al. 2002; Audretsch 2006). This trend of assigning biotechnological patents more to individuals, as opposed to

---

[2] See Norgaard 1994, pp. 24–26, for a detailed account of this co-evolutionary process.

[3] See, for instance, McKelvey (1996a) for a detail discussion on the second set of issues. See also the studies cited in the Scope Note 17, The Human Genome Project (http://bioethics.heorgetown.edu/publications/scopenotes/sn17.htm, last accessed on 9 July 2007)

firms, if true, might demand a shift in focus of the existing industrial organisation literature, where, scientists are merely treated as R&D inputs, and technologies are owned by firms. It can, perhaps, be said that the inherent science dependency of biotechnology has brought this much forgotten issue of individual 'flash of genius' back to the fore, once again. Various debates associated with it as well as the implications of such a trend are discussed.

The third issue is the consequence of patenting biotechnology for public science, and the organisations that generate it. This issue is an outcome of a strong science dependency of biotechnology on one hand, and its strong commercial prospects on the other. I have mentioned earlier that biotechnology has been subjected to patent protection from the very initial phase of its growth, mainly due to its commercial relevance. At the same time, growth of biotechnology also depends, crucially, on basic research (BR) done at universities and public laboratories (Markle and Robin 1985; Cook-Deegan 2007). Traditionally, these bodies have been entrusted with the job of enriching public 'open' knowledge (Merton 1967; Polanyi 1967). Patent protection to biotechnology has raised a fear of 'closure' of open public knowledge pool, which is commonly termed as the 'anti-common effect' of science (Heller and Eisenberg 1998; Mowery et al. 1999; Eisenberg and Nelson 2002; Sampat 2006) [4]

Biotechnology is also identified as a 'complex technology', where one end product comprises of several technological outputs. Often, patent is sought separately for these constituent (intermediate) technologies. A final product is, thus, protected by a 'thicket of patents' (Shapiro 2000; Ziedonis 2004), rather than a single patent – as the case is with traditional products. Also, biotechnological innovations are cumulative in nature. The thicket of patents at the disposal of each researcher, therefore, can be used as a strategic tool for research cooperation and negotiation. Accordingly, the role of patent in 'holding up' and 'blocking' commercialisation is increasingly being paid attention to (Ko 1992; Lerner 1995; Shapiro 2000; Lanjouw and Schankerman 2001). I give an overview of research on this (fourth) issue as well.

Finally, two issues that are intricately linked with economic development are discussed. Besides revisiting the well-known development debate on patents and technological catch up (IPR commission Report 2002, Chap. 1), I also highlight the emerging development debate on the implications of accessing biodiversity of the South by proprietary corporations of the North. While it is widely held that the progress in genetic engineering research may solve problems of health care and food security in developing countries, the proprietary control of these technologies has been a source of concern. These concerns range from the fear of overexploitation of ecological resources (Swanson 1996), to corporate ownership

---

[4] This is not to suggest that this fear is true only for biotechnology. See Gibbons et al. (1994) for a pioneering discussion on the interaction between fundamental and applied knowledge and its implications for changing research organisations. However, as mentioned by an anonymous referee, biotechnology remains one of the most science-dependent industries with substantial commercial prospect and developmental implications. The issue, therefore, draws wide attention in the context of biotechnology.

of biological diversity (Burrows 2001). The absolute advantage of the North in technology (of genetic engineering) and the absolute advantage of the South in requisite raw materials (diversity in life forms and genes) leads to a complex kind of North–South conflict, unseen in other high technology areas. Currently, at the World Trade Organisation (WTO), negotiations are taking place on the demand by the South countries to share the benefits derived by the Northern firms from commercialising products based on these biological entities, on grounds that biodiversity is not merely a natural resource. Rather, indigenous communities in many South countries have, for centuries, maintained, conserved and enriched these resources, and they form an integral part of knowledge of these communities.

The chapter has five broad sections. The following section, Sect. 11.2, will define the meaning and scope of biotechnology for our discussion, and elaborate on its various characteristics. Section 11.3 presents the basic issues of patents. Based on this discussion the thematic framework for the key section (Sect. 11.4) is formed, which analyses the implications of patenting biotechnology. Sect. 11.5 concludes.

## 11.2 Biotechnology Industry: Meaning and Scope

Despite the age-old existence of biological processes such as brewing and baking in industrial activities, the emergence of modern biotechnology refers to the use of genetic engineering techniques or recombinant DNA. In this section, an overview of its basic characteristics and the academic discussions on its historical trajectory are given.

### 11.2.1 Genetic Engineering: Basic Features

In its core, genetic engineering refers to 'controlled changes to DNA' (McKelvey 1996a, p. 80) for the benefit of humans (Taylor et al. 2002, p. 834), whose development has been much influenced by theoretical developments in the field of molecular genetics (Markle and Robin 1985). As opposed to classical genetics, where genetic information is exchanged through usual mating process, molecular genetics permits 'directed manipulation of genetic material and transfer of genetic information between species that cannot interbreed' (Gonsen 1998, p. 44).[5] One may note that by enabling genetic information to be transferred or exchanged between species that cannot interbreed, genetic engineering helped achieve a major breakthrough in genetic research by removing the species barrier (Taylor et al. 2002, Chap. 25).

It may be safely argued that biotechnology is not an industry. Rather, it is a set of technologies applicable to a spectrum of industries (Gonsen 1998). In this

---

[5] See Taylor et al. (2002, pp. 834–835) for the theory of genetic engineering.

sense, genetic-engineering-led biotechnology has paved the way for the so-called 'bioindustrialisation' by removing the technological barriers across industries (Goodman et al. 1987). Needless to mention, the removal of species barriers and technology barriers expand the domain of use of genetic engineering technologies, enabling it to reap the advantage of scale economies of a degree unmatched by many other technologies (other than, perhaps, information technology). Indeed, harnessing of genetic-engineering-led biotechnology provided a new set of life line to the economies of the West, crippled by the burden of human diseases such as diabetes and ever increasing use of chemical pesticides in agriculture. The successful incorporation of biotechnology in large-scale industrial production of human insulin, and herbicide tolerant, pest resistant corns and soybeans – major food items of the West (King and Stabinsky 1999) – immediately benefited these economies, since biotechnology reduced the uncertainties of raw material availability and hazards of chemical pollution (Goodman et al. 1987).

## 11.2.2 Genetic Engineering: Continuity or Discontinuity?

It is widely debated whether genetic engineering should be regarded as a major breakthrough over its predecessor technologies (Markle and Robin 1985; McKelvey 1996a, 1996b). Product-wise, biotechnological products are very often classified into three generations (Fairtlough 1986; Hacking 1986; Sharp 1991). The first generation products refer to simple brewed products such as beer, wine or cheese. The second generation of biotechnological products includes specialised products such as antibiotics and industrial enzymes produced by large-scale standardised modern fermentation processes. Genetically engineered human growth hormone and insulin are classified as the third generation products.

It is important to note that the core technologies of the first two generations of product largely evolved out of localised, experience-based learning, while the core technology of the third generation products is a result of formal scientific research. Another distinction between the third generation and the previous two generations are often made in terms of technological paradigms. As mentioned earlier, according to this view, genetic engineering is considered as a major advancement over and above tissue and cell-culture-based selective breeding, where manipulation is done at the gene level, and not at the level of the whole plant and animal. Nevertheless, there are differences in opinion on whether these dissimilarities are significant enough to characterise the third generation biotechnology as a revolutionary change over the first two generations. Often, these differences in opinion are country specific. European scholars maintain that the emergence of genetic engineering is a slow and continuous process over its previous generations. In USA, however, scientists prefer to view it as discontinuous jump (Markle and Robin 1985, pp. 70–71). Interestingly, US policy makers maintained a strategic distance from this view of US scientists. At the policy level, genetic engineering is often proclaimed to be incremental development (USDA 1987, p. 10), arguably, to minimise public attention against patenting and manipulation of life forms that genetic-engineering-led biotechnologies have sought to promote (Plein 1991, p. 482). This debate remains an unsettled one.

For the purpose of economic analysis, however, one would be more interested to analyse the spill over of such technological discontinuities, if any, into the economic domain. In other words, to recount the old Schumpeterian adage, one would be interested to examine whether new technologies unleash a process of creative destruction in the industrial organisation. We do not find any clear evidence of this process in the context of biotechnology. Although it is true that the emergence of modern biotechnology has helped many new start-ups[6] to emerge and grow, many old firms have also retained their competitiveness in the market (Mowery 2005). McKelvey (1996b) makes an attempt to reconcile these two by arguing that a one-to-one mapping from technological discontinuities to creative destruction may not be possible in complex technologies, where capability of firms to adopt a new technology in their otherwise 'sticky' routines (Nelson and Winter 1982) depends on a host of factors such as networks and external linkages, other than own in-house R&D. In other words, in the biotechnology industry, characterised by multiple core technologies (Chesnais and Walsh 1994), continuity of technological competence of a firm depends not only on its in-house R&D, but also on its capacity to organise additional activities to integrate externally available novel technologies into its existing routine. Understandably, this capacity might depend on various factors such as past experiences and reputation, where large, established firms may have an edge, reducing the possibility of a one to one relationship between technological discontinuity and changes in industrial organisation.

## 11.3 Patents: An Overview

### 11.3.1 Basic Issues

Economics as a discipline is concerned with appropriation of knowledge due to the importance of creativity and innovation for sustained growth and economic development. An economist's concern for effective IPRs emanates from the belief that knowledge is a public good having the characteristics of non-excludability. This has two implications. A creator of a new knowledge would be hesitant to disclose it, depriving the society of any gains in productivity and efficiency arising out of this knowledge. Second, a potential creator of a new knowledge might be hesitant to put in inventive effort if the results of such efforts are freely ridden upon by others. Although the practice of granting exclusive rights to manufacture and trade of novelty had its origin in Europe around 500 years ago, the concept of IPRs, as a formal institution, is a late eighteenth century US creation. The Patent Act of 1790 (amended in 1793) was the first of its kind with an explicit objective of promoting novelty and innovation.

---

[6] See, for instance, Gonsen (1998, Table 3.1, pp. 42–43) and Zucker et al. (1998).

The Act emphasises that '...any new and useful art, machine, manufacture or composition of matter and any new and useful improvement on any art, machine, manufacture or composition of matter...' (Section 101 {FN2: 35 U.S.C. §101}[7]) would be patentable for a limited period 'to promote the progress of science and useful arts' (Evenson and Putnam 1987, p. 403).

Any patentable item would have to conform to five standards, namely (i) novelty, (ii) utility, (iii) inventive step, (iv) reduction to practice and (v) enabling disclosure. To elaborate, an invention to be patentable should be *non-obvious*, given the current public information set; it must have some *usefulness* in the industry; it should not reflect mere skill; the idea should be embodied in a *working device* (technology) or a structure and the means to *reproduce* the invention must be made public. Maneuvering with these criteria can give rise to patent systems of diverse strengths.

The welfare reducing effect of patent through limiting competition and prolonging monopoly has, however, been a concern since its early days, especially among the policymakers. Indeed, the monopoly implications of patents refer to the oldest form of conflict between patent and public interest, leading even to abolition of patent laws in many West European countries during the nineteenth century (Machlup 1958, p. 4).[8] Thomas Jefferson, the prime architect of the US Patent Act 1790, in fact, insisted to nullify patents if they are seen in conflict with public interest.[9] In recent times, this conflict has become multidimensional with the incorporation of concerns ranging from protecting 'human, animal or plant life or health'[10] to avoid(ing) 'serious prejudice to the environment...'.[11] Consequently, these concerns are now dealt with under the premise of 'ordre public'. Broadly speaking, a threat to 'ordre-public' is taken as synonymous with a threat to the 'operation of the State and its institution' (Gold 2001, p. 8).[12] The TRIPS agreement has explicit provisions to exclude patenting of such inventions, which constitute a threat to 'ordre public' in a country. For such inventions, TRIPS has made provisions for *sui generis* protection under the ambit of national laws. Importantly, however, inventions that are denied patents on grounds of 'ordre public' shall also not be allowed to be commercialised (UNCTAD-ICTSD 2005, Chap. 19).

Conventionally, nevertheless, the academic debate on patents has focused more on the strength of the patent system, rather than the system per se. It is thus imperative to focus on the implications of varied patent strengths. Essentially,

---

[7] See Chap. 4, http://digital-law-online.info/lpdi1.0/treatise52.html. Last accessed on 10 July, 2007.

[8] See also the foreword to Machlup (1958) by JC O'Mahoney (p. III)

[9] Writings of Thomas Jefferson V (p. 47, Ford ed.) and VI (pp. 180–181, Washington ed.), cited in Graham vs. John Deere Co. of Kansas City et al., 383 US 1(1065).

[10] Health includes satisfaction of basic requirement like food, safe water, shelter, clothing, warmth and safety, along with access to medical care. See for instance, Beaglehole and Bonita (1999, p. 45).

[11] Article 27.2, Trade Related Intellectual Property rights Systems (TRIPS)

[12] See UNCTAD-ICTSD (2005, Chap. 19) for a comprehensive discussion on the evolution of meaning, concept and coverage of the term "ordre public" in the context of patent law.

patent strength is a multidimensional concept and includes characteristics such as length and breadth (scope of patent) of patents along with the rigour of patent enforcement, patent fees and the scope of compulsory licensing (Gallini 2002). Among these dimensions, the length and scope of patents have received a rather disproportionate attention in academic discussions. While patent length refers to the duration of patent protection, the breadth or scope of patents, broadly speaking, defines the 'degree of newness (or non-obviousness)' required in an invention for the grant of patent.[13] In this sense, the scope of patents defines the extent of inventive step involved in an invention. Within the discussion of patent strength, in fact, patent scope (and the issue of non-obviousness in particular) has occupied a key position. However, patent scope is purely a subjective measure, and hence highly susceptible to definitional ambiguity (Merges and Nelson 1990). As a result, definitions of patent scope have been subjected to, and shaped by, intense jurisprudential interventions, especially in the USA.

Jurisprudential interventions in the USA, to define patent scope, are essentially directed to minimise the anomaly between, so-called, 'specification' and 'claims' of a patent. 'The specification contains a discussion of the invention's background, a summary of the invention, and a detailed description of at least one embodiment of the invention...Claims usually encompass much more than this' (35 USC-112, 1988).[14] Kitch (1977) argues that the grey area in defining claims can be used in a strategic manner to block invention and prolong monopolies. The US Supreme Court, however, has outlined that 'claims are to be construed in the light of the specification and both are to be read with a view to ascertaining the invention'. To solve the litigations arising out of non-overlapping nature of specification and claim, judiciary has often resorted to 'the doctrine of equivalents'. Under the doctrine of equivalents, a new product or process may infringe an existing patent if it 'performs *substantially* the same overall function or work, in *substantially* the same way, to obtain *substantially* the same overall result as the claimed invention.' (Ko 1992, p. 781).[15] However, there is a 'reverse doctrine of equivalents' as well, to counter the doctrine of equivalents. In other words, the reverse doctrine of equivalents can be used to nullify an infringement suit when a new product or process falls well within the boundaries of claim of a previous (infringed) innovation, if it can be proved that the new innovation has been generated in a substantially different way than the existing invention (Ko 1992).

The literature on patent scope can be categorised into three groups:[16]

- Whether or not it covers fundamental scientific research along with the applied commercialisable knowledge. There are two underlying assumptions, albeit

[13] See, for instance, Gilbert and Shapiro (1990) for variation in the definition of breadth and scope of patent.
[14] As mentioned in Kitch (1977)
[15] Emphases mine.
[16] These levels are distinguished primarily for analytical convenience, and are not intended to be watertight. Nevertheless, they do address different types of strategic issues related to patents.

implicit, behind such a consideration. First, it assumes that progression from scientific research to technological invention is linear. Secondly, it also assumes, rather correctly, that any basic science research has numerous new potential lines of application. Patenting such outputs could thus prevent some of these innovations from being realised, by restricting its use (Eisenberg and Nelson 2002). Accordingly, granting patents to scientific discoveries had, indeed, for long been regarded as 'impractical and undesirable' (Machlup 1958, p. 1). The first explicit departure from this traditional position is, perhaps, the enactment of the Bayh–Dole Act in the USA, which approved granting of patents to (fundamental) research carried out at universities. This issue is important for biotechnology, due to its science dependent character. I refer to this debate as anticommon science debate, and discuss it later.

- The scope of a patent also depends on whether it covers a whole product as well as its constituent processes, or only the processes. This issue is also known as the issue of product vs. process patent. Needless to mention, a product patent would be considered broader, hence stronger, compared with a process patent (Lerner 2002). The implications for technological catch up in the context of biotechnology patents under this framework are discussed. I call it the *technological catch up debate*.

- The third level of distinction occurs within a product patent system. This is done by specifying varying degrees of inventive steps of new products. Once again, a patent system with provisions of patenting close substitutes would demand small inventive step (or non-obviousness) and would be considered as narrower in terms of patent scope (Sherman 1990), compared to a system where patent is granted only to new products, which are significantly different from the older ones. In recent years, this issue has gained importance in the light of India's amendments to Patent Laws, 2005. In an attempt to make its patent law TRIPS compatible, India has substantially altered the criteria of inventive steps, thereby, barring innovations with small inventive steps from patenting. Given that foreign multinational corporations (MNCs) and Indian firms have dissimilar capabilities to produce patented products; this has been done, perhaps, to prevent MNCs from 'ever-greening' their monopolies through insignificant incremental innovations. Clearly, it reiterates the old conviction that patent monopolies should only be extended to those inventions, which are significantly new and thus benefits the society in a major way. In the context of biotechnology, this issue is important because every biotechnological final product uses numerous (intermediate) technologies. The patent scope, in this context, would clearly define the limit (and the number) of patenting such (intermediate) technologies. In other words, the size of 'patent thickets' will be determined by the scope of patents, which, in turn, would determine the degree with which patents can be used as a tool for strategic cooperation/negotiation and 'holding up' between parties producing the final product.[17] I refer to this debate as *holding-up debate*.

---

[17] Indeed, a broad patent is assumed to provide better protection to the creators of knowledge (Klemperer 1990). At the same time, however, broad patents are accused of

The modern economics literature on patents, at least during its initial phase, remained preoccupied with understanding the intricacies of its social benefits in terms of augmenting inventive activities, net of the deadweight loss of creating monopoly (Arrow 1962; Nordhaus 1972; Scherer 1972). It is important to note that realisation of any social benefit of patents, in terms of ensuring increased flow of inventions, directly depends on the number of inventors working on diverse and non-competitive ideas (Mazzoleni and Nelson 1998). Patents would promote only a technological race in similar technologies if the fields of research of different inventors are identical (Dasgupta and Stiglitz 1980). This race might lead to a pattern of resource allocation to R&D, which is not socially optimum. In addition, the purported social benefits of patents – an increased flow of inventions – also remain illusive.[18] Moreover, contrary to the theoretical understanding that patents are imperative for inventions, a large body of empirical literature seems to suggest that patents provide useful incentives for industrial innovations only in a handful of industries and in limited situations (Lerner 2002).

## 11.3.2 Evolution of Patents in Biotechnology

The USA has been a pioneer in institutionalising the protection of biological processes as well. The US Plant Patent Act 1930 is the first formal institution to deal with protection of plant variety. Several countries, however, opposed the idea of extending patent protection to plant variety because plant variety was considered as a product of nature. Patents, also, exclude others from using a technology. The age old practice of the farming community was to produce, reuse and exchange seed varieties among themselves without being concerned much about the rights on their intellectual properties.[19] The philosophy and belief structure associated with patents were, thus, in conflict with the belief structure associated with the production of seed variety. The pressure from plant breeding industry in Europe, nevertheless, resulted into the formation of the International Union for the Protection of New Varieties of Plants (UPOV) to protect plant varieties of select plants (mainly excluding food crops), provided they are 'distinct', 'uniform' and 'stable' (DUS).[20] The strength of plant breeders' rights vary according to the definitions of distinctness, uniformity and stability. During these initial years, UPOV allowed the reuse and modifications of seeds by

limiting potential competition and strengthening monopolies both in the markets for knowledge as well as in the markets for products (Gilbert and Shapiro 1990).

[18] The society, of course, gets an invention rather fast.

[19] In a recent research Kumar (2007) finds that grass root innovators belonging to farming communities in India not only share their seed varieties, but also various other kinds of innovations and creative ideas.

[20] Distinctness refers to the unique characteristics compared with what is common knowledge. Uniformity implies possessing of that distinct characteristic by the whole population in a uniform manner. Alongside the uniformity requirement, inheritance of the distinct characteristic of the parent seed is demanded among its progeny to ensure stability. See, for instance, Rangnekar (1999, p. 131) for detail.

farmers. Any exchange of saved seeds within the community of farmers was also permitted, provided this exchange did not involve commercial trading. However, confusion prevailed as to whether protection was given only to phenotypic variations, or also encompassed genotypes. Protection only on phenotypes was considered weaker compared with a system where genotypic variations are also protected. This is because one particular genotype would include many phenotypic variations. The scope of competition between plant breeders is, therefore, quite high in the framework of protection that only covers phenotype (Wright and Pardey 2006).

UPOV was amended in 1991 to make way for protecting genotypic variations, explicitly, by incorporating the criterion to define 'minimum genetic space' of protection through 'essentially derived varieties' (EDV).[21] The amendments also restricted farmer's right to save and exchange seeds, even for non-commercial purposes. UPOV 1991 also extended its coverage of protection to include food grains and other non-commercial crops. The provision of using protected 'parent crops' for the production of subsequent varieties was also forfeited.

In a parallel development, two patent amendments in the United States facilitated the process of bringing genetically engineered inventions under the umbrella of patent protection. The Diamond vs. Chakravarty 1980 case is considered to be path breaking because it explicitly acknowledged that 'anything under the sun made by the man shall be patentable'. Kingston (2005), however, argues that this decision was, in fact, built upon the amendments made in 1952, which reduced the requirement of non-obviousness for patentability, and qualified outcomes of routinised industrial R&D to be patentable by stating that 'patentability shall not be negatived by the manner in which the invention was made'.[22] These two amendments, believed to have, paved the way for genetic engineering inventions to be brought under the umbrella of patent protection.

Accommodating genetic engineering inventions in the traditional patent system is, however, entangled with legal difficulties. The major difference between mechanical and biotechnological inventions is the impossibility of describing the latter in terms of components, parts or elements (structure), which is required under the conventional system of patents. Rather, biotechnological inventions are expressed in manipulative or functional terms (Sherman 1990; Pila 2003). It is also argued (Sherman 1990) that biotechnological inventions are more vulnerable to infringement suits due to two reasons. First, being a pioneering technology it may suffer from the absence of an adequate language of 'claim', which takes time

---

[21] EDV protects the expression of the essential characteristics that result from the genotype or combination of gentotypes (Lange 1993).

[22] In fact, until 1952 the standard practice was to allot patents to the individual scientists, who, in turn, transferred the rights to their employers. This practice had led to denial of a large amount of chemical patent as well as high transaction cost for the chemical industry, provoking them to lobby for the amendments. Indeed, 'process' became patentable, instead of 'art', only from 1952. See http://digital-law online.info/lpdi1.0/treatise52.html. Last Accessed on 10 July, 2007.

to evolve.[23] Second, it is also difficult to foresee the exact range of utility of those patents, which are filed at very early stages of inventions. Inventors, in such cases, tend to file a broad claim, making the patent vulnerable to infringement suit at a matured phase of the technology. But, such difficulties notwithstanding, granting of patents to biotechnological inventions continues. In fact, the US Court of Appeal has made explicit attempts to exempt biotechnological inventions from the requirements of non-obviousness, which would only accelerate the rate of granting patents to such inventions.[24,25]

## 11.4 Patenting Biotechnology: Implications

The six major issues outlined in the introduction are now thematically distributed. Accordingly, this section is divided into the following subsections. Section 11.4.1 gives an analytical overview of laws related to patenting life forms in different (mainly industrialised) countries (issue 1). Section 11.4.2 is rather short and discusses the issue of patent lengths.[26] Section 11.4.3 deals with patent scope and has three further subsections. In Sect. 11.4.4 I discuss the issue of patenting biodiversity through bioprospecting and its 'benefit sharing' implications.

### 11.4.1 Patenting Life Forms and 'Ordre Public': Basic Issues and Inter-country Comparison

Patenting life forms have added a new dimension to the already existing conflict between patents and public interests. Within the category of life forms, one may further distinguish among life forms of various 'orders'. Roughly, two such orders can be mentioned. Microorganisms belong to the 'lower order life forms', while 'higher order life forms' include plants, animals, along with sequences and fragments of their genes (Gold 2001, p. 5). It is the latter group of life forms, whose inclusion under the ambit of patents have raised concerns associated with 'ordre public' (Hoedemaekers 2001).

  Beside the ethical issue of 'appropriating life', granting patents to life forms runs into other, more technical, difficulties. It is well accepted that genetic engineering processes are uncertain, and thus, often non-reproducible (APO 2002), violating one important criterion of conventional patent laws (Evenson and

---

[23] Lerner (1994, p. 331) indeed provides evidence of how patent claims in biotechnological inventions evolved to become narrower and specialized over time, as the legal language grew matured to deal with biological inventions.

[24] *In re* Bell 1993, and *In re* Duell 1995 by the Court of Appeal, Federal Circuit, USA as cited in Kingston (2005, p. 8).

[25] See, in this context the discussion on the so-called "friendly court" hypotheses (conjecturing that the creation of Court of Appeal for the Federal Circuit led to a surge in patenting) in Gallini (2002, p. 138).

[26] We have not explicitly highlighted this issue in the introduction.

Putnam 1987; Kingston 2005). The lack of reproducibility has also given credence to the argument that such processes are predominantly natural, whereas patents should be given only if convincing evidence of human intervention could be found. Patenting life forms, especially, gene sequences have also been marred with problems of conforming to 'utility' aspects of patent laws (Straus 2002; Yamana 2001). In another interesting revelation, de Carvalho (2004) cites few Supreme Court orders in the USA, which emphasised that patents can only be granted to a technical idea if it can be invented in *more than one way*. In contrast, genetic engineering processes are unique. All these features of genetic engineering, allegedly, make the traditional framework of patents inappropriate for patenting inventions in genetic engineering (Thurow 1997).

Life forms, unlike their chemical or mechanical counterparts, produce progeny. A cautious approach, on ethical grounds, is thus required for patenting life forms, since such protections might have trans-generational implications for ownership and appropriation of living beings. Indeed, patent on human being is prohibited in all countries. This is also reflected in the UNESCO Declaration of 1997, which proclaimed that 'human genes are constituent of human race. Their variety and dignity should thus be protected. It also maintained that human genome is a natural state, which should not be used for economic profit making exercises'. However, the guideline had no exclusive clause pertaining to patents.[27]
Inter-country differences exist with regard to patenting lower forms of life, such as gene sequence, cell lines, animal organs, animals, animal varieties and human organs (see Gold 2001). The United States and Australia are the most pro-patent countries, permitting patents on all the above forms of higher life. Japan and Korea comes next with provisions of patents to all above forms, except human organs. Europe remains more conservative among developed countries, excluding (specific) plant and animal varieties as well as human organs from the ambit of patents (Gold 2001; Straus 2002). Canada also 'lags behind' (McMahon and Lumiere 2004) on patenting higher life forms, and the judiciary has left the matter to the Parliament to define the landscape of patentability in such cases.

These difference of opinion with respect to patenting higher life forms among the industrialised countries themselves is perhaps the reason why TRIPS has not been able to take a concrete steps in this area so far. The 'wishy-washy' guidelines of patenting life forms in TRIPS, where much has been left to the discretion of an individual country's 'sui-generis' system of protection may be seen as a failure to come to a solution, which would be acceptable to industrialised countries with diverse interests and 'ordre public'.

The concept of 'Ordre-public' may be taken as synonymous with the concept of informal institutions used in the literature of institutional economics. This literature suggests that formal institutions (laws) are shaped by informal institutions prevailing in a society (North 1990). It is also suggested that informal institutions are slow to change, giving rise to much inertia in the process of change of formal institutions. It may thus be interesting to explore the various underlying determinants in the diversity of 'ordre public' across countries. Costa-Font and

---

[27] See Yamana (2001) for detail.

Mossialos (2006) make a good beginning in this regard. They explore how increasing knowledge about a biotechnological invention may alter public belief about its usability, over time. Surely, this issue needs more research attention. A second issue for further research in this area could be to explore the various means and ways through which convergence of public orders may be achieved among these countries. Unfortunately, these issues have not been significantly addressed in the existing literature.

## 11.4.2 Implications of Patent Length

The issue of patent length is important for biotechnology, mainly for two reasons. First, because biotechnological innovations are cumulative, and second, because biotechnological research produces heterogeneous outputs, rendering it difficult to apply any uniform length of patent.

In a framework of single isolated invention, patent length stimulates inventive activities (Nordhaus 1972). But, in the framework of cumulative innovation that builds upon prior inventions, such as biotechnology, incentive to innovate may decline when patent regime is long since subsequent researchers, other than the pioneer, may have to withhold an improved technology until the expiry of the patent (Koo and Wright 2002). Horwitz and Lai (1996) find that shorter protection induces faster, but minor innovations. On the other hand, an increase in length may induce development of larger inventions, less frequently. Again, an inverted 'U' shaped relationship between the length and innovation may be found if the frequency effect dominates the size effect for a sufficiently long patent life. Gilbert and Shapiro (1990), however, argue that the optimum patent length could be infinity if the environment is stationary and the patent breadth is kept at a minimum. In an empirical study of the German synthetic dye industry, Murmann (2003) showed that during the early stage of technological capability (TC) of an industry a short patent protection encourages competition and allows more novelty to come up. The consequent evolutionary selection of the best design would, in this case, be more efficient than when competition is blocked by strong patent regime in these stages.

In sectors such as biotechnology, where the science is new, cumulative, and the rate of invention is fast, a strong patent may undermine investments on R&D (Gold 2000). Eisenberg and Nelson (2002) also argue that free availability of knowledge, especially during its early phase, boosts research activities by reducing search and transaction costs of locating the state of the art. A long patent in such formative stages, on the other hand, delays the release of such knowledge into the public domain and may prove to be counter productive. Also, unlike in many industries, biotechnological research produces varied type of research outputs, ranging from life-saving medicine to research tools based on the isolation of specific DNA sequence, cell or tissue. Medicines have to undergo stringent and expensive process of regulatory approval, for safety and efficacy, before being marketed. The marketing of research tools, on the other hand, is much less expensive and less cumbersome. It is thus argued that a 'one size fits all' type of protection (with respect to patent length) to such different types of outputs may prove to be inefficient (Thurow 1997; Gold 2000).

## 11.4.3 Implications of Patent Scope

### Patent Scope and Anticommon Science

Patents on fundamental research have often been justified on the two following grounds:

- First, parties that 'follow-up' such fundamental research into commercially viable innovations would not do so until they are certain to identify the original inventor(s), who exclusively own the invention.
- Second, the 'prospect theory' (Kitch 1977) insists that broad patent at an early stage of a 'prospect invention' prevents socially wasteful duplicative paths of follow-up developments, assuming many innovators may see very similar prospect of an invention, and might pursue with very similar type of follow up innovations, when such innovations are freely available in the public domain. Patents, by restricting their use, reduce the scope of such socially wasteful duplicative research.

The first argument assumes a conventional linear model of scientific progress and technological change, where progress in science is followed up with technological innovations. Conventionally, also, such fundamental research is supposed to be undertaken by universities while the industry is supposed to carry out applied research (Merton 1973; Eisenberg and Nelson 2002). It may also be noted that university research, traditionally, are meant for enriching the public domain of knowledge. As a result, ownership of university research is not clearly defined. According to the first argument, this lack of clear ownership impedes the exchange of such innovations, thus, deterring the process of follow up innovations and technological change. Encouraging universities to seek patent, arguably, reduces the hazards associated with entering into a licensing agreement by industry. This argument has in many ways shaped the idea of the Bayh–Dole Act (1980) in the USA (Mazzeloni and Nelson 1998). The opponents of this argument, however, belong to the school of Mertonian "open science', which proposes that the authenticity of science implies 'universality' of its results, which can be ensured only if scientists pursue their research being 'disinterested' of personal gains, as well as when the outputs of such research are made open to the community of scientists for evaluation and corrections, again in a disinterested fashion (Merton 1967, pp. 550–561).[28] Attempts to privately appropriate such fundamental research could aggravate the problems of 'anticommon effect' (Heller and Eisenberg 1998). Such anticommon effect may hinder follow up

---

[28] However, one has to be cautious in interpreting disinterestedness. It is by no means altruism. In fact, scientists can have ego and zealous. But community vigilance, actually, ensures objectivity by pitting one's ego against another (p. 559).

academic research by raising the costs of accessing upstream knowledge (Dasgupta and David 1994; Zeeman 2000; Eisenberg and Nelson 2002; Scherer 2002; Rai and Eisenberg 2003).

Emphasis on patents and intellectual property (IP) protection on fundamental research might also lead to a change in organisation of BR. Conceptually, this can occur in either of the following two ways:

- If universities remain attached to their conventional norm of open science (Argyres and Liebeskind 1998), then private firms, due to their innate concern for appropriation of knowledge, might gradually seek to replace (or at least, complement) universities as the main agent of fundamental research. An active participation of private firms in human genome project may be taken as an example of such a move.
- Universities become more conscious of appropriating new knowledge, given the prospect of revenue that can be generated from such patents. This has already happened to a great extent in chemical and pharmaceutical industries in industrialised countries. New evidences are also emerging to support such a trend in the post TRIPS regime (Sampat 2006 for USA; Geuna and Nesta 2006 for Europe; Govind 2006 for India).

In both cases, nevertheless, the flow of information about new inventions would be increasingly impaired (Cook Deegan 2007). If innovation is cumulative, follow up inventors would be at a disadvantage, and the progress of research might slow down. Further to the dimension of enhanced costs of follow-up research, one can also argue that the authenticity of scientific knowledge would become questionable in such a situation, when researches are conducted with a commercial interest and are kept out of the reach of 'disinterested' evaluation of the scientific community.

The argument of 'prospect theory' has also been criticised on the ground that the assumption that many people would perceive very similar prospects of an invention necessarily undermines the innate diversity in the creative faculty of human beings. Merges and Nelson (1990), much in line with Arrow (1962) and Scherer (1972), argue that contrary to this assumption, different people may actually view different prospects of an invention. A strong patent at the early stage may, in this case, actually prove to be socially costly by deterring entrepreneurial aspirations to explore various paths of development of such 'prospect inventions'.[29]

---

[29] A small amount of literature has also referred to the situation where a broad patent on fundamental invention puts an inventor into a safer situation vis-à-vis the threat of imitation, and may encourage inventors to license the patented technology to a third party for further development and commercialisation. This may hold true when commercialisation of an invention requires investment of an order, which is beyond the capacity of the inventor. However, Chap. 6 of Noble (1977), is replete with evidences where individual inventors had to succumb to the financial muscles of large corporations and relinquished their rights on inventions.

I limit my discussion to two broad issues. The first is the issue of academic entrepreneurship in biotechnology. The second issue is more general, and focuses on the changing practice of scientific research. Both these dimensions clearly shape the extent and nature of the 'anticommon science effect'. For this discussion I mostly draw upon the literature that emerged while analysing the impact of the Bayh Dole Act (1980) in the United States, and very similar acts that followed in many industrialised countries (for instance, France and Germany), subsequently.

It is widely held that the US economy, crippled with severe competition from Japan and other South East Asian countries, got a lifeline when the Bayh–Dole Act (1980) permitted universities to patent federally funded inventions and entitled them to engage in non-exclusive licensing of the same with the industry. It may be noted at the very outset that this Act covers scientific research across universities in the USA, and not specific to biotechnology. However, biomedical fields have been portrayed as a major beneficiary of this Act, witnessing a phenomenal increase in patents and technology licensing agreements. The share of biomedical licensing agreement went up as high as 85% of total licensing agreements in the mid 1990s.

According to some estimates (AAU 1998; OECD 2000, p. 77) the passage of this law heralded a 'new economy' by reversing the declining trend of industrial competitiveness and growth of the US economy (Nelson 2001; Mowery 2005). The resultant increased flow of technology licensing from universities to industry was portrayed as the primary force behind such a drastic turnaround of the competitiveness of US industries. The number of patents to US universities surged up by 8 times between 1979 and 1999. The entry of universities into technology transfer also accelerated sharply in the post Bayh Dole era (Sampat 2006, Figure 2). Also, the passage of the Bayh–Dole Act is believed to have given rise to a system of 'entrepreneurial university' in the USA (Audretsch 2006) by giving ownership of new technologies to the individual scientists, which raised their bargaining power in attracting (venture) capital for new start-ups. In biotechnology industry, the number of start-ups has indeed increased phenomenally in the post Bayh–Dole era (Nelson 2001). An estimate puts the figure of new biotech start-ups at a level as high as 15,000 during 1975–1989 (Zucker et al. 1998, p. 294). Mostly, these firms are believed to have been set up by the innovating scientists themselves (McKelvey 1996a), vindicating the hypothesis of 'entrepreneurial university' (Audretsch 2006). Many studies, however, point out that tacit, rather than codified, transfer of knowledge has been instrumental for the success of many such start-ups (Audretsch and Stephan 1996; Zucker et al. 2002). If this indeed is the case, one wonders to what extent enhancing the scope of *patenting* may have helped the cause! There is lack of evidence to suggest any strong correlation between transfers of patented technologies and new start-ups. Using the data compiled from US Association of University Technology Managers (AUTM 2001, 2002), Mowery (2005) reports that a technology transfer implied a new start-up only in 14–16% of cases. Around 50% of such technologies were transferred to small (less than 500 employees), but existing, firms. The rest (around 32%) was licensed out to large firms.

Nevertheless, the current euphoria about academic entrepreneurship does suggest that individual scientists seem to have regained some of their lost status, vis-a-vis firms, as owners of patented technologies. But, since many of these scientists are also university professors, who are revered more for their willingness to enrich public knowledge base through teaching and research than making monetary gains, this new trend of academic entrepreneurship has raised a new debate concerning the viability and appropriateness of such entrepreneurial activities by academics. The underlying presumption is that entrepreneurship and academic research require, at least, two different kinds of skills and cognitive attention (Polanyi 1967). Pursuing both simultaneously may not be viable in the long run because of cognitive dissonance (c.f. Akerlof and Dickens 1982). As a result, these scientists may, over time, quit academia to permanently take up the job of entrepreneurship. If we assume, which many studies in fact highlight, that these scientists also have high academic standards, the vacuum crated as a result of such job shifts may have serious implications for further progress in science. The current results of empirical research do not indicate the possibility of such drastic shakeouts (see Lowe and Gonzalez-Brambila 2007). But most of the studies are also US centric, making it difficult to derive a comprehensive 'world view'.

Entrepreneurial propensity and aspirations among the academic scientists does seem to vary across countries (Gittelman 2006). While in the US, scientists do not mind being involved in commercial activities; such involvements are still considered a taboo among French scientists (p. 1057). The paper goes on to say that 'In the US, money is not dirty. Success in the States goes with money. In France success is reputation, name not money. People want Nobel Prize (ibid.)'.[30] Interestingly, it matches well with what Tocqueville (1840, 2003) had said nearly 200 years ago about the pro-active attitude of scientists in the USA, vis-à-vis their counterparts in other countries in Europe, towards application of science and reaping commercial gains of scientific research (Vol. 2, Part I, Chap. 10).

On whether patenting fundamental research raises the costs of follow up innovations in biotechnology, we still do not have many empirical studies. In one small sample study, Walsh et al. (2003) do not find instances of any important academic 'follow up' project being curtailed or cancelled due to the problems of accessing 'upstream' patented technologies. Prima facie, this result may render meaningless much of the apprehensions mentioned earlier. However, the reasons cited for such results are interesting to note. It is reported that in many cases, patent holders have tolerated minor infringement by the university researchers on grounds that an improved technology in the public domain may become valuable for them as well. Sometimes, possibility of adverse public reaction of suing a *university* also restrained them from taking legal action. Nevertheless, this field also remains open for future research.[31]

Recent studies have also begun questioning the very tenets of the Bayh–Dole Act. These studies, for instance, suggest that a direct causal relationship between

---

[30] See also Cyranoski (2002a, 2002b) for similar concerns by scientists in Japan.
[31] Emphasis mine.

university licensing and the growth of industrial competitiveness is necessarily true only if university research and patent is considered crucial for industrial innovation and competitiveness (Nelson 2001; Mowery 2005). A small but growing empirical literature seems to contradict this assumption. Surveys by Levin et al. (1987) and Cohen et al. (2002a), in the context of the USA, came to almost similar conclusions that there is considerable inter-disciplinary variation in usefulness of university research and patents for industry. In both surveys university research and patent are regarded as 'very important' by majority of industry respondents only in engineering and agricultural sciences. The pharmaceutical science is an interesting case in point. Although, majority of the respondents rank university patent in biomedical inventions as 'very important', the ranks received by (university) patent was lower than the ranks of other (more open) sources of knowledge dissemination such as publications and conferences (see also Dasgupta and David 1994; Agrawal and Henderson 2002). A provision to grant patents to university research, therefore, is destined to help the cause of industrial competitiveness only in a limited manner. One can, however, be indifferent to such a policy change if patenting does not come in conflict with diffusion of information and public knowledge through publications and conferences. In other words, an important question is whether these two modes of information dissemination can coexist together. Some preliminary research on top US universities does not, in fact, show much trade-off between publications and patents. Top universities are able to retain their right to publish while entering into contract with the industry (Mowery et al. 1999). In an interesting endeavour, Sampat (2006) investigates whether increasing patenting reflect a move towards private appropriation of fundamental research by looking at patent citations. His regression analyses reveal an interesting story. He finds that the number and share of non-patented citations of prior scientific work are significantly higher for patents that are granted to universities (see also Trajtenberg et al. 1997). This result can be interpreted to support the apprehension that open public science is increasingly being appropriated through patents. Reconciling this finding with previous two studies, one may safely argue that although patents may not affect the number of publications, it can still contribute to anticommon effect by appropriating public knowledge, which was, hitherto, available freely.

Casual observations also suggest that academic researchers, even in top universities, increasingly, prefer to maintain secrecy about their research during informal discussions with their colleagues as well as during more formal seminars and conferences (Nelson 2001), apparently for the fear of losing potential economic value from their innovations or ideas.

Such a tendency to dodge open and candid discussions about one's research work, in the presence of a prospective patent, revives a rather old worry where thrust on patent by university was suspected to foster commercialisation and tendencies for secrecy in scientific work (Cottrell 1932, p. 222, as mentioned in Sampat 2006). However, while secrecy part remains under-explored, the limited case studies of three top universities in the USA, once again, do not support the premise that research has become more commercially oriented (Cohen et al. 2002a). Top universities seem to have sufficient bargaining power to dictate the terms of research contracts. Nevertheless, one needs to undertake further research taking comparatively larger sample, especially given the fact that many universities, other than these top ones, will have less bargaining power vis-à-vis the industry in dictating the terms of research contract, and may be forced to act much in accordance with the priorities and objectives of the industry. Such a tendency cannot be ruled out in the post Bayh–Dole environment, where collaborations with industry, often irrespective of their nature, are held in high esteem.[32]

A policy to grant patent and exclusive licensing may also be hailed if they are found inevitable for commercialisation and subsequent development of an invention. This argument is only valid for some, but not all, technologies. The case study of the Cohen-Boyer technique is widely discussed in this context. The formal licensing of this technology took place much after a few firms had already started commercialising it. Also, Zucker et al. (2002) argue that knowledge of breakthrough technologies is highly specialised, and *naturally* excludable. Contrary to the usual belief, therefore, such technologies do not appear to suffer from the conventional public good properties of knowledge, making patents redundant.[33] Granting of a patent and the scope of non-exclusive licensing, in these cases, might result in the well-recognised dead weight loss of creating monopoly.

One may not be too wrong to infer, on the basis of the above discussions, that preference for open dissemination of knowledge through publications and confe-rences vis-à-vis proprietary dissemination through the likes of patents reflects two divergent systems of scientific norms. The literature on institutional economics interprets such norms as informal institutions or values, which are 'shared mental models'(Denzau and North 1994). Such shared mental models are, often, slow to change. Thus, viewing this shift from anti- to pro-patent norms of university research, especially in the USA, as sudden and exclusive outcome of the Bayh–Dole Act contradicts one of the strong pillars of institutional economic theory. Some studies (Etzkowitz 1994; Fishman 1996), indeed, point out that the earlier-mentioned change in the norm of patenting university research, especially in the USA, has been neither sudden, nor an exclusive outcome of the Act. These studies trace the origin of this change in the decades of 1960s and 1970s, when, on one hand, many new applied disciplines such as biotechnology begun to emerge, and, on the other hand, federal funding for research was drastically reduced. According to these studies, universities gradually change their 'norms' to filing patents for their research in order to adapt to these changing environment, where universities were increasingly compelled to search for various other channels of (private) resources. The necessity to protect the outcomes of such research may have come

---

[32] Such fears are expressed by the scientists and researchers in many countries. See Ray (2004) for viewpoints of Indian scientists, and Cyranoski (2002b) for views expressed by some senior Japanese scientists.

[33] In other words, patents, according to these studies, play important roles only for those innovations, skills pertaining to which are comparatively well diffused.

as an attached conditionality.[34] Thus, there seems to be little evidence of a structural break, in the trend of patent propensity by universities, after the Bayh–Dole Act. What the act may have achieved to build up a homogenised pro-patent attitude of universities (Mowery 2005).

I further propose that the decay of the culture of open science may also raise the costs of regulation. In the framework of open science, evaluation of negative externalities and risks of new inventions were done by disinterested scientists. Such scope for unbiased evaluations gets eroded when knowledge is kept away from the public domain. The private owner of knowledge will have very little incentives to disclose risks associated with the use of its patented technology. The overwhelming interests for profit may actually lead to premature and inappropriate use of these technologies (Holtzman 1999; Koening et al. 1998). One may notice that the main justification behind the formation of the Cartegena Protocol on Biosafety Norm 2001 was to adopt 'precautionary principle' against the *uncertainty* of science and technology of genetic engineering (OECD 2002). Such regulations also call for burdensome adjustments on individual countries to build up proper institutional structures in conformity.[35] I argue that a major reason for setting up such costly systems of regulation has been the private ownership of new genetic engineering inventions, which results into disclosure of information about these technologies only in a 'biased' manner (Caulfield and Gold 2000; Cook Deegan 2007) and avoids the scope for 'disinterested' evaluation of various (unintended) consequences of these technologies.

The emergence and the historical trajectory of quality certification system in another field of science, characterised by high share of proprietary inventions, namely, pharmaceuticals, is another interesting case in point, where the haste of marketing thalidomide, without proper safety evaluations, had resulted in the birth of children with severe physical deformities. Eventually, this incident led to the establishment of a much stringent quality certificatory systems (Daemmrich 2004; Ray and Bhaduri 2003), with a spiralling effect on the costs of drug development research, the prices of medicines and a demand for stronger protection of IPRs (Cockburn 2004). Nevertheless, this argument needs further rigorous analyses before one can arrive at a definite conclusion.

## Patent Scope and Technological Catch-Up

Defining the scope of patents in terms of product vs. process patents has its implications for technological learning and TC. This has been an integral part of the development policy debate of the last few decades (IPR Commission Report 2002). A patent system is termed as 'strong' if it permits patenting of a product

---

[34] Govind (2006) in a carefully crafted study of two premier research institutes in India found that high private funding has a direct bearing on scientists' attitude towards appropriating knowledge through patents.

[35] This cost may include costs of aligning values and norms (informal institutions) of individual societies with the new formal institutions, apart from the, much anticipated, monetary costs.

along with processes, and 'weak' if only processes are patentable, not the product. Helpman (1993) argues that while strong uniform patent regime, across the globe, may raise the welfare of technology leader countries, it will not do so for the technology followers. It is now accepted that a weak patent system with only a very narrow scope of process patents encourages reverse engineering and is a prerequisite for further development of TC (Murmann 2003; Duttfield and Suthersanen 2005). Before proceeding further, I present a broad overview of the development economics literature on TC and learning.

TC operates, primarily, at the firm level.[36] Conventionally, technological progress refers to major breakthroughs and shifts, the so called technology frontier. But, especially in the context of developing countries, technological effort towards building up of TC refers to generation of capacities of minor innovation and inventing around to 'select, assimilate, adapt, modify, and improve upon a given technology' (Lall 1987; Gonsen 1998, pp. 10–19). The capability to create new technologies has been recognised as a path-dependent learning process (Bell 1984; Lall 1987; Dore 1984). The entire process of building up of TC is, conventionally, divided into three phases (Lall 1987, pp. 16–17): know-how (KH), know-why (KW) and basic research (BR). While KH refers to the capability of mastering a given technology and running it (select, assimilate and adapt) in the most efficient manner, KW implies a capability to understand (modify and improve upon) a technology, mainly, through reverse engineering. KH and KW have been treated as sequential and necessary for the building up of the next level of capability (BR).

The scope of patents can act as a facilitator in this process. The process of KW, in particular, relies heavily on this aspect of the patent system. When the patent scope is broad so as to include product as well as its constituent processes, firms can carry out KH but can never make their transition to KW (reverse engineering). The building up of BR capability, therefore, remains elusive, as understanding a technology through reverse engineering driven KW is indispensable for the development of BR capability. Indeed, many of today's industrialized countries have made their transition to BR capabilities through such uninterrupted phases of reverse engineering, either by completely discarding a patent system or by defining a very narrow scope of patenting (Machlup 1958; Duttfield and Suthersanen 2005). By allowing reverse engineering, a patent system with narrow scope also helps building up a significant competitive advantage in export markets.[37] Murmann (2003) has further pointed out that such weak patent systems allow competition in the organisational structure of firms, and helps selection of more efficient organisations, in the longer run.

---

[36] It may nevertheless be possible to extrapolate the definition of TC at the national level. However, because of externalities, such TC would not just be the summation of all firm level TCs. See Gonsen (1998), p. 6, for detail.

[37] See Murmann (2003) for the detail of export competitiveness of the German synthetic dye industry during the first half of the twentieth century, Rosenberg and Steinmuller (1988) for Japanese automobile industry during mid-twentieth century, and Bhaduri and Ray (2004) for the export performances of Indian pharmaceutical industry during late twentieth century.

Traditionally, a weak patent system is argued to reduce welfare of developing countries in situations where transfers of new technology from North to South dry out because of the threats of post-launch imitation. This argument, however, does not account for the fact that threat of imitation is not automatic, but contingent upon adequate reverse engineering capabilities of the recipient country. Until this is attained, there is no threat of imitation. Also, when domestic TC for reverse engineering is present, technologies can be (are) imitated even if not introduced locally, largely due the surge in information and communication technologies (Bhaduri and Ray 2006). Bhaduri and Ray (2006) also suggest that introduction of new technology can be quite fast even under a weak patent regime and reverse engineering capability, when the first mover advantage is sufficiently strong. A strong patent, in such a situation, can lead to large welfare losses due to the creation of patent monopoly without much gains in terms of faster access (Mrazek and Mossialos 2003; Ray 2005).

It is important to note, even at the cost of reiteration, that genetic engineering processes are unique. Patenting a process in genetic engineering effectively implies patenting of the outcome of this process and may be treated as equivalent to a product patent. A patent system in biotechnology is thus, by definition, quite strong. As discussed earlier, a strong patent regime discourages technological learning and building up of TC by technology follower countries. In fact, as we have noted in the earlier section, when a country is going through the phase of reverse engineering (KW), and is yet to reach BR capability, strengthening of IPRs, which prohibit reverse engineering, would not only halt the learning process, but would rather initiate an 'unlearning process' where countries could revert back to KII. For countries, which have reached the stage of BR capability, however, the impact of a strong patent system would depend on the type of their capability.

Conceptually, one can distinguish BR capability of major innovation from that of minor (me-too) innovations. When a country achieves BR capability of major innovation, a strong uniform patent across the globe would fetch high long-lasting competitive advantage for domestic technologies in the world market and, in turn, would ensure high commercial return. Many developing countries, however, are a long way from achieving such a capability. Their R&D focus is to develop minor, me-too type BR outputs (Upadhyay et al. 2002). To augment their capability further they continue to have intense research collaborations and tie-ups with firms and research institutes from developed countries (Pineda 2006).

Prima facie, 'me-too' type BR is undertaken for two reasons. First, the likelihood of getting a research collaborator increases when research fields overlap. Second, it allows them to take advantage of a large public domain of 'major' BR already done in this area by the leading countries. While the first reason continues to pay reward, the second reason may become restricted amidst the growing trend of patenting fundamental knowledge and research tools in biotechnology. Accessing such knowledge by the developing countries' organisations could be seriously curtailed in such circumstances. At the minimum, an additional cost would have to be incurred by these organisations, implying a diversion of physical and intellectual resources, which could otherwise have been used for research. Moreover, since the lion's share of biotechnological R&D in developing countries take place in academia or in public research laboratories, this would mean a reallocation of taxpayer's money from other (priority) areas.

Many developing countries have a poor educational infrastructure, and such renewed crunch in funds may hit them hard. However, if increased demands for funds were not met, scientific research would be hampered (Sampath 2005). It may be noted that developing countries have a rather low per capita availability of scientific personnel, often, because of brain drain.[38] Insufficient infrastructure coupled with curtailed access to research databases and frontier knowledge, due to patents, may lead to further exodus of scientists from these countries (Mkandawire 2002). Fakuda-Parr et al. (2002), in fact, argued that capacity for development is intricately linked with problems of brain drain. As a result, the process of technological catch up may be damaged, irreversibly.

One may however argue that there is little need for duplicative R&D to build up TC, when increasing institutional homogenisation under WTO ought to make transfer of technologies smoother and easier.[39] Such a doctrine, nevertheless, implicitly assumes a homogenous demand pattern across countries. In fact, implicitly based on this assumption, developed countries have often sought to compensate developing countries for their loss of competitiveness, if the latter agreed to implement a strong IPRs regime in its geographical territories (Lai and Qui 2003). But, two points need to be highlighted here. First, the demand patterns for biotechnological products, especially food and agro-biotech, are shaped by food habits, which are, often, culturally determined, and slow to change (Farbes and Armelagos 1980, Chap. 1). Second, transfers of genetically modified seeds to developing countries require their compatibility and adaptability with local ecosystems. Both these factors may come in the way of successful transfer of bio-technologies from the North to the South.

Indeed, in support of the first point, it has been highlighted that MNCs have undertaken very little research on two staple foods of developing countries – rice and wheat. James (1999) finds that the crops chosen by MNCs for field trials in developing countries are very similar to those chosen by them for field trials in developed countries. There is also variation in demand with respect to the choice of parameters within a particular crop. While the main problem of developed countries is to save their crops from herbicides, the main objective of developing countries is to increase yield, add nutritional values and protect their crops from various diseases. But, there is very little evidence to suggest that these diverse problems are addressed by the biotechnology MNCs. The prime focus of research in developed countries remains on herbicide tolerance (71%), leaving a paltry 1% effort for nutrition improvements (James 1999). Research on parameters such as

---

[38] A survey shows that 79% of 1990–1991 doctoral recipients of Indian nationals and 88% of those from China were still working in the United States in 1995. See Cervantes and Guellec (2002).

[39] The WTO document states that 'a functioning intellectual property regime should also facilitate the transfer of technology in the form of foreign direct investment, joint ventures and licensing' (see www.wto.org).

disease control and stress control, ranked by farmers in developing countries as traits of high importance (Commandeur 1997), has largely been neglected by the MNCs. Moreover, even if we take the parameter of herbicide tolerance, a successful transfer of technology to developing countries would depend on applicability of that technology to pests found in these countries. Bollworm, for instance, is often cited as a lethal pest in North America and Europe. However, in large parts of Asia, Bollworm is either not found or is present with many other, often more lethal, pests. In China, for instance, public sector research has identified six other pests having lethal effects on crops, along with Bollworm (Huang and Wang 2002).

Understandably, a more comprehensive research effort, embedded in local demand, is warranted for crops in these countries, than a simple transfer of technology. Interestingly, research projects undertaken by public R&D laboratories in India and China seem to focus more on such neglected crops or traits (Chaturvedi and Chwaii 2005; Huang and Wang 2002). A recent study by IFPRI (Atanassov et al. 2004) covering 15 developing countries in 3 continents found that poorer countries are turning to public funded research, where traits such as virus resistance, insect resistance and various agronomic properties are the primary focus of research. Also, most of the research reported to have taken place in cereals (Cohen 2005) – the main food crop in these countries. Both trends clearly show that research on genetic engineering is being redirected to suit environmental compatibility and food habits. Interestingly, the study also reveals that by diverting the research focus away from the globally profitable traits (e.g. herbicide resistance), developing countries have also been able to bypass the use of proprietary genetic resources for their follow up research. It is estimated that only 6% of all processes used research materials, which are privately appropriated abroad (ibid).

### Patent Scope and 'Hold-Up'

In this section the implications of various degrees of patent scope within a product patent system are discussed.[40] Traditionally, most of the discussions on patent strength and inventions have taken place in the context of patent length (Gallini 2002).[41] The small amount of literature on inventions and patent breadth also highlight that relationship between patent breadth and inventive activities would be contingent upon patent lengths (Gilbert and Shapiro 1990; Klemperer 1990). Conceptually, broad patents with high inventive steps (or non-obviousness) create stronger monopolies, but are also assumed to encourage more drastic innovations. In other words, society tolerates the deadweight loss of monopoly creation, but only when gains in terms of new innovations are also significantly high. By contrast, narrow patent scope gives rise to monopoly even when innovations are small and non-drastic in nature. However, one may also argue that monopoly

---

[40] The discussion, therefore, no longer pertains to the difference between product vs. process patent as in the previous subsection.

[41] With, perhaps, the exception of Merges and Nelson (1990).

under narrow patent scope will possibly be short-lived, since other firms can make some minor alterations to an innovation and replace the existing monopoly. This way, one might argue that monopolists will be able to retain only low mark-ups, since narrower patent scope, in effect, reduces the size of entry barrier. The resultant market structure could, roughly speaking, be much akin to a contestable market, where monopoly power would be substantially low (Baumol et al. 1982).[42]

This construct would be more valid when inventions are not cumulative, and the producers of final products do not have to negotiate with many inventors or patent holders to commercialise the final product. Moreover, our discussions of the previous sections also suggest that patent scopes are subjective, and hence susceptible to intense jurisprudential interventions. This construct, therefore, would also depend on the distribution of information costs (about patents) and litigation costs (in case of infringement) across firms. When these costs are symmetrically distributed across firms, this construct may be vindicated. In reality, however, these costs are often asymmetrically distributed (Lanjouw and Schankerman 2001), giving rise to a situation where firms with low litigation costs and low information costs might prevail upon their rivals to retain monopoly power, even when patent scope is narrow.

Understandably, new and small firms often do not have adequate financial resources for such activities (search of patents and litigations), and may take a cautious approach before filing patents, especially in technology clusters, where many firms exist with low litigation costs. Thus, monopoly effect under narrow patent scope can be equally strong. The society, however, would not gain as much as they would have if patent scope was broader.

A third justification for narrow patent scope pertains to transfer of patents between rival firms. Cohen et al. (2002b) find some evidence of inter-firm cooperation among Japanese firms. However, they also assert that such behaviour may be country specific.

It is common knowledge that biotechnological inventions are cumulative in nature and firms build up 'thickets of patent' for a single product (Ko 1992; Shapiro 2000; Cohen et al. 2002b). The implications of such patent thickets for 'holding up' and 'blocking' commercialisation is, also, increasingly being paid attention to (Ko 1992; Lerner 1995; Shapiro 2000). The problem of hold-up has a striking similarity, in terms of its economic consequence, with that of the classic 'problem of complements' (Shapiro 1989, p. 339), where the production of final good is hindered because of cost of accessing propitiatory (complementary) intermediate technologies.

A 'hold up' problem, apparently, arises when a firm, lacking prior information on patent domain, steps into the patent thicket of other firms, and is 'fenced up' by the patent holder (Ziedonis 2004). In other words, this problem arises not because of a wilful infringement by the 'held up' firms, but their inability to get prior information about the existence a relevant patent (Shapiro 2000). Prior access to such information, it is argued, would have enabled these firms to invent around the patent and bypass the 'hold up' problem. It is implicit in this argument that

---

[42] In a perfectly contestable market monopoly price would be equal to average costs.

involved firms have very similar level absorptive capacities (Cohen and Levinthal 1989), whereby firms' ability to innovate depends, substantially, on access to information. Given that such problems can only arise when firms are engaged in research in very similar fields, what is also implicit is that the criterion of non-obviousness for biotechnological patents is rather weak. Indeed, our discussions of Sect. 11.3 suggest that several attempts have been made to either reduce or even to do away with the criterion of non-obviousness in case of biotechnology patents.

Moreover, I have also highlighted that claims in biotechnological patents are often inappropriate, either due to early file of patents or because of lack of appropriate language of patent claims (Sherman 1990). Narrow patent scope, thus, makes the problem of overlapping claims even more acute. Firm level litigation costs, thus, becomes all the more crucial a parameter in shaping the consequences of narrow patents in biotechnology. As noted in the introduction, biotechnology is also one of the most patent-active fields, making collection of information on patent domains an expensive task. If these costs are indeed asymmetrically distributed across firms, as Lerner (1995) and Lanjouw and Shankerman (2001) seem to suggest, small and new firms would find it difficult to make much inroad into biotechnology inventions or innovations and their commercialisation. Narrow patent scope in biotechnology may not, therefore, necessarily encourage widespread innovative activities and greater competition in this sector. New monopolies would, perhaps, emerge out of incremental innovations (Robledo 2005) and ever-greening of patents in biotechnology.

Biotechnological inventions are also cumulative in nature, implying that the producer of a 'final good' may often negotiate with other firms to patent or commercialise the product. Filing patents can have some positive impact in this context, compared with the situation where firms would have kept their inventions a secret. By filing a patent, a firm discloses the existence of an invention to its potential collaborators. This step facilitates the process collaboration by reducing the search cost by the potential collaborators, which could have been prohibitively high in the absence of patents (Cohen et al. 2002b). However, such thickets have also been argued to have augmented transaction costs of collaborations and cross-licensing (Beard and Kaserman 2002; Rai and Eisenberg 2003; David and Hall 2006). Eventually, firms with higher than threshold level of transaction costs may opt for acquisition and mergers, paving the way, again, for a more consolidated market structure. One may also note that limited empirical literature on strategic patenting in biotechnology seems to suggest that such strategic use of patents to 'hold up' or 'block' inventions vary across countries (Thumm 2001, 2004). However, the reasons for this country-wise variation remain unexplored. More cross-country studies investigating the nature and extent of strategic patenting to obtain a better understanding of this cross-country variation would help policy makers design more appropriate (and perhaps country specific) standards of non-obviousness for biotechnology patents.

### 11.4.4 Benefit Sharing: 'Bio-Diversity' vis-à-vis 'Indigenous Science'

Traditionally, technological learning for the acquisition of TC by many late-coming developing nations has, often, been termed as imitation and piracy (Teece 1981). Ironically, the advent of genetic engineering technologies has reversed the fate, whereby now technologically rich Northern countries are accused of 'biopiracy'[43] by the indigenous communities in the South.[44] The genesis of the debate lies in a rather unique distribution of 'absolute advantages' of technology and raw materials across countries. While Northern countries have absolute advantage in genetic engineering technologies, the Southern countries possess an absolute advantage in the diversity of life forms. The progress of genetic engineering research inevitably depends on the access to such biological resources. This mutual dependence has led to a complex kind of North–South conflict and bargaining, often unseen in many other high technology industries.

Transfer of biological materials from the South to the North is, however, nothing new (Swanson 1996). Drayton (2005) gives a detailed account of how such transfers were expedited during the colonial rules of many such South countries as well, mainly for further research in the field of medicine. It is now well established that many of the modern medicines have been developed using biological resources, often having their native origins in the South countries. However, the trend in the post-genetic engineering era has been to explore the genetic base of every problem. Thus, starting from nutritional value and aroma of food to medicinal properties of a plant, all are supposed to be linked to their gene sequences. A patent would thus appropriate not only the phenotypic characteristics but also their genetic predispositions. Subsequently, a patent on a particular gene sequence may be used to lay claim on the entire species and their progeny having similar genetic properties. Possibly, this change in the domain of appropriation has intensified the magnitude of this conflict, where many indigenous communities fear a complete appropriation of the very base of their livelihood. An overall awareness about IPR issues may have also contributed to this dilemma. To put it differently, a trend involving greater than ever economic or commercial motive behind technological activities, coupled with heightened interest in patenting 'everything under the sun' may have made these communities conscious about their rights on their biological diversities (Rifkin 1998; Pottage 1998).

This alleged piracy of biological process (biopiracy) is of two types: the *piracy of knowledge* about the biological material (intellectual piracy) and the *piracy of material* (or resource piracy) (Burrows 2001; Shiva 2001). In a nutshell, the literature on 'biopiracy' maintains that transfer of Neem seed or Basmati variety of rice, for further research, to the West is not done at random. Rather, these plants have been selected after carefully examining their economic value, either through

---

[43] The industrialised world, on the other hand, interprets 'biopiracy' as 'bioprospecting' of raw material.

[44] It should be noted that these communities do not exclusively belong to developing countries. For the purpose of this article, however, we focus only on those communities who live in developing countries.

informal networks (Johannes 1993; Drayton 2005), or through formal research collaborations (Pineda 2006). In a rather oversimplified manner, the prime question is the following: whether the biological and genetic raw materials collected from developing world are 'natural' or their present forms are outcomes of nurture and maintenance by indigenous people? The developed countries, essentially, maintains that these resources are 'natural'. The discussion of sharing IP is, therefore, redundant. The group of developing countries (more specifically, the group of indigenous communities), on the other hand, attempt to establish that the so-called 'natural' raw materials are the results of 'millennia of study, selection, protection, conservation, development and refinement by communities of developing countries and indigenous peoples' (Burrows 2001, p. 241). Such human interventions, it is argued, should, by no means, be viewed differently from human interventions involved in research laboratories. Benefits accrued to the technology leaders using these resources should, therefore, be shared with the owners of these resources.

At one level, this controversy is related with the theoretical debate on whether biodiversity should be viewed as a 'raw material' in the standard economic production function framework (Wilson 1986), or an ecological resource, the depletion of which beyond a threshold should not be permitted (Perrings et al. 1995).[45] The majority of the indigenous communities have evolved in very close contacts with land and forests. They view biological resources as integral parts of their life, and strictly oppose the use of these resources merely as economic raw materials.

At another level, the philosophical root of this controversy that biological resources are mere natural raw materials for economic production function, devoid of any knowledge component, perhaps, lies in the long-standing controversy on what constitutes scientific knowledge. A detailed analysis of this complex debate is beyond the scope of this chapter. Rather, I shall highlight on few important differential characteristics of the two systems of scientific knowledge, namely, the Western modern science and indigenous science (Ogawa 1989, 1995; Boyd et al. 1991; Berkes 1993; Snively and Corsiglia 2002).

The Western science emphasises scientific truths to be universally valid and value free. It began with an aim to establish an overarching set of logically consistent rules to derive theory from observations. In doing so it sought to take 'science' away from mere observation and experimentation to the practice of theory justification (Duschl 1994). Through this process, it has been successful to a large extent in meeting its objective to filter out metaphysics, pseudo science and superstition from being called 'scientific'. But, the passionate involvement in theory making, allegedly, neglected a core field in the philosophy of science, namely, experiment. As opposed to the 'universal', 'precise' modern science, indigenous science has evolved in a relativist fashion, specific to its surrounding environment and culture. In other words, indigenous science has always been 'a culture dependent collective rational perceiving of reality' (Ogawa 1995, p. 588).

---

[45] However, the link between economics and ecology dates back to mid-nineteenth century, with the emergence of economic botany. See Drayton (2005, pp. 192–203).

Indeed indigenous science has grown in a relational framework between human beings, nature and socio-physical environment. In contrast, Western science views environment as a confounding factor, which must be 'controlled' for the achievement of desired outcomes. Another important difference pertains to their methodology with regard to experimentation and observation. The indigenous science is built upon timeless observations of a situation or event, in a rather holistic fashion, culminating into story telling. Modern science, on the other hand, relies more on logical assertion of theories on the basis of more short-term observations, allegedly, neglecting continuous mode of experimentation. It is also noteworthy that indigenous science, unlike modern science, does not attach any priority to human beings over nature.

Understandably, a negotiation between these two groups amounts to a negotiation between two differently held values and belief systems. It is unlikely that a solution would emerge in a frictionless manner, especially on an issue such as genetic engineering, one of the main aim of which is to 'control' nature. The solution to this negotiation would depend on how successfully these heterogeneous values and beliefs on knowledge, relations and rights are aligned together. Indeed, various kinds of benefit sharing arrangements have been proposed, including assigning property rights on natural resources (Bhat 1995), payment of royalty (Shiva 2001; CBD 2006)[46] and non-monetary benefits such as access to international research collaborations and no-cost access to improved germplasm (Raymond and Fowler 2001; Pineda 2006). But a comprehensive and operational solution is, as yet, not in sight.

## 11.5 Conclusion

Rather than attempting to summarise the main points of this chapter, I would like to note that the issue of patenting biotechnology finds its unique niche by the sheer richness of issues and diverse coverage of areas. In one extreme, the debate on 'anticommon' science is directed to shape the future directions of the progress of modern science. At another extreme, the benefit sharing debate has the potential to broaden the definition of science itself. Putting some of the theoretical propositions of these debates for intense empirical scrutiny should keep researchers busy for some years to come. In particular, one should collect cross-country evidence to examine whether it is indeed true that fundamental science is being privately appropriated, and if so, what are the costs and benefits of such a transformation. Another research issue of current relevance would be to examine whether replacement of open science by proprietary science increases the need for regulations in order to ensure safety and efficacy of using such knowledge.

One future challenge with the entrepreneurship research is, perhaps, to accommodate the issue of farm-entrepreneurship in the context of UPOV and

---

[46] See www.cbd.int/programmes/socio-eco/benefit/default.asp. Last accessed on 20 September 2006.

TRIPS. Also, even if it is established beyond doubt that university patents have been crucial for new biotech start-ups, one may further investigate whether or how patents encourage these neo-entrepreneurs to maintain their innovative spirit in the long run. More cross-country evidence should also be collected to understand the nature and the intricate dynamics of academic entrepreneurship with its consequences for growth and development of academic science.

Similarly, what could be a satisfactory solution to the benefit sharing debate: a simple extension of existing IPRs, monetary or non-monetary compensations, or something more novel? If some form of IPRs is given, what should be the penalty for infringements of such rights and how would that be made operational? All this would require intense empirical analyses by scholars of development and public policy, especially in developing countries. While inadequate data still pose a constraint, one should also not lose sight of the larger theoretical questions, while attempting to gather data. A meaningful policy prescription of these problems would, then, not be unattainable.

Future research should also take up the challenging task of modifying IPRs to better suit the requirement of biotechnology. Our discussion highlights that scholars of open science would like to see that patent scope is narrowed to exclude academic *science* from being patented. On the other hand, within the industrial research arena, a broadening of scope would at least prevent building up of thickets of marginal patents for *technological* outputs, and the consequences thereof. However, given that the 'science' of genetic engineering is interwoven with its 'technology', it becomes a daunting task to achieve these two, apparently, conflicting goals.[47]

# References

AAU (1998) University technology transfer of government-funded research has wide public benefits. Association of American Universities, 2 June
Agrawal A, Henderson R (2002) Putting patents in context: Exploring knowledge transfer from MIT. Management Science 48: 44–60
Akerlof G, Dickens WT (1982) The economic consequences of cognitive dissonance. American Economic Review 72 (3): 307–319
Alexanderson (1972) Inventors I have known. In: Alger P (ed), The human side of engineering. Schenectady, p. 137
APO (2002) Manual of practice and procedure-national. Australian Patent Office, September, Part 6

---

[47] Acknowledgement: I had many insightful discussions with Amit Shovon Ray on the analytical content and structure of this chapter. It has been a pleasure to discuss various developmental consequences of modern technologies with Rohan D'Souza. Important articles on biotechnology patenting in Japan would have remained inaccessible without Yu Sasaki's help and MV Lakhshmi's careful translations. Jagannadha Pawan Tamvada helped me with some recent studies on academic entrepreneurship and useful editorial comments. I also thank Thomas Brenner and three anonymous referees for their constructive as well as critical comments. Usual disclaimer applies.

Argyres NS, Liebeskind JP (1998) Privatizing the intellectual commons: Universities and the commercialisation of biotechnology. Journal of Economic Behavior and Organization 35: 427–454

Arrow KJ (1962) Economic welfare and the allocation of resources for invention. In: Nelson RR (ed), The rate and direction of inventive activity. Princeton University Press, New York

Atanassov A et al. (2004) To reach the poor. Results from the ISNAR-IFPRI next harvest study on genetically modified crops, public research, and policy implications. EPTD Discussion Paper 116. IFPRI, Washington, DC

Audretsch DB (2006) Does the entrepreneurial economy need an entrepreneurial university? Proceedings of the OeNB Workshop, No. 10

Audretsch DB, Stephan PE (1996) Company-scientist locational links: The case of biotechnology. The American Economic Review 86 (3): 641–652

AUTM (2001, 2002) AUTM Licensing Survey. Northbrook, IL

Baumol WJ, Panzar JC, Willig RD (1982) Contestable markets and the theory of industry structure. Harcourt, New York

Beaglehole R, Bonita R (1999) Public health at the crossroads: Achievements and prospects. CUP, Melbourne, p. 45

Beard TR, Kaserman DL (2002) Patent thickets, cross licensing and antitrust. Antitrust Bull 47 (2/3): 345–368

Bell M (1984) Learning and the accumulation of industrial technological capacity in developing countries. In: Fransman M, King S (eds), Technological capability in the third world. Macmillan, London, pp. 187–209

Berkes F (1993) Traditional ecological knowledge in perspective. In: Inglis JT (ed), Traditional ecological knowledge: Concepts and cases. International Development Research Centre, Ottawa, pp. 1–9

Bhaduri S, Ray AS (2004) Exporting through technological capability. Oxford Development Studies 32 (1): 87–100

Bhaduri S, Ray AS (2006) A game theoretic model of drug launch in India. Health Economics, Policy and Law 1 (1): 23–39

Bhat MG (1995) Trade related intellectual property rights to biological resources: Socioeconomic implications for developing countries. Ecological Economics 19: 205–217

Boyd R, Gasper P, Trout JD (eds), (1991) The philosophy of science. The MIT Press, Cambridge, pp. 247–260

Burrows B (2001) Patents, ethics and spin. In: Tokar B (ed), Redesigning life? The worldwide challenge to genetic engineering. Zed Books, London

Caulfield T (1999) The commercialization of human genetics: A discussion of issues relevant to Canadian consumers. Journal of Consumer Policy 21: 483–526

Caulfield TA, Gold ER (2000) Genetic testing, ethical concerns, and the role of patent law. Clinical Genetics 57: 370–375

CBD (2006) Access to genetic resources and benefit sharing, http://www.biodiv.org/programmes/socio-eco/benefit/default.aspx

Cervantes M, Guellec D (2002) The brain drain: Old myths, new realities. OECD Observer 230, January: 179

Chaturvedi S, Chwaii L (2005) Biosafety protocol, international trade and agricultural biotechnology: Policy inferences for India. RIS Discussion Paper No. 99, RIS

Chesnais F, Walsh V (1994) Biotechnology and the chemical industry: The relevance of some evolutionary concept. Paper presented in EUNETIC conference, Strasbourg

Cockburn IM (2004) The changing structure of the pharmaceutical industry. Health Affairs 23 (1): 10–22

Cohen JI (2005) Poorer nations turn to publicly developed GM crops. Nature Biotechnology 23: 27–33

Cohen WM, Levinthal DA (1989) Innovation and learning: The two faces of R&D. Economic Journal 99: 569–596

Cohen WM, Nelson RR, Walsh JP (2002a) Links and impacts: The influence of public research on industrial R&D. Management Science 48: 1–23

Cohen WM, Goto A, Nagata A, Nelson RR, Walsh JP (2002b) R&D spillovers, patents and the incentives to innovate in Japan and the United States. Research Policy 31 (8/9): 1349–1367

Commandeur P (1997) The DGIS special programme on biotechnology. Biotechnology and Development Monitor: 611

Cook-Deegan R (2007) The science commons in health research: Structure, function and values. The Journal of Technology Transfer 32 (3): 151–172

Costa-Font J, Mossialos E (2006) The public as a limit to technology transfer: The influence of knowledge and beliefs in attitude towards biotechnology in the UK. The Journal of Technology Transfer 31 (6): 629–645

Cottrell F (1932) Patent experience of the research corporation. Transactions of the American Institute of Chemical Engineers 22

Cyranoski D (2002a) Japanese forum urges rethink over patents. Nature 415: 354

Cyranoski D (2002b) Japan lays out 55-point patent plan. Nature 418: 116

Daemmrich AA (2004) Pharmacopolitics: Drug regulation in the United States and Germany. The University of North Carolina Press, Chapel Hill

Dasgupta P, David PA (1994) Towards a new economics of science. Research Policy 23: 487–521

Dasgupta P, Stiglitz J (1980) Uncertainty, industrial structure and the speed of R&D. Bell Journal of Economics 11: 1–28

David PA, Hall BH (2006) Property and the pursuit of knowledge: IPR issues affecting scientific research. Research Policy 35 (6): 767–771

de Carvalho NP (2004) The problem of gene patent. Washington University Global Studies Law Review 3 (3): 701–753

Denzau A, North DC (1994) Shared mental models, ideologies and institutions. Kyklos 47: 3–31

Dore R (1984) Technological self-reliance: Sturdy ideal or self serving rhetoric. In: Fransman M, King S (eds), Technological capability in the third world, Macmillan, London

Drayton R (2005) Nature's government: Science, imperial Britain and the 'improvement' of the world. Orient Longman, New Delhi

Duschl R (1994) Research on the history and philosophy of science. In: Gabel D (ed), Handbook of research on science teaching and training. MacMillan, New York

Duttfield G, Suthersanen U (2005) Harmonisation or differentiation in intellectual property protection? The lessons of history. Prometheus 23 (1): 131–147

Eisenberg RS, Nelson RR (2002) Public vs. proprietary science: A fruitful tension? Daedalus, Spring 2002

Etzkowitz H (1994) Knowledge as property: The Massachussets Institute of Technology and the debate of academic patent policy. Minerva 32: 383–421

Evenson RE, Putnam JD (1987) Institutional change in intellectual property rights. American Journal of Agricultural Economics 69 (2): 403–409

Fairtlough GH (1986) Genetic engineering-problems and opportunities. In: Jaconsson S et al. (eds), The biotechnological challenge, CUP, Cambridge, pp. 12–36

Fakuda-Parr S, Lopes C, Malik K (2002) Institutional innovations for capacity development. In: Fakuda-Parr S, Lopes C, Malik K (eds), Capacity for development: New solutions to old problems. Earthscan Publications (UNDP), London

Farbes P, Armelagos G (1980) Consuming passions: The anthropology of eating. Houghton Mifflin Company, Boston

Farnley S, More-Nase P, Sternfeld D (2004) Biotechnology – a challenge to the patent system. Current Opinion in Biotechnology 15: 254–257

Fishman EA (1996) MIT patent policy 1932–1946: Historical precedents in university–industry technology transfer. University of Pennsylvenia, Philadelphia

Gallini NT (2002) The economics of patents: Lessons from recent U.S. patent reform. The Journal of Economic Perspectives 16: 131–154

Geuna A, Nesta LJJ (2006) University patenting and its effects on academic research: The emerging European evidence. Research Policy 35: 790–807

Gibbons M, Limoges C, Nowotny H, Schwartzmann S, Scott P, Trow M (1994) The new production of knowledge – The dynamics of science and research in contemporary societies. Sage, London

Gilbert R, Shapiro C (1990) Optimal patent length and breadth. The Rand Journal of Economics 21: 106–112

Gittelman M (2006) National institutions, public–private knowledge flows, and innovation performance: A comparative study of the biotechnology industry in the US and France. Research Policy 35: 1052–1068

Gold ER (2000) Finding common cause in the patent debate. Nature Biotechnology 18: 1217–1218

Gold ER, Castle D, Cloutier LM, Daar AS, Smith PJ (2002) Needed: Models of biotechnology intellectual property. Trends in Biotechnology 20: 327–329

Gold R (2001) Patenting life forms: An international comparison. CBAC report (Canada)

Gonsen R (1998) Technological capabilities in developing countries: Industrial biotechnology in Mexico. MacMillan, London

Goodman G, Sorj B, Wilkinson J (1987) From farming to biotechnology: A theory of agro-industrial development. Basil Blackwell, Oxford

Govind M (2006) Sociology of science. Anmol, New Delhi

Hacking AJ (1986) Economic aspects of biotechnology, CUP, Cambridge

Heller MA, Eisenberg RS (1998) Can patents deter innovation? The anticommons in biomedical research. Science 280 (5364): 698–701

Helpman E (1993) Innovation, imitation and intellectual property rights. Econometrica 61 (6): 1247–1280

Hoedemaekers R (2001) Commercialization, patents and moral assessment of biotechnology products. Journal of Medicine and Philosophy 26: 273–284

Holtzman N (1999) Are genetic tests adequately regulated? Science 286: 409

Horwitz AW, Lai EL (1996) Patent length and the rate of invention. International Economic Review 37: 785–801

Huang G, Wang Q (2002) Agricultural biotechnology development and policy in China. AgBioForum 5: 122–135

IPR Commission Report (2002) Integrating intellectual property rights and development policy. Commission on Intellectual Property Rights, Government of UK, Chap. 1

James C (1999) Preview: Global review of transgenic crops. ISAAA Brief No. 12, Ithaca, New York

Johannes RE (1993) Integrating traditional ecological knowledge with environmental impact assessment. In: Inglis JT (ed), Traditional ecological knowledge: Concepts and cases. International Development Research Centre, Ottawa, pp. 33–41

Khan M, Dernis H (2006) Global overview of innovative activities from the patent indicators perspective. STI Working paper 2006/3, OECD

King J, Stabinsky D (1999) Biotechnology under globalisation: The corporate expropriation of plant, animal and microbial species. Race and Class 40: 73–89

Kingston W (2005) 'Genius', 'Faction' and rescuing intellectual property rights. Prometheus 23: 3–25

Kitch EW (1977) The nature and function of the patent system. Journal of Law and Economics 38: 463–495

Klemperer P (1990) How broad should the scope of patent protection be? The Rand Journal of Economics 21: 113–130

Ko Y (1992) An economic analysis of biotechnology patent protection. The Yale Law Journal 102: 777–804

Kodish E (1997) Commentary: Risks and benefits, testing and screening, cancer, genes and dollars. The Journal of Law, Medicine and Ethics 25: 252–255

Koening BA, Greely HT, McConnell LM, Silverberg HL, Raffin TA (1998) Genetic testing for BRCA1 and BRCA2: Recommendations of the Stanford Program in Genomics, Ethics and Society. Journal of Women's Health 7: 531 545

Koo B, Wright BD (2002) Economics of patenting a research tool. EPTD Discussion Paper No. 88, IFPRI

Kuenning MA, Makundi F (2000) Agricultural biotechnology for developing countries. American Behavioral Scientist 44: 318–349

Kumar H (2007) Motivation to innovate: A study of grassroot innovators in India. MPhil dissertation, Jawaharlal Nehru University, New Delhi

Lai E, Qui L (2003) The North's intellectual property rights standard for the South. Journal of International Economics 59: 183–209

Lall S (1987) Learning to industrialize. Macmillan, London

Lange P (1993) Derived plant varieties under the revised UPOV. Plant Variety Protection Gezzette and Newsletter, November: 51–63

Lanjouw JO, Schankerman M (2001) Characteristics of patent litigation: A window of competition. The Rand Journal of Economics 32: 129–151

Lerner J (1994) The importance of patent scope: An empirical analysis. The Rand Journal of Economics 25: 319–333

Lerner J (1995) Patenting in the shadow of competition. Journal of Law and Economics 38: 463–495

Lerner J (2002) 150 years of patent protection. American Economic Review 92: 221–225

Levin R, Klevorick A, Nelson RR, Winter SG (1987) Appropriating the returns from industrial R&D. Brookings Papers on Economic Activity: 783–820

Lowe RA, Gonzalez-Brambila C (2007) Faculty entrepreneurs and research productivity. The Journal of Technology Transfer 32: 173–194

Machlup F (1958) An economic review of the patent system. Study of the subcommittee of patent, trademarks and copyrights. US Senate

Markle GE, Robin SS (1985) Biotechnology and the social reconstruction of molecular biology. Science, Technology and Human Values 10: 70–79

Mazzoleni R, Nelson RR (1998) Economic theories of the benefits and costs of patents. Journal of Economic Issues 32: 1031–1052

McKelvey MD (1996a) Evolutionary innovations: The business of biotechnology. OUP, New York

McKelvey MD (1996b) Discontinuities in genetic engineering for pharmaceuticals? Form jumps and lock-in in systems of innovation. Technology Analysis and Strategic Management 8: 107–116

McMahon E, Lumiere J (2004) Canada lags behind on patenting higher life forms. IPL Newsletter, American Bar Association, 22 (3)

Merges R, Nelson RR (1990) On the complex economics of patent scope. Columbia Law Review 90: 839–916

Merton RK (1967) Science and democratic social structure. In: Merton RK (ed), Social theory and social structure. The Free Press, New York, Chap. 10

Merton RK (1973) The sociology of science: Theoretical and empirical investigations. The University of Chicago Press, Chicago

Mkandawire T (2002) Incentives, governance and capacity development in Africa. In: Fakuda-Parr S, Lopes C, Malik K (eds), Capacity for development: New solutions to old problems. Earthscan Publications (UNDP), London

Mowery D (2005) The Bayh–Dole Act and high technology-entrepreneurship at U.S. universities: Chicken, egg, or something else? In: Liebcap G (ed), University entrepreneurship and technology transfer. Elsevier, Amsterdam, pp. 39–68

Mowery D, Nelson RR, Sampat B, Ziedonis AA (1999) The growth of patenting and licensing by U.S. universities: An assessment of the effects of the Bayh–Dole Act of 1980. Research Policy 30: 99–119

Mrazek M, Mossialos E (2003) Stimulating pharmaceutical research and development for neglected disease. Health Policy 64: 75–88

Murmann JP (2003) Knowledge and competitive advantage. CUP, Cambridge

Nelson RR (2001) Observations on the post Bayh–Dole rise of patenting at American universities. Journal of Technology Transfer 26: 13–19

Nelson RR, Winter SG (1982) An evolutionary theory of economic change. Harvard University Press, Cambridge, MA

Noble DF (1977) America by design. Alfred A Knopf, New York

Nordhaus W (1972) The optimum life of a patent: A reply. American Economic Review 62: 428–431

Norgaard RB (1994) Development betrayed. Routledge, London

North DC (1990) Institution, institutional change and economic performance. Cambridge University Press, Cambridge

OECD (2000) A new economy? OECD, Paris

OECD (2002) Uncertainty and precaution: Implications for trade and environment. Joint Working Party on Trade and Environment. September, pp. 38–41

Ogawa M (1989) Beyond the tacit framework of "science" and "science education" among science educators. International Journal of Science Education 11: 247–250

Ogawa M (1995) Science education in a multiscience perspective. Science Education 79: 583–593

Perrings C, Mäler KG, Folke C, Holling C, Jansson BO (1995) (eds), Biodiversity loss: Ecological and economic issues. CUP, Cambridge

Pila J (2003) Bound futures: Patent law and modern biotechnology. Boston University Journal of Science and Technology Law 9 (2): 326–378

Pineda CF (2006) The impact of stronger intellectual property rights on science and technology in developing countries. Research Policy 35: 808–824

Plein LC (1991) Popularising biotechnology: The influence of issue definition. Science, Technology and Human Values 16: 474–490

Polanyi M (1967) The republic of science: Its political and economic theory. Minerva 1: 54–74

Pottage A (1998) The inscription of life in law: Genes, patents and biopolitics. Modern Law Review 61: 740–765

Rai AK, Eisenberg RS (2003) Bayh–Dole reform and the progress of biomedicine. Law and Contemporary Problems 66: 289–314

Rangnekar D (1999) Technology paradigms and the innovation–appropriation interface: An examination of the nature and scope of plant breeders' rights. Prometheus 17: 125–138

Ray AS (2004) The changing structure of R&D incentives in India: The pharmaceutical sector. Science, Technology and Society 9: 295–317

Ray AS (2005) The Indian pharmaceutical industry at crossroads: Implications for India's health care. In: Bagchi A, Soman K (eds), Maladies, preventives and curatives: Debates in public health in India. Tulika Books, New Delhi

Ray AS, Bhaduri S (2003) The political economy of drug quality: Changing perceptions and implications for the Indian pharmaceutical industry. Economic and Political Weekly 38: 2303–2309

Raymond R, Fowler C (2001) Sharing the non-monetary benefits of agricultural biodiversity. Issues in Genetic Resources No. 5. International Plant Genetic Resource Institute

Rifkin J (1998) The biotech century. Penguin Putnam, New York

Robledo JR (2005) Strategic patents and asymmetric litigation costs as entry deterrence instruments. Economics Bulletin 15: 1–9

Rosenberg N, Steinmuller WE (1988) Why are Americans such poor imitators? The American Economic Review Proceedings 78: 229–234

Sampat BN (2006) Patenting and US academic research in the 20th century: The world before and after Bayh–Dole. Research Policy 35: 772–789

Sampath PG (2005) Breaking the fence: Can patent rights deter biomedical innovation in "technology followers?" UNU-INTECH Discussion Paper 2005-10

Scherer FM (1972) Nordhaus's theory of optimal patent life: A geometric reinterpretation. American Economic Review 62: 422–427

Scherer FM (2002) The economics of human gene patents. Academic Medicine 77: 1348–1367

Shapiro C (1989) Theories of oligopoly behavior. In: Schmalensee R, Willig R (eds), Handbook of industrial organization. Elsevier, New York

Shapiro C (2000) Navigating the patent thicket: Cross licenses, patent tools and standard setting. In: Jaffe A, Lerner J, Stern S (eds), Innovation policy and the economy. NBER, Cambridge, MA

Sharp M (1991) Pharmaceuticals and biotechnology: Perspectives for the European industry. In: Freeman C, Sharp M, Walter W (eds), Technology and the future of Europe: Global competition and the environment in the 1990s. Pinter, London, pp. 213–230

Sherman B (1990) Patent law in a time of change: Non-obviousness and biotechnology. Oxford Journal of Legal Studies 10: 278–287

Shiva V (2001) Biopiracy: The theft of knowledge and resources. In: Tokar B (ed), Redesigning life? The worldwide challenge to genetic engineering. Zed Books, London

Snively G, Corsiglia J (2002) Discovering indigenous science. Science Education 85: 6–34

Straus J (2002) Recent developments and challenges in the protection of intellectual property rights. Proceedings of the International Conference on Intellectual Property. The Internet, Electronic Commerce and Traditional Knowledge

Swanson T (1996) Biodiversity as information. Ecological Economics 17: 1–8

Tatum E (1959) A case history of biological research. Science 129: 1711–1715

Taylor DJ, Green NPO, Stout GW (2002) Biological science. CUP, Cambridge

Teece D (1981) The market for know-how and the efficient international transfer of technology. Annals of the American Academy of Political and Social Science. In: Heston AW, Pack H (eds), Technology transfer: New issues, new analyses

Thumm N (2001) Management of intellectual property rights in European biotechnology firms. Technological Forecasting and Social Change 67: 259–272

Thumm N (2004) Strategic patenting in biotechnology. Technology Analysis and Strategic Management 16: 529–538

Thurow LC (1997) Needed: A new system of intellectual property rights. Harvard Business Review, September–October: 95–103

Tocqueville AD (1840, 2003) Democracy in America. Penguin, New York

Trajtenberg M, Henderson R, Jaffe AB (1997) University versus corporate patents: A window on the basicness of inventions. Economics of Innovation and New Technology 5: 19–50

UNCTAD-ICTSD (2005) Patents: Ordre public and morality. In: UNCTAD-ICTSD (eds), Resource book on TRIPS and development. CUP, Cambridge, Chap. 19

Upadhyay V, Ray AS, Basu P, Bhaduri S, Iyer P (2002) A socio economic investigation of in-house R&D in Indian industry. Report submitted to the Government of India, New Delhi

USDA (1987) Agricultural biotechnology and the public. Proceedings summary. United States Department of Agriculture. Washington, DC

Walsh JP, Arora A, Cohen WM (2003) Working through patent problem. Science 299: 1021

Wilson EO (1986) (ed), Biodiversity. National Academy of Sciences, Washington, DC.

Wright BD, Pardey PG (2006) The evolving rights to intellectual property protection in the agricultural bioscience. International Journal of Technology and Globalisation 2: 12–29

Yamana M (2001) Patenting genes and contemporary society: Problems and prospects of the proprietary information. Contemporary Society 2, 30 November

Zeeman J (2000) Real science: What it is and what it means. CUP, Cambridge

Ziedonis RH (2004) Don't fence me in: Fragmented markets for technology and patent acquisition strategies of firms. Management Science 50: 804–820

Zucker LG, Darby MR, Brewer MB (1998) Intellectual human capital and the birth of U.S. biotechnology industry. American Economic Review 88: 290–306

Zucker LG, Darby MR, Armstrong JF (2002) Commercializing knowledge: University science, knowledge capture and firm performance in biotechnology. Management Science 48: 138–153

# 12 Legal Frameworks and Public Support in the Biotechnology Industry

Dirk Engel[1] and Oliver Heneric[2]

[1]Rheinisch-Westfälisches Institut fuer Wirtschaftsforschung (RWI), Essen, Germany
[2]Center for European Economic Research (ZEW), Mannheim, Germany

## 12.1 Introduction

It is largely recognized that Germany, one of the largest European economies, failed to grasp the opportunity of upcoming key technologies such as biotechnology or information and communication technology in the 1980s, while these evolved in other countries led by the USA. After the kick off period of the biotechnology industry in the 1990s, more than 300 companies were established in Germany at the turn of the century. The slowdown of economic growth in the last 3 years affected the expected number of biotechnology companies but still resulted in 391 companies in 2007 (Ernst & Young 2007).

In this chapter we highlight the importance of the legal framework and research and development (R&D) policy in particular to explain the late development of a modern biotechnology industry in Germany. For quite a long time there was no adequate legal framework concerning the requirements for the use of biotechnology. The provisions of national genetic law were first set down in 1990. Furthermore, mistrust of the effects of biotechnology was caused by the negative association with genetic manipulation in public opinion. Legal restrictions on R&D, such as the first Genetic Engineering Act of 1990, may imply some negative effects not only for the biotechnology industry but also for the pharmaceutical industry. In contrast to that, the amendment of the law on genetic engineering in 1993 set up a regulatory framework that has the potential to promote the emergence of Germany's modern biotechnology industry.

While biotechnology firms carrying out R&D projects require considerable financial resources, legal changes and R&D policy are only two of several impact factors pushing biotechnology entrepreneurship. Access to external capital, namely, venture capital, also seems to be a most important resource and thus we will

H. Patzelt and T. Brenner (eds.), *Handbook of Bioentrepreneurship*,
doi: 10.1007/978-0-387-48345-0_12, © Springer Science + Business Media, LLC 2008

embed the role of public funding and regulation in a general discussion of impact factors.

The chapter is organized as follows. In Sect. 12.2 we discuss the rationales of state intervention in the biotechnology industry, and we summarize the main empirical findings on the outcome of state intervention. In Sect. 12.3 we provide a description of the milestones of legal changes in Germany. The background information about the aims of legal framework changes is essential for an understanding of how the legal framework works and how it can affect the behavior of scientists, entrepreneurs, and investors. In Sect. 12.4 we link important milestones of legal framework changes with the development of a modern biotechnology industry in Germany. In doing so, we will try to quantify the effects of legal framework changes. In this manner we also attempt to estimate the partial contribution of the "BioRegio contest," a major example of R&D funding programs in the "BioX" line. The chapter concludes in Sect. 12.5.

## 12.2 Legal Framework and Public Support: Rationales and Economic Relevance

### 12.2.1 Rationales for Public Support and a Legal Framework

Innovations based on radical technologies such as gene technology are closely connected with expectations of benefits to society and economic growth. The success of turning hope into reality is, however, associated with investments in a firm's R&D activity. Unfortunately, several forms of market failure may exist.

At first, market failures in the market for gene technology products may imply underinvestment by the private sector in R&D. Underinvestment in R&D may result from external effects on the one hand and information asymmetries on the other. Concerning the case for external effects, private firms will only consider their own particular benefits and choose their own level of commitment to the innovation process, i.e. R&D investments. Social rates of return from new technologies, i.e. R&D spillover to competitors, customers, and many others, are difficult to absorb by spillover-producing firms active in R&D, and thus the private sector tends to underinvest in R&D. Spence (1984) established this form of market failure by considering the issues of appropriation and diffusion of knowledge as basic characteristics of R&D activities: (a) the existence of spillover effects makes it difficult for investors to capture the full social benefits of their innovation, and (b) leading firms charge too much for their new knowledge, so that the diffusion of knowledge is less than the social optimum.

Information asymmetries on capital markets are the second argument for the expectation of underinvestment in R&D. Newly created high-tech biotechnology firms carrying out R&D projects require considerable financial resources over a long time. Significant sales are, however, absent and the entrepreneur's personal funds are usually too small. Young high-tech firms also have limited access to loans. New equity financing has some advantages over debt-financing and is often seen as a suitable means for innovative firms to overcome financial constraints. Carpenter and Petersen (2002, p. F60) point out that "equity finance does not require the firm to post collateral, investors' upside returns are not bounded, and additional equity financing does not increase the probability of financial distress." New institutional economic theory and finance theory suggest that specialized financial intermediaries, in particular venture capital companies (Lerner 2002, p. F77), are able to provide capital for some of the highly financially constrained firms.

Empirical evidence shows, however, that the supply of venture capital is limited to a specific segment of financially constrained firms. Venture capital companies avoid small-scale funding because of an extraordinary level of uncertainty about project outcomes. Furthermore, the chance to realize a sufficient return on investments depends on the existence and the wealth of stock markets (Black and Gilson 1998; Gompers and Lerner 1998; Jeng and Wells 2000). Germany's venture capital market was poorly developed for a long time. The implementation of the "Neuer Markt" in April 1997, Germany's equivalent to the United States NASDAQ, offered highly profitable exit opportunities for private equity investors. It is important to note that a well-functioning venture capital industry can only partially reduce information asymmetries

Second, biotechnology has the potential to generate negative effects for society. It brings with it a multitude of opportunities for new products and processes, but also a large degree of risk. Genetic engineering opens up possibilities to manipulate the inherited characteristics of cells, perhaps altering entire organisms. This creates the need for a legal framework, in order to prevent damage to living things and their environment – as far as is possible – and to enable the users of biotechnology to be sure that they are acting in accordance with the law.

Third, market failures in the drug market may affect the development of new drugs in Germany. Restrictive regulations in the health sector may limit the attractiveness of Germany as a lead market for the introduction of new drugs. Lead market function is, however, most important to attract R&D affiliates to stay in the country (see Beise-Zee 2001 for details of the lead market concept). As a matter of fact, Germany has lost some market shares in the production of pharmaceuticals. At present it is ranked as the fourth biggest producer after the USA, Japan, and France. It was still the third largest in the early 1990s. German pharmaceutical companies are smaller compared with their US counterparts, and have been a target for mergers and acquisitions in recent years and the present.

The above-mentioned forms of market failures on the one hand, and the expectation of high social benefits[1] on the other, lead to a special alertness on the part of the government. Concerning the specific framework conditions of modern biotechnology, the legal framework seems to be both a significant obstacle to and a driver of the emergence of a modern biotechnology industry. It is worth noting that financial constraints might, however, be the most important obstacle.

---

[1] Griliches (1992) points out that social benefits of R&D may remain significantly above the private benefit of a firm active in R&D.

Among most OECD countries, government agencies intend to bridge these gaps concerning appropriation, diffusion, and technical and market risks by similar justification of public R&D policies.

In the USA, for instance, the Advanced Technology Program illustrates these policy rationales, because "it provides cost-shared funding to industry for fledgling technologies, that are high risk in nature, but which could lead to positive spillovers." It "seeks to fund R&D where the resulting knowledge and technologies are fully appropriable; that is investors cannot fully capture the financial returns to their investment. Instead the benefits flow to other firms, industries, consumers, and the general public."

The European Commission argues that businesses have difficulties in incorporating technologies that are not part of their traditional field of activity and accessing new types of skills. In particular, "*financial risks* are seen high for innovation and profitability may be delayed by development hitches, and tax may not be neutral between success and failure." This calls for "general measures to streamline innovation processes and direct action on specific market failures" (European Commission).

The German Federal Government justifies its public R&D funding in industry by *external effects*, e.g., when third parties can use research results and thus gain an economic advantage without paying the technology developer a fee. In such cases the incentives may be too weak for innovative companies to develop private R&D activities in these areas to the extent desirable if economic profitability considerations are included. Public policy offers R&D funds "where R&D projects have long time horizons, a *high economic risk* and great financial needs and therefore are beyond the possibilities of individual companies" (German Ministry for Education and Research).

Do government agencies bridge these gaps, taking into account different "risks" by funding firms which suffer from financial, technical, or market risk? In the last decade several new technologies such as information and communication technologies, biotechnology, and nanotechnology made great progress and governments invested extensive amounts to foster these technologies. However, it is less clear whether government with its R&D policy addresses the projects and entrepreneurs it aimed to address in the sense of eliminating market failure – or if government just tends to surf on attraction and public attention to win elections. Robust empirical evidence concerning the effectiveness and efficiency of R&D policy may be a necessary condition to shed some light on this question.

### 12.2.2 The Impact of Public R&D Funding: Empirical Findings

Governments use different R&D policy instruments to overcome market failures such as a lack of appropriation by regulation (patent law), a lack of know-how diffusion by incentives to cooperate (exchange of R&D staff, collaborative R&D activities), and a lack of risks by financial incentives such as tax credits or R&D project grants. Subsidies and tax credits are market-compatible forms of direct government intervention and broadly used by policymakers.[2] The majority of European countries and larger OECD countries beyond Europe such as Australia, Canada, Japan, and the USA use tax credits (OECD 2002). France recently increased the attractiveness of this tool in July 2005 ("Tax cuts for shares in innovative SMEs or for the financing of research programs"). As a matter of fact, Germany does not apply this form of R&D policy.

Intellectual property rights are most important to protect discoveries and inventions, in particular in the modern biotechnology industry. Patents guarantee the exclusive rights to sales based on inventions and thus compensation is made for preproduction costs (about US $600 m per drug). Patentable biotechnology inventions include, for example, cell fusion procedures yielding a cell line that expresses a specific protein. In contrast to the aspect mentioned here, the patent system in Germany and Europe is known to function very well. The improvements in patent law are mostly of a minor extent.[3]

During the last decade, a rich body of studies has empirically investigated the impact of R&D policy on general and public funding of business R&D projects, in particular on the level of firms (see, for example, David and Hall 2000). As David and Hall (2000) and many others point out, most estimations in the studies reviewed are confronted with potential selection problems. In detail, governments select the most promising projects for successful implementation of research ideas. The estimated impact is overstated so long as selection bias is not eliminated. Selection bias is linked to observable as well as unobservable company-specific effects. Since the latter effects can be eliminated by parametric selection models, non-parametric procedures such as matching take into account firm-specific observables only (see Heckman et al. 1998, 1999).

Recently published studies by Wallsten (2000), Lach (2002), and Czarnitzki and Fier (2002) have applied state-of-the art evaluation methods to compensate for selection of the fittest. Lach (2000) addressed the impact of Israeli government R&D funding and applied the difference-to-difference estimator to eliminate selection of firm-specific time invariant unobserved effects. This approach handles a lot of potential selection. However, the estimator overstates the effect in the case of time variant unobserved shocks which simultaneously affect R&D expenditure and the probability of receiving a subsidy. His results suggest that the level of private R&D expenditure is higher by a factor of 11 for firms with less than 300 employees, compared with the situation of the absence of funding. Most interestingly, the coefficient has a negative sign, although not statistically significant, for large firms. Czarnitzki and his co-authors mainly apply a matching estimator und use data from the *Mannheimer Innovationspanel*, which is enriched by external microdata. The impact of public funding of R&D is estimated

---

[2] Although governments are the major players in stimulating private business R&D, private foundations offer R&D grants, too. However, non-profit foundations fostering R&D – especially technology-driven scientific foundations – are in particular more established in the USA than in Europe.

[3] See for example the "Biopatent" directive 98/44 of the European Commission, which was recently implemented in Germany.

positively, too. In contrast to Lach, the effects are, however, remarkably smaller. German firms interviewed that were funded between 1996 and 1998 report innovation expenditure on average of about 3 million Deutsche Mark. Selected nonfunded firms with similar characteristics to funded ones spent 1.49 million Deutsche Mark on average. Further analyses by Czarnitzki and Licht (2006) also suggest an above average patent outcome of funded projects, compared with that of nonfunded ones. In contrast to the study by Lach, papers from Czarnitzki and his co-authors do not focus on the evaluation of a specific program. In general we detect a lack of robust empirical evidence based on state-of-the-art science to analyze the effectiveness and efficiency of public funding in Germany. Of course, a rich body of studies deals with the evaluation of Germany's technology programs (e.g. Kulicke and Lo 2006). All of these studies do not, however, apply state-of-the-art methodology.

Lerner (1999) evaluates the long run success of firms participating in the Small Business Innovation Research (SBIR) program, a major public assistance initiative in the United States to fund the commercialization process of a new idea within a small business. Those firms receiving assistance from SBIR achieved significantly higher employment and sales growth rates than did similar firms that were not assisted by SBIR between 1983 and 1995. These differences are even more pronounced in regions with high venture capital activity and in high-tech industries. Toole (2005) analyzed whether public funding of biotechnology research, namely, fundamental and clinical research, complements industry R&D investment in the long run. His results indicate that a dollar increase in public basic research stimulates an additional \$8.38 in pharmaceutical investment after 8 years. The effect of public clinical research is smaller in magnitude and shorter in duration. An increase by \$1 results in an additional \$2.35 in pharmaceutical investment over a 3-year period.

Concerning the strategies to internalize R&D spillovers from others, a rapidly growing number of papers address the impact of firm-to-firm cooperation as well as company–scientist links. Joint R&D has become a very important mode of interfirm and science-firm collaboration in the last decade. Studies on this topic mainly show that publicly funded joint R&D outperforms publicly funded stand-alone R&D (see Czarnitzki et al. 2006). Results from Czarnitzki et al. (2006) further suggest that the outperformance of R&D-funded German firms, compared with nonfunded stand-alone R&D, mainly results from collaborative behavior. In this manner, shifting of R&D policy towards the promotion of joint R&D speaks in favor of higher benefits from public assistance.

Further studies deal with the "bridging role" of public R&D funding, also known as the "certification" hypothesis (see Lerner 1999, 2002). Brand-new ideas discovered in nonprofit-oriented research institutions are mostly characterized by technical uncertainty and uncertainty about market potential and market acceptance (for empirical evidence, see Thursby and Thursby 2002; Shane 2004). Private investors who are neither banks nor venture capitalists are disposed to fund this kind of projects. As we mentioned earlier, equity investments are more suitable than bank loans in this context. Venture capitalists need, however, a serious proof of concept. This includes a successful prototype, intellectual property rights or strategic alliances with big companies to "signal" a lower level of uncertainty. Public programs can play an important bridging role in the process of reducing the technological uncertainty of the above-mentioned projects. On the one hand, public investors should also consider social benefits and thus put less weight on the magnitude of project uncertainty. On the other, public authorities are likely to demonstrate the successful promotion of individuals, firms, or regions to increase the probability of reelection. They may have some difficulties in accepting that a part of public funds is allocated to ex post unsuccessful firms (Wallsten 2000). Further, firms may actively seek public transfers to increase their price cost margin (Eisinger 1993). In this sense, public investors will probably invest earlier than private investors. In doing so, they try, however, to avoid funding the "lemons." Fier and Heneric (2005) analyze the determinants of public R&D funding by the German Federal government for biotechnology projects. Both young, small-sized firms and old, large-scale firms have a higher probability of being publicly funded. The middle-aged and medium-sized firms are less funded. Therefore, selection by public fund managers works in line with the first predictions. Furthermore, firms with a better credit rating as well as those with patent applications have higher chances of receiving public funds, too. The evidence sheds light on positive selection by public fund management *within* the uncertain projects. It is worth noting that selection is limited. As Toole (2005) points out, the typical SBIR academic entrepreneur is not a "star scientist."

The main question is, however, whether private investors accept the bridging role and certification by public funding. Lerner (1999) arrives at the result that multiple SBIR awards do not imply an outperformance of SBIR-funded firms, however. This finding highlights the question of whether a lower level of public funding as well as a limited amount of signaling could be sufficient to contribute to certification of projects. Lerner also shows that firms winning SBIR phase 2 awards have a 3.1% higher probability of receiving venture financing, while non-SBIR funded firms have a lower probability (0.8%). Toole (2005) confirms the findings for biotechnology firms. He found that winning a phase 2 award of an SBIR program doubles the firm's chances of receiving follow-on venture capital investment. A higher level of SBIR funding also increases the chance for follow-on private investment. Altogether, the certification role of SBIR programs seems to work in reality. Further attention is drawn to the question of the impact of additional awards.

Engel and Heneric (2006) analyzed the start-up activity for participants and nonparticipants of the BioRegio contest (BRC). This contest was initiated in 1995 by the Federal Ministry of Education and Research (BMBF), and encouraged regions to apply for subsidies to be used in establishing a biotechnology industry in the region (Dohse 2000). The BMBF's main goal was to stimulate the transfer of new knowledge into new products and thereby narrow the gap between Germany and those countries leading in the application of biotechnological knowledge, i.e., the USA and Great Britain. Regions were invited to submit a development concept meant to help establish the biotechnology industry in their region for appraisal (see Dohse 2000 for details). This funding concept aimed at developing a new holistic approach for research and technology policy and was planned to integrate biotechnological capacities and scientific, economic, and administrative activities. The governmental purpose of funding biotechnology was – and still is – to ensure that the high international standard of performance in the life sciences will be maintained. BioRegio was initiated to push the commercialization of biotechnology in Germany and thus create internationally outstanding centers of excellence.

Participation in the BRC was attractive to German regions for several reasons (e.g., receiving subsidies, signaling the potential of the region to entrepreneurs and investors, networking). Taking part in the BRC leads to an exclusive possibility of having access to different valuable resources that could give rise to additional spillovers. Probably, entrepreneurs and investors are affected by the expectation of spillovers which are signalized by BRC participation. Engel and Heneric (2006) differentiated between winner regions of the BRC (Munich, Rhein-Neckar, Rhineland, Jena (special vote)) and other participants in the BRC (14 BioRegios).

**Table 12.1.** Frequency of newly founded biotechnology firms by BRC participation state

| BRC state | 1980–1994 | | 1995–1998 | | 1999–2003 | |
|---|---|---|---|---|---|---|
| | # | Intensity | # | Intensity | # | Intensity |
| BRC winner regions | 97 | 11.4 | 96 | 11.3 | 112 | 13.2 |
| BRC nonwinner regions | 92 | 8.5 | 103 | 9.5 | 206 | 18.9 |
| Other counties | 130 | 7.9 | 151 | 9.2 | 179 | 10.9 |
| *Sum* | *319* | *8.9* | *350* | *9.8* | *497* | *13.9* |

According to Engel and Heneric (2006, p. 86)
\# – Absolute numbers
Firm formation intensity: number of biotechnology start-ups related to 10,000 potential founders (= R&D employees in private sector and scientists at public R&D institutes in 1995)

Table 12.1 shows the frequency of start-up activities in absolute and relative terms differentiated by BRC participation state. In Sect. 12.4 we will discuss the development of biotechnology start-ups in more detail and thus we now emphasize the regional differences in relative terms. In BRC winner regions and BRC nonwinner ones we observe significantly higher firm formation activity in relative terms, compared with that in other BRC nonparticipating counties in each period of time.

This impression is also strengthened by the regression analysis prepared by Engel and Heneric (2006). BRC winners as well as other BRC participant regions achieve a significantly higher number of newly founded biotechnology firms, compared with regions that have not participated in the BRC. The authors do not detect, however, any kind of significant differences between the coefficient estimates of BRC winner regions and BRC participants. At this point, the outperformance of BRC winners and other BRC participants can be attributed to unobservable ability of participants and/or effects of participation in the BRC. Engel and Heneric (2006) applied the instrumental variable estimation approach to eliminate the effect of unobservable abilities. The main assumptions of these techniques were not fulfilled, however, and thus the causal effect of BRC participation cannot be deduced from this kind of empirical analysis. At this point, we can only conclude that BRC seems to be functioning well to attract regions with above average potential to build a biotechnology cluster to participate.

As a matter of fact, the firm formation intensity in BRC winner regions develops below the average over time. As a result, the share of biotechnology start-ups in BRC winner regions went down slightly from 30.4% in the first period to 27.4% in the second period and sharply between 1999 and 2003 to 22.5%. In contrast, the firm formation intensity in the biotechnology industry and the share of biotechs in BRC nonwinner regions increase remarkably. Addressing the change of the number of biotechnology start-ups between both periods, regression analysis points out that only BRC nonwinner regions are still going on to attract significantly more start-ups over time to cluster the biotechnology industry.[4]

This pattern sheds some light on the procedure for selecting winner regions. As Dohse (2000) points out, the jury seems to follow a "picking the past winner strategy": BRC winner regions are those with high inflows of public funding in the past and a high density of leading pharmaceutical companies. Based on our results, the potential to develop these clusters further seems to be more limited compared to second best regions. In this light it is questionable whether the promotion of a few best-performing winner regions from the past will generate higher outcomes than promoting second best performing regions with higher absorptive capacities. Of course, analyzing the number of start-ups provides an incomplete picture of successful clustering of the modern biotechnology industry. Further analysis should consider a broader range of economic indicators, e.g., patent applications, employment, and number of drugs, to obtain more robust evidence.

### 12.2.3 Evidence Concerning the Impact of Legal Framework Changes

Compared to public funding tools, changes in the legal framework are not the main objective of government to stimulate the commercialization of new technologies. In this section we try to summarize the main empirical findings concerning the impact of legal framework changes on the development of new industries in general and of the modern biotechnology industry in particular. To the best of our knowledge, no study has tried to test empirically the impact of legal framework changes on economic outcomes of the modern biotechnology industry. Robust empirical evidence is very rare with regard to the impact of legal framework changes in the field of R&D policy. In contrast to the lack of those studies in empirical industrial economics, many studies empirically analyze the impact of legal changes in the labor market (e.g. Bauer et al. 2007).

On the basis of this background, we envisage studies (a) that apply methodology to analyze these impacts and/or (b) that are relevant for the commercialization of

---

[4] Regression output of the zero-inflated Negbin model is available upon request to the authors. Coefficient estimates (standard error) are −0.015 (0.092) for BRC winner regions and 0.115 (0.062) for BRC non-winner regions.

biotechnology indirectly. From our point of view, the study by Gompers and Lerner (1998) addresses both conditions and gives a nice example for analyzing the effect of statutory framework and law reforms affecting the diffusion of new technologies.

The Gompers and Lerner study emphasized the impact of the clarification of the "prudent man" definition in the Employment Retirement Income Security Act (ERISA) and its effect on venture capital investments. In Sect. 1 we pointed out that venture capital is a fundamental resource for firms developing biological pharmaceuticals. Until 1978 the rule did not allow pension fund managers to invest some of the funds in high-risk asset classes such as hedge funds or venture capital funds. The basic principle for professional money management was stated by Judge Samuel Putnum in 1830: "Those with responsibility to invest money for others should act with prudence, discretion, intelligence, and regard for the safety of capital as well as income." In early 1979 the Department of Labor revised the prudent man rule that the manager must act as someone familiar with matters relating to the management of money, not just prudence. Therefore investing a small part of portfolio money in high-risk asset classes would not be seen as imprudent.

The view of venture capital commitments shows a remarkable increase immediately in the years after clarification of the prudent man rule for pension fund managers (Gompers and Lerner 1998, p. 163). Gompers and Lerner (1998) run a series of regressions to identify the partial contribution of ERISA's prudent man rule clarification (in short, ERISA's clarification). They found a positive impact of this factor on venture capital investments at the US level and the level of Federal States. As expected, ERISA affects fundraising by pension funds only and does not have an impact on fundraising by individuals. The results of aggregate analysis are interesting and suggestive, but the evaluation of effects on the individual level may be the best choice.

Gompers and Lerner also analyzed the impact on the behavior of individual venture organizations. They obtain robust results for the regression as to whether a new fund focuses on early stage investments, the segment with highest chance-to-risk profile within the venture capital asset class.

## 12.3 Legal Framework Changes in Germany

On the basis of the general discussion in Sect. 12.2, we will now make an attempt to present an overview of legal framework changes concerning the biotechnology industry in Germany. This kind of analysis is the first step in identifying the economic impact of these changes.

Genetic engineering opens up possibilities to manipulate the inherited characteristics of cells, perhaps altering entire organisms. This creates the need for a legal framework, in order to prevent damage to living things and their environment – as far as possible – and to enable the users of biotechnology to be sure that they are acting in accordance with the law. A cross-sectional view of biotechnology has already been provided in the discussion of red, green, and gray biotechnologies.[5] Biotechnology is put to use in many different ways, in many different fields of business and industries, with the consequence that it cuts across a number of legal areas. This is the background to the great number of laws that apply to biotechnology in Germany. These stem not only from Germany's national legislation, but also from Europe's legislation. In this section we will provide an overview of the history and context of legal framework changes in Germany concerning modern biotechnology. Afterwards we will try to link the dates of important changes with the emergence of the biotechnology industry.

The actual impetus for lawyers to become involved in biotechnology and genetic engineering came from the scientific community itself (Kloepfer and Delbrück 1989). At the start of the 1970s, a number of leading researchers in the field of biotechnology, which was a new area at the time, felt compelled to point to the possible dangers of new genetic engineering techniques. The techniques in question were those involved in the production of recombinant DNA and cloning. In 1974, several respected researchers published an essay in the journal *Science*, indicating possible dangers that could result from the technology (Berg et al. 1974). Among the researchers were Watson and Crick (who discovered the double helix structure of DNA) and Cohen and Boyer (who discovered how to produce and clone recombinant DNA). A new body, the Committee on Recombinant DNA, was formed under the leadership of Paul Berg, with the purpose of critically observing the new technology and holding a conference to discuss how it should be dealt with in the future (Fuchs 2000). The conference participants developed a catalogue of safety measures to prevent genetically modified organisms from spreading out into the environment (Fischer 2003). On the basis of this catalogue, the National Institutes of Health (NIH)[6] formulated the so-called Guidelines for Research Involving Recombinant DNA Molecules, which would apply in future in the USA. These guidelines include a classification of biotechnological research projects by their degree of risk, together with appropriate safety measures. Additionally, they provide a list of banned experiments.

Alongside the developments in the USA, the increasing lack of clarity in legal proceedings involving genetic engineering led to calls for a legal framework in Germany. This, in turn, provoked interest from within the political scene. The then Federal Ministry of Research and Technology (BMFT) picked up on the issue in 1978, with its guideline on protection from the dangers of in vitro recombinant nucleic acids ("zum Schutz vor Gefahren durch in vitro neukombinierte

---

[5] Based on technologies derived from the latest results in molecular biology, genetics, biochemistry, information science, or physics, the development of new therapeutics or diagnostics ("red" biotechnology), and new products or services for the agricultural and food markets ("green" biotechnology) or for environmental activities ("gray" biotechnology) frame this industry. The value chain within the biotechnology industry contains further services and supplying activities.

[6] The NIH are among the leading medical research establishments in the USA. Since their foundation in 1887, they have become a central point for medical and biological research on a federal level in the United States. NIH research aims to gain knowledge about all diseases and disabilities and to diagnose and treat them.

Nukleinsäuren") (Streck et al. 1997). The scope of this guideline proved inadequate, in that compliance on the part of private businesses was only voluntary, although it was compulsory for public research projects (Krekeler 1994). The existing guidelines did not set out a compulsory procedure to obtain permission for work on genetically modified organisms, nor did they provide legal protection for third parties. Nevertheless, industry associations had decided to adhere voluntarily to the guidelines at that time (Brocks et al. 1991). The continued success of modern biotechnological research and the new possibilities it created, along with increasing criticism of the guidelines, led the Federal Government of the time to set up an inquiry commission in 1984, to assess the opportunities and risks of gene technology. The commission had the specific task of formulating a bill of law on the subject (BTDrs.10/6775 1987). This preliminary work served as a basis for the later Gene Technology Act (Gentechnikgesetz or GenTG). Before this law on gene technology was passed, the guidelines of 1978 were virtually the only source of guidance for users of genetic engineering techniques (Brocks et al. 1991). From an industry point of view, it was hoped that a law on gene technology would make for progress in terms of the following:

- Legal certainty
- Shortening the time required to obtain a permit
- Driving down government interference
- Increasing acceptance in society

    Alongside national efforts to provide biotechnology with a political and legal framework, similar developments were taking place on an EU level. Member states were obliged to incorporate EU directives into their national law. The main sources of European influence on German gene technology law were the directive on release (90/219/EEC),[7] the directive on contained use (90/220/EEC),[8] and the directive on biological agents in the workplace (2000/54/EC). A further source of influence was the so-called Novel Food regulation (BVEL 2001).[9] The directives on release and contained use were the first EU regulations that put pressure on governments to incorporate them into their individual legal systems. The directive on contained use (90/219/EEC) was intended to provide a legal framework for work with genetically engineered organisms in a closed system. Against this background, the directive on release (90/220/EEC) was introduced to regulate the intentional release of genetically modified organisms into the environment. Legislation in Germany had to be hurried through, partially because of a particular decision made by the Higher Administrative Court (VGH) in Kassel. In 1989, the VGH had ruled against the firm Hoechst AG, forcing it to discontinue production

---

[7] The directive regulates the release of genetically modified organisms into the environment.

[8] The directive regulates the use of genetically modified microorganisms in closed systems.

[9] The regulation covers bringing new (genetically modified) foodstuffs and ingredients into circulation.

at a facility for genetically engineered human insulin.[10] The reason the VGH gave for its ruling was that the existing guidelines did not provide an adequate legal basis for the operation of genetic engineering facilities. As such, it was impossible to grant an operating license to such a facility; therefore it was necessary for the state to exercise its duty to protect its citizens and to enforce articles 2, 5 III, 12, and 14 of the constitution (to protect the life and physical integrity of third parties). This made it all the more important to create a legal framework to govern the use of gene technology (Kraatz 1993).

Before the Gene Technology Act was formulated, the existing guidelines, which were continually revised and supplemented in the period between 1978 and 1986, fell under the control of the so-called Federal Immission Control Act (BImSchG) (Brocks et al. 1991). Because of the wide range of completely different opinions on the subject among the political groups who would be affected by such a law, it took a very long time for the law itself to take shape. The first Gene Technology Act (Gentechnikgesetz – GenTG) eventually came into force in 1990. Its primary aim was one of protection (see Article 1 No. 1 GenTG) and it had the secondary purpose of promoting research (Krekeler 1994). The Gene Technology Act (GenTG) determined clearly the fields of use in which a compulsory permit would be required to operate gene technology facilities, including so-called work involving gene technology methods. This included the release of genetically modified organisms into the environment and the sale of products that contain such organisms (Articles 2 and 3 GenTG).

Permits for release had to be obtained from Robert Koch Institute. Until this point, Robert Koch Institute in Berlin, which was controlled by the Ministry of Health, was responsible for granting permits to those who applied to release or distribute genetically modified organisms. In 2002, the responsibilities of this Institute were taken over by the Federal Office of Consumer Protection and Food Safety in Braunschweig. The task of acting as a competent authority for consultation and disciplinary proceedings relating to release and distribution, which had been undertaken by the Federal Environment Agency, became the responsibility of the Federal Nature Conservation Agency. Figure 12.1 points out the central position of Robert Koch Institute in Berlin until 2002.

In addition, a large number of conditions had to be satisfied, which made for a long and complicated bureaucratic procedure. Both the public and the EU member states had to be informed when any genetically modified organisms were released. Any action of the sort had to be conducted in agreement with the Federal Biological Research Centre for Agriculture and Forestry, the Federal Environment Agency, the *Zentrale Kommission für die biotechnologische Sicherheit* (ZKBS) (central commission for biotechnological safety), and the *Bundesanstalt für Viruskrankheiten der Tiere* (federal research centre for viral diseases in animals) (Streck et al. 1997).

---

[10] The VGH compared the effects of genetically modified organisms on life in general with those of nuclear power. Although this comparison was widely criticized and adjudged to be false by the majority of legal publications, it cannot be denied that the verdict of the VGH gave added momentum to the legal process leading to a law on gene technology.

The GenTG also makes further provisions to preclude other possible dangers and defines four safety levels for genetic engineering work (GenTG Article 7).[11]

The ZKBS[12] is responsible for setting the levels and for communicating them to the relevant authorities within the particular federal state. Figure 12.1 offers a summary of the application procedure for permission to release gene-manipulated organisms (GMOs).

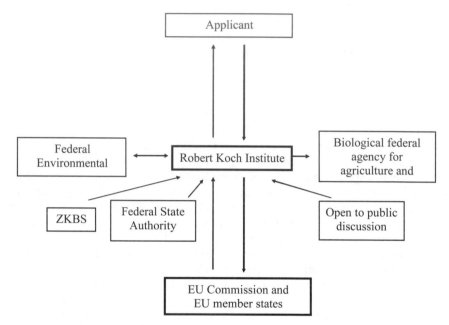

**Fig. 12.1.** Application procedure for permission to release gene-manipulated organisms

An effective regulation also requires adequate directives. The GenTG contains many authorizations to implement directives and their amendments concerning the state of the technology and science. The first five directives are the gene technology safety ordinance (GenTSV), gene technology procedures ordinance (GenTVfV), gene technology hearings ordinance (GenTAnhV), ZKBS ordinance (ZKBSV), and gene technology records ordinance (GenTAufzV). These five directives were already implemented in November 1990 (Krekeler 1994). In addition to these, more directives were implemented a few years later.[13] Table 12.2 describes the main objectives of these directives.

---

[11] No risk (S1), low risk (S2), moderate risk (S3), high risk (S4).

[12] The ZKBS is a body of experts responsible not only for assigning safety levels, but also for pointing out possible dangers associated with the release and distribution of GMOs.

[13] Federal costing ordinance to the Gene Technology Act (BGenTGKostV) of 9 Oct. 1991 (BGBl. I, p. 1972), gene technology participation ordinance (GenTBetV) of 17 May 1995 (BGBl. I, p. 734), gene technology emergencies ordinance (GenTNotfV) of 10 Dec. 1997 (BGBl. I, p. 2882), and gene technology responsibility ordinance (ZustVGenT) of 2 Aug. 2005 (GVBl., p. 328).

**Table 12.2.** An overview of gene technology law

| Ordinance/Directive | Object |
|---|---|
| Gentechnik-Sicherheitsverordnung (Gene technology safety ordinance) (GenTSV) | Contains rules for the safety assessment of individual instances of gene technology usage along with required safety measures. |
| Gentechnik-Verfahrensverordnung (Gene technology procedures ordinance) (GenTVfV) | Contains rules setting out the procedure to register and obtain permission for planned use of gene technology. |
| Gentechnik-Anhörungsverfahren (Gene technology hearings ordinance) (GenTAnhV) | Before permission is granted for gene technology facilities at the two highest safety levels, or for the release of genetically modified organisms, there must be a public hearing. |
| ZKBS-Verordnung (ZKBS ordinance) (ZKBSV) | Sets out the composition and fields of competence of the central commission for biological safety (ZKBS), a board of experts at the Robert Koch Institute |
| Gentechnik-Aufzeichnungsverordnung (Gene technology records ordinance) (GenTAufzV) | Whoever works with gene technology must keep records in accordance with the GenTAufzV and make these available to the appropriate authority on request at any time. |
| Bundeskostenverordnung zum Gentechnikgesetz (Federal costing ordinance to the Gene Technology Act) (BGenTGKostV) | Regulates the levying of fees and expenses by the Robert Koch Institute in the context of the application of the Gene Technology Act. |
| Gentechnik-Beteiligungsverordnung (Gene technology participation ordinance) (GenTBetV) | Regulates the process by which the EU Commission and member states as well as the other signatory states within the European Economic Area participate in the agreement in relation to the release and distribution of genetically modified organisms. The responsible authority is obliged to take the comments of EU member states and other signatory states within the European Economic Area into account and to put EU Commission decisions into action. |
| Gentechnik-Notfallverordnung (Gene technology emergencies ordinance) (GenTNotfV) | Emergency plans must be made for certain types of genetic engineering work at safety levels 3 and 4, to preclude danger to people and the environment outside of the gene technology facility in case of an accident. Incidents during work at safety level 2 or above, such as the escape of genetically modified organisms, must be reported to the competent authority immediately. |

| Ordinance/Directive | Object |
|---|---|
| Gentechnik-Zuständigkeitsverordnung (Gene technology responsibility ordinance) (ZustVGenT) | Responsibility for enforcing gene technology law largely rests with the federal states. The Bavarian federal government issued an ordinance assigning competencies within Bavaria. |
| EU directives | Two EU directives from 1990 are of particular importance. Directive 90/219/EEC regulates the contained use of genetically modified microorganisms, while 90/220/EEC deals with the deliberate release into the environment of genetically modified organisms. Both directives contain detailed requirements that came into force in Germany when incorporated into the Gene Technology Act. Both directives were amended in 1994 to keep pace with technological progress, the first by means of directive 94/51/EC and the second with directive 94/15/EC. More recently, Appendix III to directive 90/220/EEC was amended by directive 97/35/EC. |

*Source:* Bundesamt fuer Verbraucherschutz und Lebensmittelsicherheit (http://www.bvl.bund.de)
The unofficial, literal English translations of the names of German laws are for guidance only

The above description of the applicable regulations makes it apparent that regulating the field of modern biotechnology involves a great deal of administrative work. Official checks on the assignment of safety levels by the ZKBS created a huge amount of work, as even planned genetic engineering at safety level 1 had to be taken into account, although by definition such work involves no risk to the environment. All of this meant that modern biotechnology in Germany was in a poor state and rapidly fell behind the international competition in both research and commercial applications (Festel 1996). Companies and politicians alike strongly criticized the bureaucratic burden imposed by the law. Businesses were of the opinion that the legal framework should not regulate risk, but instead create the right conditions for the problem-free operation of gene technology (Dolata 1996).

As early as 2 years after the law came into force, there were public hearings of the parliamentary committees for health and for research, technology, and technology assessment (Hasskarl 1997; Seesing 1988). Their findings were that regulation via the GenTG was too strict and was restricting research excessively. They argued that this situation was backward-looking and thus indefensible (BTDrs.12/3658 1994). Against this background, there was a demand for a reduction of government controls on genetic engineering, along with the amount of administrative work they implied. Businesses and some politicians demanded a change in the law to cut down on bureaucracy (Dreyer and Gill 1998). Although the main emphasis remained on protection against possible dangers arising from genetic engineering and its products, the regulations laid down in the GenTG were subjected to scrutiny and the law was amended in December 1993 (BMBF 2000). The background to this was repeated criticism from the business and scientific communities, arguing that Germany ran the risk of falling behind the USA and Japan in an important technological field (Kniesel and Müllensiefen 1999; Simon and Weyer 1994). The critics of the German legal framework for work in the field of biotechnology often drew comparisons with the regulations in the USA. In contrast to its German equivalent, the American system of regulations for the use of gene technology does not take the method of manufacture into account. The organ responsible for regulatory control in America, the Office of Science and Technology, concluded on more than one occasion (1986 and 1992) that supervision by the federal authorities should be restricted to the properties and risks of products and that they should not pay attention to manufacturing processes. Furthermore, formalities were not to be allowed to get in the way of rapid progress in biotechnology and gene technology (Brauer 1995). The American regulations thus seem considerably more flexible from the point of view of companies, particularly considering that the National Institutes of Health are constantly working to keep their guidelines up to date, adapting them quickly in response to new scientific discoveries (Maluro 1986).

With the amendment to the GenTG, the German legislative successfully slimmed down the regulations in the hope of strengthening Germany's position as a location for research well into the future. A large number of corrections led to a shortening of the registration and permission-granting procedures, while government involvement and the role of the ZKBS were reduced, which in turn reduced the strain on the latter. Many changes were made within the scope of the amendment, such as the shortening of various procedures. One way in which this was achieved was by abolishing the obligation to assess work that uses gene technology at safety level 1,[14] on the basis that such work does not present any danger to the environment. Work at safety level 2 requires only appraisal and approval from the ZKBS if no permission has previously been granted for work of the sort to be undertaken (GenTG Article 7 Section 1 Nos. 1 and 2).[15] Furthermore, the idea of fostering progress, which was only of secondary importance in the initial version of the GenTG, was given more weight in the revised law, in that scientific and technical possibilities are supposed to be aligned to possible economic opportunities (GenTG Article 1 No. 2). In this way, it has been possible to improve the position of biotechnology, taking a step in the right direction to help the sector develop further in years to come. However, compared to other European countries or to the USA, conditions are still restrictive and place

---

[14] Thanks to this amendment to the law, the number of applications fell from 304 in 1991 to 0 in 1999.

[15] From the beginning, the GenTG regulated industrial genetic engineering in the chemical and pharmaceutical industries, i.e., gene technology facilities, the release of GMOs, and the distribution of genetically modified products. This almost entirely excludes the field of human genetics. The amended law contains an additional explicit reference in Article 2 section 2, to the effect that the law does not apply to the use of genetically modified organisms on humans.

considerable limits on the scientific and commercial use of biotechnological methods (cf. the debates on the release of GMOs or the use of stem cells).

## 12.4 An Empirical Assessment of the Contribution of Legal Framework Change

The discussion in the previous section suggests that legal frameworks have the potential to stimulate the emergence of the biotechnology industry. In this section we intend to discuss the stimulation effects from an empirical point of view. In doing so, we will consider important milestones in factors affecting the commercialization process of the modern biotechnology industry in Germany. Several indicators can be applied to answer the question of the emergence level of the modern biotechnology industry. The number of patent applications as well as public R&D funding in bioscience indicate the potential for commercialization at a very early stage. Since the patent activity results from the R&D process itself, public R&D funding indicates a certification of a technology by the administration. In a second stage, start-up activity and venture capital investment activity go hand in hand and may indicate a more serious level of the exploitation of opportunities.

We start with some descriptive findings concerning the federal funding of biotechnology programs in the business enterprise sector. Figure 12.2 shows the total amounts of funding, the number of funded firms, and the number of funded R&D projects. Between 1973 and 1988 all indicators increase remarkably, followed by a decrease until 1994. The time period after 1996 is characterized by a second wave of growing funding. The total number of publicly funded R&D projects increased from 52 projects in 1993 to 266 projects in 2001. In the year 2003 we observe a total number of 350 biotechnology companies in Germany. About 170 firms (49%) have been publicly funded in 219 R&D projects. The total amount of public R&D project funding in the German biotech industry is almost €28.8 million on average, and because of the matching grants requirements (cost sharing) almost €57.8 million has been invested by industry and government each year.

The picture raises the question of the determinants of dramatic changes in R&D funding over time. Related to the topic of this chapter, we would first like to highlight the role of legal framework change. It is important to note the different effects of the GenTG introduction and its slackening in 1993. Since the implementation of the GenTG in 1990 had the primary aim of protection (see Article 1 No. 1 GenTG), and the regulation excessively restricted research, a positive effect on R&D funding cannot be expected. In contrast to that, the amendment to the GenTG in 1993 focused on shortening various procedures and thus may be a reason for the moderate increase in indicators of R&D funding shown in Fig. 12.2. As expected, the figure shows a negative correlation between introduction of the GenTG and R&D funding and a positive correlation between the slackening of the GenTG and R&D funding in the following period.

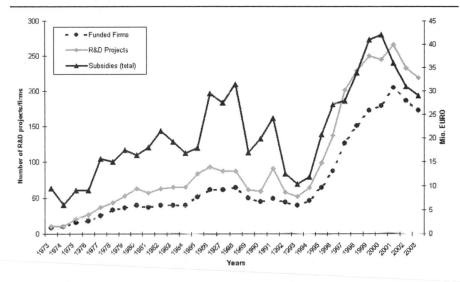

**Fig. 12.2.** Number of funded firms, R&D projects, and total amounts of public R&D biotechnology funding in the business enterprise sector (BMBF 1993–2003)

The correlation might be impressive, but it does not answer the question about a causal relationship between the GenTG and R&D funding. Several reasons may be behind the dramatic change of R&D funding after 1994. Probably, the impact of the GenTG will be zero as we check for other relevant factors. In the following, we stress the role of other determinants to explain the development of R&D funding. Both demand side as well as supply side effects may matter.

A key supply side effect was spawned by the worldwide race to decode the human genotype. In 1996 the German Human Genome Project was launched by government, science, and industry. As Fig. 12.3 shows, federal R&D funding increased from €6 million in 1993 to €20 million in 1996, the peak of annual expenses for Proteom Research between 1973 and 2003. Thus, Germany remarkably increased its efforts to take part in the race.

After 1996, the formative and booming stage of the venture capital market seems to be an essential factor. In Germany and in many other European countries, venture capital investments in biotechnology and other sectors increase dramatically after 1996. Venture capital investments in biotechnology went up by a factor of 6 between 1997 and 2001 (see OECD 2006, p. 119). The implementation of specific segments on most stock markets for young, innovative companies (e.g., the "New Market" at the German Stock Exchange at April 1997) and their rapid growth measured by number of listed companies and market capitalization stimulated the willingness of institutional investors to provide capital for venture capital companies (VCCs). VCCs invest equity in firms with the expectation of a high return on investment due to initial public offerings of funded firms 3–5 years after investment. In the boom period, the selection processes of VCCs were less restrictive. The high share of write-offs in the following years of the Internet "hype" indicates this fact clearly.[16] Both high availability of venture capital and less restrictive selection processes by VCCs until 2000 may have increased the chances to acquire venture capital and thus should have had a positive effect on the opportunity to set up a new business.

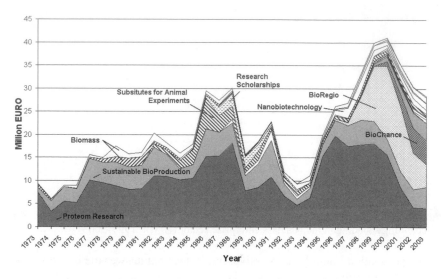

**Fig. 12.3.** Federal funding by biotechnology programs in the business enterprise sector (Germany), 1973–2003 (BMBF 1973–2003)

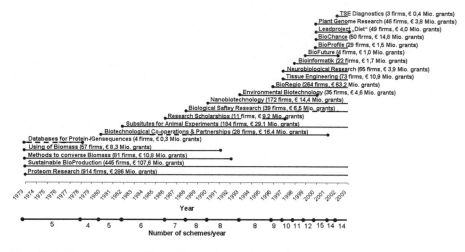

**Fig. 12.4.** Large-scale R&D funding schemes in the business enterprise sector (BMBF 1993–2003)

---

[16] According to EVCA (2001, 2002), 36.5% of all divestments in Germany in 2001 and 44.1% in 2002 were write-offs.

Third, a general change in R&D funding priorities concerning biotechnology in the mid-1990s can be observed, closely related to the above-mentioned BRC. At the same time the BRC changed the general federal government philosophy in public R&D funding: programs were restructured to increase transparency and linked with other funding programs, e.g., for health research and production engineering (see Fig. 12.3). In this context, the Federal Ministry of Education and Research (BMBF) also pushed its project management agencies. Each project proposal was embedded in research program announcements which clarified the funding objectives for each company to receive financial support. Moreover, the corporate design of funding programs for biotechnology was changed to Bio"X", beginning with BioRegio, followed by BioChance, BioFutur, and BioProfile. The corporate designs and the 15 different R&D funding programs do not just reflect policymakers' expectations concerning jobs and welfare, but also investors' hopes for profits in this technology. Figures 12.3 and 12.4 show that R&D funding provided by Bio"X" accounts for a large share of federal R&D funding in the period between 1998 and 2003. Figure 12.4 shows an upstream variety of different R&D topics; that is, the multiplicity of funding schemes represents the awareness of the different biotechnologies and their emphasis. The number of schemes increases remarkably over time. Against this background the increasing share of Bio"X" programs is impressive. With regard to the empirical findings of Engel and Heneric (2006), it is still unclear, however, whether the BRC has additionally affected the commercialization process of the biotechnology industry. The decrease in public funding since 2001 was due to the low inflow of venture capital, the downturn of the German economy, and the following recession (see Fig. 12.3).

Back to the reasons for the change in R&D funding, the role of public research activities and their outcomes have also to be emphasized. These activities are the starting point for many business solutions in the modern biotechnology industry. Toole (2005) obtains robust evidence of a positive relationship between public funding of biotechnology research and pharmaceutical R&D investments in the long run. We do not know anything about the outcome of public research over the period from 1973 to 2003, and thus, the contribution of this factor is still unknown.

Since R&D funding is a function of several reasons, the partial contribution of legal framework changes cannot be deduced directly from the figures. A multivariate regression tool could be applied to address the partial contribution of each factor. Since the number of observations is, however, very small, the estimation is based on a low variation of variables which are included in the estimation. Probably, we will be unable to secure an efficient point estimation of the partial contribution of legal framework changes because of the small sample size. In our view, cross-border comparison could be an adequate empirical strategy to increase sample size and thus to identify the partial contribution of legal framework change. Beside the empirical identification, a qualitative analysis is also helpful to shed some light on the relationship between legal framework change and R&D funding. The discussion of relevant factors shows that the most relevant of them, namely, venture capital inflow and Germany's Human Genome Project, were relevant at the beginning of 1996 and 1997, respectively. The decline of R&D funding between 1990 and 1993 as well as very low increases after the reform of the Genetics Law in 1993 could not be affected by these two factors. From our point of view, it is plausible to argue that a significant share of R&D funding change between 1990 and 1995 is affected by the GenTG's introduction and its amendment. The introduction of the GenTG might have influenced the sector and led to a restrictive entrepreneurial behavior characterized by taking no operational risks in the early 1990s.

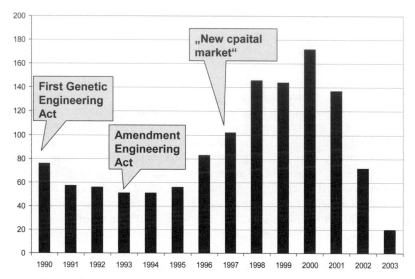

**Fig. 12.5.** Formation of new biotechnology companies, 1990–2003 (*Source:* Creditreform/ ZEW)

As a matter of fact, a similar conclusion could be drawn from the start-up activity in the biotechnology industry. Figure 12.5 shows the number of newly founded biotechnology companies applying methods and processes of modern biotechnology. The data are based on an identification procedure of biotechnology firms in the ZEW-Foundation Panel.[17] The time period after the First Genetic Engineering Act (1990–1993) is clearly marked by a decreasing number of start-ups. As recently as 1995, the number of new firms grew moderately, and increased rapidly at the end of the 1990s. For example, in 1993 less than 50 companies started a new venture compared with more than 170 new companies in 2000.

---

[17] This panel data set has been generated by the ZEW in cooperation with "Creditreform," the largest German credit rating agency (see Almus et al. 2000 for further explanations). The available information includes, among other things, the name and address of the firm, legal form, industry classification, number of employees, sales, foundation date, data regarding insolvency proceedings, date of last enquiry, free flow text with additional information about the firm, i.e., a detailed description of the firm's business activities.

The picture is very similar to the figures presenting federal R&D funding for biotechnology over time.

## 12.5 Future Research and Concluding Remarks

This chapter addresses the central theme "What do we know about the impact of R&D policy tools as well as legal framework changes on the biotechnology industry?" Here we detected remarkable blind spots on several levels:

- Many studies applying state-of-the-art program evaluation point out a positive impact of public R&D funding on firm performance. In contrast, robust empirical evidence concerning the effectiveness and efficiency of specific R&D or innovation policy programs in Germany is very rare. Of course, many studies deal with the evaluation of Germany's technology programs. Not all of these studies apply state-of-the-art methodology, however.
- It is questionable whether a "picking the winner" strategy has the potential to generate higher outcomes. Our empirical analysis of Germany's BRC points out that contest participants which did not win the contest show significantly greater changes in the number of biotechnology start-ups than do BRC winner regions. Further analysis should consider a broader range of economic indicators, e.g., patent applications, employment, and number of drugs, to obtain more robust evidence.
- To the best of our knowledge, no study has attempted to test empirically the impact of legal framework changes on economic outcomes of the modern biotechnology industry.

Following from the last fact mentioned, we focused in the second part of this chapter on a detailed description of legal framework changes in Germany, and made an attempt to link them with the emergence of the modern biotechnology industry.

Based on several reasons (risk, upcoming key technology), there was a need for regulation of genetic engineering. The first Genetic Engineering Act of 1990 set up barriers causing a negative effect not only for the biotechnology industry but also for the pharmaceutical industry. With the amendment to the GenTG, the German legislative slimmed down the regulations in the hope of strengthening Germany's position as a location for research well into the future. While venture capital inflow and Germany's Human Genome Project were of relevance since 1996, the decline of R&D funding between 1990 and 1993 as well as very low increases after the reform of the Genetics Law in 1993 could not be affected by these two factors. Therefore, it can be plausibly assumed that a significant share of R&D funding change between 1990 and 1995 is attributable to the GenTG's introduction and its amendment. In the boom period after 1995, venture capital inflow, growth perspectives of the biotechnology industry, and Germany's Human Genome Project might be the dominant factors to attract biotechnology entrepreneurs.

Compared to other European countries or to the USA, legal framework conditions are still restrictive and may place considerable limits on the scientific and commercial use of biotechnological methods (cf. the debates on the release of GMOs or the use of stem cells). The legal framework in Germany mainly reflects public opinion which is characterized by an emphasis on the risks of new technologies. The recognition and exploitation of opportunities need, however, a significant acceptance on the demand side. As the discussion about the GenTG and its amendment showed, Germany lost several years because of long discussions and the overemphasis of the risks and had to catch up on biotechnology quickly. Following from this, the legal framework has the potential to shift a little bit more towards "opportunities," which implies a less restrictive regulation.

# References

Almus M, Engel D, Prantl S (2000) The ZEW foundation panels and the Mannheim Enterprise Panel (MUP) of the Centre for European Economic Research (ZEW). Schmollers Jahrbuch 120: 301–308

Bauer T, Bender S, Bonin H (2007) Dismissal protection and worker flows in small establishments. Economica 74: 804–821

Beise-Zee M (2001) Lead markets, ZEW economic studies, Vol. 14. Heidelberg

Berg P, Baltimore D, Boyer DB, Cohen WM, Davis RW, Hogness DS (1974) Biohazards of recombinant DNA molecules. Science 185: 303

Black BS, Gilson RJ (1998) Venture capital and the structure of capital markets: banks versus stock markets. Journal of Financial Economics 47: 243–277

BMBF (2000) Bericht des Fachdialogs – Beschäftigungspotentiale im Bereich Bio- und Gentechnologie; im Rahmen des Bündnisses für Arbeit, Ausbildung und Wettbewerbsfähigkeit. Bonn

Brauer D (1995) Zur Bedeutung der Biotechnologischen Industrie in Deutschland und in der EG. In: Mohr H (ed), Biotechnologie – Gentechnik: eine Chance für neue Industrien. Berlin, pp 442–455

Brocks D, Pohlmann A, Senft M (1991) Das neue Gentechnikgesetz. München

BTDrs.10/6775 (1987) Bericht der Enquete-Kommission "Chancen und Risiken der Gentechnologie" gemäß Beschlüssen des Deutschen Bundestages, Bonn

BTDrs.12/3658 (1994) Bericht des Ausschusses für Forschung und Technologie und Technikfolgeabschätzung zum Bericht Bericht der Enquete-Kommission, "Chancen und Risiken der Gentechnologie", Berlin

BVEL (2001) Gesetzliche Grundlagen, Richtlinien, Empfehlungen, internationale Regelungen, Berlin

Carpenter RE, Petersen BC (2002) Capital market imperfections, high-tech investment, and new equity financing. Economic Journal 112: F54–F72

Czarnitzki D, Fier A (2002) Do innovation subsidies crowd out private investment? Evidence from the German service sector. Applied Economics Quarterly 48: 1–25

Czarnitzki D, Licht G (2006) Additionality of public R&D grants in a transition economy: the case of Eastern Germany. Economics of Transition 14: 101–131

Czarnitzki D, Ebersberger B, Fier A (2007) The relationship between R&D collaboration, subsidies and R&D performance: empirical evidence from Finland and Germany. Journal of Applied Econometrics 22: 1347–1366

David PA, Hall BH (2000) Heart of darkness: modeling public–private funding interactions inside the R&D black box. Research Policy 29: 1165–1183

Dohse D (2000) Technology policy and the regions – the case of the BioRegio contest. Research Policy 29: 1111–1133

Dolata U (1996) Politische Ökonomie der Gentechnik: Konzernstrategien, Forschungsprogramme, Technologiewettläufe, Berlin

Dreyer M, Gill B (1998) Pioniergeist oder Vermarktungsstrategie? Ein Hintergrundbericht über die regulatorischen Konflikte und Hürden sowie die ökonomischen Widerstände bei der Vermarktung transgener Lebensmittel, Gen-ethischer Informationsdienst 130: 14–18

Eisinger P (1993) State venture capitalism, state politics, and world of high-risk investment. Economic Development Quarterly 7: 131–140

Engel D, Heneric O (2006) Stimuliert der BioRegio-Wettbewerb die Bildung von Biotechnologieclustern in Deutschland? – Ergebnisse einer ökonometrischen Analyse. Jahrbuch für Regionalwissenschaft 26: 75–108

Ernst & Young (2007) Deutscher Biotechnologie-Report 2007 "Verhaltene Zuversicht". Ernst & Young, Manneheim

European Private Equity and Venture Capital Association (EVCA) (Different years) EVCA Yearbook. Zaventem

Festel G (1996) Zusammenhang zwischen nationalen und supranationalen Regulierungen der Gentechnik und globaler Wettbewerbsfähigkeit deutscher Pharmaunternehmen. Tectum, Marburg, Germany

Fier A, Heneric O (2005) Public R&D policy: the right turns of the wrong screw? The case of the German biotechnology industry. ZEW Discussion Paper No. 05-60, Mannheim

Fischer EP (2003) Die andere Bildung: was man von den Naturwissenschaften wissen sollte. Ullstein, Ulm, Germany

Fuchs U (2000) Die Genomfalle. Patmos, Düsseldorf

Gompers PA, Lerner J (1998) What drives venture capital fundraising? Brookings Papers on Economic Activity – Microeconomics: 149–192

Griliches Z (1992) The search for R&D spillovers. Scandinavian Journal of Economics 94: S29–S47

Hasskarl H (1997) Gentechnikrecht – Textsammlung. Aulendorf

Heckman J, Ichimura P, Todd II (1998) Matching as an econometric evaluation estimator. Review of Economic Studies 65: 261–294

Heckman JJ, LaLonde RJ, Smith JA (1999) The economics and econometrics of active labor market programs. In: Ashenfelter O, Card D (eds) Handbook of Labor Economics, Vol. 3A. Elsevier, Cambridge

Jeng LA, Wells PC (2000) The determinants of venture capital funding: evidence across countries. Journal of Corporate Finance 6: 241–289

Kloepfer M, Delbrück K (1989) Gentechnikrecht zum Schutze der Umwelt, Umwelt- und Planungsrecht: 281–298

Kniesel M, Müllensiefen W (1999) Die Entwicklung des Gentechnikrechts seit der Novellierung 1993. Neue Juristische Wochenschrift: 2564–2572

Kraatz S (1993) Die Zweckambivalenz des Gentechnikgesetzes, Nomos, Heidelberg

Krekeler N (1994) Die Genehmigung gentechnischer Anlagen und Arbeiten nach dem Gentechnikgesetz unter Berücksichtigung europarechtlicher Vorgaben, Lang, Frankfurt

Kulicke M, Lo V (2006) Untersuchung der Wirksamkeit des Foerderprogramms PRO INNO und Evaluierung des Anlaufs von PRO INNO II. Zusammenfassung der 3 Module der Programmevaluation. ISI – Fraunhofer Institut für System- und Innovationsforschung, Karlsruhe

Lach S (2002) Do R&D subsidies stimulate or displace private R&D? Evidence from Israel. Journal of Industrial Economics 50: 369–390

Lerner J (1999) The government as venture capitalist: The long-run impact of the SBIR program. Journal of Business 72: 285–318

Lerner J (2002) When bureaucrats meet entrepreneurs: The design of the effective public venture capital programmes. The Economic Journal 112: F73–F84

Mahro G (1986) Zur Zulassung einer Freisetzung gentechnisch manipulierter Organismen im Feldversuch. Natur und Recht 8: 324–344

OECD (2002) Tax incentives for research and development: Trends and issues. STI Working paper, OECD, Paris. http://www.oecd.org/dataoecd/12/27/2498389.pdf

OECD (2006) Innovation in pharmaceutical biotechnology. Comparing national innovation systems at the sectoral level. OECD, Paris

Seesing H (1988) Technologischer Fortschritt und menschliches Leben – Die Menschenwürde als Maßstab der Rechtspolitik. Campus, Frankfurt

Shane S (2004) Academic entrepreneurship: university spinoffs and wealth creation. In: Venkataraman S (ed) New horizons in entrepreneurship. Edward Elgar, Northampton, MA

Simon J, Weyer A (1994) Die Novellierung des Gentechnikgesetzes, Neue Juristische Wochenschrift: 759–771

Spence M (1984) Cost reduction, competition, and industry performance. Econometrica 52: 101–121

Streck WR, Pieper B, Becker G, Breitenacher M, Grefermann K, Meimberg R, Schüler J (1997) Die biotechnische Industrie in Deutschland: Eine Branche im Aufbruch, Ifo-Institut für Wirtschaftsforschung, München

Thursby JG, Thursby MC (2002) Who is selling the ivory tower? Sources of growth in university licensing. Management Science 48: 90–104

Toole AA (2005) Does public scientific research complement industry R&D investment? The case of NIH supported basic and clinical research and pharmaceutical industry R&D. ZEW Discussion Paper 05-75, Mannheim

Wallsten SJ (2000) The small business innovation research program: encouraging technological innovation and commercialization in small firms? Rand Journal of Economics 31: 82–100

# Index

framework change, 257, 267, 270, 271
 protection, 260
 restriction, 249
legitimacy, 4, 108, 111, 113, 117, 122,
 195
Leibniz Institute, 21
liability, 123, 200
license, 161, 162, 163, 188, 261
licensing, 32, 87, 126, 136, 142, 144, 159,
 168, 173, 183, 204, 225, 230
 agreement, 227
 fee, 187
 manager, 173
 non-exclusive, 227, 230
 technology, 227
life
 cycle, 74, 185, 205
 cycle approach, 205
 form, 212, 222
lifetime employment, 157
Lin, Kuen, 160
Lincoln, Abraham, 211
link, 66
litigation, 218
local
 economic development, 203
 ecosystem, 234
location, 44
lock-in
 resource, 123
 structural, 123
locus
 of entrepreneurship, 173
 of innovation, 61, 149
logical relationship, 153
long-term viability, 166
Los Angeles, 48
Lund/Malmö, 24, 25

**M**

M&A, 4, 133
 motivation, 4
macro-economy, 151
management, 140, 179
 experience, 140
 skill, 119, 139
 team, 137, 141, 206
managerial
 capacity, 124
 folklore, 165

leadership, 204
 resource, 202
 vision, 204
Mannheimer Innovationspanel, 254
manufacturing, 108, 163, 173
 capability, 63
 expertise, 166
 facility, 139
 process, 116, 163, 164, 265
market, 113
 capitalization, 90, 139, 268
 community, 125
 failure, 250, 251, 252
 foresight, 4, 100
 global, 189
 intelligence, 98
 launch, 2, 168
 management, 99
 orientation, 93, 98, 101
 position, 143
 potential, 122, 173
 primary, 162
 size, 68, 161, 162, 166
 structure, 236, 237
 transaction, 60
 valuation, 116, 120
marketing, 63, 70, 108, 143, 161
 agreement, 136
 department, 173
 exclusivity, 117
 partnership, 118
 right, 162, 164
mark-up, 236
Marshall, Alfred, 174
Martinsried, 21
Massachusetts, 13
 Biotechnology Council, 16
Max Planck Institute, 21
Medarex, 170, 171
medical
 biotechnology, 7
 science, 158
medicinal chemistry, 110
MediGene, 22
megacentre, 13, 16
Merck, 27, 29
merger, 4, 133, 137, 144, 167
micro-organism, 134, 155, 163
milestone, 162
Milstein, Cesar, 134
Ministry

# International Handbook Series on Entrepreneurship

Printed in the United States of America

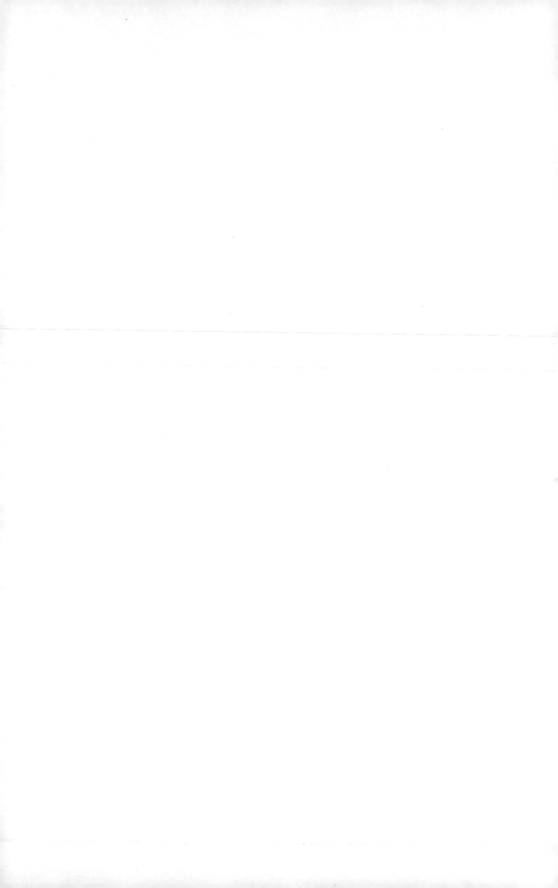